Bulls Markets

HISTORICAL STUDIES OF URBAN AMERICA
*Edited by Lilia Fernández, Timothy J. Gilfoyle, Becky M. Nicolaides,
and Amanda I. Seligman, James R. Grossman, Editor Emeritus*

RECENT TITLES IN THE SERIES

Julia Guarneri, *Newsprint Metropolis: City Papers
and the Making of Modern Americans*

Kyle B. Roberts, *Evangelical Gotham: Religion and
the Making of New York City, 1783–1860*

Timothy Neary, *Crossing Parish Boundaries: African Americans,
Catholicism, and Sports in Chicago, 1914–1954*

Julia Rabig, *The Fixers: Devolution, Development,
and Civil Society in Newark, 1960–1990*

Amanda I. Seligman, *Chicago's Block Clubs: How Neighbors Shape the City*

Aaron Shkuda, *The Lofts of SoHo: Gentrification,
Art, and Industry in New York, 1950–1980*

Mark Krasovic, *The Newark Frontier: Community Action in the Great Society*

Ansley T. Erickson, *Making the Unequal Metropolis:
School Desegregation and Its Limits*

Andrew L. Slap and Frank Towers, eds., *Confederate
Cities: The Urban South during the Civil War Era*

Evan Friss, *The Cycling City: Bicycles and Urban America in the 1890s*

Ocean Howell, *Making the Mission: Planning and Ethnicity in San Francisco*

Benjamin Looker, *A Nation of Neighborhoods: Imagining
Cities, Communities, and Democracy in Postwar America*

Nancy H. Kwak, *A World of Homeowners: American
Power and the Politics of Housing Aid*

Andrew R. Highsmith, *Demolition Means Progress: Flint,
Michigan, and the Fate of the American Metropolis*

Lila Corwin Berman, *Metropolitan Jews: Politics,
Race, and Religion in Postwar Detroit*

Bulls Markets

Chicago's Basketball Business
and the New Inequality

SEAN DINCES

The University of Chicago Press
Chicago and London

The University of Chicago Press, Chicago 60637
The University of Chicago Press, Ltd., London
© 2018 by The University of Chicago
Published 2018
Printed in the United States of America

27 26 25 24 23 22 21 20 19 18   1 2 3 4 5

ISBN-13: 978-0-226-58321-1 (cloth)
ISBN-13: 978-0-226-58335-8 (e-book)
DOI: https://doi.org/10.7208/chicago/9780226583358.001.0001

Library of Congress Cataloging-in-Publication Data

Names: Dinces, Sean, author.
Title: Bulls markets : Chicago's basketball business and the new inequality /
    Sean Dinces.
Other titles: Historical studies of urban America.
Description: Chicago ; London : The University of Chicago Press, 2018. |
Series: Historical studies of urban America | Includes bibliographical references.
Identifiers: LCCN 2018007917 | ISBN 9780226583211 (cloth : alk. paper) |
    ISBN 9780226583358 (e-book)
Subjects: LCSH: Chicago Bulls (Basketball team)—Economic aspects. | Basketball—
    Economic aspects—Illinois—Chicago. | Arenas—Economic aspects—Illinois—
    Chicago. | United Center (Chicago, Ill.) | Near West Side (Chicago, Ill.)—
    Economic conditions.
Classification: LCC GV885.52.C45 D46 2018 | DDC 796.323/640977311—dc23
LC record available at https://lccn.loc.gov/2018007917

♾ This paper meets the requirements of ANSI/NISO Z39.48–1992 (Permanence
of Paper).

Contents

Acknowledgments

A book can only be as good as the people patient enough to put up with the author. In this case it hardly measures up.

My research and writing benefited from the guidance of an incomparable group of mentors. Elliott Gorn saw the project through from start to finish. He always repeated the most important advice one can offer a student: "Keep writing." Gorn is much more than a trainer of historians and teachers; he is a good friend who has allowed me to exploit him shamelessly at every turn. He let me swim in his pool whenever I swung through Chicago and talked me through more jams than I care to admit. More than any teacher, Robert Self helped me grasp the big-picture trends, conflicts, and ideas that shaped the history of the modern United States. His editorial comments pushed me to rethink large portions of this project, and I can only hope to replicate his professionalism and generosity with my own students. Larry Bennett graciously shared his expertise on planning and politics in Chicago, consistently going above and beyond in terms of providing thoughtful feedback. He also proved uniquely generous in offering opportunities to collaborate with experts outside the field of history. John Logan's graduate seminars in urban sociology and to-the-point comments on very early versions of the manuscript motivated me to track down and analyze evidence that I otherwise would have ignored.

Several other scholars and researchers generously shared their expertise with me. Robert Edelman and Judith Grant Long each provided invaluable insight on conceptual and stylistic issues. Matthew Atkinson, Majo Boccardi, and Jeff Lundy patiently fielded my quantitative analysis queries. Tim Gilfoyle deserves special mention for providing smart, line-by-line feedback on earlier drafts. I am also indebted to the research department at the Chicago

Teachers Union, specifically Carol Caref, Sarah Hainds, and Pavlyn Jankov, for providing critical feedback and technical assistance in the data analysis process. Vaneesa Cook and Ayanna Drakos at the University of Wisconsin–Madison, as well as Joe Fitzgibbon, provided meticulous and much appreciated editorial assistance. Vaneesa, in particular, diligently met a cascade of high-pressure deadlines for fact checking and indexing in the final stages of the publication process.

Ben Joravsky deserves a paragraph unto his own. He took many breaks from his muckraking at the *Chicago Reader* to teach me about property taxes and politics in Chicago. Since our first meeting he has been both an honest critic and earnest cheerleader of this project. Much of it simply could not have been written without his help.

Many others provided invaluable logistical support. Jeffrey Cabral at Brown University helped me hurdle a raft of administrative obstacles and always provided a good laugh. Isaac Lee and Jana Valeo at the University of Wisconsin–Madison did the same, though with the added virtue of *not* being Red Sox fans. Tanya Buckingham and Soren Walljasper at the University of Wisconsin–Madison Cartography Lab transformed my ugly GIS maps into well-designed images. Tim Mennel, Rachel Kelly, Caterina MacLean, and Katherine Faydash at the University of Chicago Press proved exceedingly patient with me during the editing and production processes.

I am also grateful to those who agreed to be interviewed for this project. A sincere thanks to Charlie Beyer, Alderman Walter Burnett Jr., Thom Finerty, Earnest Gates, Annie Kostiner, Lewis Kostiner, Alex Kotlowitz, Ed Shurna, Mark Weinberg, and Bill Wilen.

A small army of civil servants from the City of Chicago, Cook County, and the State of Illinois fielded my inquiries, responded to my Freedom of Information Act requests, and helped me access relevant archival materials. A special thanks to the staffs at the Cook County Assessor's Office, Cook County Board of Review, Harold Washington Library Center Municipal Reference Collection, Illinois State Archives, and Illinois State Board of Elections (especially Monique Franklin). I am also indebted to Wayne Wilson and the rest of the staff at the LA84 Foundation Sports Library in Los Angeles, as well as the many experts at the Chicago History Museum, for helping me navigate their archives.

I am lucky to have found a professional home at Long Beach City College, where my colleagues provided the unflinching support I needed to see this project through to the end while fulfilling my duties in the classroom. Lisa Orr, my dean and former department chair, deserves a special shout out for cheering on my progress. So do Susan Chen, Vanessa Crispin-Peralta, Gilbert

Estrada, Mary Marki, David Lehman, Laura Pellegrini, Mel Ross, and Paul Savoie.

A brave cohort of friends in Chicago went beyond the call of duty by letting me crash on their couches and raid their fridges during research trips. Two couples in particular—Chris Lamberti and Milena Sjekloca, and Elena Gonzales and Simon Goldbroch—repeatedly tolerated me inviting myself to lodge at their homes on short notice. Jenny Choe, Vijay Pendakur and Katie Van Tiem, and Daniel Ussishkin also bravely opened their doors and pantries to me. Another group of comrades went out of their way to read and comment on earlier versions of this project. I am deeply indebted to feedback and friendship from William "Big Bill" Brucher, Pier Dominguez, Wen Jin, Viviana MacManus, and Gosia Rymsza-Pawlowska.

The only explanation for the list of friends and colleagues, yet to be mentioned, that have supported me throughout this project is that they are either incredibly charitable or totally desperate, or some combination thereof. In this regard, I want to thank Kevin Barry, Carolyn Bialo, Alma Carrillo, Dorie Chang, Gordon Chang, Jodi Eisenberg, Caitlin Fisher, Gintien Huang, Maria Hwang, Katharine Joo, Majida Kargbo, Charles Kim, Heather Lee, Tracy Luong, Mercedes Lyson, Koji Masutani, Jenn Mulhall, Leah Nahmias, Ronaldo Noche, Yumi Pak, Tina Park, Victoria Perez, Julie Pittman, Sarah Seidman, Tim Snow, Jacob Steele, Colleen Tripp, David Velazquez, and the inimitable Jenny Yang.

My biggest thanks go to my parents, Lucy and Jerry. Like all parents, they were far from perfect, but in more ways than they know, I could not have done this without them.

Lastly, to Derek Seidman: I have suffered no greater embarrassment in my three-plus decades on earth than having a Bills fan—yes *Bills*, not Bulls—as one of my closest friends. Please, for the love of god, give up already.

Introduction

On the night of June 12, 1991, bolstered by the stellar play of Michael Jordan, the Chicago Bulls bested the Lakers at the Great Western Forum in Los Angeles to clinch their first-ever National Basketball Association (NBA) title. The day after the victory, *Chicago Tribune* sportswriter Sam Smith foreshadowed the Bulls' emergence as a basketball dynasty when he wrote that, by beating the Lakers, they "became the team of the 90s."[1] Indeed, by 1998 the Bulls had amassed six NBA championships, and Jordan stood as one of the most worshipped athletes of the twentieth century.

The night of that first championship win in Los Angeles, a handful of Bulls fans gathered in an empty parking lot outside Chicago Stadium, the arena on Chicago's Near West Side where the Bulls played their home games until 1994, when they moved across the street to the new United Center. Adorned in Bulls gear, the fans stationed themselves around the hood of a truck with a television set mounted on top and cheered on their team. The photograph of the scene from the *Chicago Tribune* (fig. I.1) offers some important insights into professional sport at the end of the twentieth century. For one, the television's grip on the fans' attention reminds us of the crucial roles played by athletic celebrity and mass media in the growing popularity and profitability of major leagues. Jordan and the Bulls helped propel the NBA from an afterthought in the minds of television network executives and advertisers—as recently as the early 1980s CBS had aired some championship games on tape delay—to a global phenomenon that tied together fans across the planet, and profited from them, by way of broadcasts in hundreds of countries and scores of languages.[2]

As we zoom out from the television, the shadowy outline of Chicago Stadium in the background reminds us that the history of teams like the Bulls

FIGURE I.1. Bulls Fans Gather Outside Chicago Stadium During Game 5 of the 1991 NBA Finals
Source: Chicago Tribune, June 13, 1991, sec. 4, p. 5.

is about more than changes in what people saw on their television screens. Major-league franchises also played important roles in the planning and building of their respective cities. Nevertheless, the scholarly books and articles about the historical significance of Jordan and the Bulls largely overlook the fact that their rise was in many ways a story about the economic and political transformation of Chicago at the end of the twentieth century. For example, during the 1980s and 1990s, the Bulls became a pillar of the city's effort to reinvent itself as a mecca of culture and leisure for tourists and professionals. The team's home games emerged as a favorite pastime among Chicago elites. Local officials approved significant public subsidies for the team's new arena, the United Center. The new facility allegedly revitalized part of Chicago's Near West Side. Independent peanut vendors working outside the United Center made headlines by fighting the team owners in court over the right to compete for food sales on nearby sidewalks, and the Chicago City Council helped Bulls ownership get rid of the vendors while their suit wound its way through the courts.

This book is an urban and economic history of the Bulls that makes several arguments about the sports business since the 1970s. One of these claims is uncontroversial and simply adds to a growing consensus among those who have already studied the topic: new publicly subsidized sports facilities built in the wake of deindustrialization and touted by boosters as magnets for new investment were, in fact, poor engines of economic growth. What follows, especially the first chapter, takes this claim further by demonstrating that in rare cases in which professional sports franchises like the Bulls had a positive economic impact on their locales, that impact was marginal *and* accidental. By "accidental," I mean that it resulted from the quality of the team— something decidedly outside the control of politicians and planners—rather than the novelty of its stadium.

Many assume that there is little more to be said about the urban economics of sport in the late twentieth-century United States. Economists have seemingly closed the book on the relationship between the sports business and American cities. As Dennis Coates and Brad Humphreys explain in a 2008 survey of relevant scholarly publications, "The large and growing peer-reviewed . . . literature on the economic impacts of stadiums, arenas, sports franchises, and sport mega-events has consistently found no substantial evidence of increased jobs, incomes, or tax revenues for a community associated with any of these things."[3]

So why bother writing an entire book on the recent economic and urban history of a major-league sports franchise? Because mainstream economics scholarship offers a relatively narrow treatment of the question of political and economic power as it relates to the urban sports business—that is, how and why teams and stadium developments affected the distribution of resources within cities during the past forty years. To be sure, some economists describe government-funded stadiums as "massive reverse Robin Hood schemes" that transferred money from ordinary residents to rich team owners by diverting tax payments away from important public services or inducing tax hikes to cover stadium construction and operational costs.[4] This is an important conclusion and one that this book corroborates. But the economics literature typically stops there. In fact, teams like the Bulls were implicated in many other processes that emerged or intensified in the late twentieth-century American city through which the rich captured a greater share of wealth and resources at the expense of low-income people, workers, and the middle class. These processes included the privatization of formerly public spaces like sidewalks, the push to gut important government-funded social programs like public housing, and the reduction of access to leisure opportunities in inner cities for residents outside the professional and upper classes.[5]

This study also expands on what I view as an incomplete explanation from mainstream economists as to why, over the past four decades, major-league team owners witnessed a dramatic surge in the profitability of their stadiums and arenas. More specifically, the chapters that follow add to the understanding of why, in this period, owners enjoyed increasingly generous public subsidies for stadium construction and operation, and successfully implemented spectacular price hikes for tickets and concessions. Many economists argue that these trends stemmed primarily, if not exclusively, from the U.S. government's ongoing practice of explicitly or implicitly singling out the sports business for exemption from meaningful antitrust oversight. This allowed leagues to operate openly as cartels at the national level and teams to operate openly as monopolies at the local level. Leagues exploited their cartel structure to unilaterally limit the supply of franchises in American cities, granting individual teams total market control over their respective metropolitan areas. This protected team owners from local competition, thus enabling them to set exorbitant prices for tickets and concessions. Leagues also used their cartel structure to prevent the creation of new franchises in a handful of major cities—in other words, to artificially maintain a few empty markets. These conditions endowed existing franchises with an undue amount of leverage when making demands on their cities, counties, and states for government subsidies. Typically, a team threatened, with the overt or tacit support of its respective league, to relocate to one of the empty markets unless it received boatloads of public dollars for a new stadium. Usually, the league also signaled that it would not tolerate a new franchise in the city threatened with abandonment if the current team absconded for lack of subsidies. In most cases, politicians responded by throwing obscene amounts of money at the team owners so as not draw public blame for their departure.[6]

There is much truth to this line of reasoning. For the better part of the twentieth century, the U.S. government—in the form of Congress, the courts, and Justice Department—protected major-league sports from competition by actively shielding them from antitrust regulations or passively turning a blind eye to the industry's blatant violation of those regulations. The unfettered local monopoly power enjoyed by teams as a result surely helped them secure incredible sums of corporate welfare and impose steep increases in ticket prices at the turn of the millennium. But mainstream economics overplays the degree to which, in recent decades, the dramatic expansion of the local economic power of major-league team owners represented a quirky market failure specific to the government-sanctioned monopoly structure of the sports business. Consider the assertion in 1999 by economists James Quirk and Rodney Fort that "anywhere except in sports the threat [by a business to leave unless it receives public subsidies] would have been laughable" at the end of the twentieth century.[7] In fact, with increasing frequency over the past forty years, major firms from most industries successfully used such threats to extort subsidies from cities, counties, and states. Nike, for example, received more than $2 billion in subsidies in 2011 from government agencies in Oregon after threatening to relocate some of its operations and jobs outside the state.[8] Moreover, many different types of urban entertainment venues—not just major-league stadiums—jacked up prices at significant, often unprecedented rates. For instance, according to a *New York Times* report, movie-ticket prices "outpaced the effect of general inflation by more than half" between 1999 and 2011.[9]

The fact that corporate America in general—not just the major-league sports business—intensified the profitable exploitation of government and consumers at the end of the twentieth century strongly suggests that the accelerated enrichment of team owners had to do with more than just the relatively unique status of their industry vis-à-vis antitrust law. Indeed, many major-league franchises enjoyed entrenched monopolies in their respective markets for much of the twentieth century, indicating that something new was at play in terms of the dramatic growth of their economic power after 1980. In fact, the recent history of the Bulls indicates that the profitability of stadiums and arenas increased significantly at the turn of the millennium due in large part to widespread structural shifts in the American political-economic system that left few industries unaffected. By "structural shifts," I mean fundamental changes in the how government and the economy operated—for example, policy makers' abandonment of progressive taxation as a tool for maintaining robust public investment and consumer demand. These changes enabled major-league team owners to exploit their old monopoly powers in new ways and sometimes begat entirely new monopoly powers for them to exploit. Put another way, the growing impact and scope of the monopoly power wielded by teams like the Bulls largely depended on broader political and economic transformations over the past four to five decades. These transformations, discussed in more detail throughout this book, all resulted in the significant transfer of political influence and wealth from the bottom and middle to the top, as well as the return of levels of economic inequality that, by some measures, the United States had not witnessed since before the Great Depression.[10] Major-league teams like the Bulls did not exist outside of these shifts; they embraced and benefited from them.

Many refer to the major economic and political changes that led to the upward redistribution of wealth in recent decades as the "neoliberal turn" or the rise of "neoliberalism."[11] I avoid this terminology for two reasons. First, it lacks specificity because scholars invoke it to describe a dizzying array of recent economic, political, and cultural developments. Second, the word "neoliberalism" is confusing. Since the presidency of Franklin D. Roosevelt, "liberalism" in the United States has described a political orientation in support of government efforts to redistribute some measure of wealth downward.

This is quite the opposite of what people mean by "neoliberalism." Instead of "neoliberal era" or the "age of neoliberalism," I opt for the label "New Gilded Age," which suggests similarities between American capitalism in the closing decades of the nineteenth century and the early twentieth—a period remembered for producing a small class of ultrawealthy "robber barons" who used their economic power to bend government to their will—and American capitalism since the mid-1970s. Specifically, this label points to increasing economic inequality as *the* defining historical feature of both eras. This is not to deny important differences between the two. As historian Jefferson Cowie explains, the New Gilded Age differs from its predecessor not only in terms of the specific industries that dominate but also in terms of placing a much more expansive government at the disposal of corporate interests.[12]

The accumulation of wealth by Chicago Bulls owner Jerry Reinsdorf proved emblematic of the New Gilded Age. Between 1992 and 2010, the market value of the Bulls skyrocketed from approximately $155 million to $500 million (in constant 2010 dollars), a real increase of 223 percent.[13] Over the same period, median household wealth among white Americans barely budged, moving from $95,345 to $97,000. The situation proved much direr for nonwhite households. For example, within the African American community, which in Chicago has long made up a sizable portion of both the local population (roughly a third as of this writing) and the Bulls fan base, median household wealth plummeted from $16,041 to $4,890.[14] As wealthy Americans like Reinsdorf saw the value of their assets and income grow dramatically at the end of the twentieth century and the beginning of the twenty-first—as of February 2017 the value of the Bulls stood at a whopping $2.5 billion—most ordinary Americans struggled to hold on to what they had or, worse, experienced significant economic loss.[15]

While I employ "New Gilded Age" to refer to the period of intensifying economic inequality that began in the second half of 1970s, I use the term "exclusionary capitalism" to specify the political-economic system responsible for the upward redistribution of resources and power that benefited the likes of Reinsdorf. The adjective "exclusionary," as opposed to "neoliberal," more precisely describes the particular form of *urban* capitalism underwriting the New Gilded Age in American cities and how it worked to enrich teams like the Bulls to the detriment of ordinary residents. During the past forty years, urban capitalists, sports team owners or otherwise, relied on a growth model that excluded most people from enjoying its benefits in at least three interrelated ways. The first involved excluding those outside the professional and capitalist classes from certain physical spaces—for example, neighborhoods on the receiving end of significant public and/or private investment.

The second type of exclusion took the form of denying ordinary folks access to economic markets, exemplified by well-connected urban capitalists using their economic and political power to establish, maintain, and expand local monopolies. The final iteration dealt with excluding regular people from the benefits of government intervention in order to redirect public resources into the pockets of those who already enjoyed significant wealth.

Some readers may dismiss "exclusionary capitalism" as redundant because capitalism in all its forms depends on a certain degree of inequality and, hence, exclusion. This contention is a valid one, but I employ the term in a historically relative sense. That is, I use it to distinguish the urban capitalism of recent decades from the type that existed for roughly thirty years after World War II. Given that the relatively inclusive capitalism of the immediate postwar period marked a brief "exception" within American history, and in view of the many parallels between the old and new Gilded Ages, I often refer to the "resurgence" or "renewal" of exclusionary capitalism in the pages that follow.[16]

How and why did this resurgence of exclusionary capitalism happen in the United States, and how did it contrast with the system it replaced? We have to go back to 1928, the year before the stock market crash that triggered the Great Depression, when income and wealth inequality sat at unprecedented extremes. The top 10 percent of earners received more than 49 percent of national income; the top 1 percent alone commanded nearly 24 percent. The richest 10 percent of Americans held around 80 percent of the nation's total wealth (e.g., assets like real estate, corporate equity, savings). Fifteen years later, much had changed. Economic inequality in the United States stood at historic lows. By 1944 the top 10 percent's share of national income had dropped below 33 percent, and that of the top 1 percent to just above 11 percent. By 1950, the richest 10 percent still controlled more than half of the nation's wealth, but the percentage had fallen to 66. These changes were owing to not just the higher wages that came with increased wartime demand for labor but also the willingness of Franklin D. Roosevelt's New Deal coalition to institutionalize, in Cowie's words, "a new idea of collective economic citizenship and economic security." Policy makers accomplished this through the imposition of higher taxes on the incomes and wealth of rich individuals and corporations during the 1930s and 1940s, as well as government support for expanded union membership.[17]

The quarter century of economic expansion following the end of World War II proved noteworthy not only as a result of consistently high growth rates but also for the endurance of relatively low levels of economic inequality. The sustained postwar boom and the more equal distribution of its fruits owed to a joint commitment by the government and much of the business community to maintain high levels of consumer demand. This meant high wages guaranteed by widespread unionization. It also meant a willingness on the part of the government to use robust public spending on a wide array of programs and projects—the maintenance of relatively high tax rates on corporations and the wealthy helped make this spending possible—to stimulate consumer demand during recession. In sum, the economy in the immediate postwar period was geared toward including workers and consumers as beneficiaries of growth in the form of economic security and, in many cases, upward mobility. Of course, we should avoid romanticizing this system, as its inclusiveness had serious limits. People of color, women, sexual minorities, immigrants, and other marginalized groups continued to struggle to secure full economic citizenship. Overall, though, this system proved significantly more equal than its predecessor—Cowie aptly describes it as the basis for "the greatest age of equality in the United States since the onset of the industrial revolution"—and witnessed significant, if relatively modest, economic gains even among minorities.[18]

The Chicago Bulls of the late 1960s epitomized the relative egalitarianism of the quarter century after World War II. The team, created by businessman Dick Klein in 1965 with "an initial investment of $1.6 million" (approximately $12 million in 2017 dollars), began playing home games at Chicago Stadium on the city's Near West Side in 1967. Not all Chicagoans could afford tickets, but most could. In 1968, ticket prices ranged from a low of $2 to a high of $5 (roughly $13 to $33 in 2017 terms), affordable even for workers without a college education, especially the nearly one-third of the city's workforce employed in union-dense manufacturing industries (median hourly wages for a manufacturing machinist in the Chicago metro area in 1970 stood at $4.45, or $27 in 2017 dollars). There were no luxury suites or members-only club sections—just a bunch of seats the everyman could afford and a lot of basketball, all overseen by ownership that, according to available accounts, lacked anywhere near the wealth or power of Reinsdorf and his partners when they purchased the team decades later.[19]

The relatively inclusive postwar economy began to unravel in the mid-1970s as a result of several developments that threatened the profitability of American capital. Intensified competition from abroad started to eat away at the returns to U.S. firms. Compounding matters, a dramatic increase in inflation—largely an outgrowth of the embargo on oil exports called by the Organization of the Petroleum Exporting Countries (OPEC) in 1973 and the sharp rise in oil prices that ensued—significantly reduced the value of corporate profits.[20] In the second half of the 1970s, corporate America set out to restore profitability by dismantling the constraints placed on it in the post–World War II era. Firms contracted the services of a growing army of anti-unionization consultants to break strikes and undermine worker organization. They also employed expanded and better-coordinated campaign contributions and lobbying to convince lawmakers to decrease corporate tax burdens and repeal a raft of market regulations. The administration of President Ronald Reagan, whom Americans elected in 1980, embraced and encouraged these efforts. It oversaw sharp reductions in tax rates for corporations and the wealthy, the weakening of labor relations oversight, and the constriction of spending on social programs that constituted an important, if imperfect, social safety net for working and low-income Americans. Urban residents felt the effects of these changes acutely as federal aid to cities like Chicago, measured as a percentage of gross domestic product, declined precipitously after the late 1970s.[21]

The business community promised that this revival of "free market" economics would solve the problem of slowed growth in the United States. In fact, after 1980 the economy expanded at an anemic rate relative to the immediate postwar period. The new paradigm, however, proved wildly successful at concentrating ever more income and wealth in the hands of the already rich. The success of corporate America's attack on regulatory institutions, including an already-meager antitrust enforcement system, accelerated what political economists John Bellamy Foster and Robert McChesney describe as the "tendency to monopolization . . . which is demonstrably stronger in the opening decades of the twenty-first century than ever before."[22] In other words, by the turn of the millennium, monopoly (or oligopoly) was increasingly the rule in American capitalism outside, as well as inside, the sports business. The shares of national income garnered by the top 10 percent and 1 percent of earners rose to 48 percent and 20 percent, respectively, by the end of the first decade of the twenty-first century (recall that these numbers were around 33 percent and 11 percent in the mid-1940s). According to economist Thomas Piketty, today in the United States "income from labor is about as unequally distributed as has ever been observed anywhere."[23] While the concentration of wealth (as opposed to income) at the top is not quite as extreme today as it was in the decades leading up to the Great Depression, it is moving decidedly in that direction. Between 1970 and 2010, the respective shares of total wealth held by the top 10 percent and 1 percent of asset holders moved from 64 and 28 percent, respectively, to 72 and 34 percent.[24] Clearly, access to the fruits of growth in the United States has become much more exclusive, rather than inclusive, over the past forty years.

In late twentieth-century Chicago, Reinsdorf and the Bulls implicated themselves in the renewal of exclusionary capitalism in many ways, and as a result they influenced the ideological, political, and spatial histories of the city. In terms of ideology, by which I mean the general worldview or belief system of residents, the Bulls affected the way Chicagoans defined community. The success of the team helped displace versions of community grounded in economic class—versions that raised people's consciousness about the conflict between their interests and those of the wealthy—with relatively superficial definitions of community as shared support of a sports team.

With regard to politics, the Bulls' approach to doing business in the New Gilded Age encapsulated broader transformations in how the government involved itself in the economy. Reinsdorf and his partners lobbied successfully for a wide array of interventions by city, county, and state officials that helped them secure larger and more predictable profits. At the same time, Bulls ownership pressured government agencies at the local and national levels to scale back interventions in the market on behalf of working and low-income Chicagoans (e.g., subsidized housing programs) that threatened the team's profitability. All of this was perfectly in line with a more general trend in the United States at the end of the twentieth century in which wealthy and well-connected capitalists pressed for the expansion of corporate welfare while lobbying for the reduction of government action intended to help ordinary Americans. These efforts caused the transfer to private hands of what had previously existed as public wealth (e.g., corporate tax revenues spent on social-welfare programs).

The franchise's role in the "spatial" history of Chicago is the most prominent thread running through the six chapters that follow, five of which deal with the construction and operation of the United Center. By "spatial" history, I mean the history of how space was organized within the city, and in particular who had access to what within Chicago, whether a park, stadium, redeveloped apartment complex, sidewalk, or social service agency. In this regard, decisions made by Bulls ownership had wide-ranging impacts, all of which made Chicago, and especially neighborhoods in and around downtown, much more exclusive spaces in which affluence became increasingly important for gaining and maintaining access. The franchise contributed to the increasing exclusion of working- and middle-class residents from downtown leisure amenities, the expulsion of independent vendors who had competed for decades with large downtown retailers, and the mounting pressure on low-income residents to move away from downtown redevelopment.

The question of race was either explicitly or implicitly at issue in most of the Bulls' business decisions. While ownership paid lip service to racial equality in Chicago, the increasing intensity with which the team siphoned off wealth from below resulted in decidedly racist outcomes. Given the over-representation of people of color, and African Americans especially, in the bottom tiers of the income and wealth distributions, they often bore the brunt of the suffering generated by team owners like Reinsdorf. Tellingly, the fiercest resistance to Reinsdorf's profit seeking came from low-income and working-class African Americans who lived and/or worked near the Bulls' home arena.

The Bulls were not the most important force behind the revival of exclusionary capitalism in Chicago. In many cases, the franchise simply followed the lead of other firms, as was the case in its aggressive lobbying for corporate tax abatements. But in other cases, such as the tactics for marketing entertainment to the wealthy and for eliminating small-time retail competitors, the franchise's actions were more innovative. The Bulls, in other words, both shaped and were shaped by exclusionary capitalism.

Some will contend that the Bulls brought "intangible" benefits like civic pride and cohesion to Chicago. I take such claims seriously, and even agree with some of them. But after a full accounting of the social and economic costs incurred by Chicagoans as a result of the team over the past thirty to forty years, it is difficult to conclude that these were offset by the presence of a championship basketball franchise.

My "accounting" method draws on the insights of sociologists John Logan and Harvey Molotch, who argue that evaluating urban growth requires more than crunching numbers on tax receipts, business investment, and property values. Although measuring such variables helps economists understand what does or does not promote the expansion of urban economies, Logan and Molotch insist that it is equally important to grasp how particular types of development affect ordinary city dwellers' day-to-day quality of life. For example, we have to ask how certain growth strategies affected the accessibility of decent schooling and health care, the sustainability of community institutions and social networks, and the prospects for economic security for regular folks. Growth, in and of itself, does not necessarily enhance these quality-of-life indicators for most of a city's residents. In fact, it is entirely possible for impressive economic numbers to coincide with declining fortunes for the middle and working classes and those with low incomes. Thomas Piketty puts it very simply: "Growth can harm some groups while benefiting others."[25] This book thus sets out to answer the following questions: Which types of local costs and benefits did teams like the Bulls create? Who reaped the benefits and who bore the costs? In terms of the greater good, did the benefits outweigh the costs?

Making the Chicago Bulls the subject of such an in-depth case study was not an arbitrary decision. The Bulls became one of the most heralded sports franchises at the end of the twentieth century not only because of Jordan's star power and sustained success on the court but also because of the franchise's reputation as a socially responsible business operation. Relative to many other major-league franchises, this reputation was well deserved. Bulls ownership built a new arena without using taxpayer money for up-front construction costs (the aforementioned subsidies came in the form of property-tax breaks and other "hidden" forms of corporate welfare), partnered with neighborhood organizations to develop new housing and small businesses, and donated money to local schools. According to commentators inside and outside Chicago, the team set the standard for fostering a mutually beneficial relationship between sports teams and their surrounding communities, as well as for embodying genuinely free-market principles.

But this was mostly a façade for the aggressive and predatory profit seeking of Jerry Reinsdorf and his colleagues, much of which involved pressuring local government to intervene in the market on their behalf. This history thus suggests an alarming conclusion. If one of the most socially responsible sports franchises of the past generation established a fundamentally exploitative relationship with its home city, then it seems reasonable to describe the entire professional sports business as having a fundamentally exploitative relationship with urban America. I know that it is difficult for sports fans— and for what it is worth, I count myself as one—to imagine that their cities might be better off without the major-league teams they love. Unfortunately, the evidence offered up in the pages that follow suggests that this is probably the case, even when it comes to teams that enjoy stellar reputations on and off the court (or field).

This is not to dismiss the potential social and cultural benefits of sport. Rather, histories like this one serve as a call to reclaim and reshape sport in more socially constructive ways. That means, first and foremost, deprioritizing the bottom lines of team owners who have dramatically reduced the accessibility of live games, pillaged the pocketbooks of local taxpayers, and done much to disempower our cities' most vulnerable residents.

Bullish on Image: Basketball and the Promotion of Postindustrial Chicago

In the middle of the 1990s, journalists started marveling at a curious phenomenon outside the United Center, the Bulls' recently opened, state-of-
the-art arena. According to their reports, visitors from across the globe were
gathering around the statue of Michael Jordan erected outside the new facility. Writing in 1995, Richard Roeper of the *Sun-Times* noted that "tourists
from as far away as Thailand . . . posed for pictures by the . . . icon, as fans
tossed coins . . . near the base." A couple of years later, the *Tribune*'s John
Husar described a Mexican sightseer taking photos in front of the statue. The
visitor told Husar that he wanted "a memento, something to show our son or
grandchildren we were here." By decade's end, the statue was the terminus of
a pilgrimage taken by thousands of domestic and international tourists alike.[1]

The popularity of the statue corroborated the claim made by the local,
national, and international presses that Jordan and the Bulls had rehabilitated
Chicago's reputation. Indeed, it was a reputation in need of repair. When the
Bulls started winning NBA titles in the early 1990s, the city was reeling from
decades of economic decline and was dogged by a long history of vice, corruption, and segregation. Journalists and those they interviewed were nearly
unanimous in the belief that the team, and especially Jordan, supplanted images of the Second City as the seamy haunt of world-famous criminals. In
1997, R. C. Longworth of the *Chicago Tribune* asserted that "the city's symbol
is no longer a syphilitic [Al Capone] and his henchmen but a stately athlete . . . and his talented teammates." Capone's syphilis had apparently become a fixation at the *Tribune*. The following year, the paper's John Kass posited that Jordan "forced cabdrivers in almost every European country to stop
mentioning the mass murderer and syphilitic psychopath Al Capone in their
first reference to Chicago."[2]

The Bulls' alleged impact on Chicago's standing in the eyes of outsiders was well timed, arriving amid intensifying competition between cities for investment—a process prompted by slowed growth and receding federal aid to municipalities. Before the Jordan era, Chicago stood poorly positioned to compete; by the 1980s deindustrialization, political corruption, and racial conflict had convinced many investors to look elsewhere. Under the leadership of Richard M. Daley, who became mayor in 1989, Chicago politicians and business leaders launched a decades-long collaboration to develop distinctive entertainment amenities in and around downtown. In theory, these amenities would repair the city's global image and entice new visitors, residents, and employers. Working closely with the news media and local tourism industry, the Daley administration aggressively promoted the city as global tourist destination by publicizing assets like the redesigned Navy Pier and Millennium Park as well as the Taste of Chicago festival.[3] At first, the Bulls did not figure prominently in these promotional efforts. But as the franchise's dominance and global renown grew during the 1990s, the public and private sectors in Chicago incorporated the team more and more into their efforts to project a diverse, wholesome, and winning image of the city. By the new millennium, local newspapers, business associations, and government agencies had gone out of their way to stamp Chicago with the imprimatur of Jordan and his teammates.

Using the image of the Bulls to promote Chicago as a recreational paradise made sense. Jordan's talent and the team's unparalleled success during the 1990s offered a truly unique attraction for outsiders contemplating where to visit next. This proved an asset for local elites obsessed with ensuring that Chicago competed effectively in the mad dash for new spending and investment among cities that had been gutted by deindustrialization. While the team's local economic impact eluded precise measurement, journalists offered numerous examples of the team changing peoples' minds about the city and attracting tourists. One of the most stunning stories involved Japanese travelers who paid several thousands of dollars each for a "Michael Jordan Tour" of Chicago. In 1996, tour director Patrick Marume told USA Today's Jerry Bonkowski that participants typically spent $300 each on Jordan souvenirs while in the city.[4]

Such examples indicate that it was Jordan's star power and the sustained success of the Bulls on the court, rather than massive public subsidies for a new arena, that provided the appeal. In their quest for taxpayer-funded stadiums, team owners and their political allies often argued that a new facility, in and of itself, would accelerate growth by promoting increased tourism. The history of the Bulls during the late 1980s and 1990s shows that in terms of any sort of positive economic impact at the local level, team quality—a variable out of the control of policy makers—played a much more important role than the mere existence of a new venue.

This is not to say that the Bulls saved Chicago from economic ruin. Any direct impact the team had on local tourism and entertainment spending proved miniscule compared to the city's overall economy. Nonetheless, the evidence suggests that the larger effort to reengineer Chicago as a new capital of leisure—an effort in which the promotion of the Bulls by local elites played a supporting role—helped return the city to a path of robust growth. This growth, however, was distributed very unevenly. During the 1990s, Chicago's leadership funneled the overwhelming majority of new public and private investment into blocks in and around downtown, otherwise known as the Loop, which they desperately wanted to resurrect as the nerve center of an expanded entertainment infrastructure. Indeed, by 2000, the Loop had been reborn.

This rebirth did wonders for the profits of local real estate moguls, tourist industry executives, and business service firms active in the Loop, not to mention the lifestyles of urban professionals who coveted trendy downtown hangouts; but the same could not be said for Chicago's poorer neighborhoods, especially the predominantly African American and Latino ones on the city's South and West Sides. The investment poured into downtown rarely spilled over into these other areas, and the people who resided there found themselves largely excluded from the redevelopment overseen by Mayor Daley. At the start of the new millennium, economic inequality, racist policing, and segregated, underfunded schools remained deeply entrenched in Chicago. They remain so today.[5] To be clear, this chapter is not about blaming the Chicago Bulls franchise for these problems. As subsequent chapters show, decisions by the team's executives exacerbated many of those problems, but here the focus is on how politicians, the press, and other businesses in Chicago used the Bulls' cachet to help implement a local version of exclusionary capitalism in the New Gilded Age.

Chicago's elites justified their singular focus on investing in neighborhoods in and around the Loop by painting it as the only realistic option available to them. Other cities were aggressively marketing revamped downtowns in a bid for new tourist spending and business investment. The Second City had to compete by responding in kind, so the story goes.[6] This argument, however, overlooks how the administration of Harold Washington, the mayor of Chicago from 1983 to 1987 and the first African American to hold the office, offered a real alternative to the one-sided, Loop-centric model of growth. Through creative budgeting, a relatively confrontational stance toward big business, and a genuine effort to expand democratic participation in local government, Washington and his allies challenged local elites by prioritizing balanced development across the city. Not all of Washington's agenda came to fruition before his sudden death in 1987, but enough of it did to suggest that Richard M. Daley's obsession with an entertainment and leisure renaissance in and around the Loop was driven more by the politics of class than by the politics of necessity.[7]

In this context, the press and other local elites highlighted the Bulls as a much-needed source of local "community." As the *Tribune*'s Bob Greene put it in 1996, "People who may believe they have nothing in common with other people of different ethnic, racial, geographic or age-defined groups find community via the Bulls."[8] The decision by local newspapers and other media to argue aggressively that the team united disparate parts of a socially fractured city represented an attempt to resolve the tension between persistent inequality and local elites' claims that the city had put its checkered past behind it. More than diverting attention from the impact of exclusionary capitalism in Chicago, these efforts supplanted definitions of community rooted in people working together for basic economic and social well-being with superficial definitions based on shared interest in a sports team.

Before the Stampede: Politics, Economics, and Reputation in Pre-Championship Chicago

By 1990, many people inside and outside Chicago viewed the city as a segregated dystopia with few prospects for growth. Decades of deindustrialization, paired with official economic development policy that favored certain areas of the city while ignoring others, made it difficult to argue otherwise. Like many other Rust Belt cities, Chicago lost staggering numbers of manufacturing jobs after World War II to nearby suburbs, Southern states, and foreign countries. Between 1950 and 1990, Chicago's population plummeted by more than 837,000, and the number of residents working in manufacturing plunged by about 62 percent (table 1.1).

Richard J. Daley, mayor from 1955 to 1976 (not to be confused with his son and later mayor, Richard M.), managed the early stages of this decline by supporting a progrowth coalition bent on bolstering Chicago's economy with expanded office and residential development in the Loop. The Chicago Central Area Committee (CCAC), a booster and planning organization representing the interests of real estate, financial, and architectural firms, enjoyed privileged access to the mayor's office, and during the 1950s, the group helped build a consensus within the local private sector around a Loop-centered

TABLE 1.1. Selected Employment and Population Statistics, City of Chicago, 1950–1990

	Total population	Employed persons	Employed in manufacturing (%)	Unemployed (%)
1950	3,620,962	1,614,867	36.7	n/a
1960	3,550,404	1,501,731	33.5	5.2
1970	3,369,357	1,387,908	32.0	4.4
1980	3,005,072	1,235,865	26.6	9.8
1990	2,783,726	1,207,108	18.7	11.3

Sources: U.S. Bureau of the Census, County and City Data Book (Washington, DC: Government Printing Office, 1956, 1967, 1972, 1983, 1994); Chicago Community Inventory, Local Community Fact Book, 1960 (Chicago: University of Illinois, Chicago, 1963).

Notes: Post-1960 data derived from sample-based estimations, as opposed to full counts. "Unemployed" calculated by dividing number of people reported as unemployed by total civilian labor force. An individual qualified as unemployed if he or she did not have a job at the time of questioning, searched for a job in the last month, and was available to accept a job. Unemployment numbers for 1960 were for the male civilian labor force only. "Labor force" included persons age 14 years and older through 1960, but subsequent surveys raised the cutoff to 16 years old.

growth model. In support of this vision, Daley used his influence over the allocation of federal urban renewal dollars and zoning law to incentivize investment downtown. This approach placed the needs of outlying neighborhoods relatively low on the city's list of priorities, but it helped avert the wholesale gutting of the central business district suffered by other Rust Belt cities.[9]

The federal government helped pick up the slack in neighborhoods Daley neglected by increasing the amount of aid it provided to cities like Chicago during the 1960s and 1970s. This meant that, even after lavishing the Loop with funding, the Daley administration often had enough left over to maintain a relatively high level of investment in working- and middle-class neighborhoods. The leftovers helped sustain robust city services and the closely related practice of employment patronage. The latter involved doling out city jobs to Daley's relatives and constituents, which allowed him and his political "machine," or the patchwork of political offices and organizations in Chicago and Cook County dominated by the local Democratic Party, to maintain voters' loyalty. Increased revenues from the federal government also helped fund urban social programs like public housing. Chicago was no utopia during the reign of Richard J. Daley, but the expansion of federal aid made local growth more inclusive than it otherwise would have been, in turn placing some important limits on the expansion of poverty and economic inequality.[10]

However, local officials' decision making when it came to economic development and social-welfare spending exacerbated racial segregation. Convinced that the presence of low-income and working-class African Americans in and around the Loop would deter investment, Daley and his private-sector allies oversaw several massive developments during the 1950s and 1960s that forced thousands of blacks from the area. Projects like Sandburg Village on the Near North Side and the University of Illinois's Circle Campus on the Near West Side also functioned as buffers between downtown revitalization and nearby African American neighborhoods. Local officials simultaneously directed the Chicago Housing Authority (CHA) to locate new public housing projects, intended to absorb low-income African Americans displaced by downtown development, in segregated neighborhoods outside the Loop. In the words of historian Paul Street, officials designed the new CHA high-rises "to prevent the horizontal spread of black Chicago by thrusting black families into the sky."[11]

This model of development ensured that, even in an era of relatively inclusive capitalism, black Chicago faced deteriorating economic prospects. The migration of whites and well-paying factory jobs to the suburbs during the 1950s and 1960s converged with pervasive discrimination in the suburban housing market to trap most African Americans in severely segregated neighborhoods where work was disappearing. By 1970, approximately one in five of Chicago's black families lived below the poverty line; and African American families, who accounted for one-third of the population, constituted 58 percent of all families in the city officially living in poverty. The economic crises of the 1970s, which accelerated central city deindustrialization and prompted the revolt of American business against the pillars of inclusive postwar capitalism like unionization and expanded social-welfare programs, widened the economic gap between African Americans and whites in the Windy City. Unemployment among the city's African American population leapt from 7 to 20 percent between 1969 and 1989, whereas among whites it crept from 3.1 to 5.4 percent.[12]

Widely circulated images of intensifying poverty among African Americans made whites anxious about living, working, or playing in cities like Chicago. Urban planner Robert Beauregard notes that in the popular—that is, white, middle-class—American psyche of the 1960s and 1970s, inner-city blacks came to symbolize "physical deterioration . . . crime, poverty, poor schools, and unemployment," as well as social unrest.[13] Many whites responded by abandoning Chicago proper for the suburbs, eroding the local tax base and further isolating the city's African American population. By the time Richard J. Daley died in 1976, the combination of deindustrialization and white anxiety had cemented Chicago's reputation as a bad place to live and do business. In 1975, *Harper's* magazine ran an article by Arthur Louis that ranked the fifty largest U.S. cities on the basis of quality-of-life variables

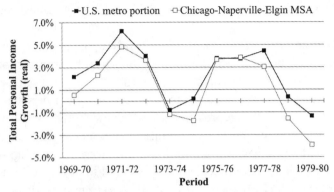

FIGURE 1.1. Real Total Personal Income Growth, Chicago-Naperville-Elgin Metropolitan Statistical Area and Metropolitan United States, 1969–1980
Source: U.S. Bureau of Economic Analysis, "Personal Income Summary," *Interactive Data Tables*, table CA1-3, accessed January 28, 2018, www.bea.gov/itable.
Notes: Personal income includes cash, certain transfer receipts like Medicaid and Medicare, lump-sum payments apart from normal earnings, and contributions by employers to health and pension funds. Inflation adjustments made using the Bureau of Labor Statistics annual average Consumer Price Index for all urban consumers (CPI-U national). All inflation adjustments for subsequent figures and tables made using the CPI-U national unless otherwise noted.

such as crime, health care, housing, and recreation. Chicago came in third worst overall, better than only St. Louis and Newark.[14] During the 1970s, the annual growth rate of the Chicago area's total personal income, a popular measure of economic expansion, lagged behind the metropolitan United States as a whole (fig. 1.1). And while Chicago averted a catastrophic fiscal crisis on the order of the one that hit New York in the mid-1970s, it did so only as a result of Richard J. Daley's ability to ignore the needs of low-income communities and cut spending at will—two practices made possible by the intractable power of Daley's Democratic Party machine.[15]

Admittedly, Chicago never enjoyed a pristine image. In 1961, sociologist Anselm Strauss noted that mention of the city conjured up visions of "crime, vice, urban disorganization . . . represented by 'Capone', 'gangsters' . . . by the well known slums and the black belt." However, for decades after World War II, an "imagery of enterprise" and "stupendous growth" counterbalanced this view. For many, according to Strauss, notions of Chicago as "Hog Butcher of the World" and the "City of Big Shoulders" somehow justified the vice and corruption.[16] During the first half of his tenure, Richard J. Daley maintained the city's status as the "City That Works" with a bevy of new infrastructural projects like the O'Hare Airport expansion.[17] But by the time Michael Bilandic became mayor upon Daley's death in 1976, that entrepreneurial reputation had receded, leaving behind stories of scandal, violence, and racism.

The victory of self-proclaimed reformer Jane Byrne in the 1979 mayoral race changed little in the city. Chicago continued to hemorrhage jobs and people. Shortly after the end of Byrne's tenure in 1983, a report from the Commercial Club of Chicago, an association of local business leaders, noted that the city still faced an "image problem" related to how "outsiders view its quality of life."[18] Byrne also reneged on promises to pay more attention to neighborhood redevelopment beyond the Loop. Her alleged reformism quickly gave way to acquiescence to forces she had vowed to undercut, such as the Democratic machine and the Chicago Central Area Committee. For example, she endorsed a ward redistricting pushed for by elites that weakened local African American political power.[19] Her capitulation ensured that most of whatever development would occur continued to take place inside the Loop. In contrast to broader trends, between 1978 and 1982 the number of private-sector jobs in Chicago's central business district jumped by an estimated 70,000, and over the same period the area added 4,600 new residential units.[20]

African American community organizations in Chicago understood the nature of the cleavage between their neighborhoods and the Loop and began mobilizing against it during the late 1960s. The result was a formidable grassroots infrastructure, and by the early 1980s this infrastructure had galvanized a base of black voters willing to cast their lot with nonmachine candidates.[21] These voters formed the backbone of a coalition of minorities and white progressives that propelled Harold Washington, an African American anti-machine Democrat, into the mayor's office in 1983.

While resistance from Democratic machine loyalists in the city council limited Washington's ability to implement his reform agenda, his administration achieved notable successes in pushing back against Loop-first development. Many of these victories did not involve the aggressive redistribution of existing wealth from downtown elites to less fortunate neighborhood residents but rather innovative efforts to distribute new resources more equitably.[22] Washington, for example, oversaw a sweeping overhaul of the city's disbursement of Community Development Block Grant (CDBG) monies, which previous mayors had funneled disproportionately to downtown revitalization. Under Washington, significant amounts of new CDBG funding found its way to struggling wards. As one researcher reports, the number of local entities receiving CDBG funds more than quadrupled during his tenure.[23] Washington's use of municipal bond issues, which funded what political scientist Barbara Ferman describes as "the largest neighborhood improvement program in the city's history," followed a similar pattern.[24]

The Washington administration paired this creative distribution of incoming resources with new forms of modestly redistributive fiscal policy. It pushed through a lease tax on commercial leases and advocated for a linked development tax that would have increased levies on new downtown construction. Washington also deemphasized costly, publicly funded festivals and mega-events meant to showcase the Loop, allowing several such initiatives to, in the words of *Tribune* reporter John McCarron, "die a quiet death." Under his tenure, the city withdrew its support for the ChicagoFest food and music festival staged annually at Navy Pier and reduced its role in the famed Taste of Chicago extravaganza. In addition, Washington ultimately withheld support for Chicago's bid to host the 1992 World's Fair.[25]

Washington also tried to incorporate low-income neighborhoods and communities of color into redevelopment efforts. He encouraged the involvement of community organizations in local planning and proved responsive to their demands. For example, as documented by political scientist Joel Rast, Washington's "local-producer" development strategy prioritized retaining and adding well-paying manufacturing jobs throughout the city over promoting expansion of the downtown real estate and service sectors.[26]

In and of themselves, Washington's policy initiatives were rather modest efforts to preserve and democratize the social programs and demand-driven growth strategies (i.e., public investments that stimulated employment among the working and middle classes) that flourished after the New Deal and World War II. However, these initiatives were downright radical when considered in the context of Rust Belt city politics elsewhere in the 1980s. By the end of the 1970s, economic recession, inflation, cutbacks in federal aid, and increasing competition for investment and jobs by suburbs, Southern states, and foreign countries severely constricted central-city revenue streams in the Northeast and Midwest. In response, political and economic elites in those regions abandoned the relatively aggressive tax-and-spend approach that had prevailed in the immediate postwar era. This meant slashing corporate tax burdens in a desperate attempt to retain and attract business, and scaling back public subsidies for social programs for the poor and working class. In many cases, it also meant the erosion of local democracy. In city after city, leaders reduced the public's ability to influence decisions about economic development by creating "quasi-public [development] entities," with members appointed by city or state executives rather than elected by citizens.[27] This new way of doing things typically involved the allocation of disproportionate sums of public resources to downtown redevelopment in order to appeal to tourists, potential residents, and corporate executives in hopes that their spending would heal the fiscal wounds inflicted by deindustrialization. Washington's policies were out of step with most of these trends, and they proved surprisingly successful, at least in the short term, given broader macroeconomic conditions.

Washington's willingness to go against the political and economic grain helps explain why, at least among African Americans and progressives, he became the most beloved black man in the history of Chicago, at least before Michael Jordan became a superstar. As his peers in other mayoral offices defined revitalization in terms of new glitzy downtown projects with little left over for working residents, Washington refused to accept superficial spectacle as a substitute for improving the lives of ordinary Chicagoans. Instead, he offered a vision of urban community defined by widespread economic security and vibrant democratic participation.

For its part, the local business community decried Washington's policies as "barriers to growth" and moved aggressively to stymie his reforms.[28] The Chicago Central Area Committee waged a protracted campaign against the lease tax and eventually beat it back. With this victory, the group's 1986 annual report declared, "The CCAC will continue to be against the imposition of new taxes on downtown development that will make the central business district less competitive with the suburbs and other regions of the country."[29] At times, then, Washington found himself outgunned by local elites who were unrelenting in their quest for expanded profits. Despite the fact that the Loop's economy boomed during Washington's tenure as a result of expansion of the local financial services sector, traditional progrowth advocates remained anxious about how, in the words of a CCAC publication, Washington's embrace of "increased political activism of [Chicago's] diverse communities" had "drastically altered the rules of the game."[30] They also feared that the heated political conflicts sparked by Washington's reformism had further undermined Chicago's reputation. Particularly embarrassing in this regard was Alderman Ed Vrdolyak, a longtime machine loyalist who appealed to racism among his white constituents by proclaiming that Washington aimed to purge them from the city altogether.[31] A 1987 Commercial Club report warned, "Chicago's image to the outside world as a place to do business remains somewhere between neutral and negative, due in no small part to the city's divisive political wars."[32]

Jordan and the Bulls: The New Icons of Chicago

News of Harold Washington's death from a heart attack on November 25, 1987, shocked supporters and adversaries alike.[33] Those who reelected him the previous year wondered whether the drive for reform had died along with the mayor. Democratic machine loyalists confirmed the fears of Washington's supporters by ramming through an eleventh-hour deal to install the machine's preferred man, Eugene Sawyer, in the mayor's office.

The day of Washington's death, it was business as usual for the Chicago Bulls. Michael Jordan led the team to victory in Milwaukee against the rival Bucks, netting thirty-three points on the way to his first of five NBA Most Valuable Player awards.[34] The winning continued in the coming years, and by the early 1990s, when the Bulls began to accumulate NBA championships, Jordan had superseded Washington as Chicago's most adored African American man. More than this, local papers proclaimed that Jordan and his teammates helped the city shed its sullied reputation. Days before the Bulls' first championship win in 1991, the *Tribune*'s Charles Madigan wrote, "A brief look at the history of word-association in Chicago proves that, with the Bulls and Jordan as ambassadors, the city is a lot better off." "Al Capone . . . Corrupt politicians . . . Racial division . . . Kids who can't read . . . Bankrupt," he went on, "these little word associations could go on and on. For the most part, they are history now."[35]

As luck would have it, the Bulls' new international prestige coincided with an aggressive push by Richard M. Daley, son of Richard J. and winner of the 1989 mayoral election, to market a revamped image of the city. This was part of the new Daley's implementation of an updated Loop-centered growth agenda focused on transforming downtown Chicago into a world-class leisure and cultural destination for tourists, professionals, and businesspeople; and it entailed a retreat from the expanded community input in planning and relatively progressive fiscal policy ushered in by Washington.[36]

This was not the only imaginable way forward—after all, the Washington administration had enhanced the equity of urban growth even in the face of federal retrenchment—but it was predictable. Despite promoting several African Americans and Latinos to powerful positions at City Hall, a nicety his father rarely indulged in, the junior Daley was not a reformer like Washington. He embraced the power brought by close alliances with traditional economic elites and the favoritism towards Loop-centric growth that such alliances demanded. As noted by one pair of researchers, Richard M. Daley depended heavily on corporate donations from sectors like legal and business services, finance, and the "convention, tourism, and entertainment industry" to fuel his repeated runs for mayor. Elite representatives from these parts of the local economy had much to gain from policies that favored public investment in Chicago's downtown, and their campaign contributions no doubt gave Daley ample reason to indulge them.[37]

Moreover, economic developments at the local and national levels made leisure-oriented growth seem sensible. Planners in Chicago and many other cities feared that the frenzied construction of downtown office space that buttressed recent growth could not sustain itself indefinitely.[38] In addition, ongoing federal cutbacks—between 1977 and 1988 federal outlays to state and local governments declined nearly 17 percent in real (inflation-adjusted) terms—meant that cities had to rely less on public investment.[39] Promoting and subsidizing downtown leisure and cultural amenities would, in theory, generate new spending more cheaply than robust public expenditures on citywide social welfare programs like affordable housing.[40]

Many inner-city mayors and their private-sector allies had already bet on an expanded tourist and entertainment economy as a panacea for deindustrialization and federal divestment, believing it would distinguish their respective locales in the eyes of consumers and investors. As political scientist Dennis Judd notes, American cities pursuing this "new downtown development strategy" built, or started building, hundreds of downtown sports stadiums, convention centers, and performing arts venues during the late 1970s and 1980s.[41] In theory, cities could lure the educated and affluent with unique leisure amenities.

Richard J. Daley and Harold Washington paid limited and sporadic attention to this approach. Richard M. Daley, however, moved quickly to make up for lost time. This meant channeling a disproportionate amount of what remained in the city's coffers toward new development in and around the Loop. Sociologist Costas Spirou reports that the City of Chicago funneled nearly $7 billion of the $11 billion it spent on infrastructure from 1989 to 2003 into "a four-mile lakefront stretch" in and around downtown.[42] This money funded projects like the expansion of McCormick Place Convention Center, the transformation of Navy Pier into a mall, and the development of Millennium Park. Daley also used taxpayer money to host 1994 World Cup matches and the 1996 Democratic National Convention in hopes that the events would showcase Chicago to the rest of the world. This was all in addition to expanded funding for downtown festivals like Taste of Chicago and the Chicago Air & Water Show. The new mayor also spearheaded a "greening" campaign that involved planting thousands of new trees in areas with dense foot traffic.[43]

Daley's moves to develop and market cutting-edge leisure infrastructure and supplement it with focused beautification efforts fulfilled the long-standing vision of downtown business interests. During the early 1980s the Chicago Central Area Committee repeatedly called for the redevelopment of Navy Pier, a new lakefront park, and extensive greening efforts as means of increasing "Chicago's appeal as a center for cultural activities and recreation" and supporting "continued growth of the city's tourism industry." Commercial Club publications echoed these desires, calling for an urban "marketing program . . . directed at correcting misconceptions of the area and improving its overall image." Surprisingly, given his fixation on Chicago's image, Daley seemed indifferent to the Bulls as they rose to international fame. After the second championship in 1992, he remarked: "It's only a basketball game. It's not going to change life."[44] Daley probably recognized that the fleetingness of an NBA championship recommended against hitching Chicago's reputation to the team.

Despite Daley's initial apathy, the meteoric ascent of the Bulls during the 1990s ultimately provided the raw material for what Costas Spirou and Larry Bennett describe as "the most effective accidental public relations campaign ever mounted on behalf of the city of Chicago."[45] As soon as Jordan and his teammates reached their first NBA finals in 1991, the local dailies described them as symbols of a new urban identity that erased popular perceptions of Chicago as the epitome of decline and disorder. In this telling, it was not only the redevelopment of Navy Pier and new trees that accounted for the transformation of the city's image. It was also the Bulls, and especially Michael Jordan. Throughout the 1990s, discussions of Jordan and the Bulls as the "City's Most Valuable Imagemaker[s]" by Chicago papers followed a consistent pattern. First, journalists acknowledged that mentioning Chicago to outsiders traditionally elicited references to urban disorder. As the *Tribune*'s Charles Madigan wrote in 1991, what people remembered before Jordan's Bulls was "the Chicago that seemed to be loosely controlled by a collection of competing barracudas masquerading as clowns." Usually, the story went on to suggest that the Bulls' prowess displaced this unflattering imagery with that of a legitimate winner. After the second title in 1992, Steve Johnson of the *Tribune* followed the script: "The river may leak . . . but at least we've got the Bulls. . . . In the afterglow of the Bulls' triumph Sunday night, Second City takes on new meanings. Try Second-Straight-Title-City. Second-to-None City." Not surprisingly, after Jordan's first retirement in 1993, the press anxiously pondered the potential consequences for Chicago's image. The *Sun-Times*' Richard Roeper compared the retirement to "waking up and finding a vacant lot where the Sears Tower used to be."[46]

The papers took up the story again after Jordan returned in 1996. Upon the fifth championship in 1997, *Tribune* columnist R. C. Longworth pontificated: "Because of moving pictures of large men in baggy shorts bouncing off satellites, Chicago has a new and better image in the world. Not so long ago, our town was known around the globe as Gangster City, synonymous with Al Capone and gangland."[47]

Indeed, more than anything else, the idea that Jordan supplanted Capone as the city's most recognizable icon underwrote arguments about professional basketball's role in rehabilitating the city's reputation. A few months after the Bulls' first title in 1991, a *Sun-Times* column by Irv Kupcinet recounted the experience of a traveler from Chicago who, upon disclosing his hometown to a customs agent in Grenada, was welcomed with, "Ah, Chicago . . . Michael Jordan!" Kupcinet rejoiced, seeing as how "Chicagoans visiting overseas invariably have been greeted with the rat-a-tat-tat of a machinegun, evoking memory of the late and unlamented Al Capone." After the second championship in 1992, the *Tribune's* editorial page got in on the action, crediting Jordan and the Bulls with having "buried the old-fashioned image of Capone in many ways," even though the paper conceded that the job was far from finished, since in some "far reaches of the globe" the images of "speakeasies, the Untouchables, [and] rat-a-tat-tat" still dominated.[48] However, by the time the team had amassed three straight championships, the local press began to assert that in most of those far reaches, Capone had become an afterthought in comparison to Jordan and company. In 1995, the *Tribune's* Rick Kogan announced that Jordan "has been able to forever eradicate the long-standing and playfully dark international image of Chicago. For decades saying 'I'm from Chicago' on foreign soil would occasion a mimed blast of machine gun fire and an 'Al Capone!' Now it elicits an 'Aaaaah, Michael Jordan.'"[49]

These were not isolated platitudes. Between 1991 and 2000, the *Tribune*, the *Sun-Times*, and *Crain's Chicago Business* published no fewer than seventy articles that mentioned Jordan superseding Capone as the city's poster boy. Many of them simply regurgitated the generic story, reminding readers that Chicago "no longer is Al Capone and machine guns and a massacre in a garage. . . . Chicago is Michael Jordan," or thanking Jordan for having "bumped off Al Capone as the worldwide symbol of our city."[50] Many other articles included anecdotes from the authors' international travels as proof. From customs checkpoints in Grenada to toll booths in Bulgaria, the story was the same: locals learned that a visiting journalist hailed from Chicago, and they burst out with their own version of, "Ahh, Cheecowgo! Cheecowgo Bools! Michael Jordan!" Tom Hundley, the *Tribune's* Rome correspondent, even recounted visiting a middle school classroom in Italy where, to his satisfaction, the children had never heard of Al Capone but blurted out "Michael Jordan" when asked to name a famous Chicagoan. Perhaps this sounded like a convenient fabrication, but it seems plausible when considered beside a 1997 article by Giorgio Viberti in the Italian paper *La Stampa* informing readers that Jordan had emerged as "the new king of Chicago, now richer and more famous than even Al Capone." In fact, many other national and international newspapers echoed these sentiments. For example, the *New York Times* and Spain's *El País* also joined the chorus of sources positing Jordan's displacement of Capone.[51] This suggests that the local press in Chicago was not an echo chamber when it came to this argument. The notion that the Bulls remade the city's reputation reached people outside Chicago and even beyond the United States.

By seizing on—some might say "manufacturing"—Jordan's succession of Capone as the face of Chicago, outlets like the *Tribune* and the *Sun-Times* took the lead in an opportunistic promotional campaign that supplemented the Daley administration's marketing of more conventional assets like Navy Pier. For the press, this was a low-risk, high-reward endeavor; it was a feel-good story that could help sell papers. A government-supported marketing effort centered on a professional sports team, in contrast, could backfire quickly for a city's tourism bureau, as one bad season might rob the promotion of its luster. In this regard, Daley's initial indifference to the Bulls made sense.

However, city officials jumped on the bandwagon once it became clear that Jordan's Bulls were much more than a flash in the pan. In 1993, the Chicago Convention and Tourism Bureau hosted a group of international tour operators and scheduled a stop for them at the new Michael Jordan's Restaurant. "Cultural Chicago," a $6 million promotional campaign launched by the Daley administration in 1997 and funded by a combination of public and private money, inserted images of Jordan in television and print advertisements running in both the United States and Europe.[52] The next year, Dorothy Coyle, the city's acting director of tourism, disclosed that an official tour coordinated by the city for international journalists included a visit to the Jordan statue in front of the Bulls' home arena. A pamphlet distributed to the journalists, as well to professionals from the travel industry, used Jordan as bait for potential downtown shoppers, urging visitors to set aside time for a stop at Niketown, the official "outfitter" of the Bulls' "superstar" guard.[53]

In the lead-up to Jordan's final game with the Bulls, Mayor Daley revealed how much his view of Jordan and the team had evolved. In an editorial for the *Sun-Times*, he wrote, "[Jordan] is one of the most beloved people in the city and one of its best tourist attractions." Clearly, local government had joined the press in viewing promotion of the Bulls as a viable response to the long-running call by Chicago's establishment for—as a 1983 report issued by the Chicago Central Area Committee put it—the "[development of] a symbol that represents the spirit and unity of Chicago."[54] Daley's change of heart should not come as a surprise. The superstar-led Bulls offered a tantalizing icon both utterly distinctive and broadly marketable. No other city could claim ownership over the most successful NBA franchise of the decade and the most popular athlete since Muhammad Ali. Jordan was not replicable, and many in Chicago recognized that exploiting the city's monopoly over him and his teammates could set it apart. *Tribune* columnist R. C. Longworth put it this way: "The Bulls have accomplished what years of civic boosterism, expensive advertising campaigns and foreign promotions failed to do."[55]

In this regard, the city received considerable help from the NBA as well as the sporting goods industry. International marketing efforts by the league, the increased global visibility of its players by way of their participation in the Olympics, and aggressive advertising by player sponsors like Nike all transformed a league with an uncertain future in 1980 into one whose 2002 "All-Star" game was broadcast in 210 countries and 41 languages.[56] This meant a level of international exposure for Chicago that exceeded the wildest dreams of the local tourism bureau.

Admittedly, the enthusiasm shared by progrowth advocates in Chicago about the Bulls' power as municipal icons tells us little about whether the team's image helped generate new local growth. Was it, in fact, realistic to imagine that Jordan's iconic status could help in the larger project of reversing postindustrial decline? More broadly, did the obsession of Daley and his allies in the media and business community with reinventing and promoting Chicago as a mecca for tourists and young professionals help Chicago regain its economic footing?

Both of these questions are impossible to answer precisely. However, the second is less controversial. Most experts, even those skeptical of Daley's agenda because it mostly ignored low-income neighborhoods, concede that the money poured into the Loop and lakefront boosted Chicago's economy, at least in the short term.[57] Indeed, a wealth of circumstantial evidence supports this perspective. First and foremost, from 1991 to 2000, inflation-adjusted total personal income in the Chicago metropolitan statistical area (MSA) grew nearly 37 percent. This was slightly faster than the metropolitan United States at large, and considerably faster than both the Los Angeles and New York City MSAs.[58] Chicago also enjoyed a boom in downtown population during the 1990s unrivaled by most major Midwestern cities (table 1.2), a fact consistent with the notion that public investment in new cultural and leisure amenities increased the Loop's appeal as a place to live for the professional and capitalist classes. This transfer of residents into the city's central business district coincided with a boom in the local service industry that offset losses in manufacturing (table 1.3). New residents often worked in white-collar "business service" jobs like consulting and generated increased demand for blue-collar service positions like janitorial work.[59]

TABLE 1.2. Downtown Population Change, Major Midwestern Cities, 1980–2000

City	1980	1990	2000	Absolute change 1980–1990	Percentage change 1980–1990	Absolute change 1990–2000	Percentage change 1990–2000
Chicago	**50,630**	**56,048**	**72,843**	**5,418**	**10.7**	**16,795**	**30.0**
Cincinnati	2,528	3,838	3,189	1,310	51.8	−649	−16.9
Cleveland	9,112	7,261	9,599	−1,851	−20.3	2,338	32.2
Columbus	8,737	6,161	6,198	−2,576	−29.5	37	0.6
Des Moines	8,801	4,190	4,204	−4,611	−52.4	14	0.3
Detroit	46,117	38,116	36,871	−8,001	−17.3	−1,245	−3.3
Indianapolis	33,284	14,894	17,907	−18,390	−55.3	3,013	20.2
Milwaukee	14,518	14,458	16,359	−60	−0.4	1,901	13.1
Minneapolis	33,063	36,334	30,299	3,271	9.9	−6,035	−16.6
St. Louis	9,942	9,109	7,511	−833	−8.4	−1,598	−17.5

Source: Adapted from Eugenie Birch, *Who Lives Downtown* (Washington, DC: Brookings Institution, 2005), 13.

Notes: Definition of "downtown" derived from queries of local officials about which census tracts constituted the downtowns of their respective cities.

TABLE 1.3. Number of Jobs in Selected Industries, Chicago City, 1991, 1997, and 2000

Year	Total (all industries)	Manufacturing	Retail and wholesale trades	Finance, insurance, real estate	Services
1991	1,196,041	192,920	249,347	168,111	445,988
1997	1,172,901	154,507	227,407	167,378	502,653
2000	1,249,249	142,485	234,571	164,999	551,620
% change 91–97	−1.9	−19.9	−8.8	−0.4	12.7
% change 91–00	4.4	−26.1	−5.9	−1.9	23.7

Source: U.S. Department of Housing and Urban Development, *State of the Cities Data Systems: County Business Patterns Special Data Extract*, accessed June 18, 2012, socds.huduser.org/CBPSE/CBPSE_Home .htm.

Notes: Includes full- and part-time positions. Because of the transition from the Standard Industry Classification (SIC) system to the North American Industry Classification System (NAICS) after 1997, the 2000 data represent estimates produced by the Census Bureau using a special NAICS-to-SIC bridge procedure. This means that comparability between 1991 and 2000 (for specific industry counts) is less precise than that between 1991 and 1997.

In addition, more people were visiting Chicago. Between 1993 and 1997 the number of tourists visiting the city each year jumped from 32 million to 42.9 million. This was especially impressive given that, according to a Commercial Club report from the previous decade, "the annual number of visitors . . . remained fairly constant" between 1978 and 1984.[60] The city's Office of Management and Budget estimated that between 1993 and 1999, combined annual attendance at the various festivals hosted by the city, about a quarter of which consisted of tourists in any given year, shot up from 4 million to more than 10 million (table 1.4).

Several of Chicago's tourist- and leisure-intensive sectors, such as amusement and recreation, as well as eating and drinking places, also experienced noteworthy growth, posting impressive numbers of new jobs during the 1990s (table 1.5). These data appear to vindicate Daley's aggressive pursuit

TABLE 1.4. Estimated Combined Festival Attendance, Chicago City, 1993–1999

Year	Combined festival attendance (millions)	Tourists as percentage of attendees
1993	4	23%
1994	6.5	26%
1995	7.5	27%
1996	8.1	26%
1997	9.4	n/a
1998	9.7	n/a
1999	10.1	n/a

Source: City of Chicago, Program and Budget Summary (1994–2000), Municipal Reference Collection, Harold Washington Library Center.

TABLE 1.5. Number of Jobs in Selected Service Industries, Chicago City, 1991, 1997, and 2000

Year	Services (total)	Personal services	Business services	Engineering and management	Social services	Tourist-intensive industries Amusement and recreation	Hotels and lodging	Eating and drinking places
1991	445,988	12,378	95,186	58,246	23,603	8,659	19,399	65,118
1997	502,563	12,826	118,770	57,897	33,610	10,580	16,447	71,726
2000	551,620	21,639	137,893	72,845	40,312	21,718	18,281	74,308
% change 91–97	12.7	3.6	24.8	−0.6	42.4	22.2	−15.2	10.1
% change 91–00	23.7	74.8	44.9	25.1	70.8	150.8	−5.8	14.1

Source: Department of Housing and Urban Development, State of the Cities Data Systems.

Notes: See table 1.3 for notes on comparability of data over time. "Eating and drinking places" technically falls under the "retail trade" industrial classification. According to the 1987 SIC codes, "personal services" includes establishments such as laundries and beauty/barber shops; "business services" includes establishments such as advertising firms, print shops, and computer maintenance and repair shops; "social services" includes establishments such as day-care centers and job-training facilities; and "engineering and management" includes establishments such as architectural and consulting firms. The stagnation of the "hotels and lodging" industry likely owed to lingering overcapacity from the 1980s. See J. Linn Allen, "Chicago's Inns Burst out of Overbuilt Slump," Chicago Tribune, February 21, 1997, ProQuest.

of tourist dollars. Indeed, there were a lot them to be had. According to the World Travel and Tourism Council, spending on leisure travel and tourism in the United States rose from $196 billion to $395 billion between 1989 and 1999 (real growth of approximately 61 percent).[61] Moreover, tourists tend to spend more per day than local consumers, and as an "export industry," tourism draws new money into urban economies from elsewhere, promoting consumer spending beyond the purchasing power of local residents.[62]

But what can we say about the role of Jordan and the Bulls in this story? Without relevant survey data, it is hard to quantify the extent to which the team influenced individuals' decisions about coming to Chicago to spend money. However, the press provided anecdotal evidence that the Bulls pulled travelers to the city. Though far from comprehensive, this evidence suggests that the *Tribune's* Rick Morrissey was serious when he asserted in 1999 that Jordan "filled hotel rooms . . . [and] shopping bags."[63] An early indication that basketball was attracting tourists to Chicago came after the Bulls erected a statue to honor Jordan outside the United Center, the team's new arena opened in 1994. *Tribune* reporter Steve Rhodes noted in November of that year that the bronze statue of "His Airness" was attracting "out-of-town visitors and . . . city and suburban residents to the West Side to pay homage to the larger-than-life basketball icon." If local reporters were to be believed, these visitors came from far-flung parts of the world like Central America and Asia.[64]

Michael Jordan's Restaurant also served as a magnet for Bulls-crazed visitors. In 1997, the *Tribune's* Dave Newbart reported that tourists from Hawaii, the Philippines, and Europe regularly stood in the middle of busy LaSalle Street to snap photos of the entire length of the mural of Jordan on the building's façade. José Luis Martínez, a sightseer from Valencia, Spain, who had come up short when he tried to score Bulls tickets, explained: "We heard [the restaurant] was one of the few things you had to do in Chicago. . . . The mecca is the stadium, but if you can't go there, you must come here." In some cases, though, these attractions simply could not make up for missing an actual game. In 1998, *Sun-Times* reporter Philip Franchine described conventioneer Alayda Linares as "heartbroken because the only thing[s] she really, really wanted to see" were the Bulls and Jordan.[65]

Unlike Martinez and Linares, many Bulls-crazed tourists made sure they had tickets before arriving. A forty-four-person tour group from Japan came to the city explicitly to attend games 1 and 2 of the 1996 NBA Finals at the United Center. The tour cost a minimum of $4,000, and it was not an isolated occurrence. By the mid-1990s tour companies organized these basketball getaways throughout the regular season. Hiromi Karasawa, a guide for one such company, told a *Sun-Times* reporter that "the airfare was cheaper than the (game) tickets." Tour participants, moreover, accounted for local spending on items other than tickets. According to another tour operator, some forked over $1,000 for an autographed Michael Jordan jersey.[66] Nimrod Armen traveled to Chicago all the way from Israel in 1996 just to see the Bulls after receiving game tickets as a bar mitzvah present. Chicagoan Bruce Woodward told the *Tribune*'s John Husar in 1997 that he had "friends in San Diego who came up a few months ago to see a Bulls game and all they wanted to do was take their pictures next to that [Jordan] statue."[67] These reports, which proved detailed and consistent enough to warrant general credibility, suggest that the Bulls were some visitors' primary motivation for coming to Chicago.

Economists justifiably scoff at the notion that sports teams and stadiums generate new spending in their host cities. Local entertainment expenditures tend to remain constant absent a real rise in wages, which means that money spent at a new arena usually comes at the expense of spending somewhere else nearby (economists call this the substitution effect). If, however, a team were to draw significant numbers of visitors from outside of their home market, one could make a stronger case for an arena's resulting in a net gain in local expenditures.[68] In other words, if the tourists and suburbanites whom the papers identified as visiting Chicago because of Jordan and the Bulls were not isolated instances, then the team exerted some sort of positive local economic impact.

This conclusion, however, comes with two caveats. First, any impact that Jordan and the Bulls had on the economy by way of increased tourist spending was marginal at best—a very small slice of a major urban economy. In 1993, a pair of *Tribune* writers credulously reported an estimate by "experts" that the draw of Jordan and the Bulls "generated" $150 million in annual tourism spending. This figure represented a tiny fraction of the Chicago metro area's gross regional product, which measured in the hundreds of billions of dollars. Moreover, the number was almost certainly a dramatic overestimate. Estimates like these regularly assumed that the tourists who spent the cash in question would not have come to Chicago were it not for Jordan and the Bulls. The evidence suggests that this was the case for some but offers no proof that it was the case for all, or even most.[69] The second caveat is that the economic impact of Jordan and the Bulls did not operate independently of other marketing efforts and entertainment infrastructure in Chicago. Some may have decided to visit the Second City largely because of the Bulls, but many would have thought twice about enduring a long, costly trip if the city offered no other diversions of consequence.

Discussions of the alleged power of sports teams to attract new spending and investment typically revolve around the alleged "big-league" status enjoyed by cities with major-league franchises. In other words, they focus on whether pro sports teams help attract new expenditures—beyond ticket sales—and investment by legitimizing a city as a major metropolis in the eyes of outsiders.[70] Debate on this issue inevitably heats up in the context of controversies over public financing for stadiums. By now, the script is well worn: opponents of public funding cite the absence of any empirical evidence that new stadiums or teams generate net gains in local economic activity, and proponents assert the presence of intangible economic benefits associated with being a "big-league" city.

Both sides of this debate tend to miss something. The Bulls of the 1990s enhanced the city's attractiveness to outsiders, but this had very little to do with some abstract status intrinsic to having a major-league team. After all, the city had hosted five major-league franchises since the 1960s. Nor did it have to do with the arena to which the Bulls relocated in 1994, as the success of and fervor around the team had started to develop well before the move. Rarely, if ever, did tourists interviewed by the local press cite the United Center, in and of itself, as motivation for their visit. What mattered was the unique success of the team. As long as Jordan and his teammates kept winning, the Bulls had the same international cachet regardless of where they played their home games. And even if, as economists Roger Noll and Andrew Zimbalist posit, there is "no systematic evidence" that businesses think about the local sports scene when making decisions on where to locate, local elites had little to lose in hawking the Bulls as ambassadors of the new Chicago.[71] Even though the impact of Jordan and the Bulls eluded measurement, this immeasurability proved relatively palatable from a fiscal perspective. The players did most of the work. The city, in concert with private firms, invested money in Bulls-linked promotion of Chicago, but the sums were paltry—on the order of a few million dollars—compared to the public subsidies often granted to teams for new stadiums.[72]

The lesson of this history is clear: cities would do well to abandon the use of tax dollars to build new stadiums and/or attract new teams. In the case of wildly successful franchises like the Bulls, it seems reasonable to incorporate them into official promotional efforts, as this requires relatively little public investment. Limiting sports-linked economic development policy in this way represents a more sensible approach than spending hundreds of millions of dollars in public monies on new stadiums that do little, on their own, to stimulate local growth. This is especially true in light of economics research demonstrating that increased stadium revenues do not necessarily translate into increased spending by teams on players—and, by extension, improved team quality—especially over the long term.[73] Hosting a dynastic franchise like the Bulls had everything to do with luck and nothing to do with the decisions of local policy makers. Urban politicians and planners, in other words, would do well to stick to addressing issues within their control rather than engaging in unproven strategies to bring perennial championships to their locales.

The Bulls and "Community" in Postindustrial Chicago

By many measures, Richard M. Daley's strategy of restructuring Chicago's economy around new cultural and leisure amenities paid off. Under his leadership, Chicago revamped its global image with new entertainment assets like Millennium Park and the championship Bulls, attracted thousands of visitors and new residents to the Loop and nearby neighborhoods, and experienced relatively impressive overall rates of growth. For the most part, however, the benefits of this growth did not trickle down to low-income and working-class residents, many of whom found themselves forced out of downtown neighborhoods as young professionals and wealthy empty-nesters moved in, driving up rents. Those already living in neighborhoods well beyond the Loop, especially on the South and West Sides, watched as the Daley administration directed most new public investment to the Loop and nearby lakefront.[74] As a result, entrenched poverty and segregation remained the norm, with few signs of change on the horizon.

This presented a marketing problem for local elites. Chicago's reputation had been dogged not only by the association with Capone but also by its protracted history of racial and economic inequality. By cultivating a new civic identity through a revitalized downtown without attending to the long-standing needs of poorer neighborhoods, especially predominantly nonwhite ones, Daley and his corporate allies risked exacerbating problems that had long fed anxieties about Chicago's hospitableness for tourists, new residents, and investors.

Local media attempted to resolve the contradiction between the glistening Loop and outlying neighborhoods starved of significant public investment by arguing that basketball united a fractured city. In many cases, the argument focused on how the Bulls unified Chicago across its segregated geography. After the first championship, a trio of *Sun-Times* reporters cataloged the diverse array of neighborhoods in which fans spilled into the streets to celebrate, ranging from the plush North Side communities off Rush Street to the notoriously destitute Henry Horner Homes housing project on the West Side. "North Side, South Side, West Side: People shot off firecrackers and took to the streets. They high-fived and hugged and cheered," the paper read. Sam Smith, the Bulls beat writer for the *Tribune*, spoke of "Chicago's team, winning with a bit of Gold Coast glamor and a lot of stockyards effort." Another *Tribune* article joined the themes of cross-class and cross-neighborhood solidarity: "Hardhats and suits, Chicagoans and suburbanites were talking to each other. . . . The Bulls' World Championship . . . for this week at least, united a diverse metropolitan area."[75] Although this coverage failed to mention race explicitly, by pointing out that the North, South, and West Sides celebrated simultaneously, journalists implied to anyone familiar with Chicago that the festivities transcended the city's racial boundaries.

Some made the point more explicitly. As the Bulls prepared for the 1991 finals, *Sun-Times* columnist Barry Cronin wrote of Bulls fans, "Young and old, rich and poor, black and white, blue collar and white collar bask in the glory of their heroes."[76] This was quite a feat since, in 1990, Chicago remained one of the nation's most racially segregated cities. According to that year's census, African Americans constituted at least 90 percent of the total population in 297 of the city's 829 census tracts, almost all of which were clustered on the South and West Sides (map 1.1). More than 87 percent of blacks living in Chicago city would have had to relocate to a different tract to achieve perfect black-white integration. Among major U.S. cities, only Cleveland ranked worse by this measure.[77] Elevated poverty rates often coincided with disproportionately black neighborhoods. In 1990, Chicago contained 140 census tracts with "concentrated" poverty—that is, with 40 percent of the population living below the official poverty line. Of these, 102 had black populations comprising over 90 percent of the tract's total population, and only 28 had African American populations comprising less than half the total (see map 1.1).

As the championships piled up, the local press continued to tout the team's ability to dissolve racial and ethnic distinctions. In 1996, *Tribune* columnist Bob Greene suggested that the Bulls functioned as a "local anesthetic," temporarily allowing Chicagoans to "forget about pain" caused by having to confront the reality of a city where blacks and whites still felt at odds.[78] And people did not have to take journalists' word for it. The night the Bulls put away the Los Angeles Lakers in the 1991 NBA Finals, Rodney Tolbert, an African American living on the West Side, told a trio of *Sun-Times* reporters: "We need this . . . Especially for the young people. It's bringing everybody together—black, white, Hispanic—they're all celebrating together." "It was like everything that was bothering you wasn't bothering you anymore," South Sider Elana Haskins-Flower told a pair of different journalists from the same paper.[79]

A handful of dissenters questioned this line of thinking. When interviewed after the Bulls 1996 championship, Chicagoan Paul Hajek sniped at

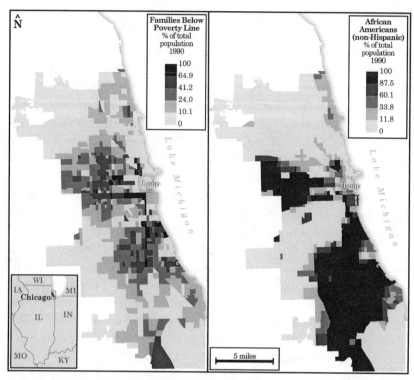

MAP 1.1. Family Poverty Rate and African Americans (Non-Hispanic) as a Percentage of Total Population by Census Tract, Chicago City, 1990

Source: Minnesota Population Center, *National Historical Geographic Information System: Version 2.0* (Minneapolis: University of Minnesota, 2011).

a pair of *Tribune* reporters: "Basketball doesn't change anything. If everyone got the day off when they won, then maybe it would be something." A few years earlier, *Tribune* columnist Mary Schmich had offered one of the only—perhaps *the* only—critique of the Bulls' alleged community building by a local journalist. She agreed with a friend who told her that "the Bulls' win has very little to do with Chicago and everything to do with the band of high-priced nomads hired to sink a ball in a basket. . . . All these guys we know by first names could all be somewhere else—and they will be before you know it."[80] For skeptics like Hajek and Schmich, it all seemed like a distraction from bigger issues.

They had a point. Richard M. Daley's growth agenda promised, if anything, to perpetuate racial and economic inequality. A study by the Boston Consulting Group found that, during the second half of the 1990s, the distribution of economic development money within Chicago was heavily weighted toward wealthy and gentrifying neighborhoods. According to Paul

Street's summary of the study, "The city's disproportionately white top two quartiles of community areas as ranked by 'economic vitality' received a total of $6.5 billion in economic development funding from 1996 to 2000," whereas the "disproportionately black and Latino bottom two quartiles received only $3.9 billion." Much of the money flowing into the top two quartiles went toward the Loop and affluent North Side in the form of infrastructural development and beautification. In many cases it subsidized projects such as the Hyatt Regency McCormick Place Hotel, which yielded millions in profits for private developers.[81]

Partisans of Loop-centered development could point with satisfaction to nominal decreases in the citywide poverty rate and a slight easing of black-white segregation between 1990 and 2000 to make the argument that the cohesion allegedly fostered by the Bulls coincided with real progress.[82] These statistics, however, masked less reassuring realities. Street reports that Chicago communities where the proportion of African American residents rose during the 1990s typically saw a decline in jobs. Moreover, between 1991 and 2000, more than 18,000 jobs disappeared from the nineteen zip codes where blacks were overrepresented, while zip codes where whites made up more than three quarters of the population added more than 19,200 positions. He also notes that, by the end of the century, fourteen of the city's fifteen poorest neighborhoods—poverty rates in these neighborhoods ranged from 32 percent to 56 percent—were disproportionately African American and eleven "were at least 94 percent black."[83] Much of this inequality owed to the ongoing decimation of decent-paying manufacturing work in the historically African American South and West Sides (map 1.2). The low-wage service jobs offered by Daley's new leisure economy proved poor substitutes, and the revitalization overseen by the mayor ultimately passed over much of the city.

Anselm Strauss, the aforementioned sociologist, noted more than half a century ago that celebrated urban symbols tend to "blot out what lies behind, or invite the viewer to disregard it, in favor of the interpretation presented by the façade itself."[84] So it was with the Bulls of the 1990s. By insisting that hosting an NBA champion provided Chicagoans from all neighborhoods with a reprieve from the pressures of their daily lives, the press encouraged readers to look away from ongoing inequities over which a basketball team had no influence. This was, in other words, at least in part about the local press using the Bulls to peddle a relatively superficial definition of "community." The urban historian Sam Bass Warner Jr. writes that at various times in the twentieth century—during the Progressive Era and the New Deal, for example—large contingents of American city dwellers defined the concept in terms of "equality of being." That is, they believed that universal access

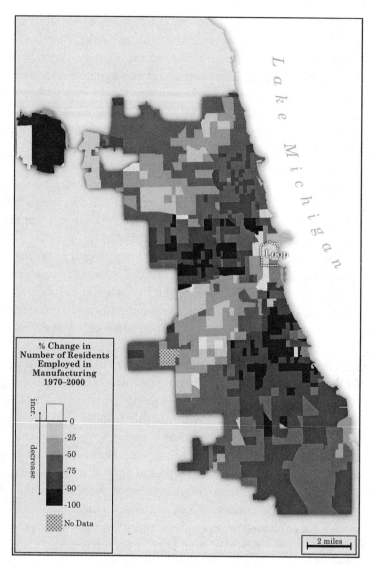

MAP 1.2. Percentage Change in Number of Residents Employed in Manufacturing by Census Tract, Chicago City, 1970–2000

Source: US2010 Project, Longitudinal Tract Database, *LTDB Downloads*, 2012, accessed January 26, 2018, www.s4.brown.edu/us2010/Researcher/LTBDDload/DataList.aspx.

Notes: Tract boundaries change from decade to decade, but the data set cited here harmonizes all the data to 2010 tract geography.

to the necessities of life, such as adequate food and housing, constituted the foundation of a healthy community.[85] This resembled the view held by members of the Harold Washington coalition in the mid-1980s. In 1990s Chicago such a definition threatened the agenda of the Daley coalition, and promotion of the Bulls as a source of civic cohesion offered an alternative conception of community: equality of fandom. The problem with this version lay in its shallowness. Basketball could entertain and distract, but it could not feed or house those excluded from the fruits of urban capitalism.

The enthusiasm with which the mainstream media, local officials, and business leaders encouraged ordinary Chicagoans to identify as Bulls fans instead of, say, residents with a shared interest in basic, "bread and butter" issues was perfectly consistent with the rise of exclusionary capitalism in the last quarter of the twentieth century. One of the ways that politicians in the New Gilded Age, such as Ronald Reagan, appealed to working- and middle-class voters shaken by the economic and social turmoil of the 1970s was to emphasize cultural rather than economic definitions of community—racial, religious, and nationalistic. This was music to the ears of big business, as these cultural definitions displaced class-based ones that pitted organized workers against employers or groups of concerned citizens against unfettered corporate power.[86] The rush of elites in Chicago to cultivate a sense of community around the Bulls was one of countless examples over the past four decades of those at the top providing shallow, alternative forms of inclusion for those left behind by exclusionary capitalism.

But touting the Bulls' success only went so far in terms of eclipsing Chicago's deep socioeconomic divisions. The limits of this strategy became all too clear when, after each of the team's championship-clinching games, celebrations throughout the city morphed into looting, property damage, and confrontations between police and residents. While disturbances broke out immediately after every championship, data collected on arrests and property damage by sociologist Michael Rosenfeld show that the most extensive unrest took place in 1992 (1,060 arrests, 347 cases of property damage) and 1993 (682 arrests, 177 cases property damage), and subsided considerably in subsequent years. Although the disturbances were concentrated in the disproportionately black and low-income South and West Sides, in 1992 they included what Raymond Coffey of the *Sun-Times* described as a "yuppieish young crowd" downtown that flipped over cars and broke the glass of several upscale Loop retailers.[87]

As Rosenfeld notes, the explanations offered by the Chicago papers for the 1992 riots provided a "mostly misleading picture," ignoring the possibility that racial and economic inequality in poorer neighborhoods fueled some of the disturbances. In many cases, the dailies lumped together the chaos in the Loop with the disorder on the South and West Sides, making it easy to avoid a discussion of the city's racial and economic geography.[88] Typical in this regard was the ever-histrionic Jay Mariotti, sports columnist at the *Sun-Times*. In 1992 he wrote, "The city has 3 million people, the suburbs another 5 million, yet a barbaric fringe drags Chicago through national newscasts as a riot capital." Mariotti saw no need to distinguish between looting a store to obtain groceries and tipping over a taxi downtown before taking the L back to the North Side. All the celebrants deserved the "barbarian" label as he saw it. "It's sad enough that the Bulls only had an hour in the spotlight before relinquishing it to Division Street, Pulaski and Madison, the South-Side, and the Not-So-Magnificent-Mile," he continued. By failing to differentiate the disturbances downtown from those in economically depressed and racially segregated neighborhoods, columnists like Mariotti preempted a discussion about why conditions in certain parts of the city might have made the unrest rational. They also took the city's leadership off the hook for asking tough questions about the root causes of the violence.[89]

When reporters covering the riot engaged with the issues of race and class, they typically posited that the unrest consisted of two phenomena: rowdy and relatively affluent fans in the Loop who took celebrating too far, and low-income blacks on the South and West Sides who looted neighborhood stores to take vengeance on Korean shopkeepers with whom they had a long history of tension. A 1992 *Tribune* article by Jennie Acker spoke to the second half of this interpretation, asserting that the looting in African American neighborhoods the previous year had hit Korean merchants hardest, and quoting residents who corroborated the uneasy relationship between the merchants and people who lived nearby.[90] Reporters like Acker were right to suggest that what happened in black neighborhoods differed from the events downtown, but the argument about blacks taking revenge on Koreans does not hold up in the face of data collected by Rosenfeld. Rosenfeld found that Arab-owned stores in South and West Side zip codes that had over ten looting incidents proved much more likely to suffer looting and damage than Korean shops. He hypothesized that the difference resulted from the fact that Arab merchants owned a larger proportion of food and liquor stores containing items of immediate utility to economically disadvantaged residents.[91]

Rosenfeld's analysis confirms that "the difference in the looting rate experienced by Arab, Korean, and black-owned stores is essentially determined by the kind of stores the different groups tend to own." In other words, whether a store sold food and drink proved a much better predictor of its probability of being looted than did the race of the owner. Rosenfeld concludes that, in passing over the fact that "looters selectively targeted" food and liquor stores "without regard for the ethnicity of the store owner," local papers neglected the possibility that hunger and deprivation were more important than interracial resentment in the looters' minds.[92]

The only reporting that offered a more historically informed interpretation came from outside Chicago. Rosenfeld notes that the *New York Times* headline "Victory Seen as Chance to Vent Pent-Up Anger" was "much closer to [the] view that the Bulls rioters were responding, in part, to a reservoir of political, economic, and racial grievances."[93] The *Washington Post*'s Michael Abramowitz also offered up the possibility that there was more to the rioting in 1992 than tension between Koreans and blacks. "Although a number of the establishments torched Sunday night were owned by Korean Americans, anti-Korean sentiment appeared to be only one ingredient in the violence," Abramowitz explained. Anticipating Rosenfeld's conclusions, the article revealed that "Korean businessmen interviewed said they did not appear to be a major target of the looters."[94] The coverage of the riots in other cities gave the impression that the Chicago media's interpretation of the events resulted not from a lack of information but from pressure to make sense of them in a way that minimized damage to the city's reputation.[95]

Legacies of Richard M. Daley and Bulls-Linked "Community"

When Richard M. Daley became Chicago's mayor in 1989, he inherited a difficult situation. The city remained profoundly segregated along lines of race and class. The federal government continued to retreat from its earlier role as an economic crutch for cities in the grip of deindustrialization. The political landscape was as polarized as ever. It thus makes little sense to place all the blame on Daley for things like the post-championship riots. He had not been in office long enough to make a significant dent in problems like racial and economic inequality.

When Daley left office in 2011, however, such problems still plagued Chicago; in some cases, they were worse. In 2010, the city ranked as having the most intense black-white segregation in urban America according to one quantitative measure popular among social scientists. Economic inequality grew considerably during his tenure; when Daley departed City Hall Chicago was just about as economically unequal as El Salvador. Many of the city's residents, especially those of color, still faced rampant police brutality and rapidly deteriorating neighborhood schools. Thousands of public housing residents found themselves with nowhere to go after the Chicago Housing Authority displaced them to make way for upscale development in and around the Loop. And Daley's willingness to borrow massive sums to finance pet projects on the lakefront, along with his resistance to raising local taxes (save sales taxes and user fees that hit working and low-income Chicagoans the hardest) left Chicago in a "fiscal mess."[96]

Such a negative appraisal of Daley's legacy invariably elicits what historian Paul Street terms the "there is no alternative" thesis from Chicago elites. It goes something like this: Had Daley not aggressively funded and promoted Chicago's downtown entertainment infrastructure, Chicago would have become Detroit. Without a herculean effort to ensure that growth of the tourism and leisure industries filled the gap left by deindustrialization, in other words, it would have spiraled into irreversible economic and social decline. Chicago had no choice but to join in the fierce competition between cities for new visitors, residents, and investors by rebranding itself as a world-class cultural destination. Even Costas Spirou and Dennis Judd, two academic experts often critical of Daley, accede to this point of view. "If the City of Spectacle that visitors inhabit did not exist," they write, "Chicago's economy would be in shambles." Spirou and Judd admit that "a price has been paid" by many low-income and working folks for Daley's successes. They insist, however, that the "cost of failure would have been immeasurably higher" and that otherwise the city would be "less prosperous, less attractive, and less diverse."[97]

If we take this perspective for granted, then touting Jordan and his teammates as a salve for intractable social divisions was not a distraction from injustices that powerful people like Daley chose to ignore. Instead, it was a welcome, if unexpected, perk for a city with no other choice but to pour the bulk of its resources into spectacular downtown and lakefront tourist attractions. In other words, settling for superficial forms of urban community rooted in sports fandom made sense in a city that allegedly had no alternative to pursuing a model of urban growth that excluded many, if not most, Chicagoans from its benefits. At least everyone, rich and poor alike, could "connect" by way of Jordan and the Bulls.

There are several reasons to question this line of thinking. For example, the "no alternative" thesis seriously downplays the political lessons taught by the Harold Washington administration. Washington was far from perfect, and many of his initiatives ran aground, but on par he ushered in a period of much more inclusive economic development for Chicago—development that incorporated neighborhoods far beyond the Loop and lakefront to an unprecedented degree. Moreover, he did so at a moment when powerful interests insisted that such a project was impossible. The needs of working and low-income people had to be ignored, elites argued, to cope with fiscal strain and free up mayors to invest more in the scramble for tourist dollars.

Washington often defied this consensus by creatively reallocating shrinking revenue streams and occasionally tapping the coffers of the wealthy to generate new revenue streams. In short, he proved the hollowness of the "no alternative" logic that still maintains a tight grip over urban elites and policy makers today.

Those who argue that Daley's only option was to flood the Loop and lakefront with billions in public investment also tend to ignore that growth in that part of the city was *not* the problem with Chicago's economy. Data collected by the Chicago Central Area Committee during the mid-1980s show that the city's downtown experienced a dramatic economic expansion under Washington. Take, for example, the CCAC's 1986 annual report. It highlighted the following downtown development milestones from that year: the opening of "five major buildings representing nearly 3.5 million square feet of space," the impending "completion of three major hotels announced in 1986," and the increase in "the number of residences in the expanding central area by 1,376 units." The story proved largely the same in 1987, when "projects totaling close to 25 million square feet of new and rehabilitated space were completed or under construction in the Central Area." Between 1980 and 1990, estimated office space in the Loop and its immediate perimeter grew from just over 81 million square feet to nearly 117 million square feet. The estimated number of residential units went from approximately 25,000 to more than 41,000, a staggering increase given the fact that there was virtually no growth in this figure during the 1970s.[98] As D. Bradford Hunt and Jon DeVries note in a recent study, "Massive private investment in new skyscraper construction and loft conversion [downtown] began in the early 1980s as office demand boomed." They go on, "A postindustrial economy centered on financial services accelerated in the aftermath of the 1981–1982 recession."[99]

Citing these data is not to insinuate that Daley had no justification for some public investment in cultural and entertainment amenities in and around the Loop. Rather, it speaks to his excessiveness in funneling the greater part of the city's economic development budget to such amenities in a part of the city already attracting a new wave of professional jobs and residents on its own. The litany of downtown projects overseen by Daley in which the city invested nine figures (or more) of public funds suggests more of an addiction to spectacle than a rational approach to economic development: $200 million to renovate Navy Pier (Daley also set in motion efforts that would culminate in hundreds of millions in additional public investment in Navy Pier after he left office), nearly $1.9 billion on two expansions of McCormick Place (site of the city's convention center), $120 million on upgrades for the lakefront Museum Campus; $400 million to renovate Soldier Field (home of the NFL's Chicago

Bears), and $270 million on Millennium Park, not to mention proposals that never came to fruition, such as Daley's promise to spend $500 million on the 2016 Olympics during Chicago's failed bid for the games.[100]

Was all of this necessary to avert economic apocalypse in Chicago? The data from the CCAC indicate that a significant amount of additional investment in and around the Loop could have happened without much help from the Mayor's Office. Unlike Detroit, where the entire city lived and died by the auto industry, a robust service economy based on sectors like finance already had deep roots in Chicago's downtown in the 1980s. The Loop, in other words, ran far less risk of wholesale deterioration than downtown Detroit. Even if downtown revitalization was a priority, Daley had some wiggle room in terms of spreading investment more evenly across the city—something already demonstrated by Harold Washington. His administration did not have a metaphorical gun to its head when it came to its spending. It made deliberate choices with the goal of directing prosperity toward certain people and away from others. The city's neglect of the "others"—for example, those who felt compelled to loot grocery stores after the Bulls' championship wins—is part of what prompted local media and elites to highlight forms of "community" that required little in the way of actual investment in projects and programs beneficial to the masses.

The contention that Daley's investment in and around the Loop paid for itself in terms of increased economic activity and tax revenue, ultimately leaving the city better off in fiscal terms, also lacks empirical support. In fact, available evidence suggests the opposite. As Daley's mayoral tenure came to a close, several bond-rating agencies downgraded the city's debt. The moves came in response to the agencies' recognition of the fact that the city's recent history of spending and taxation left it ill equipped to deal with many basic responsibilities, such as funding pension payments and preventing crime. In 2015, Chicago earned the dubious distinction of being one of only two major U.S. cities saddled with a "junk" bond rating. The other: Detroit. Ironically, rating agencies had upgraded Chicago's municipal bond grade shortly before Harold Washington's death, acknowledging what *Tribune* reporter Merrill Goozner described as the "city's improving economy and stabilization of financial operations."[101]

A final caution needs to be issued to those quick to favorably compare the recent economic history of Chicago to other Rust Belt cities like Detroit. In the epilogue to their recent study of Daley's economic stewardship of Chicago, Spirou and Judd acknowledge the mayor's "policy failures" but ultimately justify his decision making. "A visit to Detroit or Gary shows that the results of disinvestment are catastrophic, and it benefits no one at all," they posit. They add, "We confess that when we . . . stroll along the lakefront with friends or out-of-town visitors, their comments, and ours, about Chicago do not sound much different from the praise that was lavished on Daley's lakefront program when he was in the midst of implementing it."[102] These comments miss a glaring reality. If the "friends" and "out-of-town" visitors mentioned by Spirou and Judd were to move beyond the confines of the Loop, the lakefront, or the middle- and upper-middle-class North Side of the city, they would encounter something as bad as, if not worse than, Detroit. According to the most recent data released by the U.S. Census Bureau, over 40 percent of the nearly 680,000 people populating Detroit live below the poverty line. Chicago's 243 poorest census tracts contain a population approximately equal to that of the Motor City. In those tracts, the overwhelming majority of which are concentrated in large pockets on the West and South Sides, the poverty rate stands at 41 percent.[103] In other words, Chicago contains a veritable Detroit within its borders. It is two distinct cities: on one side, a glistening, tourist-friendly downtown abutted by gentrified or gentrifying neighborhoods; on the other, a sea of divestment, boarded-up windows, police brutality, and dimming hopes for some measure of economic and physical security for residents.

This reality was not inevitable. While Daley lacked total control over the economic fate of Chicago's poorer residents—rising economic inequality during his tenure had as much to do with federal as with local policy—he and his allies made crucial decisions on where to allocate resources. Those decisions had dire consequences for those without much to gain from an enhanced tourism and entertainment infrastructure in the Loop. Given the hundreds of thousands of vulnerable Chicagoans who had little to show for the overhaul of their city's image during the 1990s, it seems fair to consider the "community" fostered by the Bulls as, at best, a superficial palliative for these people's continued suffering. At worst, the "community" built by the team distracted residents from the consequences of a model of exclusionary capitalist growth that benefited the few rather than the many.

✴

When Jordan left for good in 1998, the Bulls nosedived, finishing the following season with the worst record in the NBA's Eastern Conference. With little to celebrate, some local journalists took time out to reflect on the team's remarkable run over the previous decade. In 1999, Chicago sportswriter Jay Mariotti measured the impact of Jordan and his teammates by their ability to project a winning image to faraway places not known for their basketball fandom. "I've walked into a store in basketball-dead northern Norway, not terribly far from the Arctic Circle, and seen a Michael Jordan poster," he remembered, adding,

"I've had a translator in an obscure part of Japan grin when I mentioned Michael Jordan." Less than a year after Jordan's departure, Mariotti couldn't help but wonder, "What will the town do without [him]?"[104]

For some locals, pride in Jordan quickly gave way to paranoia about who or what would prevent Capone's legacy from reasserting itself. In 2000, an editorial in the *Arlington Daily Herald*, a suburban Chicago paper, fretted over the fact that a recent *20/20* television special on political corruption in Chicago featured images of Capone for historical context and carried the headline "With Michael Gone, Capone Sneaks Back In."[105] Perhaps the concern was justified. After Jordan's departure, Chicago struggled to maintain the image of a city on the remake. Nearly two decades into the new century, its reputation today is dogged by reports of underfunded schools and intensified racial and economic segregation of students, rampant corporate cronyism, and surging violence. In a 2013 discussion of the city's long-running homicide epidemic—a problem that intensified dramatically after 2015—Kathy Bergen and Robert Channick of the *Tribune* expressed concern that the reputation of a Chicago that "has worked hard to burnish its image as a beautiful, global capital with a diverse economy and robust culture . . . is in danger of being recast."[106]

Trying to understand the value of Jordan's Bulls as a postindustrial icon is a frustrating enterprise because we have no way of pinpointing how different the city's politics and economics would have been in the absence of Jordan and six NBA titles. Nonetheless, the evidence allows for some basic conclusions. First, the Bulls' emergence as a municipal icon in Chicago probably had some limited economic benefit for the city, but this had little to do with the most frequently debated form of sports-linked economic development, namely public investment in new stadiums. In terms of the Bulls' economic impact, it was slam dunks and victories that mattered, not subsidies for new skyboxes or domes.

Despite its economic benefits, Bulls fervor masked the resurgence of exclusionary capitalism in Chicago. This growth model prioritized the leisure pursuits of the affluent over an improved quality of life for Chicagoans outside of the professional or capitalist classes. Despite the long list of excuses issued in defense of Daley's obsession with this model, the historical record, especially the brief stint of Harold Washington as mayor, suggests that the city could have done things differently without imploding economically. Had different choices been made, Chicagoans might have had less need to take temporary solace in their local NBA franchise.

"Normally, Heroes Cost You Money": Bulls Fans in the New Gilded Age

Before the sun came up on June 14, 1991, Ed Mueller of suburban Des Plaines snuck out of the house as his wife and kids slept and made his way to Grant Park in downtown Chicago. There was no late-night tryst waiting for him; he simply wanted to score a good viewing spot for the rally at which the Bulls and their fans would celebrate the team's first NBA championship. Many went to great lengths to partake in the 1991 festivities, as well as the rallies that took place after the Bulls' five subsequent titles. One person even told the *Chicago Tribune* that he lost his job for ignoring his boss's warning that he would be fired for skipping work to attend the 1992 rally.[1]

In the wake of the 1991 celebration, which drew hundreds of thousands of people, the local press highlighted the mixed origins of those in attendance. A typical account of the rally by *Tribune* reporters George Papajohn and Jodi Wilgoren noted a handwritten sign reading "Park Forest loves the Bulls." The journalists went on to mention several other neighborhoods and suburbs allegedly represented at the festivities: Palatine, Evanston, Wheaton, Hyde Park, Hanover Park, and the Near West Side.[2] Stories like this suggested that basketball *could* bring disparate parts of the metropolis together. Indeed, the Grant Park celebrations after each of the Bulls six championships offered a visible reminder that the team did more than help create profits for a select few or distract from the difficulties of urban life. The team temporarily transformed a small part of the Loop into an integrated space where Chicagoans basked collectively in the euphoria of victory.

Even if the Bulls succeeded in bringing together a mix of Chicagoans in Grant Park, not all fans celebrated the team on the same terms. For many, the rallies were their only chance to see the NBA champions in person, as the steep ascent of ticket prices that had begun in the second half of the 1980s made attending a live game at Chicago Stadium unrealistic. These heightened costs resulted in large part from the team's adoption of a business model that depended on catering to an expanding base of wealthy fans. Nothing signaled this trend more than the construction of the United Center in the early 1990s as a replacement for Chicago Stadium. The arena's design focused on maximizing premium seating like luxury boxes and club seats, which quickly emerged as a premier leisure option for the city's elite.

Team officials and the local press argued that the growing exclusivity of the United Center was the unfortunate outcome of the Bulls' obligation to keep up with rising player salaries. In theory, higher ticket prices and the expansion of premium seating would generate the revenues needed to cover increasing labor costs. However, this explanation confused cause with effect. Elevated ticket prices resulted from exponential growth in the demand for seats, particularly high-end ones, and high player salaries represented the outcome of increased revenues from costlier tickets, skybox leases, and the soaring value of television rights contracts.

The extraordinary popularity of Michael Jordan explained part of this increased demand. But the growing clamor for seats, the increasing willingness of deep-pocketed fans to pay exorbitant sums to secure them, and the resulting displacement of many working- and middle-class fans by richer ones occurred at stadiums and arenas across the country. In other words, larger forces were also at work. Chief among these was the upward redistribution of income and wealth that characterized the resurgence of exclusionary capitalism, which meant that the profitability of venues like the United Center depended more than ever on cultivating and targeting an affluent clientele. As those at the top captured greater and greater shares of economic growth, it only made sense for team owners like Reinsdorf to do whatever they could to convince them to spend their money at live NBA games. Indeed, those in the Bulls' front office expended considerable time and effort transforming basketball into a luxury product. In doing so, they dramatically enhanced the franchise's ability to exploit its long-running local monopoly power—that is, its position as the only "seller" of live NBA games in Chicago—to hike up admissions costs.

The revival of exclusionary capitalism did not mean that leagues and teams suddenly ceased promoting the physical interaction of fans from different racial and class backgrounds; the Bulls rallies in Grant Park attested to this. However, it did result in this interaction occurring less and less frequently inside major-league stadiums and arenas. Team owners, along with capitalists from other parts of the urban entertainment industry, reengineered their venues in ways that appealed to corporate executives and the professional class, and in doing so reduced access for those of more modest means. Increasingly, championship rallies and watching games on television became second-tier experiences for fans priced out of actual games.

Rallying around the Bulls: Race, Class, and Celebration in Chicago's Grant Park

Today, Grant Park stretches for more than a mile and a half along the lakefront of downtown Chicago (map 2.1). Originally designated a public park in the mid-nineteenth century, by 1930 it hosted many of the city's most venerated cultural institutions, including the Art Institute of Chicago, Adler Planetarium, and Shedd Aquarium. Decades later, the park became the setting of one of the most infamous chapters in the city's history when police attacked antiwar demonstrators gathered there during the 1968 Democratic National Convention.[3]

In addition to situating Jordan's Bulls as an antidote to the legacy of Al Capone, the media suggested that the team helped erase memories of the clash between cops and protestors. Looking back in 2006, *Tribune* columnist Richard Rothschild wrote, "Until the sublime play of Michael Jordan . . .

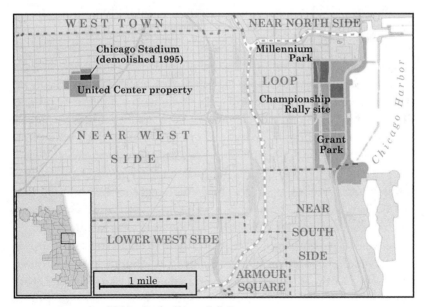

MAP 2.1. Geography of Celebration for Chicago Bulls Fans
Source: Chicago Metropolitan Agency for Planning, *Land Use Inventory* (1990, 2001), accessed January 27, 2018, www.cmap.illinois.gov/data/land-use/inventory; City of Chicago, *Chicago Data Portal*, accessed January 27, 2018, data.cityofchicago.org/.

Chicago was known as a center of gang violence, the 1968 Democratic National Convention, a less than sterling political tradition and underachieving sports teams." When the city announced the day after the Bulls won their first title in 1991 that Grant Park would be the location of an official "victory celebration," the stage was set not just for a party but also for rehabilitating the image of a downtown landmark with a checkered past.[4]

According to the local press, the event succeeded on both counts. An estimated five hundred thousand Bulls faithful turned out to witness the players and coaches brandishing their championship trophy. Rob Karwath of the *Tribune* noted the stark contrast between the Bulls rally and the tumultuous scene in 1968. "There was something missing from a typical mass gathering in Grant Park," he wrote. "Most of the pushing was polite pushing."[5]

Reporters also cited the diversity of the attendees as proof of sport's power to break down the city's socioeconomic divisions. Journalists who roamed the crowd cataloged the long list of places from which celebrants hailed: Sally Wyatt of suburban Aurora, Randall Woodward from the South Side, Tom Bare of suburban Des Plaines, and students from Brown Elementary School on the West Side, to name a few. According to one *Tribune* report, "Fans were inspired by the No. 1 team, uniting for an hour at least and forgetting the divisions that mark daily life . . . North Side and South Side and West Side, city dweller and suburbanite, African-American and German-American and Italian-American."[6]

The picture painted by such accounts was not far off the mark. The celebration held in Grant Park in 1991 *was* an astonishing display of diversity. Photographs of the crowd at the rally show African Americans, Asians, Latinos, and whites crammed together like sardines behind police barricades.[7] More than just happening to stand next to one another at the rally, people from different backgrounds interacted joyously. For example, a photo from the rally published in the *Tribune* shows two young men, one African American and one white, exchanging an enthusiastic high five.[8] One would be hard pressed to find better support for the argument of sociologists David Karp and William Yoels that, "on its most obvious level, sport provides a universal language for people and thereby lubricates the gears of social interaction."[9]

As the Bulls' championship ways continued, so did the rallies.[10] The press coverage of the celebrations thinned out after 1991, but the themes of diversity and social cohesion via sport still surfaced in the reports that did appear. In fact, by the late 1990s, the rallies had become a new benchmark for showcasing Chicago's diversity. Reporting on a conference of local clergy at the University of Illinois at Chicago in the fall of 1997, the *Tribune*'s editorial page noted that, "except for the Bulls championship celebrations in Grant Park, [the conference] may have been the most diverse mass gathering of Chicago-area residents ever. Catholic, Protestant, Jewish and Islamic clergy embraced on stage before a sea of black, brown, and white faces from virtually every section of the city and suburbs."[11]

The idea that sport could promote racial integration was not limited to journalists. In 1997, an ABC News poll asked a random sample of Americans, "Do you think that the presence of Whites, Blacks and other minorities on sports teams helps, hurts, or has no effect on integration and reduction of racial tension in other areas of life?" Overall, more than half of respondents believed that the integration of sports teams positively affected larger society (fig. 2.1). Most Americans, in other words, believed that sport had the power to undermine long-standing patterns of segregation. The Grant Park rallies seemed like the perfect case in point.

But it was more than the power of sport to transcend racial divisions that unified the fans gathered in Grant Park. According to press coverage of the rallies, what also linked them together was the fact that most of them "couldn't get tickets" to actual games.[12] Indeed, by the 1990–1991 NBA season, the cheapest ticket to a Bulls game at Chicago Stadium, a standing-room-only

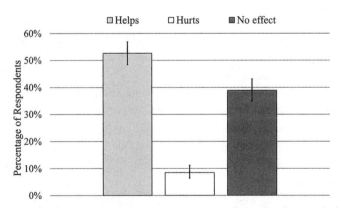

FIGURE 2.1. Reponses to February 1997 ABC News *Nightline* Poll Question: "Do you think that the presence of Whites, Blacks and other minorities on sports teams helps, hurts, or has no effect on integration and reduction of racial tension in other areas of life?"
Source: ABC News, *"Nightline" Jackie Robinson Poll* (Ann Arbor, MI: Interuniversity Consortium for Political and Social Research, 1997).
Notes: Results account for sampling weights, and error bars represent 95 percent confidence intervals. A chi-squared analysis conducted by author showed that responses were not statistically dependent on the race of the respondent ($p = 0.309$).

admission to the second balcony, cost $14, whereas the average ticket price was closer to $30 (roughly $24 and $51, respectively, in 2017 dollars).[13]

The issue of access to games often emerged when the papers described children from low-income neighborhoods on the West and South Sides who attended the Grant Park rallies. Tracy Brill, a teacher at Brown Elementary (a block east of Chicago Stadium) assumed the job of chaperone when the mayor's office reserved up-front seats at the 1991 rally for several students from the school. Speaking to reporters from the *Tribune*, Brill explained, "[The students] live so close to the stadium, and yet they don't get to be a part of it. . . . Now they finally get to be a part of the celebration and a part of the Bulls."[14] As Ray Long of the *Sun-Times* put it two years later in his coverage of the 1993 celebration: "Normally heroes cost you money . . . Not today. . . . Today you get Chicago's full cast of superheroes . . . for free. All you need to do is go to Grant Park and be prepared to do a lot of standing on tiptoe."[15]

After the 1996 rally, *Tribune* reporters Jerry Thomas and Paul Salopek covered a group of kids from the Robert Taylor Homes housing project on the South Side who attended the festivities thanks to sponsorship from a local nonprofit. These children were not lucky enough to get reserved seating, and they "were sweating in a human pyramid . . . hoping to catch a glimpse of the man of their hoop dreams." But the paper assured readers that the kids "highlighted the grit and gumption of a crowd of sports fans from all walks of Chicago life."[16]

The admission that the rallies were the best that the kids could hope for highlighted the class segregation of fandom in Chicago. The rallies were, as Neil Steinberg of the *Sun-Times* put it, a consolation prize for "the ones without clout, without connections, without cash for a courtside ticket."[17] This group included more than just people from impoverished neighborhoods in Chicago. Many suburbanites also told reporters that the Grant Park gatherings were their lone opportunity to see the home team in person. When asked by the *Tribune*'s Melissa Isaacson why he showed up in the middle of the night before the first championship rally, Tom Bare of Des Plaines explained, "I can't get Bulls tickets. . . . This is the only way to show my appreciation [to the players]." In 1993, seventeen-year-old Scott Fredericks of Evergreen Park shared a similar story. "I don't get to go to any games, so you've got to see the players somehow. . . . You got to do something to show your support," he told *Tribune* reporter Andrew Gottesman. In 1998, Carlos Medina, an Amtrak employee from Cicero, told a pair of *Sun-Times* journalists, "This is a big day . . . a day for people who can't afford to buy tickets."[18]

Instead of lamenting the fact that so many Chicagoans never had the chance to attend a Bulls game, local journalists focused on how these fans, whether they came from public housing or the suburbs, formed one big community. For example, after the 1996 festivities, Leslie Baldacci of the *Sun-Times* asked, "Who were those people standing in the sun, the mud, humidity and humanity for hours Tuesday for a brief sighting of the Bulls?" Her answer: "They were people who've never seen the inside of [the] United Center but for whom seeing isn't a prerequisite for believing. This was definitely not the fur-coat-and-diamonds, see-and-be-seen courtside crowd. . . . I don't know what the [Bulls] organization calls this element that cannot buy its way into games, but I call them great fans." As the media reveled in the grittiness of the crowds made up of "younger, less-affluent folks in T-shirts and shorts, bandanas and jeans," it was clear that the fans who attended the rallies were defined not just by their dedication but also by their exclusion from the Bulls' home arena.[19]

Class at Chicago Stadium and the United Center

Concerns among Bulls fans about the cost of attending games predated the 1990s. Throughout the 1970s and early 1980s, basketball enthusiasts in Chicago complained about repeated decisions by then Bulls owner Arthur Wirtz to raise ticket prices. In November 1973, for example, the *Tribune* published comments by several Bulls fans furious with the team's decision to charge $6.75 for seats that had sold for $3 the previous season. Geoff Hiller from suburban Highland Park fumed over "being stabbed in the back by the bush league ticket-selling practices of management." Fellow fan Dietrich Wolframm of Hinsdale, another Chicago suburb, added that despite ongoing interest in the team "fans cannot afford the Bulls."[20] According to data obtained by the *Tribune*'s Don Pierson, Bulls fans had real reason for concern: between 1967 and 1976 the price of an "average seat" at a Bulls game rose by more than 85 percent.[21]

Local commentators made special note of the ballooning cost of higher-end seats. Neil Milbert of the *Tribune* explained that, at over $10 a ticket by the mid-1970s, only those with a "corporate connection, a secret source with clout, or . . . willing to throw [themselves] at the mercy of scalpers" could hope to land courtside seats to watch the Bulls.[22] The bad news for ordinary fans in search of a spot close to the action continued during the early 1980s. In May 1981, the team notified season-ticket holders that the price of courtside seats for the following season would be $13.50 apiece, a 50 percent increase. By the 1984–1985 season, Michael Jordan's rookie campaign with the squad, courtside seats had climbed to $15 dollars a pop.[23]

However, in inflation-adjusted terms, the price of Bulls tickets held rela-

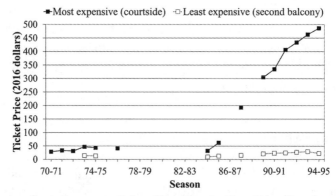

FIGURE 2.2. Cost in Constant 2016 Dollars of Most Expensive (Courtside) and Least Expensive (Second Balcony) Seats for the Bulls, 1970–1971 to 1994–1995

Source: Don Pierson, "Ticket Prices: Outa Sight!" Chicago Tribune, March 20, 1977, ProQuest; Bob Logan, "Bulls Open Here Tonight," Chicago Tribune, October 10, 1972, ProQuest; Robert Markus, "Here's Bulls' Side of Ticket Story," Chicago Tribune, February 27, 1974, ProQuest; Bill Jauss, "Bulls Return Home to 'Biggest' Week," Chicago Tribune, March 9, 1975, ProQuest; "Bulls Raise Ticket Prices," Chicago Tribune, June 13, 1985, ProQuest; "Briefs," Chicago Tribune, May 16, 1987, ProQuest; Sam Smith, "Bulls Asking Fans to Pay Dearly," Chicago Tribune, October 20, 1989, ProQuest; Lacy Banks, "Tickets Available, But Buyer Beware," Chicago Sun-Times, October 31, 1990, NewsBank; Lacy Banks, "Hottest Ticket Gets Hotter," Chicago Sun-Times, October 30, 1991, NewsBank; Dan Bickley, "Bulls Increase Ticket Prices," Chicago Sun-Times, July 15, 1992, NewsBank; Brian Hewitt, "Bulls' Center of Controversy," Chicago Sun-Times, March 20, 1994, NewsBank.

Notes: Inflation adjustments made using the Bureau of Labor Statistics CPI-U for the Chicago-Gary-Kenosha area. CPI years matched to second year of season (e.g., 1992 CPI used for 1991–1992 season).

tively steady during the 1970s and early 1980s. Unfortunately, the data necessary to calculate average ticket prices before the 1990s do not exist. But the local press reported on the maximum (courtside) and minimum (second balcony) ticket prices at Chicago Stadium (fig. 2.2). Adjusting for inflation, tickets at both extremes cost less in Jordan's rookie season (1984–1985) than a decade earlier. This suggests that anger over ticket prices owed less to the team proactively abandoning the ordinary fan than to the owners keeping pace with rising prices in the rest of the economy. As Tribune reporter Don Pierson observed in 1977, Bulls ticket prices were "popcorn compared to the general cost of living increase over the last 10 years."[24]

Things changed, however, in 1985, after the real estate mogul and Chicago White Sox owner Jerry Reinsdorf purchased a controlling interest in the Bulls. Reinsdorf quickly capitalized on the increasing demand for tickets generated by the exciting play of a young Michael Jordan and the growing popularity of the NBA in general.[25] By the 1993–1994 season the price tag for the best courtside seats in the house had surged to $300, more than a 1,300 percent increase since 1984–1985 in real terms.

The cheapest seats also became costlier, if at a slower rate. During the 1993–1994 season, fans had to fork over $19 for a nosebleed seat to watch the Bulls from the second balcony, more than 200 percent of what they cost a decade earlier, adjusted for inflation. The concurrent increase in real per capita personal income in the Chicago region—approximately 15 percent—paled in comparison.[26] If regular Bulls fans were concerned earlier about keeping up with rising prices, by the end of the 1980s they had good reason to panic.

By all accounts, the Reinsdorf-Jordan era marked a demographic shift in the Bulls fan base at Chicago Stadium. Immediately after Reinsdorf took the reins of the franchise in 1985, *Tribune* sportswriter Bob Sakamoto celebrated the fact that within a few months the new owner had "transformed a onetime blue-collar operation into an upscale franchise" by "taking a page from the Los Angeles Lakers and other NBA teams . . . selling courtside 'Jack Nicholson seats' at $30 a game."[27] Corporate clientele was nothing new at Chicago sporting events, but elites became a more central part of the fan base at Chicago Stadium after Jordan's arrival. In 1986, Bulls vice president David Rosengard bragged about prominent city officials and A-list celebrities bidding for tickets to see Jordan. "You know you're doing well when people like Burt Reynolds and folks from the mayor's staff call you up and want tickets," he explained.[28] As the team's successes mounted, so did demand from high-profile fans. A few months after the Bulls' first NBA title in 1991, director of ticket and stadium operations Joe O'Neil told a journalist at the *Sun-Times*: "Whenever there is a movie being shot in town, I can expect calls from the leading artists wanting to go to games. Last week, I got a call from Dustin Hoffman."[29]

Less recognizable fans felt threatened by the rising popularity of the Bulls among the rich. In a 1990 letter to the *Sun-Times*, Chicagoan Thomas Swanborn lamented the development: "With the high ticket prices comes a change in fans. Instead of real Bulls fans, the Stadium now is a haven for yuppies to show off their money. A fan standing and cheering now is susceptible to the wrath of a pompous yuppie. These people are turning the good old game of hoops into a high-society social event."[30] The sentiment persisted in the years to come. In 1993, Al Carli, a *Sun-Times* reader from Chicago's Archer Heights neighborhood, entreated Reinsdorf and the Bulls to cater less to celebrities and "give the little people a break." "One of these days," Carli predicted, "there just won't be enough people left with money enough to buy one of those overinflated tickets."[31] Survey research corroborates the conclusion that, by the 1990s, the demographics of live sporting events skewed decidedly toward the upper end of the income distribution. Economists John Siegfried

TABLE 2.1. Income Levels of Consumers by Attendance at Sporting Events, 1994

	Pretax family income		
	Simple mean	Weighted mean	Median
Consumers who purchased tickets to sporting events	$48,288	$56,124	$42,663
Consumers who did not purchase tickets to sporting events	$30,350	$30,350	$22,258
Ratio of purchasers to non-purchasers	1.59	1.85	1.92

Source: Reproduced from John Siegfried and Timothy Peterson, "Who Is Sitting in the Stands? The Income Levels of Sports Fans," in The Economics of Sports, ed. William Kern (Kalamazoo, MI: Upjohn Institute for Employment Research, 2000), 62.

Notes: "Consumers who purchased tickets" includes all respondents who reported spending any amount on "admission fees to sporting events" and/or "admission fees to sporting events on out-of-town trips." The difference between simple means for those who did and those who did not purchase tickets is statistically significant (99 percent confidence level). The weighted mean is weighted by total amount of expenditures made by respondents on event attendance.

and Timothy Peterson determined as much by scouring the 1994 Consumer Expenditure Survey, an annual survey conducted by the Bureau of Labor Statistics that tracks the purchases of thousands of individuals, for information about Americans who bought tickets to sports games. They found that respondents who paid for admission to a sporting event had, on average, pretax family incomes 1.85 times greater than those who did not (table 2.1). Moreover, these results likely understate the gap between the two groups during the early 1990s, since the survey "top-coded" reported family income at $300,000 (i.e., reported any incomes above $300,000 as $300,000) and also failed to capture ticket expenditures made by corporations for entertaining employees and clients.[32]

In a subsequent analysis, sociologist Thomas Wilson examined data from the 1993 General Social Survey (GSS), which asked respondents from a nationally representative sample of Americans if they had attended an amateur or professional sporting event in the previous year. Wilson's analysis revealed that, all else being equal, the higher a respondent's family income, the more likely he or she was to have gone to an event. Education exhibited a similar relationship to likelihood of attendance; people with more years of education were significantly more likely to have been in the stands.[33]

Expanding on Wilson's analysis, I used the raw data from the GSS to create "predicted probability curves" (see figs. 2.3 and 2.4 and appendix A) that show how the probability of attending a sporting event in 1992 closely tracked income and education. The statistical analysis used to generate the curves indicates that each additional $10,000 in per capita family income was associated with a 32 percent increase in the odds of having attended a sporting event.[34] Among those 25 to 44 years of age, each additional year of education was associated with a 21 percent increase in the odds of attendance (see appendix A for information on other age cohorts). Like the Consumer Expenditure Survey data, the GSS suggests that by the time Jordan and the Bulls were household names, the people at sporting events were typically wealthier and better educated than the average American.

Admittedly, these data reveal little about change over time; they provide no clues about whether there was anything novel about the overrepresentation of wealthier and more educated Americans in the stands. In fact, two surveys from the early 1980s that asked about sporting event attendance, one national in scope and the other limited to Cincinnati, demonstrate that the strong positive correlation between socioeconomic status and probability of attendance was already in play a decade earlier.[35] A skeptic of fan complaints about "yuppies" in the stands during the 1980s and 1990s might argue that there was nothing new about the phenomenon.

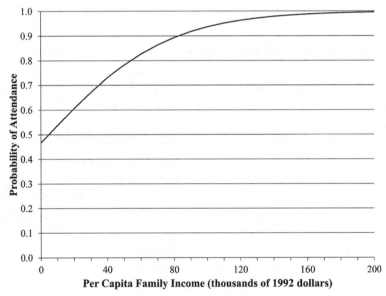

FIGURE 2.3. Predicted Probabilities of Attendance at an Amateur or Professional Sporting Event in 1992 by Per Capita Family Income
Source: National Opinion Research Center, *General Social Survey, 1993* (Chicago: University of Chicago, 1993).
Notes: Sample size for the logistic regression used to generate curve equal to 1,464.

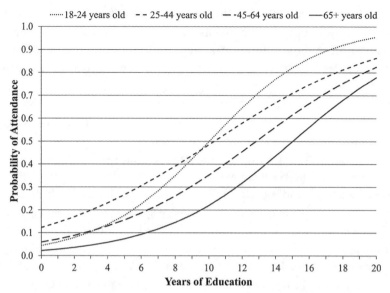

FIGURE 2.4. Predicted Probabilities of Attendance at an Amateur or Professional Sporting Event in 1992 by Years of Education

Source: National Opinion Research Center, *General Social Survey.*

Notes: Sample disaggregated by age cohort because of the possible interactive effects between age and education. Sample sizes for the age cohorts, ordered from youngest to oldest, equal to 136, 720, 432, and 298. See appendix A for more on methodology.

Other evidence, however, suggests that while this dynamic was not entirely novel, it became more pronounced in the last two to three decades of the twentieth century. In the case of the Bulls, seats affordable to regular fans became much harder to find at the end of the twentieth century. Take, for example, the dramatic increase during the late 1980s in season-ticket sales—that is, sales of tickets to all home games for a particular seat to a single buyer before the season begins. Riding the coattails of Jordan's emerging stardom, the team sold a record 4,800 season-ticket packages for the 1986–1987 season, and this number shot up to 11,200 a year later. While the Bulls promised fans in 1988 that they would limit season-ticket sales to 13,000 in subsequent seasons so as to not "shut out fans who can't afford season tickets," this meant that at least 70 percent of the seats in Chicago Stadium were typically occupied by the relative few who could afford the thousands of dollars necessary to buy season-ticket packages.[36]

To be sure, a sales strategy focused on maximizing purchases of expensive season tickets had earlier precedents. By the 1960s National Football League (NFL) teams like the New York Giants were selling nearly 100 percent of their seats as season tickets. And Major League Baseball (MLB) teams like the Los

Angeles Dodgers engineered steady expansions of the percentage of seats sold as season tickets during the 1970s and early 1980s.[37] This explains in large part why, by 1985, ticket purchases by corporations already made up about half of all gate receipts in MLB, the NBA, and the National Hockey League. But as political scientist Michael Danielson notes, and as the case of the Bulls confirms, the crowding out of working- and middle-class fans by members of the professional and corporate sets intensified at the end of the twentieth century.[38]

Average prices for the third of Chicago Stadium's seats not purchased by season-ticket holders continued to rise much faster than local incomes in the early nineties. Data compiled by the trade publication *Team Marketing Report* show that, on average, the inflation-adjusted price of attending Bulls games at the Stadium went up more than 17 percent between the 1991–1992 and 1993–1994 seasons (fig. 2.5). By the 1993–1994 season, the average ticket price had reached $36.45, and the Bulls' "fan cost index"—a figure aggregated by *Team Marketing Report* that included the cost of four average-priced tickets, four small soft drinks, four regular hot dogs, parking for one car, two programs, and two of the cheapest adult-sized caps—stood at $215.80. This represented a jump of nearly 12 percent in real terms from two seasons earlier. When one puts these figures next to the paltry 2 percent rise in per capita income over the same period in the Chicago metro area, it becomes clear that the typical

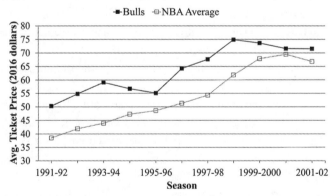

FIGURE 2.5. Average Ticket Prices in Constant 2016 Dollars, Chicago Bulls and National Basketball Association, 1991–1992 to 2001–2002

Source: Rodney Fort, "NBA Ticket Prices," *Rodney's Sports Business Data*, accessed January 27, 2018, umich .app.box.com/s/41707f0b2619c0107b8b/1/320023271.

Notes: For individual team calculations, averages weighted by number of seats at each pricing level. "NBA average" is the simple mean of the weighted averages for all teams. Figures do not account for luxury suites or boxes.

cost of attending a Bulls game was drifting further beyond the reach of regular Chicagoans.[39]

Data collected by the federal government make it possible to obtain a more precise sense of the degree to which these prices created barriers to entering Chicago Stadium. According to the Bureau of Labor Statistics, in 1994 the average annual family expenditures on entertainment fees and admissions for the third quintile (i.e., middle fifth) of families ranked in order of income amounted to $286.[40] A typical family outing to a Bulls game that year would have accounted for more than three-quarters of that total. Families at the middle or low end of the income distribution were thus unlikely to attend Bulls games, lest they spend their entire entertainment budget on one outing.

Information circulating among sports-marketing professionals during the late 1980s and early 1990s also corroborates a demographic shift at stadiums toward those with higher incomes and more luxurious tastes. In a September 1988 issue of *Athletic Business*, a sports-marketing trade publication, a trio of contributors suggested that the era of hot dogs and watery beer was giving way to something more sophisticated. "The future holds many exciting challenges as the trend away from bare necessities to convenience and luxury for the spectator continues," they told readers. In later years, the story remained the same. Another *Athletic Business* article from May 1991, this one by Andrew Cohen, quoted sports-facilities-management consultant Chris Bigelow, who asserted that "the trend is upscale products and a higher level of service." In May 1994, Cohen singled out the NBA as illustrative of this trend. "Many sports spectators—particularly in basketball, where demographics have shifted considerably toward more upscale consumers—will pay a premium for better service or accommodations," he explained.[41]

In Chicago, nothing encapsulated these trends more than the Bulls' transition to the United Center, a dual-use basketball and hockey arena that opened in the summer of 1994 across the street from Chicago Stadium on the city's Near West Side (map 2.1). Before its doors closed, Chicago Stadium contained a single, fifty-person luxury box that leased for $5,000 per game to corporations or wealthy fans willing to pay for an upscale experience. When the United Center opened, it boasted 216 twenty-, forty-, and sixty-person luxury suites (or skyboxes) that leased annually for anywhere from $55,000 to $175,000. The price included full catering, a private bar, and a dedicated attendant, among many other amenities.[42]

In addition to the suites, the new arena offered several thousand "club seats," or expensive nonenclosed seats usually purchased as season tickets, which offered patrons access to exclusive restaurants and entertainment areas for $40 per game and a $1,000 annual membership premium.[43] In 1996,

Jeff Borden of *Crain's Chicago Business* described the new club sections: "Pampered enthusiasts in the club seats never wait in line. Their orders are recorded by servers equipped with hand-held keypads. . . . Once an order is keyed in, it's transmitted to the nearest kitchen, where the order is filled and delivered in less than eight minutes."[44] Luxury boxes and club seating were not a new phenomenon; the first handful of major-league luxury suites debuted in 1965 at the Houston Astrodome. But only in the mid-1980s did professional-team owners start to envision premium seating as a centerpiece of their business strategy.[45] In 1987, the National Football League's Miami Dolphins set the trend when they moved to a new stadium containing 216 skyboxes (with annual price tags of $29,000–$65,000) and 10,211 club seats ($600–$1,400 per year). The Detroit Pistons imported the model to the NBA shortly thereafter, when the Palace of Auburn Hills opened with all 180 of its luxury boxes leased for between $30,000 and $120,000 per year.[46]

Jerry Reinsdorf and Bill Wirtz—the latter owned the NHL's Chicago Blackhawks and co-owned the United Center—allegedly hatched the plan for the new arena after noting the financial success of the Palace. By the mid-1990s a robust skybox market was the norm in the NBA.[47] In 1988 and 1989, five other NBA arenas opened in addition to the Palace at Auburn Hills, and the average luxury-box count among them (not including the Palace) stood at about thirty. Among the twelve NBA arenas opened between 1990 and 1996, that number rose to approximately ninety.[48] Premium seating offered owners expanded revenue streams. Estimates compiled by *Financial World* magazine show that "venue-related revenues" (i.e., earnings from suite rentals, concessions, parking, and in-stadium advertising) produced by the United Center amounted to three times those generated by Chicago Stadium (table 2.2).

Reinsdorf and Wirtz also realized that the demand among corporations for annual skybox leases in a major metropolitan market like Chicago made

TABLE 2.2. Venue-Related Revenues (Millions of 1996 Dollars) for Chicago Bulls and Chicago Blackhawks, 1992–1996

	Pre–United Center		United Center	
	1992–93 Season	*1993–94 Season*	*1994–95 Season*	*1995–96 Season*
Bulls	2.71	2.65	8.55	12.20
Blackhawks	8.69	7.20	23.06	24.50
Total	**11.40**	**9.85**	**31.61**	**36.70**

Source: Rodney Fort, "NBA Income and Expenses," *Rodney's Sports Business Data*, accessed January 27, 2018, umich.app.box.com/s/41707f0b2619c0107b8b/1/320022939.

Notes: Inflation adjustments made using the Bureau of Labor Statistics CPI-U for Chicago-Gary-Kenosha.

a new luxury venue like the United Center what Fran Spielman, of the *Sun-Times*, called an "architectural insurance policy" against potential down-turns in regular ticket sales.[49] John Glennon, a managing director at Lehman Brothers who helped structure the private financing deal for the new arena, put it this way: "The big advantage of having a good skybox market is that attendance can really drop off and it won't hurt your revenue stream because you have people on an annual lease."[50] Another attraction for owners like Reinsdorf was that, when the United Center opened, skybox sales were not included in the pool of NBA revenues from which players were guaranteed a percentage according to their collective-bargaining agreement.[51]

At least in terms of the skyboxes and club seating, there was little doubt that the United Center was, as *Sun-Times* reporter Brian Hewitt worded it shortly before it opened, "a pleasure dome designed for wheeler-dealers first and basketball fans second." A promotional pamphlet advertising the new club seats made it clear that one of the primary purposes of the luxury op-tions was to provide local corporations with a way to entertain current or prospective clients. "Luxurious club seating—whether to get an edge on your competition, boost sales, close deals, show appreciation or to entertain family and friends—is the ultimate way to enjoy events in style and with total con-venience and comfort," the pamphlet told potential buyers.[52]

Many major corporations with offices in Chicago immediately availed themselves of the new premium seating options. Waste Management, Bud-get Rent-a-Car, and LaSalle National Bank were among those that secured corporate skyboxes for the United Center's inaugural season. In November of that year, Barry Brown, president of Chicago Harley-Davidson (a local dealership), described his experience in a "first-tier suite"—the annual lease for such a skybox cost at least $140,000 annually—to *Crain's* reporter Joanne Cleaver. "I just about live there," he explained. "It's a totally different per-spective. You don't have to deal with smoke and people bumping into you. There's a separate hallway and entrance and exits."[53]

The local press rarely tired of adding to the list of high-profile names who frequented the United Center, whether they schmoozed in the luxury suites, sat in the club section, or rubbed elbows with players and coaches while sta-tioned in courtside seats, which were selling for well above $300 each by the time the United Center opened. Private-equity manager Marc Heisley, Hyatt Hotels magnate Robert Pritzker, and Illinois governor Jim Edgar were just a few of the notables spotted regularly at games. Not surprisingly, local lobby-ists and corporations began to use the tickets to court Illinois politicians, giving lawmakers prime seats in the hopes of getting in their good graces.[54] *Tribune* writers were probably not exaggerating when they mentioned seeing "stretch limos pulled up to the [arena's] south entrance" or noted fans "dressed as if headed to a charity ball rather than a sporting event."[55]

Longtime fans worried that these trends would reduce the quality of their experience at Bulls games, if not prevent them from going altogether. In 1994, Mike Ropa, a twenty-nine-year-old computer operator and Bulls season-ticket holder, complained to the *Sun-Times'* Brian Hewitt after learning of the team's "relocation campaign." The campaign apparently involved moving some season-ticket holders farther away from the action or to less ideal sight lines to make room for premium seating. "I think it stinks," Ropa asserted. "Pretty soon nobody's going to be going there to cheer the team, just to close deals," he added. "They're catering to the wealthy businessman."[56] Two years later, C. Wesley Johnson, who identified himself as a sophomore at Percy Julian High School on the South Side of Chicago, wrote to the *Sun-Times* in response to a call for inquiries that the paper promised it would present to Bulls chairman Jerry Reinsdorf in a special question-and-answer session. Johnson posed the following question to Reinsdorf: "How does a family of five, whose income is under $30,000 a year, purchase or get tickets to see the Bulls in the regular season? My mother has tried and was either told it's the hottest ticket in town or the price is so high you need a six-figure salary to afford it. What happens to regular people like my family who are diehard Bulls fans but can only settle for watching them on TV?" Reinsdorf responded by saying that the Bulls gave away 250 tickets for every game to local schools and referred Johnson to the team's community relations department.[57]

One could be forgiven for suspecting that Johnson had some help from a parent when he wrote his query for Reinsdorf; the prose and logic seem surprisingly sophisticated for a teenager. But whether he came up with the letter himself is less important than the content of the team owner's response. Even if Reinsdorf and the Bulls kept their word about the 250 free seats, this was just over 1 percent of the arena's 21,500-seat capacity.[58] And even if the team continued to offer nosebleed seats for less than $20 during its first few years of operation, the United Center was not intended to expand opportunities for regular fans to see games in person. As John Handley reported in the *Tribune* in 1994, despite boasting four times as much gross square footage (i.e., total floor area) as the old Chicago Stadium, the increase in non-skybox seating was modest, up only three thousand seats. Skyboxes "account for most of the increased seating," Handley explained.[59] After accounting for the addition of the new, expensive club seats, the United Center contained fewer "non-premium" seats—that is, seats outside of luxury boxes or club sections—than the old Chicago Stadium did. Moreover, by 1999, season-ticket patrons held sixteen thousand seats, or three-quarters of total capacity.[60] Only a few thousand seats remained for those who were unable to afford packages for the entire season. Despite the additional space, seats that only the well-to-do could afford were displacing those within reach of the masses.

In this regard, the transition from Chicago Stadium to the United Center encapsulated bigger trends in the history of stadium economics over the past thirty to forty years. Major-league facilities built after 1980 consistently differed from the stadiums they replaced in three regards: (1) they were much bigger in terms of gross square footage, (2) they contained significantly more premium seats in luxury boxes and club sections, and (3) they contained fewer nonpremium seats. Among a 2013 sample of seventy-three NBA, NFL, and MLB facilities built since 1987, premium seats accounted for, on average, 15.7 percent of total seating capacity, while they made up only 4.7 percent at the facilities they replaced. Just as striking, the mean decline in nonpremium seats was nearly 6,800.[61]

Rather than allowing for the preservation of affordable seats, the new square footage in venues like the United Center went toward accommodating the demand for comfort and luxury among the professional and corporate set. This meant clearing the way not only for suites but also for fancy souvenir boutiques and swanky lounges. The impulse to profit from wealthy fans has intensified so much that, by now, stories about major-league teams removing nonpremium seats from stadiums are commonplace. The motive behind such moves is, in the words of journalist Neil deMause, the desire to "sell fewer tickets at higher prices" and ensure that the only fans who enter stadiums are those "with money [to] buy more hot dogs."[62]

The prices for whichever seats remained untouched by the premium crowd or season-ticket holders often spiraled out of control, as rising demand and falling supply allowed for extortionate markups by scalpers and ticket brokers. The face value of the average (non-skybox) Bulls ticket continued to rise during the second half of the 1990s and was consistently among the five most expensive in the NBA (fig. 2.5). This, however, does not capture the fact that, at the end of the 1994–1995 season, some Chicagoans intent on witnessing Jordan's return from retirement shelled out $1,000 to brokers for tickets with a face value of $350. As the Jordan hype escalated, scalpers reported getting as much as $1,500 for tickets originally sold for $75.[63] The markups reached astronomical proportions when it became clear in 1998 that Jordan was probably in his final season with the team. According to the Sun-Times' Michael Gillis, brokers nabbed $3,000 for a ticket a few rows back from courtside during that year's NBA finals at the United Center. Courtside seats allegedly sold for $10,000, and the handful of standing-room-only tickets went for $350 each.[64]

These outlandish prices were in large part a function of the fervor surrounding specific high-profile games at the beginning or end of the season, but this does not mean that families on relatively tight budgets normally had a much easier time getting into the United Center. During the late 1990s, *Team Marketing Report* assembled a statistic called the "frugal fan index," which summed the cost of four of the least expensive tickets, four small sodas, four hot dogs, and a parking pass at each NBA arena. Not surprisingly, each of the four years for which *Team Marketing Report* computed the index, the Bulls came in well above the league average, and by the late 1990s a penny-pinching family at a Bulls game was on the hook for more than $110 per game (table 2.3). To put this into perspective, in 1997 average annual expenditures on fees and admissions for entertainment for households in the lowest income quintile (i.e., bottom 20 percent) stood at $154, enough for only one "frugal" outing to the United Center.[65]

Attending a Bulls Game was so expensive by the late 1990s that various "alternative" spectatorship options emerged for those who could not get tickets. In 1997, Bulls ownership decided to broadcast Game 4 of the NBA Finals, in which Chicago played away at Utah, on the United Center jumbo-tron and charge fans $10 for admission. In the words of *Sun-Times* reporter Dan Rozek, they "pitched the event for those who don't usually come to Bulls games," and the pitch seems to have worked. For many fans, this was their first trip to the United Center. Thirteen-year-old Bob Buckstaff, who came from the middle-class suburb of Mount Prospect, no doubt would have preferred an actual, in-the-flesh game. But as he told Rozek, "The chances of us going to a real Bulls game are pretty slim."[66]

By the end of the 1990s, never had local Bulls fans from such a wide range of backgrounds, from middle-class suburban families to public-housing tenants, faced such challenges when it came to seeing their team live. Access-

TABLE 2.3. *Team Marketing Report* "Frugal Fan Index," 1995–1996 to 1998–1999

Season	Bulls	NBA average
1995–96	$90.00	$64.60
1996–97	$111.00	$72.05
1997–98	$113.00	$76.63
1998–99	$112.00	$66.87

Source: "Frugal Fan Index," *Team Marketing Report* (1995, 1996, 1997, 1998).

Notes: "Frugal Fan Index" denotes the sum of the cost of four of the cheapest tickets, four small sodas, four hot dogs, and a parking pass.

ing the old Chicago Stadium had never been an egalitarian utopia, but the demographic transformation of the in-stadium crowd during the late 1980s and 1990s represented a real shift in how the city experienced and consumed professional basketball. Despite the unity fostered by the team's success, the shape of one's fandom became ever more dependent on economic class, and that process only intensified in the United Center era.

Justifying the Rising Costs of Access: The Player Salary Argument

What exactly caused the demographic shift in attendance? One answer that circulated inside and outside Chicago had to do with escalating player salaries. In 1988, Bulls beat writer Sam Smith explained the prospect of a new arena for the team as part of "a transition occurring here that may soon be common for America's sports teams, which must continually seek new sources of revenue to meet increasing [player] salaries." Smith went on: "One of the favored methods is to build a new arena . . . to justify higher ticket prices."[67] Two years later, another *Tribune* journalist gave the same thesis a slightly different spin, insisting that "with dramatically escalating salaries for professional athletes, skybox rentals allow team officials to keep ticket costs from soaring proportionally for patrons in less privileged seats."[68] A July 1991 piece by Andrew Cohen in *Athletic Business* echoed this latter version of the argument by ending with a quotation from Ron Turner of the stadium architecture firm Ellerbe Becket. According to Turner, "the problem in hockey and particularly in basketball is the salaries have gotten unbelievable. In order to deal with that, they [owners] need to have premium areas that cost a whole lot of money so they can always have a ticket that the average guy can buy."[69]

The idea that higher salaries were to blame for skyrocketing costs of arena access continued to surface in local papers throughout the 1990s. In 1994, the *Sun-Times*' Fran Spielman posited that the United Center provided Reinsdorf and Wirtz with "the financial wherewithal to keep pace with skyrocketing player salaries into the 21st Century."[70] Reinsdorf did his part to perpetuate this logic during the 1998 NBA lockout, when he insisted that "in the long run, I think our fans gain [from the lockout], because if we can control our [player] costs, we can control our ticket prices."[71]

Despite its popularity, this theory provided a wanting explanation for the rising cost of attendance and the proliferation of luxury facilities like the United Center. Were players' salaries in the NBA increasing? Absolutely, and at a very rapid rate (fig. 2.6). However, team and league revenues were skyrocketing concurrently, largely due to ballooning fees paid by network and cable television companies to secure exclusive rights to broadcast games.[72]

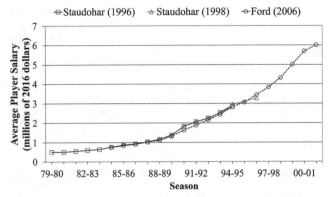

FIGURE 2.6. Average Player Salaries in Constant 2016 Dollars, National Basketball Association, 1979–1980 to 2001–2002

Source: Paul Staudohar, *Playing for Dollars: Labor Relations in the Sports Business* (Ithaca, NY: Cornell University Press, 1996), 108; Paul Staudohar, "Salary Caps in Professional Team Sports," *Compensation and Working Conditions* (Spring 1998): 4; Chad Ford, "Salary Cap for 2006–07 Season Set at $53.135M," *ESPN.com*, July 11, 2016, accessed January 27, 2018, sports.espn.go.com/nba/news/story?id=2516704.

For the 1985–1986 season, national TV revenues (the sum of network and cable payments) for the NBA came to $25 million. Four years later, the amount was $219 million.[73] In short, rising salaries were not necessarily part of some simple, zero-sum game in which team owners like Reinsdorf automatically experienced reduced profits when they paid their players more. Instead, higher salaries reflected efforts by players to capture what they saw as a fair share of expanding league revenues.[74]

During the early 1990s, some NBA teams jacked up ticket prices and built new luxury arenas despite the fact that the fraction of franchise revenues consumed by players' salaries remained relatively stable.[75] The Bulls offer a useful case in point. Between the 1989–1990 and 1995–1996 seasons, the team's estimated player costs as a percentage of total revenue went from 34 percent to 29 percent (fig. 2.7). This coincided with a more than 277 percent jump in estimated real operating income (i.e., profit before taxes and debt service). Operating margins, a rough measure of profitability and cost control calculated by dividing operating income by total revenues, averaged 35 percent—a number that would have made just about any CEO dizzy with excitement (fig. 2.8).[76] So yes, the Bulls payroll was rising during this period, but the data simply do not support the argument that Reinsdorf and company raised ticket prices because increased player salaries were destroying profitability. As long as demand persisted, the Bulls would charge more for seats no matter how low player salaries dropped.

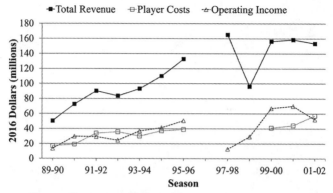

FIGURE 2.7. Chicago Bulls Core Financial Data, 1989–1990 to 2000–2002

Source: Rodney Fort, "NBA Income and Expenses," *Rodney Fort's Sports Business Data,* accessed January 27, 2018, umich.app.box.com/s/41707f0b2619c0107b8b/1/320022939.

Notes: Based on data from *Financial World* (through 1995–1996 season) and *Forbes* (after the 1995–1996 season). Operating income is total revenue less operating expenses. Player costs include salaries, deferred payments, bonuses, insurance, and workers' compensation. Gaps in the series represent missing data. All figures in constant 2016 dollars.

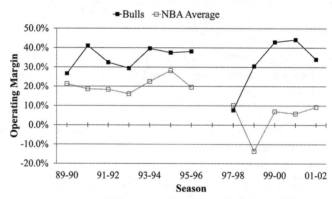

FIGURE 2.8. Operating Margins of the Chicago Bulls and National Basketball Association, 1989–1990 to 2001–2002

Source: Rodney Fort, "NBA Income and Expenses," *Rodney Fort's Sports Business Data,* accessed January 27, 2018, umich.app.box.com/s/41707f0b2619c0107b8b/1/320022939.

Notes: Operating margin indicates the percentage of each dollar of revenue left over after deducting operating costs, and indicates how well a firm controls costs. Gaps in the series represent missing data.

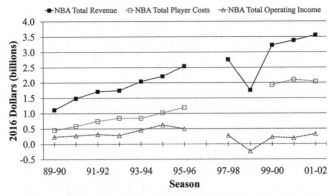

FIGURE 2.9. Aggregated Core Financial Data, National Basketball Association Franchises, 1989–1990
to 2001–2002

Source: Rodney Fort, "NBA Income and Expenses," *Rodney Fort's Sports Business Data*, accessed January 27, 2018, umich.app.box.com/s/41707f0b2619c0107b8b/1/320022939.

Notes: Operating income is total revenue less operating expenses. Player costs include salaries, deferred payments, bonuses, insurance, and workers' compensation. Gaps in the series represent missing data. All figures in constant 2016 dollars.

Admittedly, not all franchises fared as well as the Bulls during the first half of the 1990s. According to estimates compiled by *Financial World* magazine, between the 1989–1990 and 1995–1996 seasons, total "player costs" as a percentage of total NBA team revenues rose from 41 percent to 47 percent. Nevertheless, the league's overall operating income also climbed significantly—from $237 million to $498 million in constant 2016 dollars—and operating margins hovered around the more-than-respectable level of 20 percent for the entire period (figs. 2.8 and 2.9).[77] All of this is to say that increased player salaries did not necessarily translate into reduced profits or profitability, and the increase in NBA ticket prices during a period of stable—in some cases, growing—profits and profitability suggests that teams were willing to raise the cost of attending games regardless of player cost trends.

Economists James Quirk and Rodney Fort provide the clearest explanation of why ticket prices are a function not of player salaries but rather of demand for tickets:

> Fans tend to think that the high salaries drive up the prices of seats at games, and that if there were some way to put a lid on salaries, ticket prices would fall. This is simply a misunderstanding of the cause-and-effect chain at work in sports. The reason that salaries are high is because the demand for sports is high, as reflected in the prices that people are willing to pay for tickets to games and in the prices TV networks are willing to pay for the rights to tele-

cast sports games. The higher ticket prices and higher TV-rights prices increase the value of star players to teams, the amounts they add to a team's revenue, which then gets reflected in the high salaries paid to those players. Salaries are high because ticket prices are high, not the other way around.[78]

In Chicago, player costs became a convenient scapegoat for team owners and the press. The corollary of this flawed logic was that owners like Reinsdorf had no choice but to pursue a business model that priced out increasing numbers of fans. And while such reasoning provided journalists with a seemingly intuitive explanation for rising ticket prices and reduced accessibility, it obscured the real cause: Reinsdorf's desire to maximize profits and his willingness to exclude unprecedented numbers of fans from live games to do so.

Player salaries undoubtedly spiked in the mid-1990s as many teams, the Bulls chief among them, frantically ponied up to re-sign star free agents like Michael Jordan. By the 1997–1998 NBA season, player costs stood at an estimated 57 percent of league revenue, significantly above the 48 percent guaranteed by the collective-bargaining agreement. Profit margins suffered accordingly (see figs. 2.7–2.9), and owners successfully leveraged a lockout during the 1998–1999 season to impose new salary constraints (most notably a player salary cap).[79] None of this, however, altered the fact that the cost of attending games had already begun its steep ascent more than a decade earlier and had continued even through periods of effective cost control by NBA teams. Throughout the 1990s, fans paid more, and skybox-laden arenas popped up regardless of the intricacies of teams' labor costs.

Perhaps the best evidence of the absence of a tight relationship between player salaries and the cost of attending Bulls games emerged after team management disbanded the Jordan-led dynasty in 1998. Over the following six seasons, the Bulls never made the playoffs and finished with the worst record in the Eastern Conference four times.[80] Team management dumped payroll once Jordan left, but much of the demand for tickets created by "His Airness" carried over even after the Bulls nosedived. In August 1999, the *Tribune* reported that "the six-time world champions are still riding a hot streak in attendance with 567 consecutive sell-outs."[81] Given the ongoing clamor for Bulls tickets, prices remained well above the league average in the years following Jordan's departure even though the team posted one of the lowest payrolls in the NBA. In the three years after Jordan left, for example, the team's player expenses sat in the bottom three among all NBA teams.[82] That this did not result in a commensurate drop in ticket prices clarifies that lower player salaries did not necessarily translate into a cheaper United Center experience for fans.

A year-by-year comparison of the changes in Bulls player salaries and ticket prices from the mid-1990s to mid-2000s confirms the absence of any sort of

TABLE 2.4. Comparison of Changes in Chicago Bulls Player Salaries (Total) and Average Ticket Price, 1995–1996 to 2004–2005

Season	Player Salaries (total, millions)	Pct. Change from Prev. Yr.	Average Ticket Price	Pct. Change from Prev. Yr.
1995–96	$23.18		$36.00	
1996–97	$58.27	151.4	$42.97	19.4
1997–98	$61.33	5.3	$45.94	6.9
1998–99	$28.64	−53.3	$51.98	13.1
1999–00	$27.03	−5.6	$52.84	1.7
2000–01	$29.69	9.8	$52.84	0.0
2001–02	$42.59	43.4	$53.62	1.5
2002–03	$44.53	4.6	$50.67	−5.5
2003–04	$55.49	24.6	$50.67	0.0
2004–05	$57.28	3.2	$50.67	0.0

Source: Salary data from "Chicago Bulls Franchise Index," *Basketball Reference*, accessed November 20, 2015, www.basketball-reference.com/teams/CHI/. For ticket-price data, see source note to Figure 2.5.

Notes: The player cost data used for previous figures in this chapter are missing data for several years covered in this table. The data from *Basketball Reference* contain a list of individual player salaries for a given season, and there is no indication that they include payments beyond base salary (e.g., bonuses). Cumulative player salary is the sum of salaries for the entire roster for a given year. Values not adjusted for inflation.

consistent correlation between the two. Both salaries and ticket costs rose during the 1996–1997 and 1997–1998 seasons. However, the following season the cumulative salary (nominal) of the team fell by more than 53 percent while the average price of tickets climbed more than 13 percent (table 2.4). Just as telling is that in the first five seasons of the 2000s the sum of player salaries doled out by the Bulls increased erratically, spiking by about 43 percent and 25 percent, respectively, in 2001–2002 and 2003–2004, but climbing no more than 9.8 percent in 2000–2001, 2002–2003, and 2004–2005. Save a 5.5 percent drop in 2002–2003, ticket prices hardly budged over the same period. These numbers offer no compelling evidence that the cost of attending Bulls games tracked consistently with what Reinsdorf paid his players.[83]

Economists James Quirk and Rodney Fort have reiterated that, as long as fans prove willing to pay, any "reasonable" owner will maintain or increase prices even if player costs drop.[84] Even some industry insiders conceded this point. Frank Mariani, chairman and CEO of California Sports Marketing, put it this way in 1996: "Ticket pricing is just a function of what people want to pay." As long as demand for expensive seats and luxury boxes persisted after Jordan left the team, Reinsdorf had absolutely no reason to lower the costs to enter the arena.[85]

This is not to say that salaries did not play a more indirect role in rising prices at venues like the United Center. Given that the NBA's collective-bargaining agreement guaranteed players a percentage (or percentage range) of league revenues, ownership had to look to profit-maximization strategies other than squeezing labor costs. Catering to Chicago's corporate set through premium seating helped ensure that the percentage owed to players did not cap Reinsdorf's ability to increase the profitability of the franchise. But no matter how high player salaries rose, skyboxes could not increase profits without adequate demand.[86]

Creating a More Exclusive Market of Spectators

Growing demand for a more exclusive, luxurious stadium experience owed in large part to the upward redistribution of wealth that characterized the New Gilded Age. In the late 1970s, the gaps between the wages, salaries, and compensation of earners at the top of the income ladder and those lower down began to widen considerably. Despite ongoing productivity growth, low-wage and many middle-wage workers found their earnings squeezed by the replacement of manufacturing positions by nonprofessional service jobs, the disappearance of unions, the relocation of jobs offshore, a drop in the real minimum wage, and protracted periods of high unemployment (especially during the early and mid-1980s). Between 1973 and 1995, those in the 50th percentile of earners (i.e., half of the population earned more wages or salary per hour than they did, and half earned less), saw their real hourly earnings drop by 4 percent (fig. 2.10). Many top earners worked in sectors

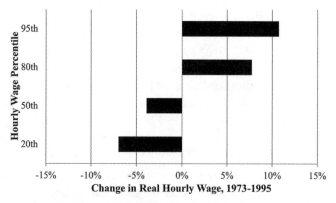

FIGURE 2.10. Percentage Change in Real Hourly Wages by Selected Percentile, 1973–1995
Source: Adapted from Doug Henwood, "Bad Recession, Bad Recovery, Bad Trends," *Left Business Observer* 135 (March 4, 2013): 4–5, 7.
Notes: "Wage" denotes earnings from hourly wages and salaries.

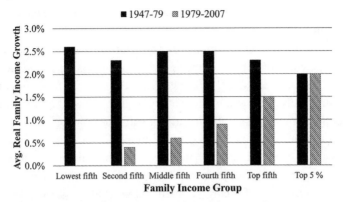

FIGURE 2.11. Average Annual Family Income Growth (Real) by Income Group, 1947–2007
Source: Economic Policy Institute, "Average Family Income Growth, by Income Group, 1947–2013," *The State of Working America*, September 25, 2014, accessed January 27, 2018, www.stateofworkingamerica.org/charts/real-annual-family-income-growth-by-quintile-1947–79-and-1979–2010/.

of the labor market less vulnerable to these changes and as a result they registered major wage or salary gains in this period. Those in the 95th percentile of earners (i.e., only 5 percent earned more than they did) saw their real hourly earnings jump by nearly 11 percent. In Chicago, these were the corporate executives and the army of professionals that supported their firms— accountants, investment bankers, lawyers, marketing professionals, and upper-level managers—whom Mayor Richard M. Daley hoped to court by revitalizing the Loop. Unfortunately, these numbers underestimate the divergent economic fortunes of low-percentile earners and high-percentile earners, since they do not account for growth in nonsalary income such as capital gains, which accrued overwhelmingly to the latter.[87]

These trends led to the exclusion of massive numbers of Americans from enjoying the benefits of ongoing economic growth. Between 1947 and 1979, growth in family income was remarkably even across American society: during this period every quintile (fifth) of the family income distribution registered average annual growth rates of at least 2.3 percent, and family incomes in each of the bottom four quintiles actually grew as fast or faster than those in the richest fifth (fig. 2.11). Things changed dramatically, however, in the period 1979–2007, during which only the top quintile of families experienced an average annual growth rate of more than 1 percent (1.5 to be exact). The bottom fifth experienced no growth at all in those years, and the second through fourth quintiles experienced significantly reduced growth rates. This shift proved so extreme that from 1979 to 2007, the richest 1 percent of households captured more of the total income growth in the United States than did the "bottom 90 percent."[88]

All of this made it more difficult for Americans in the bottom 90 percent, and especially the bottom 80 percent, to take advantage of leisure activities such as attending professional sporting events, especially as ticket prices escalated dramatically at the end of the century. Millions of workers found themselves either with less disposable income or with less time for recreation since they had to work more hours to get by.[89] Indeed, data collected by the Bureau of Labor Statistics indicate that, on average, the only pretax-household-income quintile that exhibited a notable expansion of annual expenditures on fees and admissions for entertainment activities after 1984 was the top 20 percent (fig. 2.12).[90]

Economist Robert Frank argues that growing income inequality accounted not only for the widening gap between the expenditures of top earners and the rest of American society but also for the expanded production and consumption of luxury goods and services favored by those at the winning end of this transformation. He cites several telling examples of the growth in extravagant purchases in the United States during the 1990s. In 1997, the number of luxury cars sold rose by 6.5 percent despite a 3 percent drop in total automotive sales (particularly striking was the 79 percent increase in Porsches purchased). The markets for second-home ownership, yachts, and cosmetic surgery all experienced similar booms. During the 1980s and 1990s, skyboxes

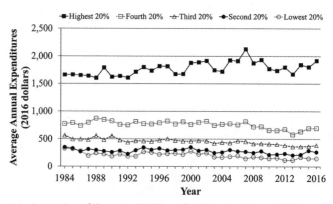

FIGURE 2.12. Average Annual Consumer Unit Expenditures, in Constant 2016 Dollars, on "Entertainment Fees and Admissions" by Pretax Income Quintile, 1984–2016

Source: U.S. Bureau of Labor Statistics, "Quintiles of Income before Taxes: Annual Average Expenditures and Characteristics, Consumer Expenditure Survey," Consumer Expenditure Survey Expenditure Tables (1984–2016), accessed January 27, 2018, www.bls.gov/cex/csxstnd.htm.

Notes: "Consumer unit" includes all members of a household.

at arenas like the United Center signaled that this "luxury fever" had thoroughly penetrated the sports spectatorship market.[91] As economist Robert Baade first noted in the mid-1990s, "The market for spectator sports has become more segmented as the distribution of income in the United States becomes more skewed . . . [and] the demand for luxury loges and stadium clubs reflects the growing inequality of income in the 1980s and 1990s."[92]

To be more precise, this growing demand reflected the convergence of increasing inequality with new efforts by the NBA and its individual teams to rebrand their product for a more elite audience. After taking over the post of NBA commissioner in 1984, David Stern moved quickly to "repackage" a league that, as a result of labor uncertainty and rumors of rampant drug use by players, was reportedly on the verge of shrinking by four or five teams.[93] In addition to implementing a strict antidrug policy and leading the effort to institute the first leaguewide salary cap, Stern assembled a veritable army of marketing experts who focused on parlaying the broad allure of stars like Magic Johnson and Larry Bird, and later Michael Jordan, into an expanded fan base.[94] The restructuring paid off. According to the trade publication *Sports Inc.*, the NBA became the only major league to register increased "average audience ratings" during the early and mid-1980s. Estimates by Nielsen Research show that the average per-game viewing audience for the NBA finals skyrocketed from 11.4 million in 1975 to 24.1 million in 1987.[95]

This increased exposure brought the NBA into line with trends already at play in the rest of the sports business. The NFL had experienced jaw-dropping growth in previous decades largely due to the skillful marketing of Monday Night Football. Quirk and Fort report that the NFL's nominal "media income" (e.g., TV, radio) went from $3 million in 1960 (the rival American Football League earned $1.6 million in media income that year) to $167 million in 1980, and up to $948 million in 1990. Nielsen data show that the number of people watching the Super Bowl went from 39.1 million in 1968 to 92.6 million in 1986.[96]

In the midst of this expanded television exposure, Reinsdorf and the Bulls took to heart the following advice from an August 1984 edition of *Athletic Business*: "It's important to think of your facility as an opportunity for revenue production, just waiting to be marketed to the right group or individual. Yes, it requires some legwork and communication with potential users, but the results can be extremely beneficial."[97] Reinsdorf and his staff did not skimp on the legwork, doing whatever they could to profitably re-engineer the in-stadium fan base. By 1990, the team had expanded its internal marketing division to twenty-two full-time employees and was publishing a six-hundred-page annual marketing plan. Not long after that, the Bulls established a separate Suite Department to service current and prospective leaseholders. On top of this, Steve Schanwald, Bulls vice president for marketing at the time, made the Bulls the first team in professional sports to task marketing staff with personally meeting "each year with every season ticket holder" to help guarantee customer satisfaction.[98]

Another tactic employed by the team's marketing department involved using the local press to manufacture mania over the alleged scarcity of Bulls tickets, thereby boosting demand and prices even further. In 1991, Schanwald told *Team Marketing Report*: "It is important to convey in the minds of current and potential season ticket holders what a precious commodity a Bulls season ticket is. Our sellout streak is publicized extensively. A waiting list for Bulls season tickets is promoted aggressively. This not only gives us a list of people to whom we can sell tickets when and if they become available, but it reinforces in the minds of current season ticket holders the precious commodity they possess."[99] Indeed, the local and national press carried stories on the Bulls season-ticket waiting lists throughout the 1990s. In 1991 Ray Sons of the *Sun-Times* reported a list of nearly six thousand names, in 1994 the *Sun-Times'* Brian Hewitt noted that it had ballooned to twelve thousand, and a 1998 piece in *Sports Illustrated* by Rick Reilly informed readers that twenty-three thousand people were officially waiting for a shot at season tickets.[100]

Similar stories about Bulls single-game tickets also appeared. Philip Franchine of the *Sun-Times* reported in June 1991 that Ticketron received more than 1.7 million phone calls for tickets to the NBA Finals between the Bulls and Lakers.[101] In 1997, local television spots on WGN and SportsChannel put a comic spin on the perceived value of Bulls tickets. One depicted traders at the Chicago Mercantile Exchange "frantically waving bids" at a man holding two Bulls tickets and "chuckling about 'a Bulls market.'" Another showed negotiations between two sets of businessmen, one American and one Asian. The Asian group agrees to a deal after receiving three Bulls tickets from their counterparts. Yet another portrayed a terrorist fending off a SWAT team by holding a lighter to two Bulls tickets. The Bulls were not alone in hyping their sellout streak to inflate demand; in recent years economists have identified similar behavior by other teams and leagues, such as baseball's Boston Red Sox.[102]

Marketing campaigns that boosted demand for games among the wealthy and gave the impression of a severe scarcity of tickets made good economic sense for the likes of Reinsdorf, irrespective of labor costs, because they empowered team owners to more aggressively exploit the market structure of professional sport. Major leagues in the United States acted (and still act) openly as cartels, granting local monopolies to franchises—that is, crowning them as the sole sellers of a major-league sport in a specific locale—by typically allowing only one team per metropolitan area. This eliminates any direct local competition within a given urban market and has created a situation in which, according to journalist Neil deMause, "trying to use your monopoly power . . . to jack up ticket prices is the plan for pretty much every sports league."[103]

But the strategy of using local monopoly power to drive up prices emerged relatively recently, even though local monopolies are old news within the business of major-league sport. For example, in major-league baseball, the only league for which we have the relevant data reaching back farther than the 1990s, the average ticket prices charged by individual teams (adjusted for inflation) remained remarkably stable between the mid-1970s and late 1980s (fig. 2.13). MLB teams in this period benefited from local monopolies, so clearly team owners were not availing themselves of their monopoly power to indiscriminately raise prices. This is the same story told by the data on select Bulls ticket prices shown in figure 2.2 (NBA teams enjoyed unchallenged local monopolies after the dissolution of the rival American Basketball Association in 1976).

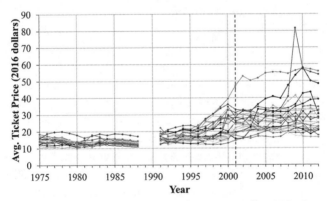

FIGURE 2.13. Average Ticket Prices by Team in Constant 2016 Dollars, Major-League Baseball, 1975–2012

Source: "MLB Ticket Price," *Rodney Fort's Sports Business Data,* accessed June 10, 2017, umich.app.box .com /s/41707f0b2619c0107b8b /1/320022665.

Notes: Roger Noll compiled the data for years 1971 and 1975–1988, and *Team Marketing Report* compiled the data for 1991 on. Each line represents the weighted average ticket price (weighted by number of seats per price level) for a team. Excludes Canadian teams and teams created after 1977. Pre-2001 data include club (premium) seating; data after 2001 exclude it. The chart thus underestimates the rise in ticket costs after 2001 (marked by the dashed, vertical line).

What changed in the final decades of the twentieth century to push team owners to dramatically raise admission costs to major-league stadiums and arenas in ways that seem more consistent with the behavior of monopolists? As outlined already, what changed was the structure of American income and wealth distribution. As a larger and larger share of economic growth in the United States accrued to those at the top, and as the wages and salaries of those at the bottom and middle stagnated or fell, team owners shifted their marketing focus accordingly—that is, to those capturing the lion's share of new disposable income. The richer this group got, the more price insensitive it became in the context of entertainment and leisure expenditures, especially in the case of scarce, high-demand tickets like those for Bulls games.[104] This intensifying price insensitivity was a dream come true for team owners like Reinsdorf, who could use the absence of direct competition as leverage to charge a small sliver of increasingly affluent fans wildly inflated prices for tickets, concessions, suite leases, and other amenities.

Monopoly power in and of itself, then, was not the sole causal force behind increasing barriers to entry at the United Center. Rather, nationwide shifts in the distribution of economic resources that characterized the rise of exclusionary capitalism created new conditions in which team owners could, through targeted marketing efforts, take greater advantage of preexisting monopolies. This is a point worth driving home, as some economists specializing in the ins and outs of the sports business identify leagues' ability to confer local monopoly power on individual teams as the singular cause of those teams' increasing economic power in recent decades.[105] These economists are not wrong to highlight the importance of this issue, but they tend to overlook the fact that monopoly power is not a historically static phenomenon; its impact can wax and wane in response to larger historical conditions. As in the case of major-league ticket prices, the ability to exploit the absence of direct competition became much more meaningful in dollar terms as a result of structural shifts in the American economy writ large. This theme will reemerge in subsequent chapters and the conclusion, as it has important implications for the types of solutions the public should consider for reigning in the power of the sports business.

That this story had to do with more than the specific market structure of the sports business is also evident in the fact that the pricing out of working-class and many middle-class consumers occurred throughout the urban leisure industry at the end of the 1990s. As historian Mike Davis documents in the context of Los Angeles, this period witnessed the dramatic expansion of a wide range of more luxurious, more expensive leisure and consump-

FIGURE 2.14. Pedestrians Pass by a United Center Security Gate
Source: Tim Boyle/Getty Images, October 14, 2004.

tion opportunities in inner cities for those lucky enough to sit at the top of
the income distribution: high-end malls and movie theaters, ritzy hotels, and
increasingly exclusive "culture" like classical music venues. Journalistic and
academic publications are replete with stories of spectacular hikes in the cost
of admissions to concerts, museums, and theater productions in recent years.
More often than not, the masses have found themselves on the outside looking in by virtue of not only lack of funds but also physical barriers like security fences and massive private parking lots, both of which have long been
in use at the United Center (fig. 2.14).[106] Ultimately, changes in the growth
model of major-league teams overlapped considerably with shifts in other
sectors of the urban entertainment industry at the end of the 1900s.

One thing that separated team owners like Reinsdorf from their counterparts in other areas of the leisure industry was that they continued to benefit
directly from working- and middle-class consumers who could no longer afford tickets for live events. This surplus fan base guaranteed a large, dedicated
TV audience, which ensured robust profits for the Bulls from the sale of local
broadcasting rights. The *Tribune's* Jim Kirk reported in 1997 that annual revenues from the team's local media contracts had risen to $17.8 million.[107] Sim-
ply put, ownership pursued a premeditated business model that depended on

a tiered structure of fandom in which most Bulls faithful watched their heroes on television, while "the more well-heeled" treated Bulls games as their
new playground.[108]

✱

In May 2010, famed NBA play-by-play announcer Marv Albert interviewed
President Barack Obama, an avowed Bulls fan, about his thoughts on the current state of professional basketball. When Albert asked the president what he
would change in the NBA if he were commissioner for a day, Obama said his
priority would be to "figure out how to price tickets so that ordinary people
can go to the games. . . . You hate to think that the only person that can go to
a game is somebody who's got a corporate account."[109] The idea that arenas
were filled exclusively with corporate elites was an exaggeration, but Obama
was gesturing to something very real.

Beginning in the late 1980s, the fan base who frequented Bulls games
changed dramatically as skyrocketing ticket costs excluded more and more
Chicagoans from regular attendance. In fact, the championship rallies in
Grant Park were important mostly because they offered many fans their only
opportunity to see the players in person. Perhaps those in attendance felt con-
soled by the chance to cheer on Jordan and company in the park, but either
way, the rallies were a form of second-class spectatorship for those without
the cash or connections to score tickets on a regular basis.

The construction of the United Center demonstrated that consumption
of the Bulls was becoming increasingly stratified by class. Reinsdorf's focus
on the expansion of premium seating coincided with the cultivation of an
elite fan base and the relegation of most fans to watching the Bulls exclusively,
or nearly exclusively, on television. The scapegoating of player salaries by
ownership and the media was a predictable, though largely unsubstantiated,
response to fans' displeasure with increasing ticket prices and reduced accessibility. These changes owed first and foremost to the conscious, calculated
efforts of ownership to cater to the small slice of the public who benefited
most from the upward distribution of income at the end of the twentieth
century.

The Bulls as "Good Business": The United Center and Redeveloping Chicago's Near West Side

Chicagoans were ecstatic over the Bulls during the 1990s, but they had good reason to dislike Jerry Reinsdorf, and it was about more than his catering to elite fans. Before the Bulls became a sensation, Reinsdorf had, in the words of *Sun-Times* reporter Tom Fitzpatrick, established a reputation as something of a "con man."[1] In 1988, he threatened to move his Major League Baseball franchise, the Chicago White Sox, to Florida in an attempt to strong-arm the city and state into paying for a new baseball stadium. The threats worked; to make matters worse, the new stadium displaced several low-income families. The *Chicago Reader*'s Ben Joravsky summed up the Sox's attitude toward the city: "We want a new stadium. . . . We want somebody else to pay for it. We don't particularly care where it goes. It's not our problem if little people with their little homes get in the way. And, yes, one last thing: give us what we want, or we leave town."[2]

Why, then, did some Chicagoans suddenly start going out of their way in the early 1990s to describe Reinsdorf as a man who, in the words of one local community leader, was genuinely "concerned about [ordinary] people?"[3] Reinsdorf's new supporters claimed that, along with Blackhawks owner Bill Wirtz, he had proved his humanity by developing a corporate-community partnership with the predominantly low-income Near West Side neighborhood around the United Center. Reinsdorf and Wirtz not only provided millions of dollars in resident-designed replacement housing for those displaced by the arena; they also contributed to a new nearby library branch and park renovation, and they provided no-interest loans to the local community development corporation for additional revitalization efforts.

The project drew widespread support, sometimes from unexpected sources. Robert Mier, commissioner of economic development under Harold Washington and an admitted skeptic of stadium-linked redevelopment, characterized the deal between the United Center and neighborhood residents in 1991 as "setting a standard for large public and private projects." He added, "The precedent is . . . in the principle that people in an affected neighborhood matter as much as the development itself."[4] Indeed, the new arena's role in neighborhood revitalization seemed like a welcome departure from the typical steamrolling of poor residents by powerful developers. Reinsdorf and Wirtz exceeded everyone's expectations by continuing to invest in non-profit development around the United Center after satisfying the terms of the initial agreement. Some observers even argued that the investment shielded longtime residents from the threat of gentrification—that is, displacement resulting from new commercial development and the influx of more affluent residents. If the Bulls accomplished the impossible on the court, it appeared that United Center ownership achieved an equally unlikely feat in the blocks around the arena: engaging in private, inner-city real estate development that facilitated longtime residents' access to new and improved services, housing, and job opportunities. At least on the surface, this seemed like a glowing exception to the resurgence of exclusionary capitalism in urban America.

However, as Larry Bennett and Costas Spirou clarify in their brief but compelling study of the United Center, this sanguine assessment overlooks the turbulent history of a neighborhood internally divided over the form of local redevelopment during the 1990s. On one side, a handful of relatively well-off, property-owning blacks came to view an alliance with the team owners as a way to both improve the livability of the community and increase their economic and political stakes within it. On the other side, some local clergy believed that the alliance's increasing emphasis on market-rate residential development excluded poorer residents from revitalization and threatened to displace them from the neighborhood altogether. Ultimately, the clergy's protests fell on deaf ears, as the lay leaders whom they criticized quickly established a monopoly over development funds from arena ownership and the city.[5]

Each side leveled accusations of self-interest against the other, but regardless of the motives, the conflict suggested that the benefits brought to the neighborhood by the United Center were not trickling down to everyone. Impoverished public-housing tenants at the nearby Henry Horner Homes confirmed this when they mounted a bold challenge to the pro-arena coalition. Proponents of arena-linked revitalization on the Near West Side from the public and private sectors saw public-housing residents as an impediment to growth. As a result, they moved to exclude most of them from the redevelopment process, and in doing so, they encouraged their displacement.

In what proved a unique, if limited, victory against the march of exclusionary capitalism through the Near West Side, Horner tenants successfully appealed to the courts to protect their right to stay in the community. If there was a force pushing back unequivocally against gentrification in the neighborhood, it was not the United Center but rather these public-housing residents.

Instead of proving that urban capitalists could balance their pursuit of profits with the needs of all neighborhood residents, sports-linked development on the Near West Side followed a blueprint that ultimately shunted aside the poor to prioritize the interests of Reinsdorf and a select group of elites. Like countless redevelopment plans imposed upon poor urban neighborhoods in the United States at the end of the twentieth century, this blueprint embraced at least two approaches to revitalization that exacerbated urban inequality: first, the retreat from programs intended to provide rental housing for low-income people in favor of initiatives to expand homeownership for the relatively affluent; and second, poverty "deconcentration" schemes that, rather than redistributing resources to the poor, dispersed low-income residents away from inner-city neighborhoods to make way for private real-estate developers.

That there were any poor people left around the arena by the end of the century owed not to an inclusive "partnership" between team owners and the neighborhood but rather to the initiative of the Henry Horner tenants. Vocal and visible advocates of the United Center development with intimate knowledge of its ins and outs, namely the team owners and their local political allies, ignored this part of the story, which rarely, if ever, came to the attention of those who lauded the project from afar.

This story points to the danger of relying too much on race alone to understand how exclusionary capitalism operated in American cities in the New Gilded Age. The arena developers fit the stereotype of white, capitalist outsiders swooping in to take charge of "revitalization" in a low-income African American neighborhood. However, conflicts over redevelopment on the Near West Side were not simply fights between low-income blacks and affluent whites. Class divisions within the African American community played a crucial role in how things unfolded. A mix of factors—personal advancement, a lack of attractive alternatives, and national shifts in politics, economics, and culture—ultimately led a few well-off African Americans in the neighborhood to throw in their lot with Reinsdorf and his colleagues. This put relatively affluent blacks, many of them homeowners, at odds with their low-income African American neighbors, many of whom resided at nearby public housing projects; and the former made repeated decisions that threatened to exclude the latter from the benefits of redevelopment. Race, in

other words, proved an imperfect predictor of whether residents would resist
or abet exclusionary capitalism on the Near West Side.

"If You Want My Land, You Have to Give Me Something"

In 1987, after two years of negotiations with City Hall, the Chicago Bears decided on a ninety-acre stretch of land just south of the Henry Horner Homes
public housing project as the site for a new football stadium. Almost all the
residents in the neighborhood, which occupied the northwestern corner of
the city's Near West Side community area, were African American (maps 3.1

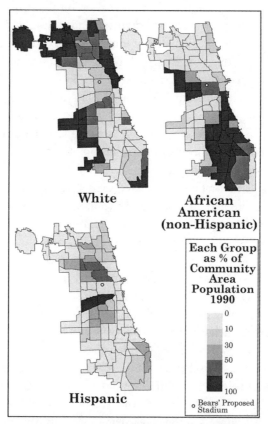

MAP 3.1. City of Chicago Community Areas by Racial/Ethnic Composition, 1990
Source: Shapefiles from City of Chicago, *Chicago Data Portal*. Demographic data from Nancy Hudspeth, "Interpreting Neighborhood Change," *Voorhees Center at the University of Illinois, Chicago*, accessed September 3, 2015, www.uic.edu/cuppa/voorheesctr/Gentrification%20Index%20Site/Main%20
Neighborhood%20Change%20Revised.htm (link no longer active but raw data available from author
upon request).
Notes: "Hispanic" encompasses Spanish-speaking persons of all races.

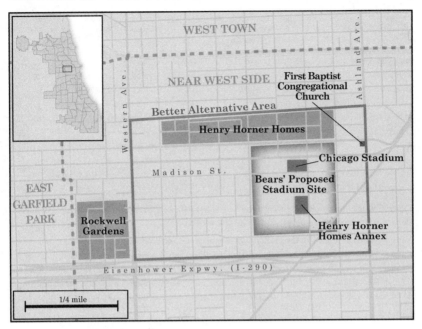

MAP 3.2. The Northwestern Quarter of the Near West Side Community Area

Source: Devereux Bowly Jr., *The Poorhouse: Subsidized Housing in Chicago, 1895–1976* (Carbondale: Southern Illinois University Press); Interfaith Organizing Project, *The Better Alternative: Near West Side Neighborhood Revitalizing Plan* (Chicago, June 1987), Municipal Reference Collection, Harold Washington Library Center; Perkins and Will, *Chicago Sports Center: A Concept Plan for Near Westside Revitalization and a New Bears Football Stadium* (Chicago, April 1987), Special Collections, Harold Washington Library Center.

Notes: The Bears stadium plan called for incorporating Chicago Stadium into its parking lots, and for the demolition of the Henry Horner Annex. The "better alternative area" refers to a set of blocks included in a 1987 revitalization proposal created by the Interfaith Organizing Project. The proposal is discussed in more detail later in the chapter.

and 3.2).[6] Most households were very low-income; their members understood what was happening. At a public hearing on the stadium plan, Horner tenant Cindi Sanders asserted that the Bears selected the neighborhood because land was cheap and residents lacked clout. "When the site on the lake was proposed, a site which would not require one displacement, no demolition for a stadium, these 30 white folks told the City that they did not want the grass nor the view of the lake disturbed, told you to go to those niggers on the West Side," Sanders told city officials.[7] She was right. Resistance from powerful community organizations like Friends of the Parks precluded stadium construction in more affluent parts of the city.[8]

Residents from Horner and the surrounding neighborhood barely had the resources to survive, let alone mount an effective campaign against the Bears.

TABLE 3.1. Selected Demographic Data for Chicago's Near West Side Community Area, 1940–1990

	1940	1950	1960	1970	1980	1990
Total population	136,518	160,362	126,610	78,703	57,305	46,197
White (%)	80.8	58.5	45.6	25.2	16.3	22
Black (%)	18.9	40.9	53.8	72.2	74.7	67
Other nonwhite (%)	0.3	0.6	0.6	2.6	9	11
Median family income (1989 $)	n/a	$14,036	$16,656	$20,421	$13,118	$10,268
All workers in manufacturing (%)	n/a	41.1	29.3	31	23.7	11.3
Civilian labor force unemployed (%)	23.6	7.3	11.7	8	15.8	20.5

Source: Chicago Community Inventory, *Local Community Fact Book Chicago Metropolitan Area* (Chicago: University of Illinois, Chicago, 1949, 1953, 1963, 1984, 1995).

Notes: Data derived from U.S. Census Bureau's decennial censuses. Economic and employment data reported by the Census after 1960 are based on sample-based estimations, as opposed to full counts. Income data is for year prior to decennial census year. Labor force included persons 14 years and older through 1960, but subsequent surveys raised the cutoff to 16 years old. Inflation adjustments made using the Bureau of Labor Statistics CPI-U for the Chicago-Gary-Kenosha area.

The Near West Side had experienced accelerated deindustrialization and demographic decline in the decades after World War II (table 3.1). Divestment was especially bad in the northwestern quarter of the community area, site of a 1968 uprising sparked by the assassination of Martin Luther King Jr. and several housing projects, such as Horner and Rockwell Gardens. When the Bears selected the stretch of land immediately south of Chicago Stadium for their proposed facility (map 3.2), 57.5 percent of families in the census tracts containing Horner and the stadium lived below the poverty line.[9] "It was an area so impoverished," wrote journalist Alex Kotlowitz, "that when Mother Teresa visited in 1982, she assigned nuns from her Missionaries of Charity to work at [the] Henry Horner [Homes]."[10]

Even as other parts of the Near West Side showed signs of recovery during the 1980s, the neighborhood around Horner continued to deteriorate. Census tracts in the southern and western portions of the community area gained population over the course of the decade, as loft development spilled westward from the Loop and residential development expanded around major urban-renewal sites like the University of Illinois at Chicago (map 3.3). In contrast, the tracts containing Horner and Chicago Stadium kept hemorrhaging residents. This uneven growth coincided with intense racial segregation. Struggling neighborhoods in the northern and southwestern parts of the community area remained almost exclusively African American, while neighborhoods closer to the Loop contained relatively tiny black populations (map 3.4).

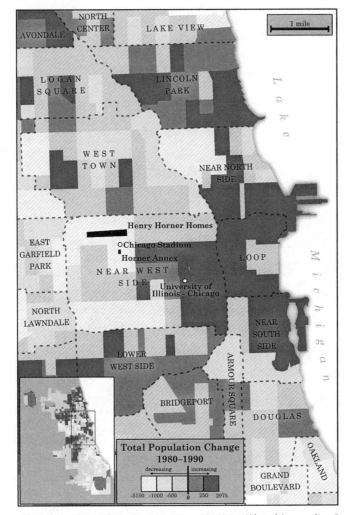

MAP 3.3. Absolute Population Change by Census Tract, Near West Side and Surrounding Community Areas, 1980–1990

Source: Shapefiles obtained from City of Chicago, *Chicago Data Portal;* U.S. Census Bureau, *American Factfinder.* Full-count census data obtained from US2010 Project, Longitudinal Tract Database.

Notes: Tracts conform to the 2010 boundaries. The LTDB database standardizes all census data from 1970 to 2010 using 2010 boundaries to facilitate better comparison across decades.

In 1985, a few years before the Bears set their sights on the Near West Side, community organizers Karen Nielson and Ed Shurna put out feelers for Chicago churches interested in collaborating with them on grassroots economic development. They were met with interest by Reverend Arthur Griffin, lead pastor of First Baptist Congregational Church, which sat a few blocks east of

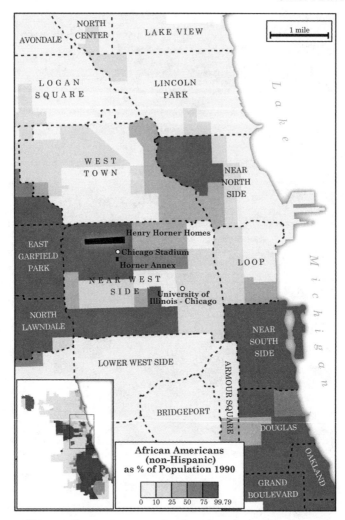

MAP 3.4. African Americans as a Percentage of Total Population by Census Tract, Near West Side and Surrounding Community Areas, 1990

Source: Shapefiles obtained from City of Chicago, *Chicago Data Portal;* U.S. Census Bureau, *American Factfinder.* Full-count census data obtained from US2010 Project, Longitudinal Tract Database.

the Horner Homes. Griffin offered Nielsen and Shurna the church basement as an office and so began a partnership that would endure confrontations with two different groups of stadium developers.[11] The organization that emerged, the Interfaith Organizing Project (IOP), initially worked on a wide range of issues. Once leaders learned of the Bears' plans, the IOP shifted its efforts almost exclusively to fighting the stadium, which local residents saw as a land grab (fig. 3.1).[12]

The IOP rallied supporters at public hearings on the stadium throughout 1987 and early 1988 and staged gutsy actions like playing a touch-football game on the front lawn of Bears owner Mike McCaskey's home to simulate the chaos of having a stadium nearby.[13] These early organizational successes owed much to the group's diverse leadership. Even though the IOP

FIGURE 3.1. Interfaith Organizing Project Flyer Calling for Residents to Attend a Meeting of Mayor Harold Washington's Stadium Site Collection Committee on April 15, 1987
Source: Robert Mier Papers, Chicago History Museum.

was ostensibly faith based, local lay leaders like Earnest Gates, who had lived near the proposed stadium site since childhood and ran a West Side trucking company, took proactive roles alongside pastors like Griffin and professional organizers like Shurna. According to Gates, it boiled down to having a common enemy: "There was a monster that had to be slain, and it was clear that it had to be slain, and the community geared up to do that."[14]

The IOP also worked with planners at the University of Illinois at Chicago (UIC) whose research suggested that most jobs created by the stadium development would not go to neighborhood residents and that the resulting increase in real estate values in the surrounding area would fuel gentrification.[15] The residents' experience with Chicago Stadium corroborated this grim outlook. Gates, speaking at a public hearing on the stadium in February 1988, lashed out against city officials, arguing that "Chicago Stadium has not provided those brothers and sisters [from Henry Horner] with jobs. A Chicago Bears Stadium will not provide those brothers and sisters with jobs. It is a sham, it is a fallacy, and we are not buying it."[16] Despite differences in social class, Gates and Horner tenants temporarily found common cause in opposing the plans of rich sports-team owners who had shown little evidence of having the best interests of neighborhood residents at heart. In response to the Bears, the IOP drafted a detailed plan for a "neighborhood-controlled revitalization option." Labeled *The Better Alternative* plan and delivered to the city and state legislature in June 1987, it outlined a "well-structured job creation strategy" as well as a proposal for financing two thousand affordable housing units in the neighborhood within ten years (see maps 3.2 and 3.5 for the area covered by the plan).[17]

The Better Alternative plan portrayed a community eager to take charge of local revitalization. Time was of the essence; as the plan pointed out, "middle class pioneers" had been moving west from downtown, driving up rents and property values. Moreover, implementation of the Bears' proposal promised significant displacement of longtime residents. "Few neighborhoods in walking proximity to the Loop remain in which to encourage the cross-section of life that would truly represent Chicago's unity in diversity," the report noted. "The opportunity to turn this vision into reality is there to be taken."[18]

The IOP's anxieties about gentrification were justified. By the 1980s the Near West Side community area contained what one local real-estate publication described as "a crazy quilt of smaller neighborhoods" (map 3.5); the boundaries between these neighborhoods coincided with the community area's uneven racial and economic geography.[19] To the east of the so-called Better Alternative Area, the West Loop and West Loop Gate neighborhoods were already drawing artists and young professionals eager to take advantage

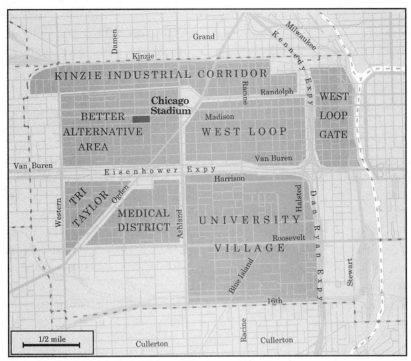

MAP 3.5. Neighborhood Geography of the Near West Side Community Area
Source: Shapefiles obtained from City of Chicago, *Chicago Data Portal.*

of inexpensive loft space close to downtown. To the south and southeast, the city had cleared out low-income residents as part of urban-renewal projects in University Village and the Medical District that, in some cases, began as early as the 1950s. In addition, by the 1980s historic preservationists had established a foothold in the nearby Tri-Taylor neighborhood.[20] Residents in the Better Alternative Area thus had good reason to fear the further encroachment of gentrification.

Despite the IOP's best efforts, the city and state ignored *The Better Alternative* plan. Eugene Sawyer, who became interim mayor after Washington's death in 1987, announced in May 1988 that the Bears had reached terms with the city to move forward with construction of a new football stadium. The Bears stadium, however, never came to fruition. What ultimately stopped it in the following months was not the IOP but a rift between Bears owner McCaskey and Chicago Stadium owner Bill Wirtz. Wirtz, whose wealth rested on a vast liquor distributorship and deep political connections, fumed when he discovered that the terms of the deal allowed the Bears to keep all revenues from parking lots that would be located on land he owned. The same month

Mayor Sawyer announced the deal, Wirtz's lawyers denied having reached any sort of legal agreement with the Bears concerning the parking lots, and Wirtz's lobbyists promptly torpedoed legislation that would have authorized state funds for the project. "We always say we defeated it," says Shurna, "but I think if Bill Wirtz had not come into play—I don't think we would have defeated it."[21]

As much as Wirtz's involvement worked in the IOP's favor, it also highlighted the tenuousness of residents' position. Redevelopment in the neighborhood continued to happen on terms set by those who had wealth and connections. This became even clearer when, in July 1988, Wirtz and his lawyers met with lenders to discuss financing for a replacement arena for Chicago Stadium on the spot where the Bears had planned to locate their new facility. By October, the Blackhawks owner had already informed the governor of his new plan, and Jerry Reinsdorf quickly signed on as a partner. Reinsdorf and the Bulls leased Chicago Stadium from Wirtz during the basketball season, but the two teams would jointly own the proposed arena.[22]

The IOP initially stuck to its no-stadium position. Even though Reinsdorf and Wirtz reached out to IOP leadership in the months after the Bears deal collapsed to find out what it would take to bring neighborhood residents on board with the new arena plans, the group remained suspicious. "All you have to do is look around Chicago Stadium to see how little Wirtz has done for the neighborhood all these years," Shurna told the *Sun-Times*' Fran Spielman in May 1989. For her part, Spielman reported that the new proposal would displace at least sixty homeowners without offering anything to the community other than cash buyouts for their homes. This made the plan a nonstarter for the IOP. Nevertheless, Reinsdorf and Wirtz moved ahead aggressively, lobbying the Illinois General Assembly for $20 million in public money for infrastructural improvements around the proposed arena site.[23]

At the end of May 1989, the IOP found an unexpected ally in the new mayor, Richard M. Daley. He temporarily derailed the team owners' efforts by insisting that they get approval for their plans from neighborhood residents, a demand the mayor could make since the city owned several parcels of land that the teams needed to build the arena. *Tribune* reporter John McCarron speculated that Daley took his stance to "minimize the political fallout associated with displacing 70 predominantly poor and black families," a view with which both Gates and Shurna agree.[24]

Daley's intervention on behalf of the Near West Siders was more than a public relations stunt. Personal and political connections likely played a role as well. By 1989 the IOP had come to count on the advocacy of Tom Rosenberg, a local real estate developer with close ties to Daley—close enough that

Rosenberg donated at least $35,000 to Daley's campaign committee between March 1989 and December 1994.[25] Earnest Gates knew Rosenberg through a local handball club, and when the latter found out about the ongoing negotiations between the IOP and the arena developers, he offered his services as a "mediator." According to Shurna, Rosenberg was not only close to Daley and Gates; he also held a long-standing grudge against Reinsdorf and Wirtz, who allegedly had interfered with some of his local development projects.[26] The combination of Rosenberg's closeness to Daley and his history of conflict with the team owners likely made his support of the IOP a significant factor in the city's decision to force the hands of Reinsdorf and Wirtz.

During the summer of 1989, with Daley having bought them some time, neighborhood residents dug in their heels and began to strategize. Some remained opposed to a new arena under any circumstances. Ed Shurna gravitated toward this position, but others began to entertain the possibility of collaborating with the stadium developers.[27] Earnest Gates, by this point the most prominent lay leader within the IOP, recalls his own thinking as increasingly pragmatic in this regard. "It was . . . a community that was on the [brink] of collapsing, and looked weak," he explained. This, along with the fact that the number of residents the new arena would displace was considerably less than in the Bears plan, made Gates "a little more amenable to talking, to having a discussion about what amenities a project like that could bring to the neighborhood."[28]

Gates had a point: The community was even poorer than it had been a decade earlier. By the end of the 1980s, more than 72 percent of families there lived below the official poverty line.[29] Moreover, help from the government appeared more unlikely with each passing day. Between 1978 and 1988, federal grants-in-aid to states and cities as a percentage of total federal outlays fell from 17 percent to less than 11 percent, and from 3.4 percent to 2.2 percent of gross domestic product.[30] In this context, Gates's change of heart resonated with other IOP members, who eventually rallied around the slogan "If you want my land, you have to give me something." At a June 1989 meeting, the IOP called on team owners to provide replacement housing for displaced residents, to fund development of additional neighborhood housing, and to help pay for a new library. With their hands tied by Daley and a group of elderly homeowners who lived within the footprint of the proposed arena site and refused individual buyouts, the team owners grudgingly agreed to negotiate with the community.[31]

Finally, on May 9, 1991, Reinsdorf and Wirtz signed a thirteen-point agreement with the IOP (table 3.2). Residents displaced by the arena would not have to move until replacement housing was ready, and United Center Joint

TABLE 3.2. Stipulations of the 13-Point Agreement between IOP and Joint Venture, May 9, 1991

1. All homeowners in the footprint of the new arena are entitled to replacement housing, and the developers must complete construction of the replacement housing before forcing said homeowners to vacate.

2. Replacement homes will be constructed in the area bounded by Damen Avenue, Western Avenue, Washington Boulevard, and the Eisenhower Expressway.

3. Those homeowners not desiring replacement housing will receive fair market value plus $30,000.

4. Renters in the footprint of the stadium will receive $6,000 in moving expenses (per unit).

5. The Joint Venture will make a $600,000 no-interest loan to the Interfaith Organizing Project to develop 75 "for sale" homes within the borders designated above in point 2. Buyers from the area delineated in point 2 will receive priority.

6. The Joint Venture will provide subsidies to resettled homeowners to cover the increased property taxes associated with the difference between the assessments of their old and new homes.

7. The Joint Venture will coordinate with the Chicago Park District to renovate and expand Touhy-Herbert Park.

8. The Joint Venture promises to refrain from acquiring any land west of Damen Avenue.

9. The Joint Venture will coordinate with the Chicago Public Library to ensure the construction of a new public library branch on Madison Avenue, between Western and Damen.

10. Local churches will be able to use stadium parking lots.

11. The Joint Venture agrees to lobby the City to provide funding for a construction trades program at Malcolm X Community College.

12. No simultaneous events will be held at the new arena and the old Chicago Stadium.

13. The IOP recognizes the $75,000 donation by the Joint Venture to the Miles Square Health Center.

Source: Interfaith Organizing Project, *The New West Side Story: The Story of the Interfaith Organizing Project* (Chicago, 1992), 33–34, Associated Mennonite Biblical Seminary Library; *Journal of the Proceedings of the City Council of the City of Chicago*, May 22, 1991, 180-227, Municipal Reference Collection, Harold Washington Library Center.

Notes: Specific wording in the table is paraphrased from sources.

Venture, the official name of the partnership between Reinsdorf and Wirtz, would establish a $600,000 escrow account to develop additional housing between Damen and Western Avenues. The team owners also agreed to lobby the city for a new neighborhood park and library, as well as a construction trades program at nearby Malcolm X Community College. Mary Schmich of the *Tribune* described it as "the rarest of wars, a war that both sides won." IOP president Arthur Griffin called it "a wonderful victory for the residents of the West Side." "It's comforting to know we have all of the neighbors behind us," Reinsdorf remarked, adding that "it's just good business."[32]

The team owners held up their end of the bargain. In 1992, residents living within the footprint of the planned arena moved into sixteen new two-flats located just west of Damen Avenue. Each one contained two 1,500-square-foot units, each with three bedrooms, two baths, oak trim, and dishwasher-equipped kitchens.[33] Coming on the heels of the Bears fiasco, it all seemed too good to be true. Mayor Daley called it "an example of what people can accomplish if they work together," predicting that the new arena would bring "jobs and economic development, but not at the expense of homes and neighborhoods."[34] An official IOP history from 1992 offered an even more celebratory interpretation. "The deal between the Stadium Joint Venture and the community rewrites history," it explained. "A largely black and low-income community was able to turn the tide of 'urban renewal' into a useful catalyst for neighborhood-based redevelopment."[35]

The joyous reception of the deal by all sides seemed justified. Economic elites could herald it as proof that for-profit real-estate development did not have to come at the expense of the already disadvantaged. Near West Siders and IOP members could claim that they scored concessions that would enhance their quality of life through expanded neighborhood resources and that they did this in the face of national trends pushing strongly in the opposite direction. The new housing, library, educational programs, and other amenities would arrive as reduced taxes for the wealthy and cuts to urban social programs were throwing most other low-income urban neighborhoods into further disarray or forcing longtime residents to abandon them altogether.

As exciting as it seemed, the deal only partially addressed the needs outlined in *The Better Alternative* plan, which called for redevelopment without a new stadium. The plan indicated that the more than forty-five acres of land eventually set aside for the new arena would be best utilized for new residential units and small-scale retail development (figs. 3.2 and 3.3). The agreement thus signaled the IOP's acceptance of the idea that revitalization on the community's own terms lay out of reach. [36]

Residents had good reason to believe that they had no other choice. Up to that point, the IOP averted defeat by virtue of the fallout between power brokers like Wirtz and McCaskey. This bought the community time, rather than shifting the balance of power between residents and outside interests. As historian Alexander von Hoffman rightly concludes in his version of the story, leaders like Gates "discovered the value of forming alliances with large institutions within or near their neighborhoods." However, Hoffman's description of residents as "a community taking charge of its own redevelopment," which echoes local journalists' notion that the deal allowed the neighborhood to "chart its own destiny," romanticizes the situation.[37]

The deal was less about residents "taking charge" than about them taking what they could get in a political environment that, to borrow from sociologists John Logan and Harvey Molotch, "required [community organizations] to join with at least some of their potential . . . adversaries" to survive.[38] This was by no means a new phenomenon in the 1980s, but the pressure on groups

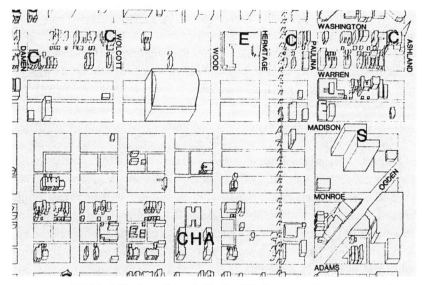

FIGURE 3.2. Detail from *The Better Alternative* Plan Land-Use Survey
Source: Interfaith Organizing Project, *The Better Alternative: Near West Side Neighborhood Revitalization Plan* (Chicago, 1987), n.p., Municipal Reference Collection, Harold Washington Library Center.
Notes: The large structure in the northwestern quarter of the detail is the old Chicago Stadium. The United Center would cover nearly the entire area west of Paulina Street, and then some.

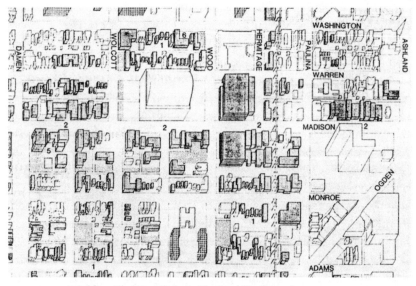

FIGURE 3.3. Detail from *The Better Alternative* Plan Land-Use Proposal
Source: Interfaith Organizing Project, *The Better Alternative*.
Notes: All the residential and commercial in-fill shown in this proposal would eventually be precluded by construction of the United Center.

like the IOP to partner with the private sector mounted as city, state, and federal government agencies pulled back from their commitments to distressed neighborhoods.

To be sure, the IOP never struck the same chords of militancy characteristic of radical black organizations in earlier decades. Nevertheless, it was reminiscent of groups organizing under the banner of "black power" during the 1960s and 1970s inasmuch as members initially demanded a self-determined alternative to gentrification. By 1991, things had changed; the commitment to self-determination had largely faded from view. The organization decided to set aside the question put forth by Reverend Griffin in 1987: "Why can't we just have the neighborhood and economic development without the sports complex?"[39]

This is not to say that the IOP suddenly endorsed the new arena as a panacea for the neighborhood's ills. After inking the deal with Reinsdorf and Wirtz, the group stayed in contact with local researchers who provided more data suggesting that stadiums resulted in little to no ancillary economic development for their respective cities and neighborhoods. An update to *The Better Alternative* plan published in consultation with an architectural and planning expert in December 1991 concluded that the northwestern part of the Near West Side "should be developed with the community's needs as the primary driving force, not the new . . . sports stadium."[40]

Nevertheless, the agreement with United Center ownership was something, and IOP members looked on with satisfaction as displaced residents moved into new housing units in March 1992. One person making the move told Maudlyne Ihejirika of the *Sun-Times* that without the deal, she would have likely "gone back to Alabama." Ihejirika gushed over the unlikely alliance between residents and arena developers. "Proud residents agree the deal was fair and generous," she reported, later quoting Reinsdorf's assessment that "in the end we [the team owners and residents] came to understand each other."[41]

In 1994, just a few months before the arena opened its doors—by then the owners had named it United Center in exchange for United Airlines' purchase of the stadium's naming rights—*Crain's Chicago Business* continued the celebratory coverage of the arena deal in a profile of Earnest Gates. The article, by Grant Pick, discussed Gates's efforts as head of the Near West Side Community Development Corporation (NWSCDC), a nonprofit founded by the IOP in 1988 to implement *The Better Alternative* plan. Gates, whose task was to use resources provided by Reinsdorf and Wirtz to jump-start new commercial and residential investment, told the paper: "People have to redo their own neighborhoods. . . . You can't depend on the government to do it, and if you don't take control yourself, some developer is going to come in and you're out."[42] Not only could neighborhoods create symbiotic alliances with big business; the formula for doing so was easy, according to Gates. All one had to do was "appeal to [investors] as businessmen," which meant reminding them that "it only makes sense to protect your investment by investing in the neighborhood and by working with the residents."[43]

The sudden appearance of mainstream press accounts that, in the words of Spirou and Bennett, transformed Gates "from conniving troublemaker to invaluable neighborhood intermediary," coincided with Gates's abandonment of confrontational language.[44] His new style was a far cry from his fiery rhetoric during the IOP's campaign against the Bears. However, it seemed like the change in approach paid dividends for the neighborhood. Per the agreement, the arena owners followed through on the promise of a $600,000 escrow account to provide no-interest loans for additional neighborhood housing, and the Bulls donated $35,000 for new basketball courts at the nearby Touhy-Herbert Park and $50,000 for computers at a new neighborhood library branch on Hoyne Avenue. To top things off, in July 1994, Chicago won its bid to host the 1996 Democratic National Convention (DNC) at the United Center. In preparation, the city and state appropriated $17 million for street improvements and beautification projects around the arena.[45] These DNC-related projects did not directly address the need for stable jobs and housing, but they promised to make the community more hospitable for retail investment and the entry-level employment it would bring.

Good news for the neighborhood continued in the months leading up to the convention. In September 1994, the Bulls announced a more than $4 million contribution for a new Boys and Girls Club next to the arena. In February 1995, United Center ownership announced the launch of the Community Economic Development Fund, which consisted of over $1 million from the team owners in support of new neighborhood businesses. By that point, Reinsdorf and Wirtz had injected upward of $8 million in grants and loans into the neighborhood.[46] New investment was finally arriving, and the community had real reason for optimism. However, during the mid-1990s, some longtime community leaders and residents started to question whether the alliance with the United Center was helping those neighborhood residents most in need of jobs, housing, and support services.

Post-Arena Development and the Decline
of the Interfaith Organizing Project

Although some of the money from Reinsdorf and Wirtz went toward the construction of new homes, the amount fell far short of that needed to build the two thousand units for low- and moderate-income families aspired to in *The Better Alternative* plan. This was where networking by Gates and the NWSCDC became crucial. The group had to mix and match funds from the United Center with a limited supply of city, state, and federal money to accomplish enough redevelopment to make the neighborhood attractive for private developers. By July 1994, the NWSCDC had used a few million dollars in Community Development Block Grant money to initiate construction of a fifteen-unit apartment building a few blocks west of the arena for moderate-income tenants who would receive rent subsidies, and by the summer of 1996, the organization had started to market single-family homes for between $150,000 and $200,000.[47]

Just as Gates and the NWSCDC began to build some momentum, however, uneasiness simmering among other IOP leaders about the new developments boiled over. In the years leading up to the NWSCDC's announcement of the deal for the new single-family homes, George Daniels, assistant pastor at First Congregational Baptist Church and Arthur Griffin's successor as IOP president, chafed at what he perceived as Gates catering to homebuyers from outside the neighborhood. Daniels believed that longtime residents, most of whom could not afford a market-rate mortgage, would not benefit from the new housing units planned by the NWSCDC. He also felt that Gates's approach to redevelopment depended more on displacing longtime residents than on protecting them. Unable to resolve their differences, Daniels and Gates severed ties. Daniels remained IOP president but ceded independent control of the NWSCDC to Gates.[48]

In December 1996, Daniels gave his side of the story to Burney Simpson at the *Chicago Reporter*. "When we began we were talking about building houses for $80,000," Daniels explained, but "when I left [the NWSCDC] they were talking about places for $150,000." He continued, "I couldn't stomach it . . . [that doesn't] represent the indigenous community. That's not the little guy."[49] Gates dismisses Daniels's claims, insisting that the real cause of the split had to do with the desire of the IOP's pastoral leadership to maintain control over neighborhood politics and their resentment of his growing public visibility. The housing brought in by the NWSCDC, according to Gates, was as cheap as it was going to get. "Now we were selling homes—brand new homes—for around $150,000 in the 90s and then there was a subsidy attached which would have dropped the price of the home $20,000. . . . You couldn't beat that."[50]

Gates's argument about home prices held water. After the split, Daniels and the IOP developed a few three-bedroom homes in the Better Alternative Area that sold for around $80,000 each. However, rising land costs precluded development of additional units at such a low price. According to a 1996 *Sun-Times* article, nominal land prices in the area had jumped 1,400 percent since the early 1980s. By 1997, the IOP could no longer develop units priced under $100,000 east of Western Avenue, so it shifted its focus to residential development further west in East Garfield Park, leaving Gates unchallenged around the arena.[51] In this context, one reading of the conflict between Gates and Daniels is that the former's pragmatism prevailed over the latter's idealism. Even if he compromised, at least Gates got things done.

There is some truth to this interpretation, but it papers over the legitimacy of Daniels's concerns over escalating land values. Admittedly, had the NWSCDC built homes priced at $80,000 as Daniels wanted, most residents still could not have afforded them. But homes like the ones Gates developed, which required around $30,000 in annual income to qualify for a mortgage, foreshadowed more dramatic gentrification and a more serious threat to the IOP's original vision of executing redevelopment that would directly benefit *all* longtime residents. As Shurna told a pair of *Sun-Times* reporters back in 1988, the IOP's "goal [was] to revitalize the whole neighborhood—that includes the businesses, the schools and Henry Horner Homes."[52]

In Daniels's eyes, Gates had lost sight of this broader commitment. Interpersonal politics aside, this was far from an unfounded critique. Gates certainly engaged in efforts to aid longtime residents, like helping to set up the new Boys and Girls Club and administering various youth and job-training programs. But as the next chapter details, after the signing of the thirteen-point plan, Gates and the NWSCDC focused more and more on constructing private, market-rate housing for new, not existing, residents—precisely the opposite of what *The Better Alternative* plan called for. This would, in theory, revive the tax base and lure retail investment much faster than longer-term initiatives like poverty reduction, job creation, and substance-abuse treatment.[53] But prioritized to the exclusion of a sustained, comprehensive program of socioeconomic uplift for longtime residents, market-rate residential development risked leaving the neighborhood's low-income population to fend for itself. Moreover, it created a new problem for the poor, namely escalating rents.

Daniels felt that Gates's increasing closeness to Reinsdorf and Wirtz also threatened the neighborhood's neediest residents. When Gates decided to stack the NWSCDC board with Bulls officials in the early 1990s, Daniels was outraged. "This was not the vision. IOP stood in opposition to the Bulls," he said in a 2000 interview.[54] He was alarmed by how the NWSCDC had emerged as the official clearinghouse for redevelopment funds that, because of the legitimacy lent by support from the team owners and the city, could unilaterally define the best interests of the community. Daniels, it turned out, was not the only one with serious concerns.

The Horner Homes and the Fight for Inclusive Revitalization around the United Center

The Henry Horner Homes were one of eleven high-rise public housing projects built by the Chicago Housing Authority (CHA) during the 1950s and 1960s. In theory, projects like Horner, where by 1957 the CHA had completed 920 units of subsidized rental housing for working and low-income families, represented the fulfillment of the promise made by the federal government during the New Deal to guarantee Americans access to adequate housing. The 1937 Wagner-Steagall Housing Act institutionalized this commitment by empowering the federal government to distribute funds to local housing authorities. A little more than a decade later, by way of the Housing Act of 1949, Congress committed to funding 810,000 new public-housing units. By 1961, the CHA had added 736 new units to Horner in the form of the adjacent Horner Extension. In 1969, 109 additional units became available in the form of the Horner Annex, located just a few blocks south of the original Horner Homes (map 3.2).[55]

Many tenants who lived at Horner during the 1950s and 1960s recall it as a nice place to raise a family, but in subsequent decades the project fell into disarray. By December 1991, residents and housing activists described Horner as the CHA's "most troubled development" and "one of the most distressed public-housing properties in the nation." In that year, the vacancy rate reached 49.5 percent, the worst of any development, and far above the CHA average of 15.9 percent.[56] According to a local public-housing advocate active in the neighborhood at the time, the list of maintenance and sanitation issues included "broken, boarded-up and leaking windows, broken trash chutes . . . missing . . . fire escape signs . . . defective stairway handrails . . . [and] human and animal waste in public areas." Moreover, the development was thoroughly segregated. In 1991, 100 percent of the residents were African American, 90 percent received some form of public assistance, and single women led three-quarters of the households.[57]

What transformed the promise of a place like Horner into what historian D. Bradford Hunt calls a "devastating urban policy failure"?[58] The answer lay in a combination of poor design and administration, racist housing policy, and the decline of the postwar economy. In the first place, the federal government elected to build on the cheap in order to produce large numbers of units quickly. Moreover, the growth of conservative opposition to expanding public-housing appropriations after World War II, driven in large part by Cold War hysteria about public housing being too socialistic, limited its funding and encouraged systemic neglect of the program. As a result, local housing authorities depended increasingly on below-market rents paid by public-housing tenants for maintenance and upkeep of projects, but on its own this revenue stream proved inadequate.[59]

As African Americans continued to flood into Northern cities from the South in search of work in the two decades following the war, middle- and working-class whites, including many who had previously lived in public housing, resettled comfortably in the suburbs by taking advantage of federal home-loan programs. Inner-city firms and jobs followed. Racist real-estate practices such as steering nonwhite home buyers away from predominantly white communities, violent resistance from white community groups, and "redlining"—the systematic exclusion of African Americans from eligibility for government-backed home loans—trapped blacks within central cities. As a result, most lacked access to the new jobs and capital (especially low-interest home loans) that underwrote the growth of the postwar middle class. In Chicago, local officials used high-rise public housing to warehouse African Americans who had been cut off from the suburban boom, keeping them away from white neighborhoods and creating "second ghettos" in the process.[60]

The containment of working-class and low-income blacks in public-housing projects crippled them within a changing economy. Between 1967 and 1973, as growth slowed and manufacturing jobs continued to leave the city, the fraction of CHA tenants relying on welfare assistance rose from less than a quarter to more than two-thirds. Gang activity and a black market in drugs started to fill the "social void" left by widespread unemployment.[61] By the mid-1970s Congress had effectively abandoned federally funded public-housing construction by introducing the Section 8 program, which provided vouchers to subsidize rents in the private market. In theory, this encouraged the deconcentration of poverty in housing projects and boosted efficiency by increasing the private sector's role in programs run by the Department of Housing and Urban Development (HUD).[62] Unfortunately, Section 8 subsidies often proved too meager to convince landlords and developers to open units to low-income families, and voucher recipients often left public housing only to end up in substandard shelter elsewhere. Moreover, local housing authorities did not provide enough vouchers. By 1985, Chicago's Section 8 waiting list stood at forty thousand families.[63]

Given this history, it should come as little surprise that Horner residents were skeptical of the ability of a new stadium to help them. In fact, the Bears' stadium plans called for locating one of the end zones on top of the Horner Annex.[64] At a public hearing on the Bears plan in February 1988, Maurine Woodson, who lived in the Annex at the time, voiced her frustration with the lack of information regarding how displaced residents would find new housing. "HUD says there is no money for new housing. You said you are going to put us in new housing, new structured housing. . . . I want to know how you are going to do it," she told representatives from the Chicago Department of Planning. Because residents had waited in vain for HUD to approve a CHA request for $1.9 million to renovate the Annex in 1985, Woodson's cynicism made sense.[65]

During its struggle against the Bears, the IOP viewed Horner tenants as an important stakeholder. *The Better Alternative* plan included a commitment "to work hard to improve public housing in the neighborhood and to help public housing residents help themselves improve their conditions—their housing, their access to jobs, their health care and their generalized needs as a vital continuing part of this community." When he first linked up with the IOP, Earnest Gates loudly advocated on behalf of Horner residents, asserting during a passionate public oration in 1988 that Horner "is destined to be torn down if we allow [the stadium] to happen."[66]

However, the thirteen-point plan did not reference improvements to public housing. By 1991 the Horner Mothers Guild, a group of concerned mothers living in the Horner Annex, decided that they could not afford to wait for the promised spillover effects from the United Center. Residents were leaving, the CHA had stopped repairing and releasing vacant units, and the residential development headed up by the NWSCDC and United Center ownership offered little hope to public-housing tenants. [67] Seeing no viable alternative, the Mothers Guild appealed to the courts.

In November 1991, aided by attorneys from Chicago's Legal Assistance Foundation, the guild sued the CHA and HUD for violating federal housing policy by pursuing "de facto demolition." According to the plaintiffs and their lead counsel, Bill Wilen, "By failing to maintain the Horner developments, the defendants have, in effect, demolished Horner in violation of the U.S. Housing Act." The legislation in question not only required that local housing authorities get approval from HUD prior to tearing down any public-housing structure; it also mandated the consultation of affected tenants prior to such action. The suit demanded that the CHA halt the de facto demolition and take immediate measures to restore higher occupancy levels.[68] Decades later, Mothers Guild member Annette Hunt explained her involvement in the suit: "I didn't want my kids to grow up in an environment that wasn't safe. . . . My take on the lawsuit was to try to make it better for them, to let them know that . . . you don't have to live this way if you speak out about some of the things you feel are not right."[69]

The case dragged on for several years. In the meantime, rumors started to circulate that the city and United Center ownership wanted Horner residents gone.[70] The rumors had to do with alleged plans to tear down the Horner Annex to make room for additional arena parking (map 3.6). In July 1994, on the heels of the announcement that the arena would host the 1996 DNC, Fran Spielman of the *Sun-Times* asked, "Is the 1996 Democratic National Convention behind plans to demolish the 109-unit annex?" State senator Rickey Hendon, who had served previously as the local alderman, told Spielman that the city had convinced the DNC site selection committee to hold the event at the United Center by assuring them that the Annex would not be in the way. "The city said to them when they did the tour, 'Don't worry about those people. They won't be there. That's where the parking lot will be for you all,'" Hendon alleged.[71]

Although Hendon has since had his integrity called into question—he stepped down from his state senate seat in 2011 after his campaign manager pled guilty to trying to bribe public officials—the local press and Horner residents corroborated his claims about the Annex.[72] A few weeks before he made the accusation, *Tribune* reporters Dorothy Collin and Mike Conklin noted that the city had closed down large stretches of the streets around Horner before the visit of the site selection committee, suggesting that officials wanted the Annex out of the picture for conventioneers. CHA chairman Vincent Lane initially admitted to a link between the new arena and the CHA's plan to scrap the Annex, but he insisted that the DNC had nothing to do with it. According to him, discussions about demolition "were going on long before Chicago made its convention bid. . . . [T]he Bulls people have acquired all of the real estate around the Henry Horner Annex. They're going to have hundreds, if not thousands, of cars and people swarming over the development."[73] Horner tenants agreed that the new arena was a factor but rejected Lane's crowd-control explanation. Annex resident Stacy Springfield later recalled being "sure that to the owners of the United Center and the yuppies that generally attend games, our building was an eyesore." Tenant John Maddox concurred with Springfield, adding his dismissal of earlier assurances from Lane that residents would have the last word on whether the building would survive. "Lane kept telling us we would have the final say," Maddox told Maudlyne Ihejirika of the *Sun-Times*, but he "knew all along they were going to tear this down for that stadium." Yet another Annex resident, Sarah Ruffin, claimed that Lane informed her and her neighbors "that the stadium wants the property, so we need to make plans to see where we're going to go."[74]

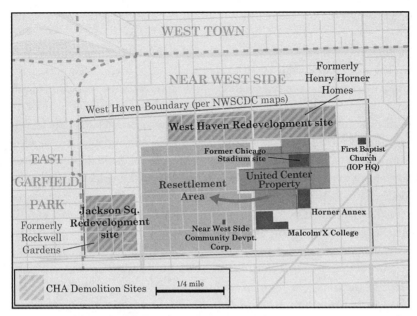

MAP 3.6. The Better Alternative Area, Post–United Center Development

Source: Bill Wilen, "The Horner Model: Successfully Redeveloping Public Housing," *Northwestern Journal of Law and Social Policy* 1, no. 1 (Summer 2006): 62–95; Local Initiatives Support Corporation, *West Haven: Rising Like the Phoenix, LISC Chicago's New Communities Program* (October 2007), accessed May 13, 2013, www.newcommunities.org/cmadocs/WHaven_NCP_Plan_07.pdf; "Community Directory," *Near West Side Community Development Corporation*, accessed March 17, 2013, www.nearwestsidecdc.org/directory/index.html# (link no longer active but PDF copy available from author upon request); Interfaith Organizing Project, *The New West Side Story: The Story of the Interfaith Organizing Project* (Chicago, 1992), Associated Mennonite Biblical Seminary Library.

Notes: The West Haven boundary indicates the NWSCDC's stated area of operation according to its website and published planning documents. Some earlier NWSCDC planning documents show West Haven as having the same boundary as the "better alternative area," but I use the boundary including the stretch of land between Western Avenue and the western border of the Near West Side Community Area. I based this decision on the fact that, given the history of planning and infrastructural development on the West Side, this stretch melded more seamlessly into West Haven than any other neighborhood (the next chapter addresses this issue in more detail).

Stadium officials responded ambiguously to the rumors. When the CHA applied to HUD in early August 1994 for permission to demolish the Annex, Lane stuck with the story that the structure would interfere with stadium operations and expose children to safety hazards. But United Center executive vice president Howard Pizer contradicted Lane, at least initially. When asked by Ihejirika about the arena's role, Pizer denied being a "player" in the controversy, insisting that the Annex land was "not needed for normal United Center events." A few days later, though, Pizer admitted to her, "We did at one time talk about whether or not it (the Annex) might come down, and whether we could use it for parking, but that was two years ago." He added that his bosses might still have interest in the land if it became available.[75]

The most direct evidence of United Center executives' attempts to push Horner residents out of the neighborhood emerged in the context of a quid pro quo struck between the owners and Dexter Watson, the alderman of the ward containing the arena, in the summer of 1994. In exchange for Watson agreeing to introduce an ordinance that would ban independent vendors from selling peanuts within one thousand feet of the United Center, Reinsdorf and Wirtz hired a few of Watson's constituents to work in the facility's food stands. Watson dragged his feet on carrying out his end of the bargain while he bickered with the owners over the details of the arrangement; ultimately, Watson's successor as alderman, Walter Burnett Jr., introduced the ordinance in 1995 after cutting a similar deal with arena ownership. In the meantime, a disgruntled United Center employee leaked an internal memo detailing the cronyism between the owners and Watson to Mark Weinberg, an attorney helping the vendors fight United Center ownership's efforts to evict them from nearby sidewalks. Weinberg's interest in the memo, which Howard Pizer drafted for Wirtz and Reinsdorf on July 26, 1994, had to do entirely with its reference to the ordinance. But the memo also referenced the Henry Horner Annex:

> It would be made clear that the [United Center] Joint Venture is only agreeing to this [deal] reluctantly and would not do so unless it resolved existing problems and disagreements with Senator Hendon and Alderman Watson. Therefore, it is expected that we will receive the cooperation of these parties so far as the Horner Annex, the West of Damen Parking, and the 1,000 foot ordinance are concerned.

If the documents leaked to Weinberg were authentic—and no evidence to the contrary has surfaced—then at some point the negotiations between Pizer and local politicians touched on the latter pressuring the city to demolish the Horner Annex.[76]

The preponderance of evidence thus indicates that Reinsdorf and Wirtz wanted Horner tenants gone and that they invested some measure of time and resources in getting rid of them. This calls into question characterizations of the United Center as a clear win-win for both the team owners and longtime residents. In fact, the stadium developers moved to exclude Horner tenants from resources and opportunities flowing from new investment in the community. Why the push from United Center ownership to knock down the Annex? Answering this requires some informed speculation. Reinsdorf and Wirtz probably had designs on cashing in on rising property values in the neighborhood through ancillary real estate development. Indeed, by the time of this writing, Reinsdorf had invested in several luxury apartment developments in the Near West Side, including one a few blocks northeast of the Annex site.[77] Another possible explanation is that Reinsdorf and Wirtz wanted to insulate affluent fans, especially white ones, from public-housing residents. Team owners regularly buffered their new facilities from nearby poverty with massive parking lots. In fact, Reinsdorf had previously executed this strategy at the new Comiskey Park.[78]

Given that the United Center coalition appeared to be pushing for their relocation, Horner tenants in the shadow of the arena were justified in feeling excluded from sports-linked redevelopment. As Horner resident Lena Kimbrough replied when asked by a pair of *Sun-Times* reporters about the controversy: "To tell you the truth, I really didn't expect them to leave us close to that new multimillion-dollar stadium, us being low-income and black and all. I knew this was coming."[79] However, when Lane requested permission from HUD to tear down the Annex in 1994, the saga was far from over. Despite reports in mid-August that he had worked out a plan to provide replacement housing nearby, HUD officials and Horner residents refused to sign on. By this time, Lane had changed his story, insisting that neither the stadium nor the DNC had any bearing on the situation. The real issue, Lane explained, was that "the neighborhood surrounding the Henry Horner Annex has changed from residential to commercial/industrial and therefore does not provide the necessary infrastructure to promote residential life."[80]

Nobody bought the explanation. If it was a zoning issue, why were the arena developers working with Gates to build new housing nearby? And why the rush to take down the Annex when it was in the best shape of all the Horner buildings? It had the lowest vacancy rate—only 8 of its 109 units were vacant—and the fewest problems with crime. As Annex resident Gwen Woodson summarized, "The stadium wants this land and the city doesn't want us here when the convention comes to town."[81]

To their surprise, Horner residents learned in September 1994 that HUD had rejected Lane's proposal to demolish the Annex. In a letter to Lane, Joseph Shuldiner, HUD's assistant secretary for public and Indian housing, wrote, "The present proposed approach of demolishing buildings that are almost fully occupied when the CHA has several vacant high-rise buildings at the [Horner] site is hard to understand."[82] Even better news came in March of the following year, when district court judge James Zagel found the CHA guilty of de facto demolition and approved a consent decree mandating a complete overhaul of the Henry Horner Homes. Zagel granted all current

residents the right to move into new or refurbished housing in their existing neighborhood as long as they remained lease compliant.[83] Per the initial
decree and a series of amended versions issued between 1995 and 1999, all
of the high-rises and mid-rises would be demolished, tenants in the structures slated for demolition would receive new townhomes or two-flats in the
same neighborhood, and Annex residents would receive the right to vote on
whether to rehabilitate or demolish their building. The ruling also obligated
the CHA and its private contractors to consult with a group of tenant leaders, the Horner Resident Committee (HRC), throughout the process.[84] The
ruling represented a remarkable victory for tenants. With the courts behind
them, they had hope of fending off the CHA and team owners.

The consent decree helped insulate Horner residents from upheavals in
federal public-housing policy. In 1992, HUD launched the Urban Revitalization Demonstration Program, later renamed HOPE VI, which offered large
grants to public-housing authorities for the demolition of blighted projects
and the expansion of Section 8 voucher programs. Under the Clinton administration, the grants also provided seed money to local housing authorities for
the redevelopment of demolished projects as "mixed-income" sites with limited numbers of new public-housing units dispersed among mostly market-
rate ones. In many cases, private developers jumped at the opportunity to
partner with local housing authorities and invest in these redevelopments.
Because many of the sites sat on real estate in or near revitalizing downtowns,
private investors stood to make handsome profits on the market-rate units
(and receive tax credits for developing properties with below-market-rate
units).[85] Ideologically, HOPE VI relied on the increasingly popular notion
that poor people could better exercise "personal responsibility" when ex-
posed to the influence of the middle class. In theory, interacting with more
affluent neighbors would provide low-income residents with positive examples and an aspirational worldview, encouraging the latter to lift themselves
out of poverty.[86]

HOPE VI also came packaged with tougher restrictions on access to public housing. Not long after it authorized the program, Congress mandated
stiffer work requirements for tenants receiving federal housing assistance.[87]
The new regulations echoed the mandates of the Personal Responsibility and
Work Opportunity Act signed into law by Clinton in 1996, which imposed
stricter employment conditions on those receiving direct cash assistance
from the government and set narrow time limits on the receipt of aid. In the
second half of the nineties, welfare "reform" in the United States reduced access to benefits, decreased the generosity of benefits for those who still qualified, and took a much more punitive approach to dealing with the poor.[88]

New urban housing policy in the United States also provided city governments with the rationale and federal support necessary to advance central city revitalization by "deconcentrating" poverty, rather than taking meaningful steps to address its political and economic roots.[89] The use of federal funds for the demolition of public housing enabled mayors like Richard M. Daley to clear out poor public-housing residents as part of larger downtown revitalization efforts. When Congress suspended a law requiring cities to replace every demolished public-housing unit with a new unit (the one-for-one rule) in 1996, it gave Chicago the green light to take the wrecking ball to projects near the Loop without having to worry about constructing replacements.[90]

The Horner Resident Committee and its attorneys rejected this approach. They believed that having stable housing to begin with would better help people find good employment than would threatening them with eviction. HRC leaders and their attorneys fought to ensure that the consent decree precluded the CHA from imposing requirements beyond standard lease compliance, such as mandatory drug testing and "hours-based work requirements." In practice, this meant that the CHA could deny Horner tenants replacement units in the same neighborhood only if they voluntarily vacated their old Horner apartment while waiting for the new one, if they stopped paying rent or utilities before the replacement unit became available, or if the courts convicted them of a felony that threatened somebody's physical safety. Crucially, the consent decree specified that this final condition would not be retroactive, giving Horner tenants what Wilen and his colleague Rajesh Nayak characterize as a "blank slate" and ensuring that existing residents "controlled whether they would be eligible for a replacement unit" in the same neighborhood.[91]

Meanwhile, Earnest Gates appears to have kept Horner residents relatively low on his list of priorities. Although the NWSCDC eventually signed on to help develop some of the replacement units for Horner tenants, this happened after the court issued the consent decree—that is, after the courts empowered Horner residents to stay in the neighborhood. In fact, Byron White of the *Tribune*, in detailing the efforts by the City Council and CHA to move the replacement units into East Garfield Park, an impoverished area further west of the United Center, described Gates as "more than happy about the possibility." According to Thom Finerty, a former CHA official who later consulted for the Horner residents' legal team, Gates's apparent excitement over this prospect had to do with his concern that replacement units for Horner residents would interfere with market-rate development already planned by the NWSCDC.[92]

Nevertheless, the redevelopment of Horner remained on track because of the consent decree and pressure on the city to get to work on the project so that the Clintons could showcase it at the DNC. Wilen and Finerty recall that when Hillary Clinton visited the site, she insisted that the Annex be either demolished or rehabilitated in time for the convention. When Annex residents voted to rehabilitate instead of demolish, the CHA quickly went to work.[93] The combination of the consent decree and the Clintons' publicity concerns ensured that Horner would become the national symbol of "the CHA of tomorrow" and that, at least in the near term, many CHA tenants were there to stay.[94] Phase 1 of the Horner redevelopment, eventually dubbed "West Haven"—the name now refers to the neighborhood encompassing the northwestern quarter of the Near West Side—was completed in 2000. The end product entailed 551 new or rehabilitated public-housing units (323 of which were allocated to longtime Horner residents) in and around the blocks where demolished Horner structures previously stood.[95]

Why had Gates, given the fact that he had spoken out in their defense during the Bears fiasco, become less attentive to—some might say antagonistic toward—Horner residents? Little doubt it had something to do with ensuring that money from Reinsdorf and Wirtz kept flowing. The owners had announced more than $1 million in additional low-interest loans for local businesses in February 1995, and it made little sense for the NWSCDC to bite the hand that fed it. But this was about more than pragmatism. As a local homeowner, businessman, and new political insider, Gates was coming to embody a class politics that prioritized property values in West Haven over inclusive redevelopment. As political scientist Preston Smith II clarifies, "both racial *and* class interests" have shaped the behavior of black elites in Chicago and other American cities.[96] It should come as no surprise that Gates came to see Horner tenants as a liability, especially given the "common sense" among real estate developers that their presence made the neighborhood less attractive to outsiders and depressed property values. Janita Poe of the *Tribune* summed this up in 1996, asserting that Gates "speaks for the middle class, the homeowners. . . . He is the strategic community planner who can leave the 'hood,' put on a blue suit and hobnob with Daley . . . Reinsdorf . . . and Wirtz."[97]

The evidence in support of this reading of Gates's transformation mounted in the second half of the 1990s. In June 1997, Don Adams, editor of *Our Voices*, a community newsletter published by Horner residents, reported that Gates withheld the transfer of several new West Haven units developed by the NWSCDC to Horner families. While short on explanations, the article noted, "Some residents of Horner feel that Gates is not trying to create a mixed community but rather trying to replace residents that now reside in the area with more affluent people" and "feel that he does not want a community of people who rent but just people who own homes." It went on, "This so-called Haven is turning out to be everything but a haven. It's turning out to be a community of segregation and separatism."[98] The same week, a report by Leon Pitt in the *Sun-Times* provided some insight into Gates's motives, noting that he had refused to hand over additional units as required by the consent decree because of alleged tenant vandalism in some townhomes that had already been opened to Horner residents. Before releasing any more units, Gates wanted to beef up work requirements and screening criteria, and he insisted on re-screening Horner tenants who had yet to move into new units.[99]

Stacy Springfield, who had recently moved with her children into a renovated three-bedroom apartment in the Annex, characterized Gates's call for increased screening as "a tactic to keep CHA residents out of what easily could be market-rate apartments."[100] Springfield acknowledged some problems with a few Horner tenants who had transitioned into new housing in West Haven, but she insisted they were aberrations. Her assertion gained credence when the CHA went to court to ask for an amendment to the consent decree mandating Gates's desired screening requirements; the judge denied the request based on a lack of evidence.[101] Springfield also took offense at Gates's attempt to place restrictions on who could live in the new units. "I wonder if people really believe that vandals, gang bangers and drug addicts are all that reside in CHA," she wrote in *Our Voices*. "CHA residents made this revitalization, not just Earnest Gates."[102] For tenants like Springfield, Gates's push for tougher screening clearly encroached on the inclusivity of the consent decree and neighborhood revitalization more generally.

Nobody at Horner argued that tenants who violated their West Haven leases should be allowed to stay, but they did believe that, in the words of Don Adams, "the vast majority of Horner residents are law-abiding citizens," and that as many of them as possible should have a chance to "make a new start." Moreover, Horner residents pointed out that persistent drug and gang activity, mostly in the high-rises still to be demolished at that point, had less to do with shortcomings of public-housing residents than with the shortage of jobs.[103] By the end of the 1990s, however, Gates seemed convinced that ongoing problems at the Horner redevelopment boiled down to tenants' personal failings. He explains his continued, unsuccessful campaign for tougher screening requirements this way: "We knew and we argued that if you're a crackhead on the eighth floor of the high-rise that you're going to be a crackhead in a new condo." As Ed Shurna admits: "Earnest could be a conservative Republican in some regards. . . . You know, pull yourself up by your bootstraps, 'I made it, you can make it.'" In West Haven, then, a complex tangle of

competing class interests and ideologies within the African American community ensured that conflicts over redevelopment transcended stereotypes
about poor urban blacks versus white gentrifiers.[104]

In fairness to Gates, not all Horner tenants saw (or see) him as the enemy. Catherine Fennell, an anthropologist who studied the redevelopment of
Horner and volunteered at the NWSCDC as part of her research, observed a
generational split among tenants over whether Gates posed a threat. Women
in their fifties and beyond tended to trust lawyers like Wilen who helped them
secure the consent decree, whereas many younger residents suspected that
their elders had become pawns of lawyers out of touch with the best interests
of the community. Although Fennell does not delve deeply into the concerns
that some residents had with Wilen, the fact that some opted to work with
Gates at the NWSCDC points toward a lack of trust in the former.[105] Moreover, some Chicago public housing residents in new mixed-income developments welcomed tougher screening requirements. These tenants saw Gates
as doing what he had to do to insulate new public-housing units from rapid
deterioration due to crime and neglect.[106] Acknowledging different views on
these issues among public-housing tenants, however, does not change the
key distinction between Wilen and Gates: the former saw keeping all Horner
residents in the neighborhood as a top priority, and by most accounts the
latter did not.

Gates's politics were far from unprecedented within black Chicago. As
Preston Smith II argues, in the decades immediately after World War II, African American elites in the city rallied around urban policy that fostered
class segregation in the black community by promoting middle-class homeownership while largely ignoring the pressing need for affordable housing among low-income and working-class African Americans.[107] But while
Gates's outlook and behavior had historical precedents, he adopted them
only after abandoning a vision of economic empowerment that included all
the Near West Side's African American residents. The pragmatism informing
Gates's transformation was no doubt encouraged by larger political developments at the end of the twentieth century. As the political scientist Philip
Klinker explains, the election of Bill Clinton in 1992 marked the culmination
of a process begun in the early 1980s through which a large segment of the
Democratic Party tacked sharply to the right on social and economic issues.
Panicked by the effectiveness of Republicans' appeal to "traditional values,"
as well as white backlash against black political militancy, many Democrats
followed Clinton's lead in embracing a relatively ruthless law-and-order approach to crime, as well as increasing hostility to affirmative action and social
welfare programs.[108]

Clinton played to the racist belief that responsibility for the country's problems lay squarely in the hands of inner-city communities of color who refused to pull their own weight. It was in this context that he expressed, in his own words, "understanding" of the "fears" of "white people [who] have been scared so long that they have fled to the suburbs" and highlighted increased personal responsibility as the key to social and economic uplift.[109] At a moment when the Democratic Party adopted many of the individualistic positions and policies championed by their Republican counterparts, "bootstrap" advocates like Gates emerged as local power brokers. Born in 1952 a block east of the old Chicago Stadium, Gates watched the neighborhood burn in 1968 and lived through its subsequent decline. Instead of using the money he made with the trucking business he founded in the late 1970s to move away, he took it upon himself to rebuild the neighborhood one block at a time by rehabbing crumbling houses. Conveniently, the media's praise for Gates usually left out the fact that he, unlike most residents living around the new arena, was born to parents economically stable enough to move into the neighborhood when it was still predominantly white.[110] Minus this information, he was a timely poster boy for the politics of self-help.

None of this is to say that Gates was purely hostile in his dealings with public-housing residents in West Haven after the mid-1990s. Because many Horner tenants protected by the consent decree were in the neighborhood to stay, the NWSCDC eventually allocated significant resources to integrating them into local economic revitalization. For example, it used grant money to fund the Home Visitors Program, which helped public-housing tenants find employment and access counseling from social workers. The politics of funding such programs, however, probably encouraged Gates to abandon the unconditional support he had voiced during the 1980s for Horner tenants and to assume a more tough-love approach in his dealings with them. Grants from nonprofits and city or state agencies were the main sources of a scarce pool of money for things like the Home Visitors Program. By the late 1990s, these entities were not only uninterested in funding efforts run by organizations that took radical stands on questions of social justice but also unlikely to award grants to programs that did not embrace the idea that teaching personal responsibility was the key ingredient in fighting poverty.[111]

It also bears mentioning that Gates's growing fixation with drawing new homeowners and commercial investment to the neighborhood was not necessarily bad for public-housing residents. After all, for those residents' lives to improve over the long term, they needed economic growth in and around the blocks where they lived. New growth could bring access to new and better jobs, healthier and cheaper food, and improved physical infrastructure.

But more and more, the actions of Gates and his allies implied agreement with the consensus among economic and political elites that such growth depended on the exclusion of the poor. Rather than situating the ongoing struggles of all public-housing residents as a problem that local economic redevelopment could solve humanely, Gates and the NWSCDC increasingly situated these residents as an obstacle in the way of redevelopment.

The point, then, is not that Gates was a sellout but that his actions were shaped by structural shifts in the American political and economic landscapes at the end of the twentieth century. Recounting the efforts of Horner residents to resist these larger historical forces shows that celebratory accounts of Gates ignore the fact that "black politics" around the United Center was far from unified. In the end, the allegedly inclusive redevelopment strategy championed by Gates and the NWSCDC proved elusive on the ground. According to a report coauthored by the NWSCDC in 2002, the group supported an approach that "welcomes higher-income residents while calling for tougher management of the various subsidized developments and strong support systems for the existing low-income population."[112] More affluent residents and "tougher management" of low-income ones were certainly parts of the actual equation, but "strong support systems" for the neighborhood's less fortunate families were less evident. If anything, Gates and company worked to distance their efforts from the community's most vulnerable residents, many of whom resided at Horner.

This approach foreshadowed broader shifts in public housing's relationship to redevelopment in Chicago, particularly the implementation of the Plan for Transformation, a $1.5 billion HOPE VI initiative announced by the CHA in 1999. The plan combined aggressive demolition of traditional public-housing units—Chicago's net stock of 38,700 total units in 1999 had declined by almost half by 2010—with a dramatic increase in Section 8 vouchers and very limited new-unit construction in "mixed income" redevelopments. Unfortunately, mixed-income revitalization has too often equated "neighborhood improvement" with rapidly "removing a large share of the public housing population" by way of housing vouchers.[113]

While some voucher recipients made their way to communities less dangerous and depressed than the ones they inhabited before—"a relatively low threshold," as scholars D. Bradford Hunt and Jon DeVries point out—the much anticipated proximity effects of such relocations (e.g., jobs through networking with new middle-class neighbors) largely failed to materialize.[114] This means that the best-case scenario for most residents relocated from traditional CHA units with vouchers was marginally improved surroundings, not improved economic mobility. Rightfully skeptical of the promise of vouchers, eager to preserve social networks built over the course of decades, and keen on participating in the economic revitalization of neighborhoods near the Loop that housed now-demolished CHA high-rises, many CHA tenants looked forward to returning to new mixed-income developments in those neighborhoods. At the outset of the Plan for Transformation, CHA guaranteed the right of return to these developments to the tens of thousands of public-housing residents who had to relocate with vouchers due to demolition.

However, by 2009 less than 10 percent of temporarily relocated residents had successfully moved back into mixed-income communities. In some cases, increasingly rigorous screening and work requirements made them ineligible while they waited for new units. In others, construction delays led frustrated families to break off contact with CHA relocation officials. Those forced into a tight rental market with vouchers often ended up in substandard housing in poor and segregated neighborhoods, the exact opposite of the voucher program's stated intent. As both public-housing residents and advocates argue, it appears that a primary outcome of the Plan for Transformation has been the expulsion of poor and working-class families from neighborhoods coveted by real-estate investors.[115]

Because of the consent decree, the only one of its kind within the CHA system, Horner residents have avoided some of the pitfalls of the Plan for Transformation. Well over half of the residents at Horner exercised their right to stay in the neighborhood, and nearly all of those who did received a new or rehabilitated unit in West Haven by the end of 2008. Fifty percent of the families affected by phase 1 of the West Haven redevelopment elected to stay, as did 75 percent of the families affected by phase 2, which replaced additional demolitions with a new mixed-income development. Moreover, according to Wilen, as of 2006 all the Horner residents affected by phase 2 who opted to stay *remained* in West Haven.[116]

Among the CHA's mixed-income developments, West Haven boasts the highest percentage of units set aside for low-income families. Per the consent decree, about half of new units in West Haven belong to CHA tenants, whereas most other mixed-income developments set aside barely a third for such families.[117] Because the decree barred relocating residents before developers completed new units in West Haven, the CHA could not use vouchers to force tenants into an inhospitable rental market. The fact that former Horner tenants in West Haven enjoyed work and education requirements considerably more flexible than at other mixed-income developments provided added security in the face of a lackluster economy. Moreover, the decree's mandate that tenants play an active role in any modifications to the development placed some limits on the power of private developers to unilaterally pursue their own agendas in West Haven.[118]

Unfortunately, West Haven has not fully escaped the trend to exclude those without the resources to cover escalating housing costs from meaningful participation in central-city revitalization. Although Horner residents wishing to stay in West Haven all secured new or rehabilitated units there, phase 2 of the redevelopment (originally scheduled for completion in 2010) failed to yield agreed-on targets for new public-housing units for others on the CHA rolls. As of February 2014, the private developer contracted by the CHA for the project had delivered only 237 of 271 of the public housing units promised as part of phase 2.[119]

Even more concerning, in 2013 the CHA secured an amended consent decree that threatened some of the historic protections won by Horner residents during the mid-1990s. During the first decade of the twentieth century, phase 1 of the Horner redevelopment—unlike phase 2, phase 1 was not developed as a mixed-income site and housed only low-income public-housing residents—drew increasing scrutiny from several sources. The CHA argued that phase 1 units had deteriorated rapidly and required rehabilitation. Affluent residents from market-rate phase 2 units, as well as private developers active in the neighborhood, claimed that the persistence of concentrated poverty at the phase 1 site encouraged crime, fostered disorder on local streets and sidewalks, and ultimately deterred new local investment. In response to these concerns, the amended consent decree mandated the redevelopment of the phase 1 units as a mixed-income site, which would eventually reduce the total number of public-housing units in West Haven by more than one hundred. The new decree also resulted in tougher lease-compliance rules for public housing residents who remain.[120]

These changes raise serious questions about the durability of the gains made by ex–Horner residents. Unfortunately, it appears that redevelopment around the United Center is taking on a more exclusive character under pressure from private developers who view public-housing tenants as an impediment to profitability and from well-off residents who view low-income neighbors as an eyesore. Annette Hunt, one of the original Mothers Guild leaders, admits that the future seems scarily uncertain. "Most of the time when we sat in these negotiations [about the consent decree], it's like we're always giving and they're always taking," she lamented in a recent interview.[121]

Such is the case with exclusionary capitalism in neighborhoods like West Haven in the New Gilded Age.

*

In February 1988, at a public hearing on the Bears stadium plan, a Near West Sider named Loretta Roland made a bold proposal to city officials. Roland told them that she would welcome a new stadium if neighborhood residents could jointly own the facility and receive a percentage of its profits. While officials brushed aside her idea, Roland clearly understood the stakes of constructing a new stadium in her neighborhood.[122] If Bears ownership had its way, residents would receive none of the value generated by the facility and likely experience a decline in quality of life as a result of stadium-linked nuisances like increased traffic. Public ownership of the stadium might have gone a long way toward solving this problem.

When Reinsdorf and Wirtz swooped in to take advantage of the scuttling of the Bears' plan by developing a stadium of their own, Roland's idea was still off the table, but in this case neighborhood residents did secure millions of dollars in development subsidies from the owners. In the end, though, the charitable disposition of United Center ownership provided a weak and, at times, insidious substitute for ambitious plans developed by the residents themselves, who prior to 1990 consistently rejected a sports stadium as a centerpiece of revitalization.

As much as its proponents argued to the contrary, the redevelopment of the community now known as West Haven did not stand out because of an exceptionally equal partnership between a professional sports arena and neighborhood residents. Instead, it stood out because of the efforts of a small group of largely forgotten CHA tenants whom Reinsdorf and Wirtz actively moved to exclude. United Center ownership, ever committed to maximizing profits from the new arena, offered no real solutions to the problem of exclusionary capitalism in central-city neighborhoods. In fact, the resources funneled by Reinsdorf and Wirtz into the community encouraged a core characteristic of exclusionary capitalism in cities at the end of the twentieth century: "redevelopment" that depended, at least in part, on the removal of those most in need.[123]

Anchor or Shipwreck? The United Center and Economic Development in West Haven

Shortly before he left office in 2011, Mayor Richard M. Daley kicked off a "neighborhood appreciation tour," a series of appearances at which he waxed poetic about Chicago's progress under his leadership. According to *Tribune* reporter John Byrne, who paraphrased Daley's comments at the tour stop in the Near West Side, the mayor described the United Center as "an anchor for revitalization."[1] If skeptics had a hard time taking the mayor's word for it, sources outside the city backed up Daley's description. In a television report on recent trends in urban redevelopment aired by *PBS NewsHour* in 2005, correspondent Elizabeth Brackett assured viewers that "it was private investment [in] the United Center that started the revitalization of the [Near] West Side." By reminding everyone that arena ownership "continued to stay involved in the neighborhood," Brackett reinforced the idea that the stadium was a boon not only for the team owners but also for longtime neighborhood residents.[2] In the new century, planning documents from the Near West Side Community Development Corporation, still under the leadership of Earnest Gates, affirmed the inclusiveness of stadium-linked "revival" in West Haven. One such document asserted that redevelopment "should continue to find a place for—and not displace—those who have weathered the lean years."[3]

As the previous chapter showed, things were not so simple. The priorities and actions of the United Center coalition often conflicted with the needs of low-income residents. But in and of itself, this antagonism tells us little about the tangible transformations of West Haven in the United Center era. That the team owners and their allies promoted the exclusion of public-housing residents from their revitalization plans does not necessarily prove the prediction of scholars Costas Spirou and Larry Bennett that the United Center would "speed a one-sided gentrification" of the surrounding neighborhood.[4]

In fact, the Horner consent decree cast real doubt on how much displacement would occur. Moreover, recounting the conflict between the Gates and Daniels factions, on its own, does not answer the question of whether the arena functioned as a catalyst for economic growth in West Haven.

A detailed history of the economic and demographic changes that accompanied sports-linked development on Chicago's Near West Side reveals a different picture than that presented by Daley, the local and national press, and the United Center coalition. Mapping population change in West Haven during the 1990s and 2000s shows a sustained exodus of longtime residents, one that outpaced similar processes in adjacent neighborhoods. This is not to say that the arena was directly responsible for people's departure; important institutions and historical forces aside from the United Center were at play. However, the data indicate that arena-linked redevelopment did little to nothing to curtail the process. Moreover, the revitalization efforts funded in part by the team owners and implemented by Gates—efforts centered on expanding homeownership—likely placed indirect pressure on longtime residents to abandon the neighborhood. By 2010, huge numbers of the low-income folks who lived around the new arena when it opened were gone. It thus makes little sense to speak of redevelopment around the United Center as "balanced" or "inclusive"; many of those who needed the benefits of revitalization the most were no longer around to take advantage of them.

The argument that the arena attracted new investment to the Near West Side beyond the team owners' charity was presumptuous at best and misleading at worst. The evidence suggests that growth in West Haven during the United Center era would have occurred even without the arena, as the neighborhood sat in the path of a new wave of real estate investment radiating outward from the Loop since the early 1980s. Put another way, the one form of ancillary development that the arena did the most to promote, the financing of expanded private homeownership, was likely imminent even before its construction. The most optimistic reading of the evidence is that the buzz around the arena helped accelerate this preexisting pattern. Reinsdorf and Wirtz, however, took credit for revitalization that would have happened even in their absence.

Furthermore, those with an intimate knowledge of the area's history argue that the United Center impeded additional investment in West Haven. Considerable evidence supports this perspective. For example, planning documents produced by the city after the arena opened criticized the project for monopolizing local economic activity at the expense of additional commercial investment. So, while the owners' promotion of their own philanthropy suggested that their investment trickled down in significant ways to residents, their actual business practices pushed in the opposite direction. Their constant efforts to internalize as much local revenue as possible within the United Center reduced West Haven's capacity to sustain small-scale entrepreneurs or larger firms from industries with proven track records of providing good jobs and generating positive economic "ripple effects" across neighborhoods. The design of the arena, which grew directly out of Reinsdorf and Wirtz's efforts to monopolize the neighborhood's economic activity, also made the area less livable for new and longtime residents. For instance, the facility proved a major impediment to vibrant pedestrian traffic.

The deeper one digs, the clearer it becomes that the United Center failed to fulfill its promise as an anchor of "balanced" redevelopment. It did not reduce inequality in West Haven, unless by that we mean allowing for, and likely encouraging, the departure of low-income residents. Moreover, the arena obstructed an even distribution of new investment across space, not by accident but by design—a design intended to deliberately minimize competition and control as much locally generated revenue as possible. The planning and design of the arena ultimately enabled Reinsdorf and Wirtz to hoard the revenues generated by new economic activity in the neighborhood. As a result, residents found themselves largely excluded from whatever new prosperity the private sector brought to the community.

The Logic of Development around the United Center

During its struggle against the Bears, the Interfaith Organizing Project rejected the media's claim that a new sports facility promised, in the words of one *Tribune* journalist, "economic salvation for the community."[5] The stance was far from a knee-jerk reaction. Researchers from UIC who collaborated with the group found little evidence from other cities to suggest that a new sports facility would help reverse the fortunes of residents. A 1988 report written by planners at UIC noted that "in only 9 of the 22 cities [that have built or remodeled stadiums in the last 25 years] is there commercial activity in the area immediately adjacent to the stadium. In 5 of the 9 cities the growth around the stadiums was part of expanding downtown areas. . . . Only in Kansas City did a stadium by itself, in the opinion of the planner interviewed, spur growth around it."[6] However, these details suddenly seemed less relevant when, in the wake of the Bears' failed stadium development efforts, Reinsdorf and Wirtz made significant concessions to the IOP in the thirteen-point plan. As the ink dried on the agreement, Mayor Daley proclaimed that it was the "first step in the rebirth of the economically depressed West Side."[7]

In subsequent years, local officials went further, asserting in interviews

with credulous journalists from Chicago's dailies that by catalyzing revitalization without displacement, the United Center succeeded where other stadium developments had failed. In 1996, for example, spokespeople for Chicago's Department of Planning reiterated that "the United Center has totally
spurred the area's development" while reassuring Chicagoans that it had also
helped "preserve the existing community during the process."[8] Such praise
was not limited to an echo chamber of Chicago papers and political insiders.
As indicated by the PBS NewsHour coverage mentioned previously, the story
was largely the same according to reports filed outside the city. Luke Cyphers
of the New York Daily News wrote in 1998 that "the replacement homes [fi-
nanced by the team owners] anchor a rebounding neighborhood a few blocks
from the United Center."[9] As I detail here, some academics also joined the
chorus of cheerleaders for arena development. Chicago boosters, in other
words, seemed to be peddling fact.

What made this project different from the many stadium developments
that failed to stimulate economic activity nearby or threatened longtime residents with displacement? Supporters pointed to the millions of dollars in direct investment—grants, loans, and charitable contributions—made by the
team owners, and especially by Reinsdorf and the Bulls. The thirteen-point
agreement between arena ownership and the IOP committed the former to
upward of $3 million of direct investment in the neighborhood for replace-
ment housing, seed money for the NWSCDC, and upgrades to community
infrastructure (table 4.1). This influx of capital convinced editors at the Chicago Sun-Times that the new arena was "the lifeline to economic revival on
the west side."[10]

Money from the thirteen-point plan did make a difference in the neighborhood. Historian Alexander von Hoffman estimates that funds from the
United Center helped the NWSCDC construct seventy-five new homes, albeit
for new residents, in the years following the agreement. Moreover, the team
owners impressed local media by continuing to funnel resources into the
community beyond the terms of the thirteen-point plan, and in some cases
longtime residents benefited (table 4.1). For example, in 1996 Reinsdorf donated the proceeds from a $100,000 fine levied by Bulls management against
player Dennis Rodman for an "obscenity-laced tirade" to the NWSCDC.
The money ultimately went toward residential beautification, and the press
rushed to quote Margaret Glenn, a longtime homeowner who received a new
fence and refurbished façade as a result. "I love Rodman because he gave me
this [fence], he can say anything he wants to say," Glenn told Tribune reporters Ron Grossman and Flynn McRoberts.[11]

Another justification for hailing the United Center as exceptional had to

TABLE 4.1. Direct Neighborhood Investment by United Center Ownership, 1991–2009

Investment	Source	Amount	Year Reported
Replacement housing (16 two-flats)	United Center	$2,500,000	1991
$600,000 escrow account for low-interest home loans (managed by NWSCDC)	United Center	$600,000	1991
Property tax subsidies for longtime, local homeowners	United Center	n/a	1991
New basketball courts for Touhy-Herbert Park	Bulls	$35,000	1991
Computers for Mabel Manning Public Library	Bulls	$75,000	1991
Malcom X College Scholarship Fund	United Center	$85,000	1991
Donation to Miles Square Health Center	United Center	$75,000	1991
James Jordan Center/Boys and Girls Club	Bulls	$4,700,000	1994
United Center Economic Development Fund	United Center	$1,000,000	1995
Rodman fund (donation of money collected from fine of Dennis Rodman)	Bulls	$104,878	1996
Expansion of scholarship program and upgrading of athletic programs at Malcolm X	United Center	$1,600,000	1996
Computer upgrades at Mabel Manning Library	Bulls	$50,000	1998
Donation to Chicago Housing Authority to fund Home Visitors Program (overseen by Gates)	Bulls	$1,000,000	1999
Contributions (in-kind and monetary) to Adopt-a-School program (William H. Brown Elementary and Victor Herbert Elementary)	Bulls	n/a	n/a
Founding grant for Noble Street charter school campus (Bulls College Prep)	Bulls	$2,005,000	2009

Source: "Area Briefs," *Chicago Sun-Times*, April 25, 1996, NewsBank; Burney Simpson, "City Plots New West Side Story"; "Charitabulls," *Sports Philanthropy Project,* accessed May 13, 2013, www .sportsphilanthropy.com/content/index.php?pid=350; John Barron, "United Center Area Gets $1 Million Boost," *Chicago Sun-Times*, February 2, 1995, NewsBank; John Handley, "In Play: West Side Story Getting Positive Rewrite with Help of New Stadium," *Chicago Tribune*, July 24, 1994, ProQuest; Sean Terry, "Planning Strategy for the United Center: A Redevelopment Plan for the United Center and Its Surrounding Surface Parking Lots" (master's thesis, University of Illinois Chicago, 2006), 3–4.

Notes: Dollar values *not* adjusted for inflation. All figures reflect the highest estimates encountered by author. The money transferred to Malcolm X College did not consist of donations but rather payments in exchange for the right to use the college's north parking lot for overflow parking on game nights. Greg Hinz, "Malcolm X's Comeback," *Crain's Chicago Business*, September 20, 1997, ProQuest; *Chicago City Junior College District v. Department of Revenue of the State of Illinois*, State of Illinois Department of Revenue, Office of Administrative Hearings, Chicago, No. 10-PT-0014 (08-16-768), 2008 tax year.

do with its alleged role in encouraging public investment in West Haven and other nearby neighborhoods. The project's advocates pointed to the impetus created by the arena for infrastructural investment by local government. The city and state chipped in over $18 million for infrastructural improvements such as street upgrades around the stadium, and the city and state later dedicated more than $30 million to additional neighborhood beautification, demolition, and street improvements in preparation for the 1996 DNC (table 4.2). City officials also successfully convinced federal agencies like HUD that the United Center offered an ideal node around which to invest Community Development Block Grant monies. As a result, they secured several multimillion-dollar grants for additional infrastructural improvements and the financing of community development efforts. This supplementary investment excited local boosters because it exemplified how the city could combine relatively modest infrastructural investment with privately funded anchor projects to fill the void left by reduced federal funding for neighborhood revitalization. As a promotional packet from Chicago's campaign to host the 1996 DNC told readers, "We're a city that works *together* forging public/private partnerships to maximize our civic resources."[12]

A third line of reasoning concerned the arena's alleged promotion of the neighborhoods in the northern half of the Near West Side as trendy places to

TABLE 4.2. Public Investment in Support of the United Center

Investment	Source	Amount	Year Reported
United Center surrounding infrastructure (street improvements, etc.)	City of Chicago	$18,000,000	1989
Renovations at Touhy-Herbert Park	City of Chicago	$600,000	1991
Construction of Mabel Manning Public Library Branch	City of Chicago	$3,200,000	1991
Strategic Neighborhood Action Program Funds (for demolition, infrastructure, low-interest financing)	Department of Housing and Urban Development	$2,100,000	c. 1992
New Homes for Chicago Program	City of Chicago	n/a	n/a
Infrastructure improvements in support of Democratic National Convention	City of Chicago, State of Illinois	$36,300,000	1994–1996
Other Community Development Block Grants (CDBGs) for infrastructure, housing, and job creation	Department of Housing and Urban Development	$5,000,000	1995

Source: Charles N. Wheeler III and Mark Brown, "Senate Backs a New Bulls-Hawks Stadium," *Chicago Sun-Times*, June 23, 1989, NewsBank; Cheryl Ririe-Kurz, "West Side Story," *Chicago Sun-Times*, August 6, 1995, NewsBank; Jill Schachner Chanen, "A Gritty Part of Chicago Gets a New Sparkle," *New York Times*, April 20, 1997, ProQuest; Patrick Reardon, "Stadium Agreement Has a Winning Look," *Chicago Tribune*, May 10, 1991, ProQuest; "Mabel Manning Branch Library," *Ross Barney Architects, Inc.*, accessed May 13, 2013, www.r-barc.com/places/?name=Mabel+Manning+Branch+Library; Scott Fornek and Fran Spielman, "Un-Conventional Facelift," *Chicago Sun-Times*, May 27, 1996, NewsBank.

Notes: Dollar values not adjusted for inflation. All figures reflect the highest estimates encountered by author.

live and do business. According to Scott Fornek of the *Sun-Times*, by 1996 city officials were already talking of a "business and housing boom sparked by the 1994 opening of the United Center," and a couple of years later a pair of *Tribune* reporters emphasized the arena's role as "the cornerstone of a Near West Side reborn as an attractive place for people of all incomes to live."[13] After 1994, new home purchases in West Haven increased significantly, and between 2000 and 2009 the number of neighborhood households earning at least $50,000 went from 207 to 1,063 (a considerably faster rate than in Chicago as a whole).[14] In 2001, West Haven experienced a major injection of private retail investment when a Walgreens drug store opened at the intersection of Western and Madison. The consensus seemed to be that these trends owed to the cachet brought to the neighborhood by the United Center. As Earnest Gates told a reporter in 1994, "People are looking at the community differently [after the United Center deal]."[15]

The combination of fresh investment and positive notoriety ushered in by the arena led boosters to herald it as the foundation of a "balanced mixed-income community that welcomes new residents without displacing those already in the neighborhood."[16] As Gates explained in 1998, "If it had not been for the United Center . . . the indigenous community could have been priced out of the neighborhood."[17] This story persisted. A report co-published in 2002 by the NWSCDC and one of its nonprofit development partners described the collective "vision" of the neighborhood: "West Haven will become a vibrant mixed-income community that offers opportunities for public housing residents and other long-time community members as well as newcomers." The report went on to recommend that housing "subsidy programs stay in place to avoid displacement of long-time residents."[18]

Some researchers posit that "balance" accurately describes what unfolded in West Haven. Hoffman, for example, compares the recent urban history of the community around the United Center favorably with that of neighborhoods like the Near South Side, where gentrification proved more "unmistakable" during the 1990s. In his telling, West Haven was exceptional because its leaders skillfully navigated a "central problem" of neighborhood development in late twentieth-century America: "improving a low-income neighborhood but not allowing a wholesale replacement of the population by high-income groups."[19]

Census figures aggregated at the community area level support Hoffman's view. Although the data indicate significant increases in white population, median income, and educational attainment in the Near West Side, the increases proved far less dramatic than in the Near South Side (see table 4.3). The numbers imply that the neighborhood around the United Center, the

TABLE 4.3. Selected Statistics from Hoffman's *House by House, Block by Block*

	Near South Side		Near West Side	
	1990	2000	1990	2000
Total population	6,828	9,509	46,197	46,419
Percentage white	5.4	25.2	18.8	25.3
Percentage black	93.6	64.4	66.8	53.3
Percentage below poverty level	61.0	32.3	51.1	37.5
Average family income (1999 $)	$19,822	$70,835	$32,242	$56,325
Percentage with some college	27.7	62.7	35.1	52.0
Percentage housing units vacant	7.0	16.0	23.6	15.1

Source: Adapted from Alexander von Hoffman, *House by House, Block by Block: The Rebirth of America's Urban Neighborhoods* (New York: Oxford University Press, 2003), 265.

only part of the Near West Side Hoffman discusses, avoided the degree of gentrification that overwhelmed other neighborhoods near the Loop.

Supporters of the arena development appeared to have the facts on their side. Reinsdorf and Wirtz poured a significant amount of money and resources into West Haven, the construction of the arena and the 1996 DNC brought millions in supplementary public investment, and by the end of the 1990s the reputation of West Haven had changed for the better.

The Catch-23 of "Balanced" Redevelopment

The history of Horner residents' fight against relocation calls into question the United Center coalition's commitment to inclusive revitalization. It says little, however, about whether what took shape around the arena actually resembled a neighborhood where longtime residents could enjoy stability alongside new, relatively affluent arrivals. After all, many public-housing residents stayed put because of the Horner consent decree. Perhaps labels like "mixed income" and "balanced" really do capture what was going on in West Haven.

The reality on the ground proved very different. Evidence of displacement of low-income folks from the blocks around the new arena appeared in local papers a few years after it opened. In 1998, Rosalind Rossi and John Schmid of the *Sun-Times* reported that schools in the Near West Side had lost "nearly 2,500 students, mostly African Americans, since 1991." They pointed to attrition at many of the struggling public schools in the immediate vicinity of the United Center and Horner as a culprit.[20] Two years earlier, the *Tribune*'s Evan Osnos had identified the Near West Side as one of several community areas near the Loop where "countless residents fall into the cracks of the housing system . . . mak[ing] too much money to live in Chicago Housing Authority facilities, but not enough to qualify for subsidized home ownership programs."[21]

These reports seemed at odds with the NWSCDC's stated goal of adding new residents next to, rather than in place of, people who lived in the community before 1991. Reports prepared by the NWSCDC and its development partners never provided actual statistics to support the assertion that stadium-linked development created stability for longtime residents. Instead, most of the numbers in the publications dealt with the influx of new middle-class residents. Apparently, the assumption on the part of these nonprofits was that more affluent newcomers were joining, rather than displacing, community members.

Resolving the contradictions between the news reports and the claims made by Hoffman and the NWSCDC requires an examination of demographic change within West Haven specifically, rather than the Near West Side as a whole (Hoffman's data deal with the latter).[22] The remainder of this section offers precisely this sort of analysis, based largely on census data. Most of the methodological details are relegated to the footnotes, but a brief discussion of two technical points will make the analysis easier to understand.

First, in addition to zooming in on change in West Haven, the following analysis considers demographic transformation in nearby neighborhoods including the Loop, West Loop Gate, West Loop, and East Garfield Park (map 4.1).[23] Looking at this narrow corridor of neighborhoods extending

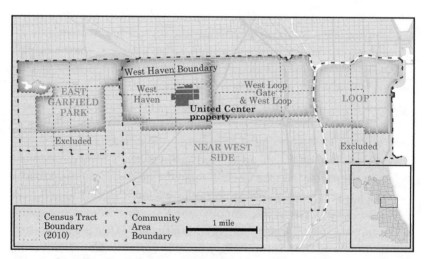

MAP 4.1. Census Tract Geography in West Haven and Nearby Neighborhoods
Source: Shapefiles obtained from City of Chicago, *Chicago Data Portal*; U.S. Census Bureau, *American FactFinder*, accessed August 25, 2013, factfinder2.census.gov/.
Notes: West Haven boundary reflects the neighborhood as defined by the NWSCDC.

west from Lake Michigan, which is largely buffered from residential development to the north and south by industrial zoning and the Eisenhower Expressway, respectively, generates several useful points of comparison.[24] East Garfield Park, physically demarcated from West Haven by rail lines, remains a prototypically poor West Side neighborhood. The community has experienced little investment since the 1960s. By contrast, the West Loop and West Loop Gate gentrified rapidly during the 1980s and 1990s, and the same process began even earlier in the Loop.[25] If the popular wisdom about the effects of investment ushered in by the United Center holds water, the recent history of the tracts encompassing West Haven should reveal more population growth than in East Garfield Park. Moreover, such growth should have occurred without significant displacement and at a less dramatic pace than that within the West Loop and West Loop Gate, leaving West Haven with a high degree of stable socioeconomic diversity relative to its adjacent neighborhoods.

The second technical issue concerns the specific census tracts employed to define the neighborhoods in question. The tracts used to measure change in West Haven extend slightly to the north and south of the official neighborhood boundary as defined by the NWSCDC, which at first glance suggests that they are a poor proxy for tracking change within that boundary. Fortunately, the difference between the residential population within the tracts and the residential population within the NWSCDC's West Haven boundary is negligible. The area within the tracts extending beyond the boundary to the north is exclusively industrial, a neighborhood with no residential population in recent history. Moreover, as of 1990 the area within each of the two tracts extending beyond West Haven to the south contained relatively insignificant residential development (map 4.2).[26] In the westernmost of the two tracts, the section south of the expressway contained only 4.5 percent of total residential development. In the tract to the east, that number was 1.7 percent.[27]

In defining the East Garfield Park "neighborhood" the analysis here excludes census tracts in the East Garfield Park community area below the Eisenhower Expressway, a large physical barrier that acts as a de facto divider of actual neighborhoods. It also excludes the tracts on the eastern and western edges of the community area that contain land both north and south of the expressway. This owes to the fact that considerable portions of the residential land in each one lie south of the expressway (30.5 percent in the case of the tract on the eastern edge and 76.8 percent in the case of the one on the western edge).[28] This means that population change in distinct neighborhoods south of the expressway could have exerted a major influence on census measurements for the larger tracts. Luckily, the stakes involved in this

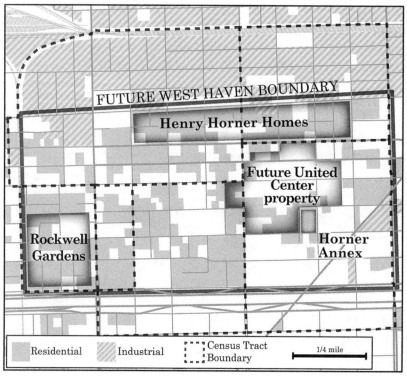

MAP 4.2. Land Use in West Haven, 1990
Source: Shapefiles obtained from Chicago Metropolitan Agency for Planning, *Land Use Inventory, 1990*, accessed May 17, 2013, www.cmap.illinois.gov/land-use-inventory; U.S. Census Bureau, *American Fact-Finder*.

decision are low. I included the two tracts in question in a previous iteration of the analysis, and it had no effect on the general trends observed or on the conclusions drawn.[29]

Mapping changes in the racial composition of these neighborhoods at the end of the twentieth century suggests a very different picture than the one provided by Hoffman and United Center advocates. Admittedly, changes in racial makeup do not reveal everything when it comes to evaluating the degree of gentrification in a neighborhood like West Haven. Gentrification is, at its core, a class-driven process characterized by higher-income residents displacing lower-income ones. Furthermore, scholars have documented instances of high-income people of color displacing low-income residents of the same racial background. Nevertheless, rapid influxes of white residents into historically black neighborhoods typically indicate affluent newcomers pushing out longtime, lower-income residents.[30]

By certain measures, the changes in this regard were less than dramatic in

West Haven. The proportion of the neighborhood's population comprised of
African Americans fell from 94.5 to 89.3 percent over the course of the 1990s
and to 74.8 percent between 2000 and 2010 (map 4.3). Nevertheless, the 2010
number was still high compared to the gentrifying neighborhoods directly to
the east. Between 1990 and 2010 the percentage of the population represented
by blacks in the West Loop and West Loop Gate (combined) dropped more
than 25 percentage points, from 36.5 to 11.1 percent. To be sure, West Haven
was becoming less "black" than East Garfield Park, but a clear racial gradient
remained along Ashland Avenue twenty years after the IOP struck its deal
with the arena developers. The dilution of the African American population

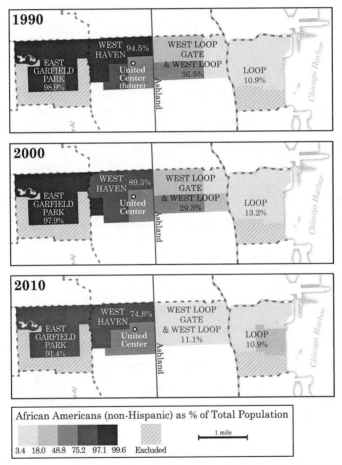

MAP 4.3. African Americans (Non-Hispanic) as Percentage of Total Population in West Haven and
Nearby Neighborhoods, 1990–2010
Source: Shapefiles obtained from City of Chicago, *Chicago Data Portal*; U.S. Census Bureau, *American
FactFinder*. Full-count census data obtained from US2010 Project, *Longitudinal Tract Database*.

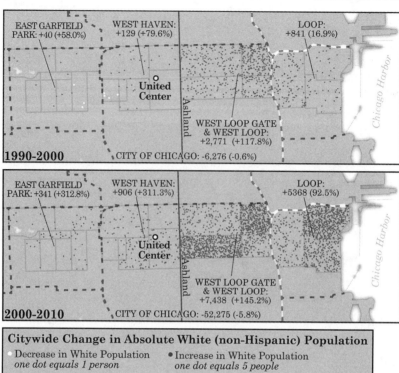

MAP 4.4. Change in Absolute White (Non-Hispanic) Population in West Haven and Nearby Neighborhoods, 1990–2010

Source: Shapefiles obtained from City of Chicago, *Chicago Data Portal*; U.S. Census Bureau, *American FactFinder*. Full-count census data obtained from US2010 Project, *Longitudinal Tract Database*.

Notes: The location of the population dots is randomized.

in West Haven quite possibly had less to do with the displacement of blacks than with the gradual addition of nonwhite residents.

Indeed, while whites moved into the tracts around the arena, it was at a much slower rate than into the West Loop and West Loop Gate. Taken together, the latter neighborhoods saw the number of white residents jump by more than 10,000 between 1990 and 2010 (map 4.4). This seems consonant with the "balance" celebrated by champions of stadium-linked development. New residents were arriving in West Haven but at a relatively slow pace.

The balance argument becomes harder to sustain, however, after accounting for the change in the absolute number of African Americans in West Haven. Between 1990 and 2000, the neighborhood experienced a net loss of more than 3,330 blacks (map 4.5). This represented nearly a quarter of the African American population in the tracts surrounding the United

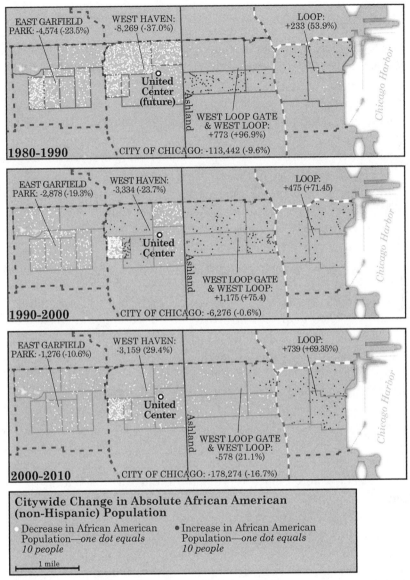

EAST GARFIELD PARK: -4,574 (-23.5%)   WEST HAVEN: -8,269 (-37.0%)   LOOP: +233 (53.9%)

Chicago Harbor

United Center (future)

Ashland

WEST LOOP GATE & WEST LOOP: +773 (+96.9%)

1980-1990   CITY OF CHICAGO: -113,442 (-9.6%)

EAST GARFIELD PARK: -2,878 (-19.3%)   WEST HAVEN: -3,334 (-23.7%)   LOOP: +475 (+71.45)

Chicago Harbor

United Center

Ashland

WEST LOOP GATE & WEST LOOP: +1,175 (+75.4)

1990-2000   CITY OF CHICAGO: -6,276 (-0.6%)

EAST GARFIELD PARK: -1,276 (-10.6%)   WEST HAVEN: -3,159 (29.4%)   LOOP: +739 (+69.35%)

Chicago Harbor

United Center

Ashland

WEST LOOP GATE & WEST LOOP: -578 (21.1%)

2000-2010   CITY OF CHICAGO: -178,274 (-16.7%)

Citywide Change in Absolute African American (non-Hispanic) Population

○ Decrease in African American Population—*one dot equals 10 people*

● Increase in African American Population—*one dot equals 10 people*

|— 1 mile —|

MAP 4.5. Change in Absolute African American Population in West Haven and Nearby Neighborhoods, 1980–2010

Source: Shapefiles obtained from City of Chicago, *Chicago Data Portal;* U.S. Census Bureau, *American Factfinder.* Full-count census data obtained from US2010 Project, *Longitudinal Tract Database.*

Notes: The location of the population dots is randomized.

Center. The decline continued apace in the next decade, as the neighborhood experienced another net loss of more than 3,150 blacks. During each of these decades, the rate of decline in, and the absolute loss of, African American residents in West Haven exceeded the numbers for East Garfield Park, which had few, if any, links to the United Center or the NWSCDC. Moreover, these figures almost certainly underestimate the decline in the black population from its pre–United Center levels. Since Earnest Gates and the NWSCDC marketed West Haven to middle-class African American renters and home-buyers, blacks moving into the neighborhood around the same time offset some of the loss indicated by the census.[31]

At the same time, the African American population increased dramati-cally in the neighborhoods to the east of the United Center. But the fact that these areas contained little subsidized housing stock indicates that the blacks who relocated there consisted of homebuyers from outside of West Haven. The tracts around the arena were not in the midst of stable, mixed-income revitalization. They were undergoing what one urban policy expert describes as a "typical gentrification pattern" in 1990s Chicago, in which the city's tradi-tionally black neighborhoods "improved" in socioeconomic terms but "con-tinued to lose substantial portions of their population."[32] If nearly 6,500 Afri-can American residents who remained in the neighborhood in 1990 departed over the following two decades, it goes without saying that stadium-based revitalization excluded a major portion of the community.

This is not to say that the United Center caused, or even accelerated, gen-trification. The departure of African Americans from the neighborhood was already in full swing by the 1980s. In fact, the decline of the black population in West Haven appears to have slowed after 1990. Thus, one might reasonably argue that the United Center helped limit African American out-migration. But this interpretation misses the mark for three reasons. First, the net popu-lation losses in West Haven since 1990 underestimate the shrinkage of the longtime black population, as the arrival of African American homebuyers offset the numerical impact of some departures. Second, while the pace of black depopulation in East Garfield Park tapered off during the 1990s and 2000s, the rate of decline in West Haven eased in the 1990s but hardly budged during the 2000s. In theory, the alleged anchor effects of the arena should have been more pronounced during the 2000s, since by the end of the de-cade the arena had enjoyed more than fifteen years of highly profitable op-eration. Instead, the neighborhood around the United Center continued to suffer from more demographic instability than its impoverished neighbor to the west. Finally, the magnitude of this instability would have been much more pronounced in the absence of the legal protections won by residents at Horner, which owed nothing to the United Center.

To understand this final point, one must look closely at the fate of Rockwell Gardens, the other major public-housing project in West Haven. Rockwell Gardens, which sat just a few blocks to the south and west of Horner—the CHA originally planned it as part of Horner but later constructed it as a separate project—consisted of more than 1,100 units built during the 1960s (map 3.2). Like Horner, Rockwell Gardens suffered rapid deterioration in subsequent decades, but by some notable measures it was in better shape than Horner in the early 1990s. For example, in 1991 its vacancy rate stood at 12.5 percent, nearly 37 percentage points below Horner's.[33]

The number of African Americans living in the census tract containing Rockwell Gardens (in the southwestern corner of the West Haven cluster) fell by more than 2,400 during the 1990s (map 4.5). This was, by far, the highest rate of African American depopulation among the neighborhood tracts. In fact, the census numbers underestimate the severity of the outflow from Rockwell. CHA records show that the number of public-housing residents at the project, almost all of whom were black, plummeted from 4,033 in 1991 to 1,265 in 2001 (table 4.4).[34] The reasons behind this exodus mirrored those in Chicago's other public-housing developments: the seemingly unstoppable momentum of decades of divestment from the surrounding neighborhood, negligence by the CHA, and unchecked gang activity. Rockwell's instability persisted into the 2000s. In 2003, the CHA began to demolish the project as part of the city's Plan for Transformation, which used HOPE VI funds to

TABLE 4.4. Number of Public Housing Residents at CHA Developments in West Haven

Year	Henry Horner (West Haven)	Rockwell Gardens (Jackson Square/West End)
1974	8,750	5,375
1980	7,765	5,274
1991	3,057	4,033
2001	2,137	1,265
2008	1,847	232

Source: Chicago Housing Authority, CHA Facts 1974 (Chicago: Chicago Housing Authority Executive Office, Division of Information and Statistics, 1975), Chicago Housing Authority Development Records, 1948–1992, box 22, folder 4, Chicago History Museum; Chicago Housing Authority, Statistical Profile: 1991 to 1992, n.d., Municipal Reference Collection, Harold Washington Library Center; Chicago Housing Authority, Moving to Work (MTW) Annual Plan (Chicago, 2002 and 2009), accessed January 27, 2018, www.thecha.org/documents/?CategoryId=41&F_All=y.

Notes: Parentheses underneath the original project names contain the names of the mixed-income redevelopments that replaced them.

replace public housing with mixed-income developments. By 2008, only 232 public housing residents, less than 5 percent of Rockwell's 1980 population, remained at the site.[35]

Unfortunately, this was the norm when it came to "redevelopment" of public housing under the Plan for Transformation. To make the new developments more attractive to market-rate buyers, the CHA designated only a tiny number of mixed-income units for very low-income public-housing residents. After receiving notice that their units would be demolished, most residents received "housing choice vouchers" to use in the private rental market, and the CHA assured them that they would eventually have the right of return to the new mixed-income sites. However, as Casey Sanchez of the *Chicago Reporter* documented during the mid-2000s, only a tiny fraction of residents ever made it back to the new developments.[36]

While demolition happened at a breakneck pace during the late 1990s and 2000s, construction of new mixed-income units lagged far behind. Budget shortfalls and an insistence on strict caps on the number of low-income residents by the CHA and the private developers it contracted to construct the mixed-income developments meant that only a handful of the families forced to accept "temporary" vouchers would realize their right of return. All of this was enabled by the suspension in 1996 of a federal mandate that local housing authorities replace every demolished public housing unit with a new one.[37] Tougher restrictions on qualifying for new public-housing units disqualified scores of families, often for petty transgressions like late utility bills. According to sociologist Jason Hackworth, these changes, combined with the fact that the CHA pursued one of the most aggressive demolition schedules in the country, made the problem of displacement of public-housing residents in Chicago "among the worst nationwide."[38]

The consent decree secured by Horner residents shielded them, at least initially, from many of the uncertainties surrounding the right of return. The order mandated that the CHA could not demolish units until it completed replacements, and it guaranteed more humane qualification requirements in terms of work status and criminal background. While many Horner residents also left the neighborhood, these losses would have been much more severe had redevelopment at Horner followed the same trajectory as at Rockwell. Between 1991 and 2008, the number of residents living at Horner dropped from 3,057 to 1,847, a decline of about 40 percent (table 4.4). Over the same period, Rockwell's population plummeted from 4,033 to 232, a decline of more than 94 percent. Clearly, the consent decree gave residents there a meaningful defense against the wholesale displacement occurring at other projects in Chicago.

To reiterate, none of this proves that the United Center caused residents to leave West Haven. Skeptics would be right to point out that the demolition and "redevelopment" of large public-housing projects like Rockwell Gardens—not the construction of the arena—proved the primary engine of African American population loss in West Haven (and, by extension, the primary engine of West Haven's demographic instability relative to neighborhoods like East Garfield Park). However, the maps and data presented here do unequivocally prove that the arena was far from the miracle anchor that its proponents described. As boosters spoke of a "balance . . . that supports newcomers, but not at the expense of existing residents," those existing residents were leaving the community in droves. It was either shortsighted or dubious on the part of arena ownership, city officials, and the NWSCDC to argue that a new sports facility would salvage or stabilize a neighborhood plagued by what one local activist described as a "long evolutionary process of disinvestment," as well as by extensive public housing demolition.[39] The tens of millions of dollars in direct and indirect investment linked to the United Center were a drop in the bucket relative to what was required to provide enough socioeconomic support to keep longtime residents in place.

That these resources were not forthcoming from the government was a matter of priority rather than fiscal capacity. The United Center did not represent the private sector's ability to revitalize communities where publicly funded redevelopment efforts had failed. Instead, it represented the private sector parading as a "free market" fix for a neighborhood in crisis as officials poured most local taxpayer money into glitzy projects on the lakefront and in the Loop. In terms of generating new investment for the benefit of longtime, low-income residents, the Horner consent decree proved more meaningful than the United Center. The two-phase redevelopment of Horner forced local and federal housing authorities to pony up approximately $250 million for public-housing redevelopment.[40]

There is more to this story, however, than the inability of a new professional sports facility to rejuvenate a decimated community for the benefit of those yet to leave. By way of the NWSCDC's development efforts, money from the team owners very likely exacerbated the pressures forcing the departure of many low-income African Americans. In particular, the dedication of much of this money to "homeownership growth" meant fewer housing options for poorer residents. During the 1990s, Gates and the NWSCDC focused on developing "affordable" for-sale properties, but at a cost of around $150,000 each, these units remained well beyond the reach of most of the neighborhood's longtime residents.[41]

Residents in West Haven who failed to qualify either for a mortgage or for public housing found themselves with few options for stable shelter, and many no doubt packed up and left. Especially for "hard to house" residents like grandparents caring for grandchildren, victims of domestic violence, and individuals with limited work histories, the neighborhood went from what a trio of housing experts describe as "troubled," offering "stable, if less than ideal, housing," to a community that offered no viable long-term housing options. Indeed, as CHA records confirm, many of those forced to leave Rockwell with vouchers relocated to impoverished, segregated neighborhoods on the city's western fringe such as North Lawndale and Austin.[42]

The experience of former Rockwell residents and others in West Haven who fell outside the protections of the Horner consent decree encapsulated larger trends in Chicago, and urban America more generally, during the late twentieth century. Many public-housing residents who relocated with vouchers during the 1990s found rental units in areas with lower relative poverty rates, but this represented a hollow victory. As geographers Todd Sink and Brian Ceh report, in Chicago most of the new neighborhoods that received voucher users suffered from "highly concentrated" poverty—just not quite as bad as the origin neighborhoods—and were located "away from the central city."[43] In other words, they were further away from the parts of Chicago attracting the most public and private investment. Drawing on national data, housing expert Susan Popkin adds that among voucher recipients "a substantial proportion are struggling to meet basic needs," like rent and utilities, "that previously were covered in public housing."[44]

Decision makers in West Haven like Reinsdorf and Gates did not orchestrate some master plan to purge low-income residents. They did, however, provide the money and manpower for implementation, at the neighborhood level, of national pro-homeownership policies that shunted aside low-income residents to make way for profitable real-estate investment. During the 1990s, the Clinton administration pushed through a patchwork of legislation and initiatives that reallocated federal housing resources from programs designed to provide shelter for the poor to programs designed to increase working- and middle-class homeownership in low-income neighborhoods. Major pillars of this shift included the 1992 Federal Housing Enterprises Financial Safety Act, the rewriting of the Community Reinvestment Act, and the 1995 launch of the National Homeownership Strategy. Supposedly, increased homeownership rates in depressed communities would result in stabilization and revitalization by increasing the economic stakes of residents in the local community. New homeowners, in other words, would bring an enhanced sense of "personal responsibility" to their neighborhoods.[45]

Predictably, these new policies drove a 31 percent jump in mortgage originations in low-income areas between 1993 and 1997.[46] But while they placed new assets in the hands of some who had previously fallen just short of qualifying for a mortgage, they also fueled significant gentrification. Such was the case in West Haven. From 1997 to 2006, the number of loans issued for owner-occupied home purchases increased exponentially and accrued relatively equally to white and nonwhite buyers (fig. 4.1). However, only 2.2 percent of those loans went to borrowers defined by HUD as "very low income," and only 14.1 percent went to "low income" ones. In other words, a full 83.7 percent went to middle- or high-income borrowers, with the latter category becoming more prevalent over time (fig. 4.2). This process generated significant amounts of new wealth in the neighborhood but distributed it overwhelmingly to the already well-off. Earnest Gates and the NWSCDC seemed more than happy with the situation. A report coauthored by the organization in 2007 bragged, "The number of upper middle income households—a key demographic needed to support retail development—has nearly tripled in the last fifteen years."[47]

In 1996 Horner resident Rubin McClellan displayed impressive prescience when he told Don Terry of the *New York Times*: "Before Michael Jordan came along and built that stadium over there, the city never thought about us. . . .

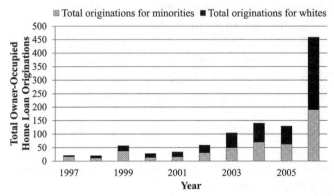

FIGURE 4.1. New Owner-Occupied Home Purchase Loans in West Haven by Minority Status, 1997–2006.

Source: Author's analysis of Kathryn Pettit, "Urban Institute Home Mortgage Disclosure Act (HMDA) Summary Data," *Harvard Dataverse* (2013), accessed January 27, 2018, dataverse.harvard.edu/dataset .xhtml?persistentId=hdl:1902.1/19436.

Notes: These data cover loans for one- to four-family dwellings and manufactured homes for which information on the race of the recipient was available. The data set uses census tracts harmonized to the 2000 boundary definitions, which allows for a more focused neighborhood definition for West Haven (tracts 2804–2816).

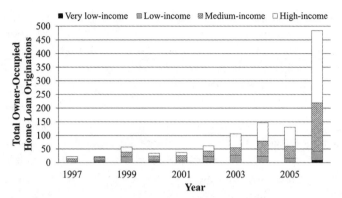

FIGURE 4.2. New Owner-Occupied Home Purchase Loans in West Haven by Income Level, 1997–2006. *Source:* Author's analysis of Kathryn Pettit, "Urban Institute Home Mortgage Disclosure Act (HMDA) Summary Data," *Harvard Dataverse* (2013), dataverse.harvard.edu /dataset.xhtml?persistentId=hdl:1902 .1/19436.

Notes: Totals differ from Figure 4.1 because of differences in the number of records missing race data and the number of records missing income data. Very low-income borrowers include households with 50 percent or less of the HUD area median family income. Low-income borrowers include households with 50 to 80 percent. Middle-income borrowers include households with 80 to 120 percent. High-income borrowers include households with 120 percent or more.

Now, they want to chase the black man out of here." Two years later a pair of *Tribune* reporters paraphrased another skeptical Horner tenant: "As he figures it, within 10 years the Horner high-rises will be parking lots for the condos of white urban professionals. . . . 'That's the Catch-23,' he said, mixing Michael Jordan's jersey number with Joseph Heller's classic novel."[48] Ironically, many at Horner would fare relatively well given the consent decree, but the cynicism was ultimately vindicated by the form taken by redevelopment in the rest of the neighborhood.

The tragedy confronted by poor people in West Haven who fell outside the protections of the Horner consent decree is best summed up by housing experts Larry Bennett, Nancy Hudspeth, and Patricia Wright. They note that, especially in neighborhoods near the Loop, scores of very low-income residents had to leave their homes and communities "just at the point when new private investment and, very likely as well, ancillary public investment in infrastructure and schools promise[d] to greatly improve both economic opportunity within the neighborhood and the local quality of life." In West Haven, advocates of stadium-linked development constantly reaffirmed a commitment to "the delicate balancing act [of] welcoming our incoming residents . . . while at the same time ensuring that those who have lived in

West Haven for decades are not chased out."[49] In practice, they did a much better job fulfilling the former goal.

The United Center and Economic Revitalization on the Near West Side: Credit Where It Wasn't Due

Whether the odes to balance misrepresented the nature of neighborhood change in West Haven had little bearing on the broader argument made by local boosters that the arena catalyzed the economic revitalization of the Near West Side. The press in Chicago repeatedly rejoiced in reminding readers, as Bill Rumbler of the *Sun-Times* did in 1996, that "in the Near West Side neighborhood, the building of the United Center seemingly has sparked a housing rebirth." A few months later, the *Tribune's* Ellen Martin repeated the same, noting that "loft developments are sprouting from the Eisenhower Expressway to Fulton Street," and adding: "Without question, the United Center has spurred development in the area."[50] This line of reasoning was not limited to journalists. Some academics also argued that the arena deserved credit for new private investment in the surrounding area. Urbanist Sean Zielenbach, for example, posits in his 2000 book on neighborhood change in Chicago that "the United Center . . . sparked considerable redevelopment in the community."[51]

Not everyone was convinced. In 2007 Larry Bennett, an urban planner at DePaul University, questioned whether the change in the area had much to do with the United Center. Over a decade after the arena opened, Bennett told Kirsten Miller of the *Sun-Times*, "There's been redevelopment to the west of the stadium, lofts have been built to the east and restaurants have sprouted up on Randolph." However, reversing the popular logic, he added: "I think a lot of that occurred without the United Center influence. It could well be that the United Center has benefited more from the neighborhood flux." A few years later, fellow urban planner Rachel Weber expressed a similar view, commenting that nearby development "happened in spite of the United Center . . . not necessarily because of the United Center."[52]

This skepticism echoed one of the arguments against stadium-linked development made by the Interfaith Organizing Project during the late 1980s. During its struggle against the Bears, the group maintained that new private investment in West Haven was imminent with or without a stadium. As IOP president Arthur Griffin told reporters in 1987, "The neighborhood is so well-situated, close to the Loop and transportation lines, that it is bound to come back, even without a stadium."[53] The IOP insisted that the city rebuff

the Bears and focus its efforts on helping longtime residents resist displacement as development swept westward from the Loop. The UIC researchers
working with the IOP agreed. One of their reports pointed out that "there is
considerable evidence that development activity is already moving westward
[from downtown]." Between 1984 and 1987, private developers working in
the West Loop "invested $100 million to rehab more than 1.5 million square
feet of former distribution and light industrial space into loft office space
and condominiums."[54] A subsequent report released by the researchers in
1988 listed several stadiums around which growth "was found to be related to
downtown expansion" rather than to the stadiums themselves. It concluded
that "if a sports center is built on the [Near] West Side . . . there is likely to be
commercial growth to the east because that is already occurring."[55]

If these arguments held water, then not only was the United Center a
disappointment in terms of promoting balanced revitalization; it also had
a dubious claim to anchoring economic revitalization of any kind. Indeed,
archival documents confirm that, well before Reinsdorf and Wirtz hatched
plans for the arena, a wave of reinvestment was pushing westward toward
Horner from the Loop. A 1987 memo circulated within Chicago's Department of Planning mentioned that the neighborhoods between the Loop and
West Haven were "experiencing tremendous growth in the residential, office
and commercial market from the conversion of obsolete manufacturing facilities and redevelopment of large tracts of vacant land."[56]

Long before the media latched onto the idea that the United Center was
driving redevelopment in the northern half of the Near West Side, it reported
extensively on the westward push of investment from the Loop into the area.
In June 1985, David Ibata of the *Tribune* alerted readers to an "accelerating
renaissance" in West Loop Gate. "Institutions and corporations are laying
plans to move to the . . . neighborhood, and developers are ready to launch
loft renovations," Ibata explained. In April 1986, *Chicago Magazine*'s Patrick
Barry pointed to the massive Presidential Towers residential high-rise in
West Loop Gate and the nascent "loft district farther west" as parts of the
"Super Loop" emerging from "the steady outward movement of redevelopment" from downtown. A year later, M. W. Newman of the *Sun-Times* com-
mented on the "advancing offices, apartments and light industry edging in
[westward] from a multibillion-dollar downtown," and the *Tribune*'s Patrick
Reardon observed "an encroachment of strong-hearted yuppies who are pio-
neering the renovated loft apartments and offices" in the southern part of the
West Loop.[57]

In the late 1980s and early 1990s, most observers agreed not only that, in
the words of a pair of *Sun-Times* reporters, "a tidal wave of renovation and

new construction [was] spreading west" from the Loop, but also that the new development promised to reach the blocks containing the old Chicago Stadium and Horner Homes. As Newman put it in a different piece for the same paper, by the time the Bears and the city settled on the Near West Side for a new football stadium, private investment was already "knocking on the door of very poor people who live behind barred doors on strategic turf."[58] Alex Kotlowitz, a journalist who spent several years interviewing Horner residents in the late 1980s, agreed. In his 1991 bestseller *There Are No Children Here*, Kotlowitz writes, "Since the city's downtown . . . can't expand to the east because of Lake Michigan, it has crept westward, past the Chicago River and through the city's once notorious skid row, certain to bump eventually right up against Henry Horner."[59]

The recollections of real-estate investors active in the area during the 1980s suggest a similar history. Annie and Lewis Kostiner, who began converting old manufacturing spaces in the West Loop into residential and commercial properties in the second half of the decade, emphasize that by 1988 they had started buying up land just a few blocks east of parcels eventually occupied by the United Center. As Annie recalls, they got involved in real estate development in the area because it was close to downtown and the land was cheap, not because of a sports arena. "What I remember the most was the emphasis on the location, on being confident that this would be a good project because of the proximity to the Loop. . . . So we ran with [it] because the property was affordable," she explains. As the Kostiners continued their development efforts during the 1990s, they "never talked about the United Center" except in the context of the Democratic National Convention in 1996, which they admit provided a boost to the area by prompting the city to complete infrastructural improvements between the Loop and the arena at a quicker-than-usual pace. Otherwise, the United Center was an afterthought, something that other developers in the West Loop could have done without.[60]

Building permits from the pre–United Center era back up the conclusion that investment was headed for West Haven with or without a new sports facility. Map 4.6 shows the location of all building permits filed for new construction in the Near West Side and the Loop from 1987 through 1990. The map confirms that investors had already made significant forays into both West Loop Gate and the West Loop. According to the *Tribune*'s William Mullen, much of this new investment consisted of loft conversions for use by commercial tenants attracted to "cheap office rents and the area's proximity to the Loop."[61] For example, one of the new construction permits was for a Federal Express facility that opened just a few blocks east of Chicago Stadium at Madison and Racine. Other permit records show that, by 1990, banks,

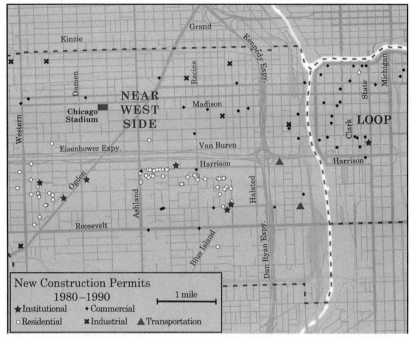

MAP 4.6. Permits Issued for New Construction by the City of Chicago, Near West Side and Loop, 1987–1990

Source: Shapefiles obtained from City of Chicago, *Chicago Data Portal*; building permit data obtained from City of Chicago Department of Planning and Development, *Chicago Neighborhood Development: New Construction 1987–1990* (Chicago, February 1992).

Notes: New construction south of the Eisenhower Expressway resulted from ongoing development in University Village and the influx of historic preservationists into the Tri-Taylor neighborhood.

restaurants, and even a couple of new single-family homes had popped up west of the Kennedy Expressway, easy walking distance to the old home of the Bulls and Blackhawks.[62]

Unfortunately, building permits issued for new construction offer only a partial measure of new development since they tell us nothing about renovation or conversion of old structures. This is especially true in a city like Chicago, where in recent decades artists and young professionals enamored of "loft living" have gobbled up old industrial space. Map 4.7 provides a partial corrective by plotting all new development in the West Loop and West Haven, new construction or otherwise, mentioned by local journalists and realtors from 1983 through 1990. This, too, is an inexact representation of local development history. However, like map 4.6, it documents a significant amount of activity by investors immediately to the east of West Haven prior to the United Center deal. In 1987, IOP president Reverend Arthur Griffin told the papers: "Developers are salivating to get in here with or without a stadium. The catalyst is our geographic proximity to the Loop."[63] These maps suggest that he was right.

In the years after the arena opened, a handful of press reports conceded that, rather than surrounding the United Center on all sides, most new development was popping up between the arena and the Loop, where it had been occurring for years. In 1996, Ellen Martin of the *Tribune* observed, "The rapid growth in the last two years has been east of Ashland Avenue [in the West Loop]." In 1997, *Crain's Chicago Business* reporter Jane Adler stated plainly, "Most new development is still east of Ashland Avenue." A full decade later, a report issued by a nonprofit collaborating with the NWSCDC in West Haven observed "increasing development activity principally moving in from the east."[64] According to these accounts, not much had changed since the 1980s. Development appeared to be moving toward the United Center from the Loop, not radiating outward from it. Indeed, if we return to the census data on changes in racial composition in the corridor of neighborhoods extending west from the Loop, this is the pattern that emerges. Between 1990

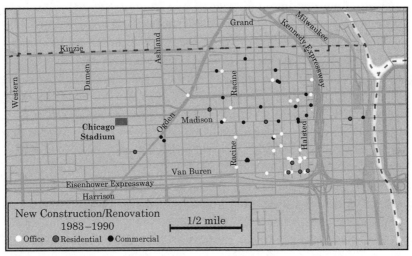

MAP 4.7. Sites of New Construction or Renovation Noted in Local Newspapers and Real Estate Publications, Northern Half of Near West Side, 1983–1990

Source: Shapefiles obtained from City of Chicago, *Chicago Data Portal*. Address data obtained from Don DeBat and Gary Meyers, "Near West Side Property Values Get High Grades," *Chicago Sun-Times*, June 22, 1990, NewsBank; Danuzio Lima and Stephen Steinhoff, *Community Resource Book*, Technical Report No. 1-87 (Chicago: Nathalie P. Voorhees Center for Neighborhood and Community Improvement, University of Illinois at Chicago, August 1987), 76, prepared for the Interfaith Organizing Project, Municipal Reference Collection, Harold Washington Library Center; Chicago Applied Real Estate Analysis, *Real Estate Market Trends Affecting Chicago's Near West Side: A Final Report* (Chicago: Applied Real Estate Analysis, 1988), Municipal Reference Collection, Harold Washington Library Center.

and 2010, for example, net increases in the white population progressively intensified in the Loop, West Loop Gate, and West Loop, eventually spilling over into West Haven (map 4.4). In other words, residential in-migration into these neighborhoods followed a pattern of gradual westward diffusion.

The point is not that the United Center had zero economic impact on the surrounding neighborhood. Money from Reinsdorf and Wirtz helped the NWSCDC lure some homeowners to West Haven, and the 1996 DNC certainly lit a fire under the city to make infrastructural improvements near the arena. Even Spirou and Bennett admit that the arena likely had an important "showcasing" effect for the area.[65] But arguing that the United Center played a seminal role in neighborhood revitalization relies on several bad assumptions. In the first place, it assumes that development in West Haven during the late 1990s and 2000s had little historical connection to previous investment to the east. Given the dramatic depopulation and surplus of cheap land in West Haven, it is hard to believe that developers would have stopped their push east of Ashland Avenue in the absence of the United Center during the late 1990s and early 2000s. Aberrant macroeconomic conditions in those years, such as significant real income gains—Chicago's real median income jumped 9.3 percent during the 1990s—and low interest rates nudged real estate developers to move into trendy neighborhoods close to downtown.[66]

The "United Center as revitalizer" thesis also assumes that new investment by the city would never have materialized without a new arena. In fact, most infrastructural investment made by the city for the DNC occurred east of the arena or in other community areas altogether.[67] Under Richard M. Daley, the city was quick to inject funds for infrastructure into gentrifying neighborhoods without new stadiums, especially ones near the Loop. It thus remains up for debate whether the DNC generated new public investment or simply accelerated investment by the city in the West Loop that was already imminent.[68] Perhaps the stadium sped up these efforts, but there is little compelling evidence that they would have never happened without the United Center.

In the end, United Center ownership took full credit for nearby revitalization.[69] Local politicians and press outlets, even the national media, rushed to reiterate that it was Reinsdorf and Wirtz who ultimately had saved West Haven. This sort of public relations coup had, by the 1990s, become typical of the urban sports business. For example, public and private boosters for Coors Field, built in Denver's Lower Downtown (LoDo) during the first half of the 1990s to house baseball's Colorado Rockies, boasted of its unparalleled importance to successful downtown revitalization. Stadium experts Kevin Delaney and Rick Eckstein note, however, that much of the development linked by boosters to the new stadium "began well before Coors Field was built and before the Rockies were awarded a franchise."[70]

For team owners like Reinsdorf and Wirtz, peddling stadiums as miracle cures for underdeveloped neighborhoods during the 1990s was critical to sustaining popular faith in the idea that the sports business played a positive role in urban development. In response to independent studies showing no measurable impact of teams or stadiums on economic growth at the level of city or metropolitan area, stadium boosters increasingly focused on the apparent role of the facilities in economic revitalization at the smaller scale of a neighborhood.[71] In the case of the United Center, even these scaled-back expectations relied on wishful thinking.

"Built with the Imagination of a Chipmunk": The United Center as Planning Failure

After the United Center opened, Chicago's press occasionally took note of the fact that, despite the money from the team owners and the NWSCDC's marketing of new homes, a stark contrast still existed between the West Loop and West Haven. In 1996, *Tribune* architecture critic Blair Kamin conceded that West Haven "no longer looks shabby" but insisted that there were still "two Madison Streets—one east of Ashland [Avenue], a gentrifying landscape where yuppie restaurants set tables along the sidewalks; the other west of Ashland, a depressing landscape where unemployed men and women mill around on the sidewalk."[72] Perhaps it was unrealistic to expect dramatic change so soon, but more than a decade later the divide persisted. In 2006 *Sun-Times* reporters David Roeder and Fran Spielman explained: "Since its opening in 1994, the United Center has been credited with leading a turnaround of the Near West Side. But stretches of Madison Street near the stadium are still empty or hold only small decayed stores."[73]

Some attributed the continued unevenness of development to the thousands of public-housing residents who remained in West Haven because of the consent decree. In 1997, Jane Adler of *Crain's Chicago Business* cited unnamed sources who claimed that "developers are leery about getting too close to public housing projects west of [the] United Center."[74] Looking back on the history of development in the neighborhood, Earnest Gates agrees. "As soon as folks realized that there's public housing on the street, it [took away] the economic incentive for some [to move in]," he recalls.[75] Gates even told the *Chicago Reporter* in 2009 that he and other community leaders had lobbied to maintain a high density of public-housing residents to, as journalist Kelly Virella described it, "booby-trap" West Haven against gentrification.

"We put scattered-site public housing in the neighborhood to make it distasteful for really, really higher income," he explained in his own words.[76]

Given the contentious relationship that developed between Gates and many public-housing residents during the 1990s, the notion that he orchestrated the retention of subsidized housing to "booby-trap" the community against gentrification seems like a romantic rewriting of history. In any case, the continued presence of CHA tenants in West Haven quite possibly deterred potential investors and homebuyers. According to some urban planning experts, during the 1990s Chicago's real-estate industry applied a rule of thumb that the proportion of a neighborhood's public-housing population had to drop below one-third before investors could generate sufficient demand for market-rate housing and commercial development.[77]

Blaming the slow pace of revitalization in West Haven entirely on the continued presence of public-housing residents, however, diverted attention from another culprit: the design and planning of the United Center. Surface parking sited around the arena impeded ancillary development by taking up an inordinate amount of space and inhibiting the free movement of residents and visitors. As Charles Leroux and Ron Grossman of the *Tribune* noted in 1996, "Much of the surrounding neighborhood [has] been paved over to form a sea of parking lots in the middle of which the new United Center sits like a stranded concrete-and-glass whale." From an economic development perspective, this was unfortunate. Planner Eran Ben-Joseph explains that the expansive surface lots around sports facilities are "probably the most wasteful and underutilized type of lot." Even Earnest Gates agrees. "You can't get the businesses, the stores and the stuff that is vital to a community's day-to-day life because it's vacant," he explains.[78] Gates blames much of the parking problem on lot owners unaffiliated with the United Center who set up shop on the outskirts of the arena, but this makes little sense. Available land-use data show that United Center property alone, the overwhelming majority of which consisted of parking lots, ate up nearly fifty-five acres in West Haven. Moreover, Gates concedes that Reinsdorf and Wirtz bought out several of the non–United Center lots during the 1990s and maintained them for their own profit.[79] The domination of the local landscape by surface parking was, first and foremost, the responsibility of arena ownership.

It was not as if Reinsdorf and Wirtz lacked alternatives. When construction crews broke ground on the United Center, some other NBA arenas—New York's Madison Square Garden is the best example—had thrived for decades without big surface lots. The same was true of the Chicago Cubs' baseball stadium, Wrigley Field, less than six miles to the north of the United

Center. The team owners chose not to mimic these facilities' dependence on multilevel parking structures and public transportation.[80]

They also ignored a straightforward way of reducing the arena's dependence on surface parking: lobbying for a new elevated train stop near the arena. There were two viable options in this regard: first, a new Green Line stop at Damen Avenue and Lake Street, four blocks north of the United Center; and second, a new stop at the intersection of Madison Street and a previously out-of-service connector track between the Green and Blue Lines that runs two blocks east of the arena and is now part of the Pink Line (a stop had existed at this location at least until the late 1940s).[81] Reinsdorf and Wirtz solicited funds from the state for infrastructural improvements around the arena site in the late 1980s, and the 1996 Democratic National Convention brought new money for nearby infrastructure from the city. The team owners, however, never pushed openly for using the funds for a new train stop. In the new millennium, outside pressure for such a project accumulated. As a consortium of local planning experts from the public, private, and nonprofit sectors argued in 2008, rebuilding a new Pink Line stop at Madison Street "could provide an opportunity for the United Center to strengthen its connection to the Near West area, and reduce the current amount of parking required for games and events."[82]

A decade and a half after the arena opened, the parking lots remained an impediment to redevelopment. When a May 2008 *Tribune* editorial asked, "Why hasn't [the] Near West Side neighborhood been redeveloped as dramatically as Chicago officials expected," the first answer it came up with was the moat of parking around the arena. "There's so much space," the paper explained, "the blocks around the United Center's 40-plus acres don't yet have the anchor institution that would make the area as vibrant in the daytime as it is on game nights."[83] The irony here was likely lost on most readers. The voice of the Chicago establishment, which had gushed over the United Center's promise as an anchor development west of Ashland, now argued that the slow pace of development owed to the arena's design. Local officials were conceding that, as urban planning professor Rachel Weber offered in a 2011 interview, the "sea of surface parking lots" was "not exactly . . . the kind of setup you want to have if you want . . . an institution to have effects on the surrounding area."[84] Ironically—perhaps "tragically" is more appropriate—the Interfaith Organizing Project predicted these problems with impressive precision in its *Better Alternative* plan of 1987, which presciently warned that "the neighborhood would be irreparably damaged" by a new large-scale stadium development.[85]

Perhaps the starkest evidence of the United Center's failure from a design perspective came from a series of studies published jointly in 2008 by public agencies including the Chicago Department of Planning and the Regional Transportation Authority, as well as local nonprofits such as the Metropolitan Planning Council. The research candidly concluded that the arena had hindered more robust development in West Haven. One of the reports explained, "The United Center and its associated surface parking lots are an impediment to creating a cohesive neighborhood," and noted the arena's role in creating "barriers to connecting [the West Haven] and West Loop areas." "Yet, this underdeveloped land also presents an opportunity to plan for large-scale infill which can create new retail and hospitality uses, as well as employment," it went on. The study recommended a targeted redesign of the arena's periphery in line with "a new vision for the Madison [Street] corridor" in which "future infill development" could replace "the large area of surface parking lots surrounding the arena." The research also pointed out that the physical layout of the arena transformed West Haven into an unwelcoming space for residents and visitors. "The pedestrian environment for day-to-day movement around the area is uncomfortable due to open expanses of parking. . . . The presence of this intimidating space inhibits local pedestrian movement in all directions," the report noted.[86] A map created by the Department of Planning (fig. 4.3) marked several pedestrian routes blocked by

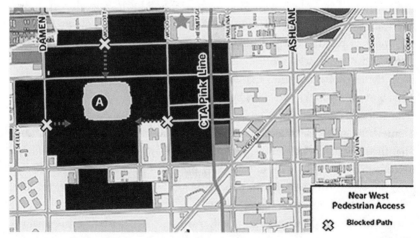

FIGURE 4.3. Detail from Chicago Department of Planning Map Showing the United Center's Interference with Pedestrian Traffic in West Haven

Source: City of Chicago, Regional Transportation Authority, Metropolitan Planning Council, and HNTB, *Existing Conditions Report: Near West Study Area* (Chicago: Chicago Reconnecting Neighborhoods, February 2008), 10, accessed May 17, 2013, reconnectingneighborhoods.org/resources/pdfs/WestExConReport_May6_2008.pdf (link no longer active but PDF available from author upon request).

the United Center and its lots. The map verifies that the "House that Jordan Built" was no exception to what political scientist Charles Euchner describes as the tendency of stadiums constructed at the end of the twentieth century to "destroy . . . 'linkage-rich' space" and preclude "tight-knit neighborhood patterns."[87]

The Department of Planning even called for the use of public money to "target the area surrounding the United Center . . . for service and entertainment-oriented retail development . . . in conjunction with structured parking to serve visitors."[88] That the city felt the need to step in with taxpayer dollars to help correct the situation betrayed the absurdity of the history of stadium-linked development in West Haven. City officials had billed the United Center as the ideal public-private partnership, only to concede decades later that the arena was, in the words of the *Toronto Star*'s Damien Cox, "built with the imagination of a chipmunk"—that it was less a solution to the neighborhood's problems than a source of them.[89]

The United Center's design made the neighborhood not only less livable for residents but also less attractive to investors interested in profiting from dense residential and commercial development close to downtown. By impeding development marching west from the Loop, the arena parking lots likely negated any showcase effect. The facility's design also clashed with the second Mayor Daley's larger effort to transform neighborhoods in and around the Loop into pedestrian-friendly locales appealing to Chicago's new urban gentry. Few United Center boosters argued that a new arena would lead to the expansion of Chicago's economy as a whole; the fact that Reinsdorf and Wirtz picked up the tab for initial construction costs effectively dispensed with the need for the type of farcical economic impact statements often used to bilk taxpayers into supporting public funding for sports facilities. However, claims that the United Center would revitalize a small part of the Near West Side were not totally outlandish. As economists John Siegfried and Andrew Zimbalist note, big-league facilities can, in theory, "reposition economic activity within a metropolitan area" and facilitate the redevelopment of individual neighborhoods or urban cores.[90] This might have happened in West Haven if locals and visitors had redistributed their entertainment spending to businesses in the immediate vicinity of the United Center. The arena's design, however, precluded this from happening.

This was intentional. The seemingly irrational design of the arena made perfect sense when it came to generating profits for Reinsdorf and Wirtz. Property-tax records from the Cook County Board of Review show that by the early 2000s, the team owners were pulling in upward of $2 million a year in parking receipts.[91] Moreover, they had an interest in ancillary commercial development not occurring near the arena. A proliferation of restaurants, bars, and other entertainment facilities near the United Center would have thwarted ownership's efforts to monopolize the local market of food and drink sales in West Haven on game nights.

The efforts by Reinsdorf and Wirtz to vacuum up every cent of event-related spending not only discouraged investment in the surrounding community; it also guaranteed what economists refer to as leakage of stadium-generated revenues out of the local area. Because most of the revenues found their way into the pockets of the team owners and players, people who did not spend much time in West Haven on non–game nights, little of this money recirculated as spending in the immediate vicinity.[92] It may have been the "House that Jordan Built," but Jordan and his teammates lived and spent their cash elsewhere.

In the end, the United Center's design undercut its potential to increase the day-to-day quality of life of longtime residents in West Haven. Roger Watson, a senior citizen and public-housing resident living in West Haven during the 1996 Democratic National Convention, bluntly summed up the situation for a *Sun-Times* reporter. "They don't care about people like us," Watson said of United Center ownership and city officials. "Concrete. Blacktop. Fences. These aren't for the people here. What are we going to do with that stuff?"[93]

Little wonder that, during the struggle against the Bears, the IOP criticized the surplus of "underutilized development opportunities . . . like the surface parking lots around [the old] Chicago Stadium."[94] Given the fact that low-income residents at Horner had won the right to stay in the neighborhood with or without a new arena, they probably stood a much better chance of benefiting from Loop-linked development based on high-density residential and commercial investment.

✳

When the Interfaith Organizing Project drafted the original *Better Alternative Plan* in 1987, it proposed converting the land eaten up by inefficient surface parking around Chicago Stadium into "neighborhood-scale housing."[95] Residents and organizers knew from decades of experience with Chicago Stadium that arena-linked "development" would be more problem than solution. Despite early optimism around the deal cut with Reinsdorf and Wirtz, what emerged in West Haven was the opposite of the IOP's original vision. By the time the United Center opened, residents had to contend with more parking lots. It did not take long for many to realize that the new arena made the area less hospitable for residents, visitors, and investors.

Except for the redeveloped Horner units, most of the new housing that sprouted up in West Haven underwrote a model of development inherently hostile to longtime, low-income residents. The steering of stadium-linked community investment toward the expansion of private homeownership, reinforced by broader shifts in local and federal urban housing policy, very likely encouraged the displacement of thousands of impoverished Near West Siders (at least those without protection from the courts). As in countless other cases of central-city gentrification during the New Gilded Age, revitalization in West Haven after 1990 rested in large part on the transfer of neighborhood resources like land, housing, and consumer spending from poor and working-class residents to wealthy newcomers.

Gentrification in West Haven did not, however, coincide with a full-fledged economic recovery. Arena design intended to funnel as much consumer spending as possible into the pockets of Reinsdorf and Wirtz ultimately reduced the appeal and viability of the neighborhood for prospective residents and investors. Perhaps the cachet of the new stadium helped accelerate investment between the Loop and the United Center, but most of the evidence indicates that the United Center, to borrow from Larry Bennett, "barely registers as a local economic force."[96] That development was on the march toward West Haven since the 1980s begs the question of whether the arena had a significant economic impact on the neighborhood other than getting in the way of the expansion of development outward from the Loop.

In the end, the economic benefits of the United Center were far from inclusive. Significant numbers of poor residents who were supposed to benefit from arena-linked redevelopment found themselves swept aside. Even for many private real-estate developers, the arena represented more bane than boon because of its sprawling, inefficient design. Wealthy homebuyers who poured into West Haven may have been pleased with their new digs a stone's throw from the Loop, but the United Center's dominance of the landscape limited the neighborhood's livability, not to mention its ability to support additional commercial development. The only clear winners in this story, then, were the team owners.

"Peanut Envy": The United Center's War against Sidewalk Vendors

When the United Center opened its doors on Chicago's Near West Side in 1994, the state-of-the-art arena offered the ultimate in fan experience. Bulls season-ticket holders suffering through the first of Michael Jordan's many retirements could at least take solace in the "carbon dioxide-powered condiment dispensers," the "computerized heating and cooling system," or any of the United Center's many other accoutrements that were, according to Jeff Borden of *Crain's Chicago Business*, "designed to pamper paying customers."[1] But something more than Michael Jordan was missing. Peanuts, the snack food of choice for thousands of fans at the old Chicago Stadium, had disappeared. Bulls and Blackhawks fans could not buy them inside, and the vendors from whom they used to buy them outside the old Chicago Stadium were suddenly gone.

The disappearance of peanuts might seem like the logical outcome of the teams' efforts to cultivate and cater to a market of fans eager to indulge in the highbrow cuisine introduced at the United Center, which included an assortment of more than forty wines to wash down menu items like Norwegian salmon and prime rib.[2] While some elite patrons may have preferred caviar to peanuts, the absence of the latter was not about the evaporation of demand. After all, the United Center continued to offer less luxurious items like hot dogs and domestic beer.

In fact, Bulls owner Jerry Reinsdorf and Blackhawks owner Bill Wirtz waged an aggressive, two-part campaign against the peanut vendors in their quest to monopolize food sales and carefully police the space around the new arena. The first part was a prohibition on outside food brought into the United Center by fans, many of whom had long toted peanuts purchased from street vendors into Chicago Stadium. In the face of legal challenges to the food ban mounted by the peddlers, the owners took advantage of the resurgence among federal judges of a logic that endorsed monopolists' "freedom" to operate unhindered by government intervention, no matter how predatory their business practices. The second part was a city ordinance banning street vendors from within one thousand feet of the United Center. Introduced by the neighborhood alderman Walter Burnett Jr., and passed unanimously by the City Council in October 1995, the ordinance ensured the departure of the vendors regardless of the courts' actions in response to the food ban.[3] In the end, the arena owners eliminated their primary competitors in the local market for food sales.

Experts in the fields of economics and law have written extensively on monopoly power and the U.S. sports business. The topic's allure owes to the unique place of leagues and teams in the history of business competition policy in the United States. In 1922, the Supreme Court handed down a ruling exempting Major League Baseball from federal antitrust law. In theory, antitrust statutes prohibit firms, or groups of firms (i.e., cartels), from willfully obstructing competition within their industries to establish and maintain monopolies or monopolistic practices that harm consumers (e.g., through higher prices or fewer options). The exemption has allowed MLB to behave openly as a cartel and engage in many anticompetitive behaviors without fear of intervention by the courts or prosecution by the Justice Department. For example, it has permitted the league to unilaterally restrict the creation of new franchises and to endow each team with an "exclusive territorial franchise"—in other words, a local monopoly over the production and sale of major-league baseball. This not only has shielded teams from local price competition but also has made it easy for them to use the threat of relocation to secure public subsidies for new stadiums. Because MLB has not only restricted the number of teams within a city (usually to one) but also deliberately obstructed the creation of teams in a handful of viable markets, it perpetuated an artificially high demand for franchises. Teams seeking public money have exploited the situation by using threats of moving to one of the empty markets to strong-arm local officials into doling out taxpayer dollars for new or upgraded facilities.[4]

MLB is the only professional sports league with an official exemption from antitrust law, and during the twentieth century other major leagues like the NBA, NFL, and NHL faced repeated legal challenges to many of their monopolistic, anticompetitive behaviors. Many of these challenges dealt with league labor practices, and the results varied. Nevertheless, the Justice Department often assumed what economists James Quirk and Rodney Fort describe as a "hands-off position" in its treatment of anticompetitive behavior by all major leagues. This was particularly true in the case of the leagues' artificial restriction of franchise supply and the granting of local monopolies to individual teams.[5]

The history of the vendor purge from the sidewalks around the United Center reveals that in the New Gilded Age, many teams successfully expanded their local monopoly powers beyond the realm of franchise rights. Historically, the market for sales of food and souvenirs on the public sidewalks surrounding stadiums remained outside the crosshairs of team owners. This changed after the luxury stadium boom began in the 1980s. Thus, the resurrection of exclusionary capitalism did more than enhance the ability of teams like the Bulls to profit from existing monopoly powers—for example, using the absence of local competition to implement unprecedented price hikes for tickets. It also created opportunities for them to establish *new* forms of monopolistic control.

Recounting the campaign against vendors around the United Center also reveals that there was more to the growing economic and political power of major-league stadium owners in recent decades than the special treatment of the professional sports business by the government. While explicit or implicit exemption from antitrust law certainly empowered franchises to use threats of relocation to extract more and more lucrative public subsidy deals (and other concessions) from their home cities and states, this was not a factor in Reinsdorf and Wirtz's successful offensive against the peanut vendors. The campaign occurred immediately after the United Center opened, when there was zero risk that either the Bulls or Blackhawks would relocate.

In fact, the outcome of the vendor saga was part of the federal courts' renewed acceptance of predatory and coercive business practices by corporations throughout the economy, not just by the sports business. The economic crises of the 1970s provided an opening for several influential, probusiness legal scholars to revive an understanding of "free markets" that dominated the late nineteenth and early twentieth centuries—one that defined "freedom," first and foremost, as the right of private capital to profit infinitely regardless of the consequences for others. As a result, after 1970 the judiciary increasingly sanctioned efforts by large corporations to undermine smaller competitors by unilaterally blocking or sabotaging the latter's market access rather than by selling a superior and/or less expensive product. Consumers lost out by having fewer viable options and facing artificially inflated prices. By the new millennium, corporate-friendly forces had reestablished the federal courts as a mechanism for transferring wealth from working- and middle-class Americans to the rich.

The accelerated privatization of public space throughout the United States at the close of the century also contributed to the disappearance of vendors from the periphery of arenas like the United Center. The passage of the antivendor ordinance by the City Council, which effectively handed control over nearby streets and sidewalks to team owners in return for generous campaign contributions to key aldermen, encapsulated this trend. In addition to banning the vendors, the ordinance also mandated the use of public resources—in this case, the Chicago Police—to enforce it. By the end of the 1990s Reinsdorf and Wirtz had not only commandeered all the revenues previously produced by the peddlers; they also convinced the city to subsidize the costs of maintaining their newly established monopoly.

The passage and enforcement of the thousand-foot ordinance yielded consequences borne overwhelmingly by low-income people and working people of color. The law wiped out the livelihood of a group of predominately African American small-time entrepreneurs and it went so far as to criminalize their presence. This was perfectly consistent with efforts throughout the urban entertainment and retail industries at the time to repel people that investors feared would, because of their class or skin color, make patrons uncomfortable.

The economic history of peanuts at the United Center also clarifies the synergy between the federal courts' embrace of unfettered monopoly power and cities' acquiescence to demands by capitalists to privatize public space. The courts, by endorsing the ban on outside food, effectively nullified United Center patrons outside the arena as a viable market for the peddlers. The City Council, by passing the ordinance, guaranteed that if the vendors persisted in their efforts to sell peanuts to those patrons, they would be harassed, fined, and perhaps even arrested. So, while judges granted Reinsdorf and Wirtz implicit control over the economic activity on the streets and sidewalks around the United Center, local aldermen supplemented their work by offering the owners much more explicit—and, if need be, coercive—power to enforce that control.

The role of Reinsdorf and Wirtz in this story exemplified the gap between the rhetoric and reality of exclusionary capitalism within and beyond the sports business. The owners invoked the idea of free-market economics to argue against courts intervening on behalf of the vendors while pressuring aldermen to pass the ordinance. Thus, capitalists like Reinsdorf and Wirtz justified the upward redistribution of wealth by touting markets unhindered by government. However, whenever the objectives of free-market competition and upward redistribution came into conflict—that is to say, whenever

big business needed the government to guarantee upward redistribution—
economic elites like sports-team owners invariably abandoned their commitment to the former.[6]

Food Bans and Free-Market Monopoly

In 1985, Charlie Beyer returned to Chicago after a stint in the Peace Corps.
One thing he knew for certain: he did not want to wear a suit in a nine-to-five
job. On a whim, he decided to work as an independent peanut vendor on the
sidewalks surrounding Wrigley Field, home of the Cubs. What Beyer initially
thought of as a temporary gig ended up lasting more than a decade, during
which he sold peanuts and programs to fans outside of Wrigley, the old and
new Comiskey Parks, Soldier Field, and Chicago Stadium.

Beyer's fondest memories are of selling outside of Wrigley because of the
carnivalesque atmosphere created by the tight integration of the ballpark into
the surrounding neighborhood. That said, the public ways and sidewalks
around the old Chicago Stadium offered vendors the best access to customers of all the city's major-league facilities. "The thing about the Stadium was
that it was probably the most liberal of any of the places," Beyer remembers.
"There we were standing right by the entrance doors at each of the gates. . . . I
still remember when I first saw that I went, oh my goodness now this is amazing, being allowed to do this—this is incredible."[7]

The other fifty or so peanut vendors working the gates of Chicago Stadium
tended to come from backgrounds different from that of Beyer, who was
white and college educated. Most were African American, and many hailed
from low-income neighborhoods on the West and South Sides. "People definitely saw me as a novelty," Beyer recalls, "and people definitely said, 'What
are you doing out here?'" Some of those working beside Beyer had few other
employment options, and some sold peanuts to supplement other wages. In
a few cases, the vendors were elderly men who used sales to pad their meager
Social Security checks. Vendors could pull in a few hundred dollars before a
game on a good night, and they generally worked outside multiple venues
throughout the year.[8]

In the late 1980s, changes in the professional sports business threatened
the vendors' position outside of Chicago's stadiums. Up to that point, most
revenues generated by major-league facilities came from ticket sales. Earnings
from the sale of food and drink, programs, and advertising were relatively insignificant.[9] During the 1980s, however, teams transformed their venues into
all-inclusive entertainment zones for the minority of fans who could afford
not just tickets but a luxury experience including gourmet food and pricey

souvenirs. As a result, revenues from in-venue food sales shot up for teams with new facilities (table 2.2).

In cities like Boston, Chicago, Denver, and Pittsburgh, the new high-stakes food and beverage sales sparked efforts by stadium owners to eliminate competition from independent street peddlers.[10] Vendors in Chicago first felt the squeeze of policies against peddling outside of Wrigley field in 1988, right after the Cubs installed lights and began playing a limited schedule of night games, which increased the surrounding neighborhood's cachet as a trendy hangout. Soon after Wrigley's lights went on, the local alderman mounted a public campaign against the vendors, claiming that they were "harassing" Cubs fans. In 1990, the City Council passed an ordinance barring peddling on public streets and sidewalks in the ward containing Wrigley. Some street vendors managed to carve out spots on private property around the stadium, but the ordinance initiated a purge of those who were not so lucky.[11]

While the vendors continued to work the gates of Chicago Stadium during the late 1980s and early 1990s, other venues in the city shut them out. In 1993, two years after the new Comiskey Park opened on Chicago's South Side, the City Council passed an ordinance banning all forms of peddling on public property within one thousand feet of the facility. Local officials alleged that the vendors presented a safety hazard by impeding foot traffic.[12] As Beyer remembers it, the Comiskey purge happened much less gradually than the one at Wrigley. The vendors' only recourse was to sell peanuts to cars on off-ramps of the Dan Ryan Expressway—a situation that presented a genuine safety hazard and produced far fewer sales. By the end of 1993, peddling around Comiskey was finished.[13] Soldier Field, home of the Chicago Bears, came next. In April 1994, pressured by downtown businesses intent on eliminating competition during World Cup matches at Soldier Field, the City Council created a no-peddling zone encompassing most of the Loop and Near South Side, an area that included the football stadium.[14]

When the City Council initiated the purge from the sidewalks in the Loop and around Soldier Field, the United Center was only a few months away from opening, and the vendors sensed that their days selling outside of Bulls and Blackhawks games were numbered. Mark Weinberg, who sold an alternative fan program called the *Blue Line* outside Chicago Stadium before Blackhawks games, remembers the vendors who also peddled outside the other venues commenting on how they had been, in his words, "fucked" by the various ordinances. The peddlers predicted that once the Bulls and Blackhawks transitioned to the new facility, the teams would move to push them out entirely.[15] "The pattern had already been established," Beyer recalls.

"Lights at Wrigley, vending ordinance; new stadium at Comiskey, vending ordinance."[16] In their minds, it was only a matter of time.

The Bulls and Blackhawks proved the vendors right, but instead of an anti-peddling ordinance, the teams instituted a ban on all outside food items in the United Center immediately after it opened in 1994.[17] The fact that the old Chicago Stadium allowed fans to bring in peanuts purchased outside, combined with the cheap prices offered by street vendors, ensured a steady stream of business for the peddlers before 1994. While a handful of fans continued to purchase peanuts from the vendors and sneak them inside during the Bulls' 1994–1995 season, the food ban discouraged most, and the vendors' revenues plummeted. Thornton Elliott, one of the elderly African Americans who sold peanuts outside the arena, packed up for good not long after the ban went into effect. "I guess most fans figured, what's the use of buying peanuts if you have to sneak them in?," Elliott told *Chicago Reader* reporter Ben Joravsky. "I used to make $300 at a Blackhawks game. That first preseason game I made $40. The next game I made $22. It wasn't worth it."[18] The food ban unilaterally destroyed the viability of the public ways around the new facility as a market for the sale of peanuts.

Because Weinberg peddled programs rather than peanuts, the food ban did not cut into his sales the way it did those of the peanut vendors. Nevertheless, the ban seriously irked Weinberg, who viewed it as Reinsdorf and Wirtz "stepping on people who were powerless."[19] Weinberg was even more of an anomaly among the vendors than Beyer. A Jew from Highland Park—the same affluent North Side suburb where Reinsdorf lived—he graduated from law school at the University of Chicago and went to work for Katten Muchin Zavis, a high-powered Chicago law firm. Weinberg's time at the firm helped him develop a greater understanding of the power wielded by men like Reinsdorf. Reinsdorf joined Katten Muchin Zavis in 1968, and the firm was the conduit to many of the professional connections that eventually facilitated his move into the real-estate business.[20]

Uneasy about working in the Chicago establishment, Weinberg walked away from the firm to pursue what, by that time, was an all-consuming passion: lambasting the dismal performance of Chicago Blackhawks management and questionable business practices of owner Bill Wirtz. In 1991, Weinberg started publishing the *Blue Line*, an underground program containing spoof advertisements and lurid, merciless satires of Wirtz. The topics ranged from Wirtz's alleged alcoholism to accusations of financial deceit levied against him by close friends and family. After the food ban took effect at the United Center, one issue of the *Blue Line* listed the "Top 10 Reasons Why I, King Bill, Have Banned Peanut Sales." Among them: "If those homeless

FIGURE 5.1. Mr. Peanut Gets the Boot from the United Center
Source: *The Blue Line*, c. October 1995. Courtesy of Mark Weinberg and Blue Line Publishing.

peanut vendors make too much money, they might build their own stadium and buy their own hockey club and then where would I be?" Another program featured a cartoon depicting Mr. Peanut handcuffed, escorted out of the United Center at gunpoint by security (fig. 5.1).[21]

Even though fans could still bring the *Blue Line* into the United Center, Weinberg could not stomach a fellow Jew like Reinsdorf stomping out the livelihoods of a group of men trying to scrape by. "You know the Jews were peddlers," Weinberg explains. "That's what the Jews did when they came over on the boat. . . . The powerful interest [pushing out the peddlers] in this case is ironically a wealthy Jewish man named Jerry Reinsdorf. . . . I'm sure Reinsdorf's grandparents were peddlers." It was a good guess. In fact, Reinsdorf's father worked as a peddler at various times, including a stint buying and reselling seized property at Internal Revenue Service and bankruptcy auctions.[22]

In September 1995, after convincing eighteen of the peanut vendors who had worked outside the United Center to sign on as plaintiffs, Weinberg filed suit against United Center ownership, alleging that the food ban violated the Sherman Antitrust Act's provisions against "predatory" monopolization. The suit called for a preliminary injunction against the ban and demanded that the United Center pay "compensatory" and "punitive" damages for what vendors claimed amounted to the loss of $500,000 in annual income.[23]

The plaintiffs had to do more than prove that the United Center established a monopoly on food sales. Per the Sherman Act, the possession of a monopoly by a firm did not, in and of itself, warrant intervention. To elicit legal action, a monopolist had to be guilty of "maintain[ing] or enhanc[ing] monopoly power improperly" through "exclusionary, anticompetitive, or predatory conduct." In other words, the U.S. government accepted the existence of monopolies so long as they resulted from "fair" competition in which one firm came to dominate a market by offering a product that consumers preferred to that of competitors rather than by using coercive methods such as political favors, intimidation, or collusion. The government sanctioned the former type of monopoly as "innocent."[24] Moreover, the lack of precise guidelines for what constituted "improper" monopolization gave judges a lot of room to support seemingly anticompetitive business practices. This explains in large part why, as historian Ellis Hawley notes, "The great era of business consolidation, the years from 1897 to 1904, came [immediately] after the Sherman Act and not before."[25]

Weinberg and the plaintiffs argued that the monopoly over food sales established by the ban was not "innocent" because it deliberately established a barrier to entry that had nothing to do with consumer preference. They argued that the monopoly harmed consumer welfare by preventing Bulls and Blackhawks fans from taking part in the long-standing "tradition" of purchasing peanuts on their way to games. They also pointed out that the arena constituted an "essential facility" for the sale of peanuts in Chicago. Sherman prohibited denying a competitor use of a facility, even in the case that the firm denying access owned the facility, "that cannot reasonably be duplicated and to which access is necessary if one wishes to compete."[26] Weinberg and the plaintiffs insisted that the United Center qualified as such, and that the owners were thus prohibited from taking direct or indirect measures impeding vendors' access to arena patrons.

Initially, the peddlers appeared to be on strong footing regarding both claims. They clearly went out of business not because of their inability to offer a competitive product but because of an artificial barrier erected between vendors and fans. Moreover, precedent already existed for treating sports arenas as essential facilities. Coincidentally, Bill Wirtz's father, Arthur, the previous owner of Chicago Stadium, lost an antitrust case in the early 1980s based on the essential-facilities clause. After a business rival purchased the Chicago Bulls basketball team in 1972, Arthur Wirtz refused to allow the team to play in Chicago Stadium even though, as the courts ruled and reaffirmed, it was the only facility in the city at the time that could reasonably accommodate a professional basketball franchise.[27]

Despite the seeming strength of the vendors' claims, Rebecca Pallmeyer, the U.S. district court magistrate judge who first considered the suit in February 1996, denied the request for a preliminary injunction and, in turn, rejected each of the legal rationales offered by Weinberg and the plaintiffs. Pallmeyer reasoned that the ban did not single out peanut vendors in a predatory fashion, because it applied to food in general rather than peanuts alone. She also rejected the essential-facilities argument made by Weinberg, insisting that there was no "reason to conclude that, regardless of the popularity of peanuts at the game, professional sports games are the only places that peanuts can be sold or consumed." In other words, Pallmeyer implied that the vendors could hawk their snacks at other unspecified locations within the city.[28]

Diane Wood, one of the two judges who subsequently upheld Pallmeyer's findings when the case reached the Seventh Circuit Court of Appeals in 1997, added that since the United Center announced that it would not sell peanuts inside, the owners were not even engaged in the peanut sales market. "The United Center is obviously not monopolizing the market for peanuts," Wood explained; "it is staying strictly out of the peanut business."[29] But even had the arena continued to sell peanuts, the courts reasoned, the ban would be no different than the long-accepted practice of movie theaters confiscating candy purchased outside. While both Pallmeyer and Wood acknowledged that the ban posed real difficulties for the peanut peddlers, they agreed with the defendants' attorneys that these hardships constituted the outcome of the "legitimate desire to maximize profits" through "operating the United Center as a business."[30]

The opinions written by Pallmeyer and Wood made sense in the abstract. The assumptions underlying them, however, bordered on the preposterous. Pallmeyer's suggestion that "access to United Center fans is simply not essential to peanut sales" exemplified the gap between her legal reasoning and the material reality faced by the vendors. In theory, the peanut vendors, most or all of whom were licensed through the city, had the ability to set up shop on any public street corner in Chicago. But as the plaintiffs argued, there was no conceivable way that Chicagoans passing a random street corner constituted a "market" comparable to hungry basketball and hockey fans.[31] The fact that vendors like Thornton Elliott quit the enterprise altogether after the ban went into effect threw this into sharp relief. Perhaps access to United Center ticket holders was not "essential" to selling a bag of peanuts on a random street corner. However, the vendors absolutely needed this access to sell enough inventory to make a living. Neither Pallmeyer nor the Seventh Circuit judges identified a specific market within Chicago with a comparable customer base for the vendors.

The notion that the food ban failed to meet the standard of predatory business practices laid out by the Sherman Act because it did not specifically target peanuts, but rather food in general, also strained credulity. Pallmeyer noted that "the policy not only discourages peanut sales; it also discourages new business that might cater to hungry Bulls fans—popcorn vendors, hot dog stands, doughnut shops, and convenience stores are a few examples."[32] Putting aside the fact that doughnuts were rarely, if ever, the game-time choice of American sports fans, this logic ignored the history of food peddling around the old Chicago Stadium. Justice Wood even acknowledged that "peanuts are the only food sold directly outside the United Center to United Center patrons," and neither the courts nor the defendants offered any evidence to suggest that the food ban would have an impact on other types of vendors or local businesses.[33] Moreover, anyone who regularly attends games knows that peanuts have enjoyed unique popularity among fans because they can tote them through the gate and to their seats with much more ease than other fan favorites like hot dogs and cotton candy. Thus, Pallmeyer's suggestion that a victory for the vendors would set some sort of viral precedent threatening the larger community of food concessionaires was laughable.

Pallmeyer, Wood, and the other judges hearing the case also agreed that because Reinsdorf and Wirtz decided not to sell peanuts inside the United Center, they could not be accused of monopolizing the peanut business. By this reasoning, the monopoly over the food sales market resulted from a combination of "historic accident" and "business acumen" rather than "improper" predation on competitors.[34] Weinberg and the vendors tried to preempt this reasoning by designating the market in question as that for food concessions in general rather than peanuts alone. The judges pushed this aside, ignoring the fact that customers who previously purchased peanuts outside the arena now either had to go without food during games or satisfy their cravings by purchasing a different type of snack inside the United Center.[35] Regardless of which outcome predominated, it is safe to say that the latter occurred with some frequency. Even if, as Wood claimed, the team owners "stayed strictly out of the peanut business," the fact that they remained squarely in the larger food-sales market meant that the ban helped them absorb business previously secured by the vendors. Ultimately, the courts sent the message that the owners' desire to maximize profits trumped vendors' right to compete in a market where consumers still wanted the latter's product.

Although it is impossible to pinpoint the food ban's role in revenue growth

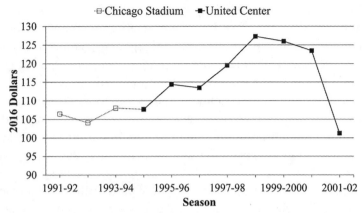

FIGURE 5.2. Price in Constant 2016 Dollars for Typical Family Basket of Concessions at a Chicago Bulls Game, 1991–2002

Source: Rodney Fort, "NBA Fan Cost Index," *Rodney's Sports Business Data*, accessed January 27, 2018, umich.app.box.com/s/41707f0b2619c0107b8b/1/320022929.

Notes: "Typical basket" defined as the sum of two small beers, four small soft drinks, four regular hot dogs, parking for one car, two game programs, and two of the least expensive adult-sized hats. Inflation adjustments made using the Bureau of Labor Statistics CPI-U for the Chicago-Gary-Kenosha Area.

at the United Center, it definitely coincided with significant price increases on items sold inside. According to data collected by *Team Marketing Report*, the real cost of a typical basket of concessions for a family of four at a Bulls game rose by more than 18 percent during the United Center's first five seasons (fig. 5.2). One of the effects of pushing the vendors out was to increase demand for food inside, which helped Reinsdorf and Wirtz create a market conducive to price hikes. Admittedly, inflation-adjusted concessions prices dropped back to their pre–United Center levels in the first few years of the new millennium, but it is probably imprudent to compare directly the costs of food and drink in the arena during the Jordan era and the costs in the years that immediately followed. The standing-room-only crowds and elevated excitement during the Bulls championship days likely supported a level of demand for in-stadium snacks and libations unparalleled in the team's history.

This seemingly small story—literally, peanuts—was about something much bigger. In sanctioning the food ban, the courts not only gave their blessing to a policy ostensibly dealing with customer behavior inside a private facility; they also empowered Reinsdorf and Wirtz to control economic activity on public property (e.g., nearby sidewalks) that they did not own. The judges' endorsement of this far-reaching corporate power was not an accident. It coincided with the federal courts' increasing embrace after 1970 of monopolists' "freedom" to maximize profits at all costs.

This shift marked a return to an unapologetically pro-corporate judicial common sense that prevailed throughout American courts during the late nineteenth and early twentieth centuries. Passage of new antitrust statutes in this earlier period came in response to the widespread view, spurred by the populist and progressive movements, that extreme concentration of capital threatened ordinary folks' economic and political freedom. According to this perspective, monopoly posed a threat not only to consumer welfare but also to democracy itself; the accumulation of unprecedented wealth by monopolistic or oligopolistic corporations endowed them with undue influence over government. However, before the Great Depression the courts' interpretation of these laws tended to enhance corporate power rather than contain it. This was particularly true in context of labor relations. In the decades following passage of the Sherman Antitrust Act in 1890, judges used the statute primarily to shield large employers from efforts by workers to organize, treating unions as an illegal restraint on trade.[36]

According to historian Andrew Wender Cohen, criminal antitrust prosecutions of workers actually increased after the 1914 passage of the Clayton Antitrust Act, which was supposed to have the opposite effect. Organized labor in cities like Chicago ultimately found enough ways to "circumvent the law" to survive and revitalize themselves during the New Deal.[37] Until then, however, the trend was clear: antitrust law favored efforts by employers to discipline workers and craftsmen. Between the opening of the twentieth century and World War I, the Justice Department and courts took high-profile antitrust action against a handful of firms, such as the Northern Securities Company and Standard Oil, charged with anticompetitive behavior. But these actions ultimately proved isolated concessions to public outcry rather than trend-setting decisions. With the onset of the First World War and the government's increasing support of business "associationalism" (cartel behavior within industries to avert price instability), policy makers turned more of a blind eye toward anticompetitive business practices like price-fixing. At the same time, they posited that monopolization was the centerpiece of an efficient and profitable industrial economy (indeed, there was some truth to the "efficiency" rhetoric). According to this logic, the real threat to the dynamism of American capitalism was not the growing concentration of economic and political power in the hands of a select few but the activists who railed against corporate power. By the 1920s, this "common sense" was deeply entrenched among lawmakers, and the government effectively ceased antitrust prosecutions of big business.[38]

The privileged treatment enjoyed by monopolists vis-à-vis antitrust law eroded somewhat with the Great Depression. Widespread economic suffering fueled an emerging consensus that the right to unrestrained profitability for the few should not necessarily trump economic justice for the many. In the context of labor relations, this emerging common sense took the form of New Deal legislation like the National Industrial Recovery Act (NIRA) of 1933 and the Wagner Act of 1935, which established workers' legal right to organize regardless of antitrust rules. These new laws did not address concerns that many Americans had about the concentration of corporate capital or anti-competitive market behavior. In fact, as historian Jefferson Cowie recounts, the NIRA encouraged anticompetitive practices like price-fixing among large firms by "suspending" antitrust regulations for business, which the government hoped would "prevent cutthroat competition" and, by extension, help stabilize markets. Nevertheless, the new legislation signaled the growing embrace by legislators and their constituents of government regulation of markets in the name of the working and middle classes' economic security. The Supreme Court soon followed suit in 1937, upholding state minimum-wage laws and the Wagner Act (in 1941 the court ruled in favor of sweeping exemptions from antitrust law for unions).[39]

During the late 1930s, government officials used antitrust law more liberally to punish powerful firms for anticompetitive practices, such as predatory pricing, that hurt consumers. Nobody embodied this trend more than Thurman Arnold, who President Franklin D. Roosevelt appointed to head the Justice Department's Antitrust Division in 1938. While Arnold roundly rejected the traditional populist refrain that big necessarily equaled bad when it came to business, he acknowledged that many large corporations used their privileged market position to exploit and abuse consumers and smaller competitors. During his first two years in the post, Arnold oversaw the dramatic expansion of the budget, staff, and caseload of the Antitrust Division, and ultimately helped foster what historian Alan Brinkley dubs the "anti-monopoly moment" of the New Deal.[40]

The moment was short lived, at least in terms of the zeal that characterized Arnold's leadership during 1938 and 1939. As Brinkley explains, the government's antimonopoly crusade lost steam as a result of several developments, including a shift in the government's attention to mobilizing for war, as well as the increasing priority given to "less controversial" forms of economic regulation such as fiscal policy (e.g., taxing and spending) after 1940. But while Arnold's campaign petered out, after the New Deal a residual skepticism of monopolists' tendency toward corporate malfeasance lingered within the federal government and courts. Part of this no doubt had to do with the appointment of Arnold and many like-minded New Dealers to federal judgeships after their service in the Roosevelt administration.[41]

This skepticism, along with the postwar emphasis on driving growth through widespread access to consumer goods at competitive prices, led the federal government to maintain a mildly adversarial stance toward the abusive application of monopoly power after World War II. To be sure, between the end of the war and the late 1960s, antitrust enforcement failed to stymie—in fact, the Justice Department and judges mostly ignored—the steady increase in large firms' market share. That said, relative to their pre–New Deal predecessors, federal agencies and courts in the quarter century after World War II remained more willing to entertain the possibility that market domination by a single corporation or a small cadre of firms could pose problems for the public that necessitated government intervention.[42] Specifically, the Justice Department and courts remained concerned about monopolistic "coercion": the use of what legal scholar Rudolph Peritz describes as "grossly unequal bargaining power" to force the hand of consumers, competitors, or small businesses. For example, in cases like *Klor's v. Broadway-Hale Stores* (1959) and *Simpson v. Union Oil* (1964), the courts rejected the legality of efforts by monopolists to dictate the specific terms by which local retailers could sell the monopolists' products, and they generally defended the rights of small-business owners to operate independently of larger firms.[43]

This changed as the economic crises of the early 1970s provided an opening for reactionary critics of postwar competition policy to push the pendulum back toward the unqualified defense of firms' freedom to maximize profits. A new vanguard of antitrust scholars at the University of Chicago, most notably Robert Bork and Richard Posner, popularized a set of theories about market competition that aligned seamlessly with business's assault on relatively inclusive economic policy that redistributed wealth downward. They argued that monopoly represented the natural and legitimate outcome of free-market competition because, according to them, market dominance inherently signaled consumer preference for the monopoly firm's product. These scholars also insisted that rather than engendering artificially high prices, monopoly firms inevitably reduced costs by streamlining production under a single entity, that barriers to entry represented a fiction of leftists' imagination, and that all markets remained open to competent competitors.[44]

Ignoring a long history of coercive practices by monopolists, jurists like Bork and Posner assumed that monopoly necessarily represented the outcome of free-market competition and had nothing to do with firms' power to influence policy decisions. As one trio of political economists points out, this emerging school of legal scholarship swept aside the possibility that powerful firms could use coercion against their competitors, and it did so "by fiat at the level of pure theory."[45] For the likes of Bork and Posner, monopoly simply could not pose a threat to competition. In their view, a monopolistic firm always represented the apex of efficiency within a given market, so its dominance confirmed that competition was working as it should. Any government efforts to interfere in the marketplace thus threatened individual "liberty" by penalizing those who had legitimately cornered a market.

Bork, Posner, and their adherents distorted the definition of free-market competition offered by economists, even those who shared their commitment to wealth maximization. For example, Milton Friedman, the high priest of American neoclassical—that is, pro-free market—economics, explicitly rejected the notion of competition as "personal rivalry, with one individual seeking to outdo his known competitor." He insisted that "free" markets depended on a situation in which "no one participant can determine the terms on which other participants shall have access." For Friedman, monopoly was the legitimate outcome of freely competitive markets only if it resulted from the merit of a firm's product and the efficiency of its production practices, not from active efforts by the firm to sabotage its competitors. By contrast, the Chicago School legal theorists arbitrarily expanded their definition of "competition" to include the latter, championing a no-holds-barred view of the marketplace.[46]

The Chicago School followers were right to argue that large-scale production, in and of itself, was not necessarily harmful to consumers. Contrary to the pronouncements of die-hard antimonopolists, large firms often achieve greater efficiency from a more streamlined division of labor. If properly regulated, this increased efficiency could translate into lower prices and wider availability of certain products.[47] But even if the Chicago School legal theorists were correct to link the scale of production to efficiency, they ignored the obvious point that large corporations would be free to manipulate markets through financial and political power if left unregulated. Big firms with the resources necessary to influence political and judicial decision making did not have to best competitors by developing better manufacturing processes or offering up superior products and services. Instead, they could rely on strong-arm tactics such as intimidation and collusion, as well as political lobbying, to ensure that they never had to risk being out-competed. The Chicago Bulls' campaign against peanut vendors was a perfect case in point.

By the time the peanut vendors took their case to court, the American legal, political, and economic establishments had thoroughly undermined any form of progressive antitrust regulation. The reactionary positions of the Chicago School enjoyed wide purchase within the American judiciary by the 1980s. Moreover, as economist Edward Herman points out, U.S. presidents Ronald Reagan and George H. W. Bush "aggressively dismantled" antitrust enforcement by slashing funding for the Justice Department's Antitrust Division and replacing its leadership with cronies sympathetic to the Chicago School. The gutting of antitrust enforcement continued under Clinton, a high-profile action against Microsoft notwithstanding. At the same time, large firms amassed small armies of economists and lawyers to assist in mounting antitrust defenses, a move that further inoculated big business against successful prosecution.[48]

Unfortunately for the vendors, some of the country's most ardent defenders of the Chicago School sat on the Seventh Circuit Court of Appeals. In fact, Posner himself served as chief justice of the court during the period that the vendors filed both the initial suit and their appeals. While Posner did not weigh in on the peanut case, the judges who did embraced his stance on the monopoly question. They equated actions that clearly violated Friedman's notion of free-market competition with smart business practices as opposed to predatory manipulation of the marketplace. For Pallmeyer and Wood, the fact that the food ban served the economic interests of the United Center was enough to conclude that it was instituted for "valid business reasons."[49] In the judges' minds, protecting market freedom was synonymous with protecting large firms' ability to maximize profits, and so there was little that the arena owners could do that would violate antitrust law as long as it enhanced profitability.

Not surprisingly, Pallmeyer, Wood, and the other district and circuit court judges who heard the case did their best to sidestep the issue of consumer welfare. Obviously, fans who wanted to buy peanuts outside the United Center were being disadvantaged not only by being deprived of a product that they wanted but also by having to replace it with something more expensive from inside the arena. The fact that some fans tried to sneak peanuts into the facility even after the ban went into effect proved that the vendors' disappearance had little to do with the natural workings of the market. At one point in her opinion, Pallmeyer flippantly noted, "To the court's knowledge, the unavailability of peanuts has not, in this amazing basketball season, apparently deterred attendance at Bulls games."[50] This simply avoided the question at hand, as the vendors had not argued that the food ban harmed consumer welfare in the market for tickets; their suit dealt specifically with the market for food sales. The effort to equate the high spirits of Bulls fans in general with the impossibility of predatory business practices on the part of United Center ownership reiterated the courts' refusal to conceive of the arena and its management as anything but a marvel of free-market competition.

Tellingly, none of the legal rationales offered by judges like Pallmeyer dealt with the fact that the defendants were in the business of major-league sports, as opposed to some other industry. Someone familiar with the history of the sports business might assume otherwise. The U.S. government had a long history of shielding the major-league sports business from antitrust legislation. The tolerance of monopolistic behavior of leagues and teams by the judicial branch and Justice Department reaches back to the 1922 Supreme Court decision in *Federal Baseball v. National League.* The plaintiffs in the case sued major-league baseball teams for colluding to block franchises from competitor leagues from participating in the market for professional baseball. The court ruled, however, that major-league baseball—the ruling did not apply to other sports—was exempt from antitrust law by reasoning that it was not "commerce" in the conventional sense of the term. According to a unanimous decision by the judges, it was more game than business, and thus the government should not hold it to regulatory standards imposed on other sectors of the economy. While several defendants challenged the ruling in ensuing decades, none of the challenges led to a decisive reversal of the original decision. As sports economist Andrew Zimbalist notes, MLB's antitrust exemption remains intact, albeit with a high degree of "ambiguity" as to its exact extent.[51]

Other major leagues like the NBA never received the same sort of sweeping antitrust exemption enjoyed by MLB. However, they did receive more limited, special protections from the government. These included the passage by Congress in 1961 of the Sports Broadcasting Act, which explicitly permitted major leagues without an antitrust exemption to sell broadcasting rights to network television as leagues (i.e., cartels) instead of as individual teams. This eliminated competition between franchises in the selling of rights, allowing leagues to fix the fees networks paid to broadcast their games at exorbitantly inflated prices. The Justice Department also tolerated other forms of anticompetitive behavior by major leagues other than MLB, namely repeated mergers with smaller competitor leagues. The department also did nothing to prevent the new consolidated, monopoly leagues from artificially limiting the number of franchises in individual cities to one, or sometimes two, teams. This antitrust immunity has enhanced teams' ability to practice a range of predatory, inefficient behaviors harmful to consumers, ranging from price gouging to artificially denying new pro sports teams entry into urban markets that could support them.[52]

The courts never cited this long history of special treatment of major-league sports in taking Reinsdorf and Wirtz off the hook for blocking market access for the peddlers. This story, then, was not about the unique history of antitrust law as it related to professional sports. It was about the sports business availing itself of much larger transformations in the American legal

system. These transformations empowered corporations from many industries to employ anticompetitive tactics for manipulating markets, helping
them capture wealth previously held by smaller competitors and consumers.
As former secretary of labor Robert Reich points out, in recent decades the
government has sanctioned expanded monopoly powers that harm consumers and enhance corporate political power in industries like banking, phar-
maceuticals, health care, telecommunications, and agribusiness. The driving
force behind the vendor purge, in other words, was the national campaign by
pro-corporate legal scholars and their allies to ensure that the federal courts
and Justice Department reverted to their traditional role of justifying and
enforcing exclusionary capitalism.[53]

Economists tend to overlook the role of these larger historical forces in
their explanations of the expanding market power of teams like the Bulls in
the past thirty to forty years. Instead, they focus overwhelmingly on the specific historical relationship between the major leagues and the government.
For example, James Quirk and Rodney Fort, two of the foremost authorities
on the economics of sports, suggest that "all of the many problems of the pro
team sports business" emanate from the government's allegedly unique tolerance of monopolistic, anticompetitive behavior by the major leagues. They
advocate for Congress to eliminate the exemption of major leagues from antitrust law so that "the role of the government and the courts in pro team
sports would be what it is in every other industry, as a corrective to monopolistic abuses if they arise again in the future."[54]

Such diagnoses and prescriptions hold some water but tend toward over-
generalization. Few would dismiss the formal and informal antitrust exemptions enjoyed by pro sports as irrelevant. Moreover, enabling the Justice Department to take antitrust action against the industry (e.g., by breaking up
leagues) might curb some of its abuses of power; but other abuses, like the
purge of independent street vendors, had nothing to do with the specific relationship between the sports business and the courts and Justice Department.
As a result, eliminating formal and informal protections from antitrust law
for the sports business would do little to stop such behavior, provided team
owners remain wealthy and well connected. A big reason that economists
like Quirk and Fort miss this point is that they fail to acknowledge that the
government tolerated a significant and increasing amount of anticompetitive
action in many sectors of the economy at the end of the twentieth century.
This explains the fact that key measures of the degree of monopolization in
American markets have risen markedly in recent decades. For example, according to John Bellamy Foster and Robert McChesney, between 1950 and
2007 "the total gross profits of the top two hundred U.S. corporations as a

percentage of total business profits in the U.S. economy" went from 13 percent to more than 30 percent. Data such as these strongly suggest that orthodox economists like Quirk and Fort are wrong to posit that, in general—that is, outside of major-league sports—"markets work."[55] Thus, forcing the courts and Justice Department to treat major-league sports just like "every other industry" is no panacea for the predatory conduct of team owners like Reinsdorf and Wirtz.

All this emphasizes the point that the scope and influence of monopoly power within the sports business changed over time in response to trends that transcended the major leagues. In the case of skyrocketing ticket prices in the 1990s, teams like the Bulls took greater advantage of an existing monopoly power—that is, status as the sole local seller of NBA tickets—to profit from growing income inequality. When it came to forcing peddlers out of local markets in food sales, owners like Reinsdorf succeeded in creating a monopoly power never before seen because an increasingly probusiness judiciary gave them the green light to do so.

The Thousand-Foot Ordinance: Government Intervention on Behalf of Free-Market Monopoly

The ultimate outcome of the vendors' suit remained in question until the U.S. Supreme Court refused to hear an appeal by the plaintiffs in March 1998.[56] In the meantime, facing a potentially protracted legal struggle and uncertainty as to whether the vendors might eventually stumble across a sympathetic judge during the appeals process, Reinsdorf and Wirtz moved to ensure that the vendors could never return regardless of the outcome of their lawsuit. To do so, they solicited the help of local politicians in Chicago. In August 1995, just days after Weinberg and the vendors filed their initial suit, Walter Burnett Jr., the newly elected alderman of the Twenty-Seventh Ward (which contained the United Center) introduced a city ordinance banning licensed street vendors from within one thousand feet of the arena.[57]

As in the case of the new Comiskey Park, arena ownership and city officials cited pedestrian "congestion" and concerns over vendors forcing fans to walk in the street, and the City Council passed the ordinance unanimously in October 1995. While Weinberg and Beyer tried to organize the vendors to pressure the City Council to reverse the decision, their efforts quickly stalled.[58] The passage of the ordinance meant that, even if the courts struck down the food ban, the vendors would still be out of work, and Reinsdorf and Wirtz would enjoy an indefinite and uncontested monopoly over all food sales in and around the arena. Moreover, it extended the scope of the existing measures against peddling, because it affected not only the peanut vendors but also those selling souvenirs.

This was Chicago, where no political favor goes unpaid, and passage of the ordinance was no exception. Years later Burnett explained that United Center officials "tried to make it look like it wasn't just greed . . . but it was clear from the beginning that what they really wanted was the peddlers' business. . . . I've never been pushed so hard on anything in my life." In exchange for introducing the ordinance, Burnett asked Reinsdorf and Wirtz to employ a handful of the alderman's constituents to work in United Center concessions stands. Reinsdorf and Wirtz agreed.[59]

That was not all they doled out. On March 25, 1995, a few months before the introduction of the ordinance in the City Council, United Center ownership donated $2,000 to Alderman Burnett's campaign committee. The donation was the first made to Burnett by Reinsdorf and Wirtz—the contributor was officially listed as the United Center—and the largest to Burnett's campaign committee during the fund-raising cycle that spanned the first half of 1995.[60] The contribution falls short of the legal definition of bribery; it was not against the law. But even if the arena owners did not make it explicit that they expected Burnett to introduce the ordinance in exchange for the donation, we know from extensive research by political scientists that large campaign contributions create a "generalized sense of obligation" among politicians toward major donors.[61] Burnett's willingness to do the bidding of Reinsdorf and Wirtz helped him secure their ongoing financial support in his runs for reelection. Between February 1996 and December 2015, United Center ownership donated at least $41,500 to campaign committees controlled by Burnett.[62]

Burnett was not the only alderperson who received significant financial support from team owners before and after using their clout in the City Council to get rid of independent vendors. Eleventh Ward alderman Patrick Huels, who represented the part of the city with the new Comiskey Park and served as Mayor Daley's "whip" in the City Council, the councilman who bears responsibility for "rounding up" votes in support of the mayor's proposals, was also involved in the process in a way that mirrored, and in some ways went beyond, Burnett's role.[63] The new Comiskey Park (renamed U.S. Cellular Field from 2003 to 2016 and Guaranteed Rate Field thereafter) was the home of Major League Baseball's Chicago White Sox, the other major-league franchise owned by Jerry Reinsdorf. Between the beginning of 1987 and the end of 1992, Reinsdorf (by way of the Chicago White Sox) contributed at least $6,750 to Huels's campaign committee.[64] Then, in 1993, Huels personally introduced the same thousand-foot ordinance for the new Comiskey Park, which passed shortly thereafter. This raised eyebrows not only because of the donations but also because Huels's actions generated a clear conflict of interest: he owned a security firm on Reinsdorf's payroll. City Council records of the vote on the Comiskey ordinance show that Huels abstained from voting on the measure—this would have been consistent with ethics guidelines—but John Carpenter and Charles Nicodemus of the *Sun-Times* reported that Huels voted in favor of it on the basis of an audio recording of the meeting.[65]

After the passage of the ordinance at the new Comiskey Park, Reinsdorf continued to funnel donations to Huels—between July 1993 and May 1997 they amounted to at least $7,000—and in 1995 the alderman eagerly threw his weight in the City Council behind the newly proposed antivendor ordinance at the United Center.[66] As chair of the council's Committee on Transportation, Huels endorsed Burnett's proposed ordinance on the council floor, brought it to a vote, and personally voted in its favor. Given his position as Daley's floor leader and his reputation for, in the words of two *Tribune* staff writers, "using persuasion, favors and arm-twisting" to ensure that legislation that he (and Daley) coveted sailed through the City Council, Huels's backing was crucial.[67] Moreover, he lent his vote even though his security firm remained on Reinsdorf's payroll. He thus influenced the adoption of ordinances with clear financial benefits for both the Bulls and White Sox while not only receiving considerable campaign financing from Reinsdorf but also being in his employ. The former arrangement constituted a legal form of influence; the legality of the latter is questionable at best. Huels eventually had to step down in 1997 because of another controversy, and neither Reinsdorf nor Wirtz ever received any form of reprimand.[68]

The enlistment of aldermen like Burnett and Huels by United Center ownership epitomized the inner workings of municipal politics in the Windy City in the New Gilded Age. While the first Mayor Daley depended in part on contributions from the local business community to fund his runs for reelection and maintain his grip over the "old" Democratic machine, these contributions were not the primary source of his political power. More important was the vast system of patronage he exploited. Daley the elder and his political allies used their control over the distribution of city and county employment to secure votes, campaign labor, and campaign contributions from ordinary Chicagoans. The machine demanded that, in exchange for their livelihoods, municipal employees vote for Daley Sr. and the aldermen he endorsed, "volunteer" to work on their campaigns (e.g., by door knocking), and sacrifice some of their wages in the form of donations to machine candidates. This arrangement guaranteed the repeated reelection of the first

Mayor Daley, as well as election of a solid majority of aldermen who willingly rubber-stamped his legislative proposals.[69]

By the time Richard M. Daley became mayor in 1989, several developments had severely curtailed the viability of the old patronage-based machine tactics. First, slower economic and tax revenue growth limited the funding available for expanding municipal payrolls. Second, federal courts intervened by issuing the Shakman decree in 1972. The decree and its subsequent amendments outlawed compelling city employees to provide political support, campaign labor, or campaign contributions, and prohibited political considerations in municipal hiring decisions. Third, Harold Washington not only endorsed the Shakman decree but also diverted Community Development Block Grant money away from funding patronage jobs in favor of grassroots organizations. And finally, the cost of running effective political campaigns, even at the local level, had spiraled out of control because of the expanded use of television advertising, advanced polling techniques, and more sophisticated public relations and political consulting operations. Modest contributions from public employees could not cover these escalating costs.[70]

In response, Daley the younger fashioned what political scientist Dick Simpson terms the "New Daley Machine." This apparatus depended far more than its predecessor on corporate contributions, particularly from the service industries that formed the backbone of the postindustrial Loop, such as high-powered law firms, banking, stock and options trading, and tourism. The cash from these sources funded "modern high-tech" campaigns that mirrored national races in their ballooning investment in professional media and consulting services. In his 1995 reelection run alone, Daley spent $5.6 million. His expanded trove of campaign cash also helped him establish his own rubber-stamp coalition in the City Council, as transferring funds to the campaigns of aldermanic candidates or using his enhanced media presence to disseminate endorsements cultivated political loyalty.[71]

The fund-raising trends embodied by Richard M. Daley trickled down to aldermanic campaigns. Candidates for seats in Chicago's City Council also had to rely less on patronage, so they compensated by following Daley's lead in vying for votes using state-of-the-art tactics. Daley often, but not always, contributed generously to aldermanic candidates he endorsed from his own war chest. This meant that those running for City Council seats started depending more on corporate donors of their own, especially within their respective wards. By 1995, successful aldermanic candidates engaged in what Simpson describes as "the most contentious races" were spending, on average, more than $93,000 on their campaigns. In that year, approximately

40 percent of contributions to such campaigns came directly from corporations, and much of the remainder came from individual donors who owned local businesses.[72] The contributions by United Center ownership to the likes of Burnett and Huels demonstrate the outsized roles of corporate donors in campaign finance at the aldermanic level. Reinsdorf and Wirtz regularly handed over four-figure donations to candidates in these races, and sometimes the amounts were downright staggering given the average overall spending. For example, within the span of eight days in January 2015, they gave Burnett a total of $12,500 in cash and in-kind contributions![73]

Reinsdorf and Wirtz did not stop with Burnett and Huels. Between 1987 and 2016 they contributed to at least twenty-nine different aldermanic candidates running in at least twenty-one different wards.[74] This wide distribution of campaign funds to City Council incumbents and hopefuls translated into increased influence over municipal policy making in two ways. Most basically, it put United Center ownership on the political radar of many lawmakers casting votes in the City Council. If an issue affecting local sports stadiums (or their team owners' investments) came up for consideration in a committee or on the council floor, aldermen who received donations from United Center ownership would be more likely to see things as Reinsdorf and Wirtz did. Spreading around their donations also ensured that they placed themselves in the good graces of aldermen who, while not necessarily representing wards containing Reinsdorf or Wirtz developments, wielded significant influence within the council. Such was the case with Ed Burke, the Fourteenth Ward alderman who served as chair of the City Council's powerful Finance Committee from 1983 to 1987, and again since 1989. It seems doubtful that Burke's position as the most important decision maker, after the mayor, on fiscal matters in Chicago had nothing to do with the fact that United Center ownership gave him at least $72,450 in campaign contributions from 1989 to 2015.[75]

Reinsdorf and Wirtz's cultivation of influence over council members by way of campaign finance gives the lie to the claims made by the team owners' lawyers that their food sales monopoly resulted from "nonpredatory" (i.e., free-market) business practices, and by extension that the government had no right to interfere in defense of the vendors. Reinsdorf and Wirtz recognized that, given fans' preference to pay less for peanuts, the vendors posed a legitimate competitive threat, and eliminating them required more than engaging in idealized free-market competition as envisioned by economists like Friedman. The moment that actual free-market competition threatened their bottom line, the owners muscled local government officials into rigging the market in their favor. Reinsdorf and Wirtz, in other words, endorsed government intervention in the economy only so long as it helped them increase their profits.

Even the *Tribune*, the mouthpiece of Chicago's elite, struggled to come to terms with the inconsistent and self-serving embrace of allegedly free-market competition on the part of United Center ownership. Lambasting the new ordinance, the paper's editorial page opined, "For examples of the sort of enterprise that economists extol and politicians praise, it would be hard to beat the men and women who sell peanuts . . . outside the United Center."[76] The *Tribune*'s dismay notwithstanding, the ordinance was consistent with broader trends in urban capitalism in the New Gilded Age. After 1970, municipal governments dramatically expanded efforts to insulate private investment from risk through mechanisms like massive tax breaks (much more on this in the next chapter). Ironically, as municipalities intervened to protect the interests of capitalists, the capitalists themselves often backed brutal cuts to government aid to the poor because that aid violated the tenets of "individual freedom" and "personal responsibility." In practice, this resulted in what one pair of political economists describe as "one rule for the masses and another for elites," and the United Center anti-peddling ordinance exemplified this double standard in action. Indeed, Reinsdorf himself denigrated public "welfare" programs while demanding that the City of Chicago threaten coercive action against a group of independent entrepreneurs who had played by the rules of free-market competition all along. The peddlers, who paid the city for their yearly operating license, faced fines of up to $500 and possible arrest if they braved selling their wares around the arena.[77] The police patrolling the area around the stadium thus became a publicly funded security service for Reinsdorf and Wirtz.

The methods used by Reinsdorf and Wirtz to secure passage of the ordinance are noteworthy. While there is no evidence that the owners' success in court owed to personal or political connections (e.g., with the judges), things worked differently with the ordinance. Reinsdorf and Wirtz's personal, professional, and political connections, as well as their vast economic resources, provided them with privileged access to the City Council. Any number of "incentives"—jobs for constituents, free Bulls tickets, campaign contributions—might have convinced local lawmakers to do the team owners' bidding. The disproportionate political influence of urban capitalists in their cities was nothing new, but this influence grew significantly at the end of the twentieth century along with the skyrocketing corporate money funneled into politics through "legal" channels like campaign committees. Expanded political influence among the wealthy was both cause and effect of the massive redistribution of wealth and income over the previous thirty to forty years. The rich used campaign contributions as leverage in pushing politicians to enact profit-friendly policies; and as those policies helped them capture more of the wealth pie, they spent increasing sums on influencing lawmakers.[78] This allowed team owners like Reinsdorf and Wirtz to augment the scope of their monopoly powers and come to dominate previously "free" markets.

What was thus emerging on the Near West Side during the 1990s was a process through which private commercial landholders simultaneously mobilized federal judges and municipal officials in support of their bid to assert total control over a market that had historically operated on public street corners and sidewalks. The favorable view of the food ban by the monopoly-friendly district and circuit courts meant that the Bulls and Blackhawks could use decisions ostensibly pertaining to conduct within the United Center to manipulate the viability of public spaces outside the arena as sites for the independent sale of peanuts. On their own, the court rulings made the street corners and sidewalks useless to the vendors; they did not make the vendors' presence illegal. The ordinance changed that, supplementing the implicit control over public property bestowed upon Reinsdorf and Wirtz by the courts with the option of calling on local law enforcement to forcibly remove vendors from any city-owned land within a seventy-plus-acre area surrounding the United Center.[79] Ownership of the sidewalks, street corners, and alleys in the area still technically resided with the city, but this mattered less than the fact that the ordinance transformed the City Council and police into proxies for arena ownership.

The ordinance exemplified a more general push at the end of the twentieth century to privatize Chicago's public space for the benefit of private corporations. The anti-peddling ordinances at stadiums in the 1990s—the City Council passed all the stadium and arena ordinances between 1990 and 1995—constituted only part of a larger campaign against vendors that also involved the introduction of ordinances at sites in or on the periphery of the Loop, as well as a cluster of gentrifying North Side community areas like Lake View and Lincoln Square (map 5.1). The transformation of Chicago's municipal code into a staunchly anti-peddling document in the last decade of the twentieth century signaled a new, more systematic embrace by local officials of restricting access to public space in the interests of the leisure, hospitality, and real-estate industries. It also marked a stark departure from the policies of the populist administration of Harold Washington during the 1980s. According to a 1986 *Tribune* report, Washington "encouraged food vendors to set up their stands along the State Street Mall" and initiated the licensing of local street entertainers.[80]

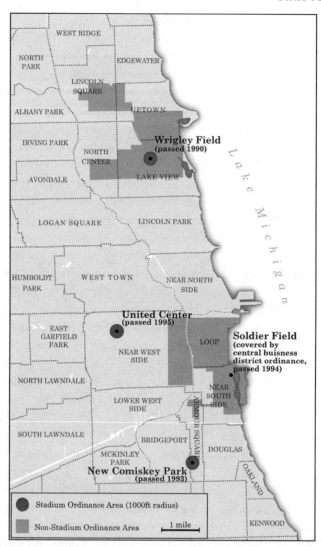

MAP 5.1. Selected Antipeddling Ordinances in Chicago's Loop and North Side Passed during the 1990s
Source: Shapefiles obtained from City of Chicago, *Chicago Data Portal*. Non-stadium antipeddling ordinances mapped using street boundaries provided in Municipal Code of Chicago, 4-244-140, accessed
January 27, 2018, www.amlegal.com/codes/client/chicago_il/.

Richard M. Daley, however, saw peddlers as eyesores or, at best, pesky
competition for his corporate allies. In addition to backing stadium owners' war against food vendors, he waged a high-profile campaign during the
early 1990s against independent newsstand operators, many of whom sold
papers and magazines in the Loop. He claimed that it was his desire to "clean

the city" that led him to back the passage of a 1991 ordinance limiting the number of newsstands in Chicago and imposing steep licensing fees that put many existing stands out of business.[81] The desire must have been especially strong, because between 1992 and the end of Daley's tenure as mayor in 2011, the City Council passed no fewer than twenty-six ordinances or ordinance amendments dealing with the prohibition of peddlers from certain stretches of public sidewalk.[82] Today, no-peddling placards are ubiquitous throughout the city's affluent and up-and-coming neighborhoods (fig. 5.3).

Chicago was not the only city where street vendors found themselves under siege by alliances between wealthy landholders and urban policy makers during the 1990s. The campaign waged against peddlers by business improvement districts (BIDs) in New York City began around the same time as Daley's crusade. BIDs are private associations of property owners that bankroll what urbanist Ryan Devlin summarizes as supplemental "sanitation, security, maintenance and planning" services for a particular grouping of blocks in the hopes of growing local commerce and property values. During the 1990s, several prominent BIDs in the Big Apple threw their weight behind council measures intended to reduce the amount of sidewalk that vendors

FIGURE 5.3. Chicago No-Peddling Placard
Source: Paul Sableman, www.flickr.com/photos/pasa/4472114122, accessed October 22, 2017 (used under Creative Commons license).

could legally use; council members used the same sort of flimsy arguments about pedestrian "congestion" as their counterparts in Chicago.[83]

The passage of one of these measures, Local Law 45, significantly reduced the availability of sidewalk space to vendors by instituting a new series of requirements on legal peddling operations—for example, a new mandated distance between a magazine vendor's table and subway entrances. According to sociologist Mitchell Duneier, up to that point New York City law provided for "plenty of space for those who wanted to engage in entrepreneurial activity on the sidewalk." But the new ordinances, the BIDs' successful efforts to increase the harassment of vendors by private security and city police, as well as their strategic placement of new planters in spots traditionally occupied by peddlers, made such entrepreneurial activity much more difficult.[84]

The assaults by public officials and corporations against the street economy in New York and Chicago were part of a larger trend in the urban United States toward using new land-use regulations to privatize sidewalks and flush out street vendors who lacked significant political or economic power. The desire of more established retailers to eliminate direct competition only partially explains this trend. As Duneier explains, it also owed to the rise during the last two decades of the twentieth century of a new "law and order" politics allegedly geared toward improving urban residents' quality of life. Ongoing central-city deindustrialization and cuts to social welfare spending under Reagan contributed to burgeoning homeless populations in central cities, and mayors obsessed with cultivating a positive image for their locales mounted "unrelenting campaign[s]" against the unhoused.[85]

These campaigns targeted not just the homeless and panhandlers but also sidewalk peddlers who allegedly offended the senses of the urban gentry. Vendors, even those with places to live, found themselves caught up in massive police and private security dragnets. In many places, officials justified the new approach not only by citing pedestrian safety but also by pointing to then-new ideas about urban disorder such as the so-called broken-windows theory. The theory, popularized by social scientists George Kelling and James Wilson in the early 1980s, posited that any form of visible "minor disorder" would set off a chain reaction of crime by indicating to potential criminals that the neighborhood in question lacked sufficient monitoring by residents and police. One of many problems with such justifications, as Duneier points out, is that they assumed that vendors engaged in "innocent entrepreneurial activity" signaled the same form of "disorder" as vandalized vehicles or broken store windows.[86]

The hollowness of such an assumption becomes apparent when one takes a closer look at street vendors and realizes, as Duneier did while conducting his sidewalk ethnography in Greenwich Village, that "many citizens enjoy the presence of the vendors on the sidewalk."[87] The available firsthand accounts from the peanut vendors in Chicago corroborate this claim. According to Charlie Beyer, prior to the vendor purge, fans on their way to see a game at one of Chicago's sports venues genuinely enjoyed interacting with the peddlers: "The feedback I would get from other people was that they loved—it wasn't just that they loved the cheaper prices, they loved the interaction with folks. . . . I think people enjoyed that sense of community . . . that was like part of the game for them, was getting their bag of peanuts before they went in or even just saying hello to me before. . . . I know a lot of people knew who the vendors were that they passed by, whether it was Jerry or me or Ralph."[88] The irony here is hard to miss. As many touted the Bulls as a key to breaking down social barriers within the city, the elimination of the vendors marked the end of one of the few concrete contexts in which affluent fans interacted face to face with Chicago's working classes.

The disappearance of the vendors also made little sense in terms of economic development in West Haven and Chicago more broadly. Research on street vendors suggests that they have a positive economic impact locally because they tend to buy their supplies from wholesalers and retailers inside or not far from the neighborhoods in which they work. This helps sustain and grow local businesses and employment.[89] The successful efforts of United Center ownership to monopolize food and souvenir revenues in West Haven precluded such positive ripple effects. Since owners and players typically live outside the neighborhoods—and often outside the cities—where their teams play, revenues that go into their pockets tend to leak out of the local area.[90]

Those versed in sports economics might argue that anti-peddling ordinances at major-league venues owed to the refusal by the courts, Congress, and Justice Department to invoke antitrust law to rectify the artificial scarcity of teams engineered by league officials. This explanation makes sense intuitively. The absence of antitrust enforcement encouraged teams to act with impunity in threatening to relocate unless local governments bowed to their demands, especially because league officials regularly promised to punish host cities refusing to comply by blocking the import of a new franchise. Reinsdorf's use of threats of relocation to secure massive government subsidies for the new Comiskey Park exemplified this sort of exploitative behavior.

However, the nationwide proliferation of anti-vending legislation confirms that the extension and entrenchment of major-league teams' monopoly powers in the early 2000s sometimes arose from trends operating beyond the pro sports business. Local governments in this period rushed to privatize public space around many types of commercial real-estate developments;

stadiums were not unique in this regard. Moreover, threats of relocation by Reinsdorf or Wirtz were simply not in play when the City Council passed the anti-vendor ordinance. The arena had just opened. The Bulls and Blackhawks were not going anywhere, and the refusal of local politicians to pass the ordinance would not have changed that. City Hall handed the owners exclusive rights to food and souvenir sales during basketball and hockey games even though Reinsdorf and Wirtz were stuck on the Near West Side for the foreseeable future. What mattered, in the end, was not the fact that they owned major-league teams but that they belonged to a larger class of wealthy and well-connected urban capitalists.

Race and Revenue at the United Center

Daley's equation of pushing out peddlers with "cleaning" the city suggests that there was more to the anti-vending crusades at the United Center and elsewhere than sparing powerful landowners from a little bit of competition.[91] This choice of words put a palatable gloss on what amounted to using the privatization of once-public spaces to remove low-income and working-class people, especially nonwhites, from new sites of urban consumption. Mayors obsessed with refashioning their cities as tourist-friendly, as well as team owners set on cultivating a moneyed fan base, feared that such residents would scare away potential patrons.

Although team owners rarely voiced these fears publicly, occasionally their anxieties over occupying stadiums and arenas in neighborhoods they perceived as too black came to light. One such instance occurred back in 1958, while *Chicago Daily News* reporter Bill Furlong successfully eavesdropped on a private meeting of Major League Baseball owners by listening through an air vent in an adjacent room. Furlong heard the Washington Senators president Calvin Griffith explain the team's impending move to Minneapolis: "The trend in Washington is getting to be all colored."[92] Among franchise executives, Griffith was far from alone in harboring these sentiments, and by the 1980s and early 1990s they were anything but a relic. Amid persistent segregation and economic decline, owners desperately wanted to flee inner cities with large low-income black populations to bring their operations closer to what market studies indicated were increasingly suburban, white fan bases.[93] Reinsdorf admitted as much in a 2007 interview in which he talked about efforts, eventually aborted, to move the White Sox to the western suburb of Addison: "If you draw a circle around Comiskey Park/US Cellular Field of 25 miles, 40% of that circle is Lake Michigan, you know? Another 20% or something like that was the projects; *those people* didn't go to baseball games.

When you're in a retail business, which is what baseball is, you want to be in the middle of your market area. So we had 60% of our market area that didn't produce customers. If we went to Addison and we drew a circle of 25 miles around it, we were right in our market area."[94] Reinsdorf's account confirms that teams remaining in blighted areas within city limits worried that placing well-to-do ticket holders in proximity to poor neighborhood residents, especially African American ones—his use of the term "projects" has an unmistakably racial connotation—might be bad for business.

Similar issues were at play at the United Center. As early as 1987, one local community activist predicted that plans to renovate Chicago Stadium or build a new sports facility on the Near West Side would include measures to "better buffer its fans' parking from the negative elements within the Henry Horner Housing Projects."[95] United Center ownership's actions validated this hypothesis. They surrounded the United Center with acres of surface parking so that, as urban planner Rachel Weber notes, it was "easy in, easy out" for fans coming in from the suburbs and the Loop (map 5.2). Weber describes the facility as a "kind of fortress" built "to make suburban fans feel more 'comfortable.'"[96]

In this context, getting rid of the mostly African American vendors was just another part of fortifying the parking buffer and insulating fans from inhabitants of the ghetto surrounding the arena. Thus protected, these fans could enjoy an anxiety-free outing to watch the black players inside. According to Charlie Beyer, vendors "were seen as riffraff, and so [the team owners wanted] to get rid of the riffraff . . . clean up . . . make [the arena surroundings] spiffy clean."[97] This suggests that Reinsdorf and Wirtz viewed the peddlers in much the same way that they viewed nearby public-housing residents—as an unsightly and unsettling liability that arena ownership needed to remove or render less visible.

Real-estate developers' use of privatization as a means of screening out low-income people and people of color from leisure spaces and retail establishments has a postwar history that stretches back much farther than the 1990s. Particularly in the urban South, in places like the greater Atlanta area, white suburbs that emerged or expanded after World War II often used privatization to sidestep federally mandated racial integration. Instead of refusing nonwhites access to public swimming pools, public buses, and other public accommodations, many middle- and upper-class white suburbs simply abandoned their commitment to public resources. As an alternative, they turned increasingly to private spaces and assets like backyard swimming pools, private country clubs, and self-owned automobiles.[98] By the 1990s, however, developers in Chicago and beyond were transferring the privatization model

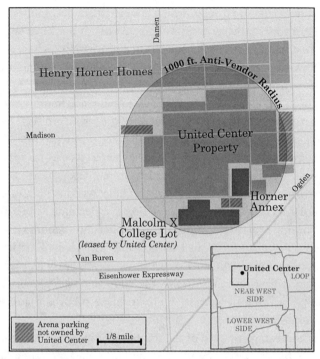

MAP 5.2. Geography of the Antivendor Ordinance and United Center Parking
Source: To determine the ownership status of the arena parking lots, the Property Index Numbers (PINs) assigned by Cook County to the associated parcels were cross-checked with local tax payment records available in hard copy at the Office of the Cook County Clerk. PINs determined using Cook County Assessor's Office, *CookViewer* applet, accessed January 27, 2018, maps.cookcountyil.gov/cookviewer/. On the Malcolm X lease, see Ben Meyerson, "Malcolm X College to Get New Building," *Chicago Journal*, February 21, 2012, accessed January 27, 2018, chicagojournalarchive.com/Blogs/Near-Loop-Wire/02-21 -2012/Malcolm_X_college_to_get_new_building.

back into central cities, creating well-protected oases of consumption amid the ruins of the urban crisis. The anti-vending measures were one small part of what historian and cultural critic Thomas Frank describes as a nationwide process of "reconceiving [urban American] along new lines" during the New Gilded Age. Specifically, "the poor were to be expelled, and room was to be made for . . . a green zone wherein cosmopolitan citizens with cash and taste could safely play."[99]

✳

After the thousand-foot ordinance permanently wiped out the peanut vendors, Weinberg managed to continue selling the *Blue Line* until the late 1990s. Even though arena officials and local police continued to harass Weinberg and Beyer—Beyer began peddling the program with Weinberg after the peanut ban—the special protections for the sale of printed material under the First Amendment helped them skirt the ordinance. The partnership ended in the late 1990s, when Weinberg walked away from publishing the program. Weinberg kept trying to irritate Wirtz, though, and he returned to the sidewalks around the United Center at the start of the new century to sell *Career Misconduct*, a hilarious book he wrote chronicling Bill Wirtz's notorious history of corruption.

Despite attempts by the police to forcibly remove Weinberg for violating the anti-vending ordinance, Weinberg successfully sued the City of Chicago in 2002, securing his right to peddle his muckraking exposé. Ironically, after losing in district court, he won his appeal in the Seventh Circuit by asserting his First Amendment rights.[100] Weinberg's newfound luck in the Seventh Circuit likely benefited from the fact that he framed the issue as an example of the government infringing on his individual freedom of speech rather than on his rights as a small businessman. Within the Seventh Circuit, claims to individual freedom gained more traction when they did not directly threaten the profits of people like Reinsdorf and Wirtz.

Weinberg's victory resonated far beyond the United Center. Entire professional sports leagues recognized that the case threatened their teams' ability to control the space around their respective facilities. Officials from several leagues filed amicus briefs in support of the city's appeal to the Supreme Court, contending that barring vendors of all types from around pro sports facilities remained a priority "because terrorists masquerading as vendors could strike outside a stadium."[101] The Supreme Court concluded it had better things to do than protect the nation from al-Qaeda operatives gone undercover as peanut vendors. It refused to hear the city's appeal.

But Weinberg's victory had no bearing on the status of the peanut vendors, who never returned to the United Center. Their permanent absence signaled not just sports franchises' expanding market power at the end of the twentieth century but also the resurgent synergy between federal and local arms of government bent on clearing the way for unfettered profits and political influence by corporate America. As political and economic elites touted theories defending the sanctity of free markets unhindered by state intervention, team owners like Reinsdorf and Wirtz tolerated competition only if it justified predatory business practices and minimized the risk of their own investments. When it did not, the owners quickly enlisted the aid of government officials, who were all too willing to help them snuff out their competitors. And while the legislation passed by the City Council played an obvious role in Reinsdorf and Wirtz's campaign to remove any semblance of economic competition in the local market for food and souvenir sales, its utility for the owners went further than this. It also fulfilled their desire to rid the sidewalks and parking lots around the United Center of people—specifically, low-income folks—who they believed scared away moneyed fans.

The actions on behalf of United Center ownership by both the federal courts and the Chicago City Council did not result directly from formal or informal antitrust exemptions granted to the sports business. They were outcomes driven mostly by sea changes in how corporations interfaced with politicians and judges at the end of the twentieth century. Perhaps economist James Galbraith best sums up the behavior of the powerful capitalists who, like Reinsdorf, profited from these transformations. He writes: "None of these enterprises has an interest in diminishing the size of the state. . . . For without the state . . . they would not themselves exist and could not enjoy the market power that they have come to wield."[102]

"Nothing but Net Profits": Public Dollars and Tax Policy at the United Center

United Center ownership's willingness during the vendor saga to depend on government to enhance profitability while paying lip service to free markets was no aberration. As the press lauded their decision to privately finance the new arena, Reinsdorf and Wirtz successfully pressured lawmakers to authorize significant public subsidies for the United Center through several tax-abatement schemes. The most valuable was a special property-tax formula for valuing the facility that saved the owners hundreds of millions of dollars.[1]

The tax breaks, which significantly offset Reinsdorf's and Wirtz's private investments in the arena, encapsulated two important trends in stadium finance. First, in the face of growing skepticism during the 1980s and 1990s about the fiscal prudence of using taxpayer money to subsidize professional sports facilities, some team owners opted to "privately" finance new stadiums. But these nominally private deals always involved considerable, unreported public costs. While the mainstream press doled out accolades for teams allegedly willing to assume the full risks of the free market by coming up with private financing, the same teams devised backdoor mechanisms for shifting costs back to the public. Second, in the decades following World War II, public stadium subsidies typically depended on a local government's right to a significant portion of facility revenues. By the end of the century, however, teams building new stadiums secured exclusive or near-exclusive rights to those revenues. In other words, while public money still flowed to teams, teams were providing little, if anything, in return.[2] Such was the case at the United Center.

Placing the United Center tax breaks in broader historical context reveals that, much like the vendor purge, they stemmed not just from the unique market structure of major-league sports but also from systemic changes in late twentieth-century urban capitalism. In response to a flurry of historical developments during the 1970s that threatened corporate profits, American capital rebelled against a fiscal status quo that, since the New Deal, had depended on progressive taxation to support a relatively robust array of social programs that helped ordinary citizens. An important component of this rebellion was the successful push to dramatically expand corporate subsidy programs available to a wide variety of industries, and many of the programs involved various tax-exemption and tax-abatement "incentives" at the municipal, state, and federal levels. Proponents argued that these programs spurred new economic growth by freeing up capital that firms would have otherwise sunk into public taxes. In practice, they proved largely ineffectual in terms of stimulating broad-based economic growth but wildly successful in terms of redistributing wealth upward. The United Center tax breaks were just one example of this explosion of corporate welfare programs inside and outside the sports business.[3]

The breaks granted to Reinsdorf and Wirtz also exemplified the particular ways in which this process played out in Chicagoland. Major commercial property owners in Chicago successfully undermined a local property-tax system that remained, even after the 1970s, relatively progressive. Chicago policy makers avoided the sort of tax revolts that paralyzed other parts of the country, and as a result they continued to depend disproportionately on commercial property taxes, as opposed to those levied on ordinary homeowners, to fund municipal services. The city's real-estate industry responded by applying political pressure at every level of local and regional government— pressure that came in many forms, including direct lobbying and generous campaign contributions—to convince lawmakers to chip away at progressive tax policies that transferred resources from the rich to the less fortunate.

Local politicians still feared popular blowback from dramatic increases in residential property taxes, and they turned to regressive excise taxes, sales taxes, and user fees to fill the holes left by reductions in commercial property taxes. In response, owners of valuable commercial real estate regularly secured exemptions from the new (or increased) taxes. Reinsdorf and Wirtz, for example, convinced the City Council to reduce their amusement-tax liabilities on revenues generated by the United Center. Firms from industries as varied as aerospace engineering and low-cost retail secured similar breaks, shunting responsibility for the taxes to the working and middle classes. Ultimately, the government's role in minimizing the risk of private investment in the United Center shared much in common with its role in doing the same for firms outside the pro sports business. Teams like the Bulls did not act apart from the normal structures of capitalism. They were deeply embedded in those structures.

The United Center and Public-Private Stadium Finance

United Center boosters reveled in pointing out that Reinsdorf and Wirtz used their own money to build the arena. In 1994 Peter Bynoe, a local financier who had helped structure the public funding deal for the new Comiskey Park a few years earlier, described the United Center to *Tribune* reporter John Handley as "a model for this kind of facility around the country, especially with its mostly private financing."[4] A few years later, *Crain's Chicago Business* emphasized the exceptional nature of the arena's financing. "[Reinsdorf and Wirtz] have performed a public service," the paper's editors insisted, "by showing . . . the city and the state that private—rather than public—stadium ownership is the only rational approach to building a new sports facility."[5]

This rhetoric was not limited to local partisans; independent economists also highlighted and praised the financing behind the United Center. In a 1999 study, James Quirk and Rodney Fort acknowledged that the arena was "built by team owners primarily with private money" and cited it as proof that "it is not inconceivable that a new facility could pay for itself under private ownership." Writing in *USA Today* in 2000, economist Raymond Keating also offered acclamation for the project. He admitted that the financing was not "perfect" because the public picked up the tab for about $20 million in infrastructural upgrades around the new arena, but he insisted that the deal was "pretty good" by the standards of the day.[6]

Private funding made economic sense for the team owners. New revenue streams created by the United Center, as well as the dual occupancy of the Bulls and Blackhawks, kept enough cash flowing year-round to make the investment a safe bet. Private funding also guaranteed that the teams would maintain exclusive rights to all stadium-generated revenues. Other factors convinced Reinsdorf and Wirtz that they could pay. For example, the threats made by Reinsdorf during the late 1980s to relocate his major-league baseball franchise, the White Sox, away from Chicago if the city and state blocked public financing for a new ballpark left a bad taste in the mouths of Chicagoans. The threats worked. Not only did the city and state pick up the construction costs for a new stadium; they also allowed the Sox to keep nearly all stadium revenues. The deal led the *Chicago Reader's* Ben Joravsky to refer to the new park as "home of the sweetheart deal."[7] Reinsdorf recognized that asking for a similar plan for a new basketball arena would likely unleash even greater public outcry.

Shifts in attitudes among policy makers and the public regarding stadium finance also made the use of private funds to construct the United Center seem like the most pragmatic course of action for the owners. By the late 1980s, many local and state governments were wary of using public money to build major-league facilities amid reductions in federal aid to cities and a growing consensus among economists that stadiums did not generate new local economic growth. In this context, U.S. Congress tried to make it harder for cities and states to fund stadiums with taxpayer money. The Tax Reform Act of 1986 attempted to curb public involvement in stadium finance by restricting use of municipal tax-exempt bonds to pay for sports facilities. Although the legislation contained loopholes that eventually paved the way for cities to pay even greater shares of stadium costs, its passage indicated growing popular disapproval of using public money to build private sports venues.[8]

Reinsdorf and Wirtz were not the only owners who apparently dug further into their pockets for new facilities. Data collected from popular press reports and secondary sources by stadium-finance expert Judith Grant Long suggest that, nationwide, the share of stadium financing shouldered by the public fell significantly after the 1970s. According to these figures, the average reported public share of financing (taking into account the publicly reported costs of building, land, and infrastructure) among facilities built for NBA teams went from 87 percent for the period 1970–1979 to 65 percent for 1980–1989, and down to 34 percent during the first half of the 1990s (the trend was similar in other leagues).[9] By the end of the twentieth century, the world of stadium finance had seemingly changed.

According to stadium boosters, a new generation of public-private partnerships allowed team owners and local governments to share investment risk more equitably. Sports franchises would get access to benefits like cheap land, and cities would purportedly benefit through the private redevelopment of underutilized lots and increased property-tax revenues.[10] Indeed, Long's data on reported public shares of facility financing suggest that, from a fiscal perspective, the United Center represented a great deal for Chicagoans. According to the readily available sources that Long culled, the public share of financing for the United Center stood at 0 percent. By contrast, the same types of sources show that taxpayers paid 84 percent of the cost of buildings, land, and infrastructure for the new White Sox park.[11]

But reports of the 0 percent figure ignored a more complex reality. For example, the State of Illinois and City of Chicago contributed at least $18 million for infrastructural improvements around the new arena. In late June and early July 1989, journalists covering the Illinois General Assembly for the *Sun-Times* reported on state legislators also authorizing a property-tax break for the planned arena "that could save [the owners] millions of dollars over the course of the 22-year agreement." They offered no additional details other than the fact that "Wirtz said the project would not be economically feasible if the state did not come up with the assistance package that includes a 22-year property tax break."[12]

The House bill amendment containing the tax break sparked heated debate in the Illinois General Assembly. Several of the forty-seven state representatives who opposed the amended bill—sixty-two voted in its favor—claimed that it was a needless handout to corporate elites at the expense of ordinary residents. Monique Davis, representing Illinois's Thirty-Sixth State House District, described as "strange" the fact that "we have so many hospitals closing in the State of Illinois and we don't see so many 'green' votes up there when we're trying to keep those hospitals alive, but when it comes to these civic centers and these ball parks and these stadiums, we all of a sudden can find the money." Others charged that complex jargon masked the true nature of the legislation. Representative Anthony Young, from the state's Seventeenth District, urged his colleagues to "look at the Bill," warning that "it contains one of the most incredible real estate tax giveaways." "That's very hard to decipher," he complained, "but it's certainly in there."[13]

Sun-Times reporter Chuck Neubauer concurred. "The tax breaks the United Center received from the Illinois General Assembly will save the owners tens of millions of dollars in real estate taxes," he concluded in a 1995 report. According to Neubauer, the legislation required the Cook County Assessor's Office, the local body that valued real estate in Chicago, to assess the United Center differently than other commercial properties.[14] Cook County normally assessed commercial properties on the basis of the net income (i.e., profits) they generated. However, the special legislation allowed Reinsdorf and Wirtz to dramatically understate United Center net income by deducting mortgage interest, as well as federal and state income taxes. In addition, the new law mandated a reduced assessment level for the arena. At the time, the Assessor's Office normally calculated a commercial property's assessed value as 38 percent of its fair market value (a function of net income). The special legislation, though, enabled the assessor to value the arena at only 20 percent of fair market value. It also arbitrarily capped certain multipliers used in the calculation of commercial property taxes. As a result, from 1997 through 2011 —the numbers for which complete data are available—Reinsdorf and Wirtz paid an estimated total of $147 million less in property taxes, measured in constant 2016 dollars, than they would have under standard statutes (fig 6.1; see appendix C for calculations and an explanation of why this figure differs from previously published estimates).[15]

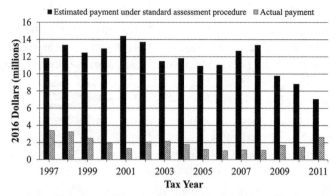

FIGURE 6.1. United Center's Actual Property-Tax Payments versus Estimated Property-Tax Liabilities under Standard Assessment Procedure, in Constant 2016 Dollars, 1997–2011
Source: Author's calculations using data from Cook County Assessor's Office, Freedom of Information Act Request, Order No. 62939, Transaction No. 62013, March 28, 2013.
Notes: "Tax year" refers to year of assessment. Inflation adjustments made using the Bureau of Labor Statistics CPI-U for the Chicago-Gary-Kenosha area.

For tax years 1997 through 2011, actual property-tax bills for the United Center averaged $1.9 million in 2016 dollars. By contrast, standard assessment formulas would have required annual tax bills in excess of $11 million in most years. Such figures might sound extreme. Keep in mind, however, that except in 2004 and 2005, the years in which United Center revenues dipped because of NHL work stoppages, annual net income generated by the new arena averaged more than $32 million.[16] In other words, the owners would have taken home tens of millions of dollars in annual profits even without the breaks. Moreover, when expressed in terms of the arena's property-tax rate—that is, the ratio of property taxes paid to property value—eight-digit tax bills suddenly seem far less onerous. Under standard assessment procedures, the rate would have ranged from an estimated 3.0 to 5.7 percent (and averaged 4.6 percent) from 1997 to 2011—figures generally consistent with other major commercial properties in the city (see table 6.1). They also represented a reasonable cost of doing business for Reinsdorf and Wirtz. After all, property taxes funded the municipal services that maintained the economic viability of such a valuable property and sustained the well-being of the workers and consumers inside (e.g., infrastructural maintenance, sanitation services, libraries, schools).[17]

A more general reason to dismiss charges that standard commercial property assessment would have overburdened Reinsdorf and Wirtz is that the United Center's financial statements capture only a fraction of the economic benefits that accrued to them as franchise owners. The accounting records for the arena reveal nothing about the stratospheric increase in the television revenues captured by teams—earnings from television probably appeared in team-specific accounting records (e.g., for the Chicago Bulls corporation rather than the United Center)—or about the resulting surge in franchise values over the past quarter century. Between 1991 and 2017, in line with general trends in major-league sports, the estimated value of the Bulls leapt from $100 million to $2.5 billion. These jumps in team-specific revenues and team values dramatically expanded the income and wealth of owners like Reinsdorf to the point that $10 million in additional property taxes each year represented a drop in the bucket. Ordinary assessment would not have come anywhere near jeopardizing the financial viability of the United Center or the Bulls. Instead, it would have marginally reduced the team's profitability, an outcome incompatible with the tenets of exclusionary capitalism.[18]

To be clear, the aggregate property-tax savings estimate cited earlier, $147 million, represents the inflation-adjusted savings on property taxes over a fifteen-year period—that is, the purchasing power, in 2016 dollars, of the savings during each year from 1997 to 2011 added together. This is not to be confused with what economists would refer to as the "present value" in 1994, the year the United Center opened, of all the arena property taxes forgone in the decade and a half covered by figure 6.1. Technically speaking, a cash flow of a nominal amount set to take place in the future—for example, a stadium subsidy granted in the form of a tax exemption ten years from now—is, in the present, worth less than the nominal future amount. Why? Because in theory one could invest a lesser sum right now in interest-bearing investments and have it equal the nominal future value after ten years. To borrow from stadium-finance guru Neil deMause, "the true cost in present-day dollars," or the present value, of annual subsidies granted in the future "is how much you'd have to set aside now [at the outset] to pay off those future costs."[19]

All this may seem like abstract, technical minutiae. Indeed, in real-life Chicago officials did not set aside a lump sum to offset taxes that Reinsdorf and Wirtz were not going to pay. But knowing the present value of the future tax breaks in 1994 allows for a more accurate comparison of the public costs incurred by the city over the twenty-two-year life of the United Center property-tax deal and the up-front costs of constructing the arena. Using a simple extrapolation technique to estimate the forgone property taxes for years for which precise data are unavailable, the present value at 1994 of twenty-two years of property-tax breaks was $85.9 million. This corresponds to 49 percent of the $175 million Reinsdorf and Wirtz spent on the arena—a significant recuperation of their initial investment and the fiscal equivalent of local government footing nearly half the bill for the United Center's up-front construction costs (accounting for public spending on surrounding infrastructure would raise the percentage even higher—to around 60 percent).[20] Moreover, the savings were well in excess of the total amount of money injected into local redevelopment efforts by arena ownership (the sum of the present values at 1994 of the figures in table 4.1 is approximately $12.6 million).[21] The tax relief constituted a less visible government subsidy at a moment when public tolerance for taxpayer-funded stadiums was on the ebb. While the United Center still represented a good deal for the city relative to the new Comiskey Park, this was an extremely low bar given that the public picked up more or less the entire tab for the latter. Ultimately, the hidden tax benefits empowered United Center ownership to tout what was, in fact, a heavily subsidized project as a miracle of private initiative.

These hidden costs encapsulated the dramatic understatement of the public liabilities involved in public-private partnerships struck between local governments and major-league sports franchises across the United States in recent decades. As Judith Grant Long demonstrates, popular sources and many academic studies regularly overlook taxpayer expenditures on stadium infrastructure, ongoing municipal support services such as the use of police for crowd control, maintenance and upkeep, and property-tax exemptions. After accounting for these often-invisible costs, Long estimates that the share of major-league stadium costs covered by taxpayers actually crept upward in recent decades despite journalistic reports to the contrary. According to her figures on financing for 121 major-league facilities operating in 2010, "these uncounted public costs exceed[ed] $10 billion."[22]

In defense of the tax-abatement scheme, Bill Wirtz argued that private banks would not have financed the arena in the absence of such huge property-tax breaks.[23] In other words, the forgone tax revenue was the price the public had to pay to cement its "partnership" with the teams. A more likely explanation is that that the banks wanted proof that the team owners secured the tax breaks not as a precondition of lending to them but as a precondition of lending to them at lower interest rates (a lower tax burden meant reduced costs of doing business, thereby lowering the risk of default). The tax breaks thus functioned as a double subsidy, not only reducing the fiscal burden borne by arena ownership but also depressing the cost of capital required to finance the facility "privately."

This property-tax history highlights other contrasts between the financing of facilities like the United Center and that of the previous generation of stadiums. In addition to a lucrative tax subsidy, United Center owners secured the rights to keep all venue-related revenues while local government still absorbed the bulk of the costs. This despite the fact that the cost of the new arena, like the price tag of other similar facilities opened after the mid-1980s, far exceeded that of stadiums from earlier generations. This was a departure from past practices. In the decades following World War II, the use of public expenditures to build stadiums was common, but it was usually contingent on local governments collecting a sizable share of the cash flows generated by the facilities, often through rents paid by teams. By the early 1990s, teams captured more subsidy dollars and provided less, if anything, in return.[24] Particularly telling in this regard was the Chicago City Council's 1991 statement of compliance with state legislation authorizing the tax breaks. City Council minutes containing the statement read, "It is an appropriate and desirable public purpose for government to assist and cooperate in such development and construction in order to stabilize and reduce the risks and burdens associated therewith."[25] However, the statement never mentions taxpayers' right to some portion of United Center revenues in exchange for their role as reducers of risk.

More egregious examples exist of this shift toward unconditional public expenditures on stadiums; the new White Sox park is an obvious case in point. But the formal tax abatements enjoyed by United Center ownership represented a move in the same direction. No evidence has surfaced that Chicago Stadium enjoyed a government-mandated reduction in its property-tax liabilities. Thus, the United Center tax formula likely signaled the willingness of local policy makers to sanction new, unconditional mechanisms to subsidize the Bulls and Blackhawks.

The property-tax breaks also exemplified how teams relied on the complexity of new subsidy schemes to avoid public scrutiny. Cook County property-tax law and assessment procedures are notoriously intricate, and few journalists or concerned citizens had the resources to thoroughly document what was happening. As Long notes, the new generation of stadium-financing arrangements of the 1980s and 1990s depended on the "opacity of partnership deals" to keep taxpayers in the dark, removing decisions about government funding from democratic processes like public referenda.[26]

The United Center Property-Tax Deal in National Context: Corporate Welfare in Late Twentieth-Century America

The economic history of the United Center broadens our understanding of the range of causes behind team owners' recent success in shifting the risk of stadium development further onto the public and reducing teams' public accountability in the process. Rodney Fort, echoing the consensus in the economics literature, identifies teams' local monopoly power, which "derives from the special legal treatment of leagues," as the "ultimate culprit" behind the unconditional doling out of public money for sports facilities.[27] The government has allowed professional sports organizations like the NBA to operate openly as cartels, artificially limiting the supply of franchises. This suppression of supply takes two forms: granting individual franchises exclusive rights to operate in a specific market and preventing franchise expansion in or relocation to a handful of markets that could sustain the franchise economically. With the support of their leagues, teams in search of publicly funded stadiums have threatened to move to one of the open markets unless local government coughs up major subsidies for a new facility. Leagues have typically signaled that the abandoned city will not receive a new franchise, thus placing extreme pressure on local officials to concede to the demands in hopes of avoiding charges of "losing" a major-league team.[28]

The government-sanctioned monopoly power wielded by leagues and teams was an important force behind the proliferation of massive, unconditional public subsidies for major-league stadiums. As the White Sox debacle illustrated, the government's refusal to subject leagues to meaningful antitrust action, and the resulting impunity with which teams have resorted to the relocation racket, placed enormous pressure on taxpayers to pick up the tab for new stadiums without asking for anything in return. Reinsdorf admitted as much in discussing his threats to relocate the White Sox if local taxpayers failed to fund the new Comiskey Park. "We had to make threats to get the new deal," he explained. "If we didn't have the threat of moving, we wouldn't have gotten the deal."[29]

But relying solely on the monopoly power thesis to explain the stadium subsidy phenomenon raises a puzzling question: Government-sanctioned monopoly power in American professional sports is very old news, so why did it result in structural changes in the political economy of stadium building only after 1980? Both the NFL and the NBA failed to fully consolidate their monopolies until the 1960s and 1970s, respectively. It is conceivable that the effects of this consolidation only became evident in the final two decades of the twentieth century. But major-league baseball enjoyed an explicit government exemption from antitrust law, as well as the unchallenged market dominance that went with it, since 1922; and Long's analysis suggests that during and after the 1980s stadium finance in major-league baseball also underwent many of the same concerning transformations as it did in other major leagues. Namely, the real, absolute public costs of baseball stadiums rose dramatically and public rights to revenues generated by new facilities evaporated.[30] More explanations about these recent trends are therefore in order.

Judith Grant Long offers an important one in her analysis of the history of stadium subsidies. As she points out, deindustrialization and receding federal aid boosted demand for new teams and stadiums among cities by encouraging them to pursue tourism-led growth strategies. This increased demand, combined with the ongoing limitation of franchise supply by major leagues, intensified stadium-subsidy bidding wars between cities that were competing to acquire or retain a team.[31] Long's observation reiterates that the economic and political impacts of the long-running monopoly power enjoyed by major-league sports varied over time and depended a great deal on trends affecting the American urban economy as a whole.

The case of the Bulls' special property-tax deal suggests that, at the turn of the millennium, these trends were not limited to central-city mayors' turn to tourism as a form of economic salvation. Tellingly, research for this study did not yield evidence of relocation threats by the Bulls or Blackhawks. Moving outside of the Chicago metropolitan area made little sense for either team, as such a move would have entailed relinquishing sole control, within their respective leagues, over the third-largest market in the United States. In the absence of a record of relocation threats, what explains the Illinois General Assembly's willingness to grant such a lucrative tax-abatement subsidy to Reinsdorf and Wirtz? Larger shifts in the politics of taxation and government spending in the United States are at least part of the answer. In the decades following World War II, corporate America typically understood the progressive taxation system that emerged from the New Deal—that is, a system that imposed significantly higher tax rates on those with more income and wealth—as part and parcel of stable growth. Relatively high tax rates on corporations and wealthy individuals enabled the government to spend liberally to better regulate demand and maintain the high wages, employment levels, and consumption that underwrote steady economic expansion and profitability throughout the 1950s and 1960s.

This understanding ended with the crisis of profitability faced by American capital during the 1970s, a scenario sparked by a variety of developments, including steep rises in inflation and the growing competitiveness of firms in Europe and Asia. Big business responded by mounting a concerted political offensive against progressive taxation at all levels of government and, among other things, pushing for expanded public subsidies for corporations. Corporate America argued with increasing forcefulness that a "good business climate" and, by extension, a return to robust growth, depended on the success of such initiatives.[32] The endgame of all of this was clear: cutting taxes and regulation on business and the rich while expanding corporate welfare would result in a massive, upward transfer of wealth, and along with it the exclusion of growing numbers of Americans from the ranks of the economically secure.

To accomplish this agenda, business leaders and other economic elites poured unprecedented amounts of resources into an expanded pro-corporate political infrastructure intended to counter the organizational power of labor unions and other progressive groups. By the end of the 1970s, these efforts had blossomed into a formidable, well-oiled national movement supported by a sweeping network of propaganda outlets and think tanks, political action committees (which poured mountains of new money into campaign finance), and trade associations. For these groups, pushing the government to enact massive tax cuts for big business and the wealthy was a top priority. They justified their push in two ways. First, new supply-side economic theories claimed that tax cuts, especially on the rich, would "pay for themselves" by freeing up more cash for new investment, which would expand employment, consumer spending, and profits. Supply-siders argued that tax cuts would not deplete government revenues because, according to them, lower rates charged on an expanded labor force and increased profits would yield as much or more revenue as higher rates charged on a smaller workforce and stagnating profits. Second, proponents of reduced corporate tax burdens claimed that lower taxes would force the government to cut back on or halt spending on the social welfare programs that the wealthy resented.[33]

The business counteroffensive achieved quick, decisive victories. At the national level, for example, the Economic Recovery Tax Act of 1981, signed into law by President Reagan, initiated a precipitous decline in the top marginal income tax rate: over the course of the 1980s the top rate plummeted from 70 percent to 28 percent.[34] According to economic historian Bruce Bartlett, this move had some "stimulative effect" and played a role in the "rebound of growth" in the early 1980s. But growth rates had returned to more anemic levels by the end of the decade, and the intellectual justifications of supply-side economics faltered against mounting evidence of its lackluster effects. Most analyses indicated that lower taxes paid on the new economic activity stimulated by reduced tax rates offset only a small fraction, at best, of revenue lost as a result of the application of lower rates to previously existing economic activity. Over and over in the years after 1980, Reaganesque tax cuts failed to pay for themselves. Furthermore, economists struggled to establish a solid empirical connection between tax cuts for the rich and sustained improvements in economic growth, or between those cuts and reduced government spending. In the face of this information, why did many corporate executives and their intellectual and political allies continue to push aggressive tax cuts? Because while they failed to improve growth over the long term, the cuts succeeded magnificently at redistributing wealth upward.[35]

The assault on taxation also played out at the local level. Corporations successfully secured more, and more generous, government subsidy programs under the guise of incentives for private investment. These often came in the form of new tax-abatement or tax-exemption programs. Local tax-incentive programs were not unheard of before 1970. In fact, lawmakers in Southern states pioneered their use during the New Deal in hopes of luring industry from the North. However, in the words of one expert, they "really matured" during and after the 1970s, proliferating rapidly across and within states (fig. 6.2). Property-tax abatements, tax-exempt bond programs used by local governments to make loans to private firms at below-market interest rates, and exemptions from corporate income tax all underwent major expansions at the century's end. By 2005, the typical state boasted more than thirty "economic development subsidies" related to property taxes or otherwise.[36] The rapid expansion of these programs owed in part to corporations and consulting firms bombarding legislators and the public with specious economic "studies" by hired "experts." The reports preyed on localities' growing desperation to retain and attract new investment in the face of deindustrialization and fiscal crisis, and corporations played states and cities off

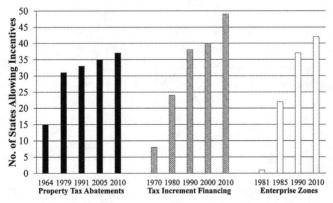

FIGURE 6.2. Increasing Use of Property-Tax Incentives in the United States after 1960
Source: Daphne Kenyon, Adam Langley, and Bethany Paquin, *Rethinking Property Tax Incentives for Business* (Cambridge, MA: Lincoln Land Institute, 2012), 5.
Notes: The authors who compiled this data note that "property tax abatements are stand-alone programs that are not part of broader economic development programs" (5).

one another with more frequency, inciting a race to the bottom in which local governments competed to offer the most lavish corporate welfare packages to retain or attract private capital.[37]

A key motor driving this trend nationally and locally was the dramatic expansion of corporate campaign contributions intended to aid in electing legislators friendly to the probusiness agenda. Much of this money came through new corporate political action committees (PACs), which collected donations from like-minded individuals and transferred bundles of cash to candidates aligned with their interests. (PACs became convenient tools for the wealthy to increase their giving to candidates, since donations to them do not count against limits on contributions directly from individuals to candidates).[38] Between 1977 and 1988, the number of corporate PACs went from fewer than 600 to more than 1,800 (over the same period the count of labor-union PACs never exceeded 400). This proliferation of probusiness PACs drove the extraordinary increase in PAC contributions to candidates (of both major parties) running for federal office: from $35.2 million during the 1977–1978 election cycle to $217.8 million during the 1995–1996 one.[39]

Corporate donors and corporate donation recipients typically deny the existence of a relationship between campaign contributions and policy change. But only the most naive observer could possibly maintain that the mountains of cash from businesspeople do not significantly impact legislative decisions. Little surprise, then, that in their recent study of more than 1,770 proposed federal policy changes between 1981 and 2002, political scientists Martin Gilens and Benjamin Page found that one of the best predictors of a proposal being enacted into law was whether it enjoyed support among wealthy Americans (the top 10 percent in terms of income). They ominously report that "the preferences of the average American appear to have only a miniscule, near-zero, statistically non-significant impact upon public policy."[40]

And just as one would expect in the context of exclusionary capitalism, the influence over policy makers exerted by business interests has only furthered this "pay-to-play" system of politics in the new century. The initial barrage of increased corporate campaign financing unleashed in the 1970s paved the way for the enactment of policies, such as reduced marginal tax rates for the rich, that allowed those with the most income to command more and more of America's wealth. Big business then plowed significant chunks of increased wealth back into ongoing campaign-finance efforts. This smoothed the way for even more extreme legislation in favor of corporations, including looser laws on campaign donations and new campaign-finance loopholes that facilitated increased corporate spending. The cycle continues unabated today.[41]

The intensification of pay-to-play politics also occurred at the state and local levels. In 1993, Jay Fitzgerald and Kevin McDermott of the *Springfield State Journal-Register* reported that "total political contributions to the individual campaign funds of the four legislative leaders [in the Illinois General Assembly] increased more than 10-fold, from less than $310,000 in 1983 to more than $3.1 million in 1993." In Illinois, the problem of outsized campaign contributions from corporate donors was particularly acute prior to 2011. Before that year, state law placed no limits on individual contributions to candidates for political office.[42]

United Center ownership was knee-deep in efforts to shape the legislative landscape by filling the campaign coffers of state, county, and city politicians. Reinsdorf, Wirtz, and other Bulls and Blackhawks executives offered up large contributions to powerful lawmakers in their own names, in the name of the United Center Joint Venture, and in the names of the wide array of firms they ran. For example, Reinsdorf funneled money to candidates not only through donations on behalf of the Chicago Bulls and Chicago White Sox, but also through real estate companies such as Encounters Ltd., JMR Trust, and Westwood Pointe. The precise amount of money United Center ownership injected into political campaigns over the past four decades is impossible to quantify. Campaign-finance records from Illinois are notorious for their incompleteness, disorganization, and illegibility.[43] This is particularly true for records from before the mid-1990s, which are available only in microfiche form (as opposed to a searchable online database), often not alphabetized (making systematic research onerous), and sometimes written in indecipherable script. Nevertheless, available data suggest the magnitude of the arena owners' involvement in campaign finance. Those data also reveal where they focused their contributions and why.

Even if we exclude contributions to corporate PACs, the sum of recorded donations by Reinsdorf, Wirtz, and other long-serving team and arena executives (board members, limited partners, and vice presidents) from 1980 to 2016 reached seven figures. During these years, United Center ownership contributed more than $383,000 to candidates running for the Chicago City Council, more than $432,000 to Chicago mayoral races, more than $110,000 to candidates for the office of Cook County Assessor, more than $913,000 to campaigns for seats in the Illinois General Assembly (House and Senate), and in excess of $535,000 to Illinois gubernatorial candidates (see appendix B for methodology behind these figures and a detailed definition of "United Center ownership" as used here). Moreover, these contributions significantly underestimate the total amount of money injected into Illinois campaigns by the arena owners not only because they exclude giving to corporate PACs but also because they discount missing or illegible data from microfiche records, as well as smaller contribution totals to candidates for other offices such as Illinois state treasurer and president of the Cook County Board of Commissioners.

That United Center ownership expected the contributions to pay off economically is suggested by the fact that they targeted the bulk of their giving at offices with significant power over policy affecting the arena's profitability. From 1985 to 2012, the arena owners gave at least $121,000 to campaign committees controlled by Michael Madigan, who has been speaker of the Illinois House of Representatives since 1983 (save the years 1995 and 1996).[44] As speaker, Madigan holds huge sway over the legislative agenda of the Illinois House, largely by transferring money from Illinois Democratic Party PACs under his control to junior legislators. According to campaign-finance activist Tracy Litsey, serving as this sort of conduit for campaign funds is how high-ranking state legislators like Madigan keep "the other legislators in line and control the votes."[45] Proposed state legislation has fared little to no shot of passage without the blessing of Madigan during his tenure as speaker, and United Center ownership no doubt had this in mind when they contributed to his campaign in the lead-up to the Illinois House vote on the tax breaks. Notably, state representative Richard Mautino, to whom Madigan earlier transferred resources from the Friends of Michael Madigan PAC, proved one of the most outspoken supporters of the tax breaks during the relevant floor debate.[46]

Because the governor of Illinois has the power to veto General Assembly legislation, it made sense for Reinsdorf and others with a financial stake in the United Center to also donate generously to Republican governor Jim Thompson during the 1980s. By the time the General Assembly passed the United Center property-tax deal in 1989, they had contributed at least $34,750 to Thompson's campaign committee. Between then and February 2015, they donated more than $500,000 to the committees of gubernatorial candidates.[47]

Why did the United Center owners keep donating to power brokers like Madigan and Thompson after getting their coveted tax breaks? First, they had other economic and political interests that extended beyond the United Center. Reinsdorf, Wirtz, and other team executives had their hands in a wide swath of industries, including residential real estate and alcoholic beverage distribution. Ongoing donations kept them in the good graces of legislators as issues relating to those other businesses arose. Just as important was the fact that continued donations to powerful politicians protected the property-tax deal from criticism or potential reform efforts by politicians with the power to repeal it or limit its benefits.

Consider the available records of donations made by United Center ownership to the candidates running for Cook County assessor, the office in charge of implementing the special property-tax assessment formula. Reinsdorf and his partners contributed $110,600 to candidates for the office of assessor between 1988 and 2010. Most of this largesse—99 percent—came after the state legislature passed the deal.[48] This strongly suggests that these donations had less to do with getting legislation passed and more with staying in the favorable graces of whomever ran the Assessor's Office, thereby avoiding any movement to "overvalue" the property or draw public attention to the arena's special tax status. Similar considerations were probably at play in large, ongoing contributions to Chicago mayoral and aldermanic campaign committees. These donations thus protected the United Center's privileged relationship with the government from the threat of genuine democratic reform.

The favorable tax treatment enjoyed by United Center ownership and other major campaign contributors was not a partisan issue. Reinsdorf, Wirtz, and other United Center executives, in line with the behavior of other wealthy donors, gave liberally to both parties—more than $2.2 million to Democrats and more than $760,000 to Republicans—between 1980 and 2016 (the advantage for Democrats owes to the historical dominance of Democrats in Illinois, especially Chicago).[49] The explosion of corporate money in political campaigns in the final quarter of the twentieth century drove up the price of running successful political campaigns, and it became more and more difficult for candidates to keep up with opponents unless they took corporate money. Many Democrats, who had historically maintained a relatively antagonistic relationship with corporate power, assumed an "If you can't beat 'em, join 'em" posture—President Bill Clinton is a good case in point here—and increasingly accepted and courted contributions from big business. Not surprisingly, Democrats like Clinton became ever more amenable to policies that reduced tax burdens and increased government subsidies for powerful corporations.[50]

Sometimes, government officials in the pockets of the rich and well connected wrote legislation for a single firm, as in the case of the United Center's special assessment formula or Illinois's Corporate Headquarters Relocation Act of 2000. The latter law granted airplane manufacturer Boeing $30 million in financial incentives in exchange for making Chicago home to its new corporate offices.[51] Other times, they made new subsidy programs available to a wide swath of corporate interests. In Illinois, the General Assembly's offerings in this regard include, but are not limited to, the 1977 authorization of tax-increment financing (TIF) in municipalities, particularly Chicago, which funneled increases in property-tax revenues in certain districts to private developers; the Illinois Enterprise Zone Act of 1982, which provided property-tax abatements as part of a much larger basket of benefits for corporations willing to invest in "underdeveloped" areas referred to as enterprise zones; the High Impact Business Program, approved in 1985 as a mechanism to dispense tax breaks for corporate construction projects outside of enterprise zones; the 1993 creation of the Business Development Public Infrastructure Program, which doled out grants and low-interest loans for infrastructural development in support of commercial real estate; and the 1999 introduction of corporate tax credits under the Economic Development for a Growing Economy (known as EDGE) program.[52]

In Chicago, as elsewhere, corporations outside the sports business regularly availed themselves of these programs to shift the risk of their investments to the public. In 1993 and 1994, the State of Illinois and the City of Chicago provided RJR Nabisco with $90 million in subsidies to convince the company to stay in Chicago (Mondelez International, which later took over RJR Nabisco, moved about six hundred jobs at its Chicago factory to Mexico in 2015). Seven years later, Ford Motor Company found itself on the receiving end of more than $100 million in handouts for investing in a new "supplier park" on the city's Southeast Side. In 2010, a subsidiary of U.S. Steel received a tax-increment-financing subsidy of $97 million for a development project just north of the Ford facility. The list goes on and on.[53] These subsidies, like most instances of public stadium funding at the end of the twentieth century, were often unconditional. That is, they usually lacked binding stipulations compelling private developers to provide concrete public benefits, such as a guaranteed number of new, good-paying, permanent jobs. Typically, the subsidy deals also failed to include requirements for independent cost-benefit analyses or other empirical data justifying the use of incentives. Moreover, the subsidies regularly ended up in the hands of firms that were already so profitable they could easily absorb the risk of investment without corporate welfare, or they were earmarked for development in parts of the city already attracting significant private investment in the absence of subsidies.[54]

The lack of binding conditions and oversight empowered Chicago policy makers to aggressively—or recklessly, some would argue—implement tax incentives and other business subsidy programs approved by the state. Between 1990 and 2000, for example, the land area covered by Chicago TIF districts soared from approximately 47 million square feet to 1.3 billion square feet.[55] This might prompt speculation that the Chicago metropolitan area's impressive growth during the 1990s—in percentage terms it outpaced Los Angeles and New York by significant margins—owed in part to liberal approval of tax breaks and public subsidies for private firms. However, given the findings of economists regarding the impact of such incentive programs

on local economic growth, such a conclusion is speculative at best. As a literature review from 2012 notes, "The majority of studies suggest that property
tax incentives have little impact on local economic growth." In studies that
have revealed a positive impact of property-tax breaks on growth, the effect
tends to be short term. Moreover, the research indicates that property-tax
abatement proves more effective at convincing firms to relocate within metropolitan areas than between them. The evidence of the impact of other types
of business subsidies is equally disappointing.[56]

This is not to say that all public subsidies for private business are bad; well-
designed incentive programs may productively supplement larger economic
development strategies. Such programs would rely on careful research to determine whether the incentives would tip the decision of certain businesses to
invest in a specific area rather than simply lining the pockets of those already
intent on investing there regardless of the subsidies on offer. They would
also focus on export-intensive industries likely to result in net gains in local economic activity. Moreover, thoughtful subsidy programs would impose
binding conditions on recipient businesses (e.g., wage minimums for new
jobs, clawback provisions empowering local government to recoup the value
of subsidies if the recipient fails to comply with the initial agreement). The
United Center tax deal failed to meet these criteria, and unfortunately it was
more representative than exceptional. As a result, existing incentives have
proved much more effective at redistributing wealth upward—not to mention shifting tax burdens downward—than at producing growth with widely
enjoyed benefits.[57]

In the end, the United Center property-tax deal demonstrates how, after 1970, government intervention in the U.S. market increasingly favored
the fortunes of large private firms and wealthy individuals, bestowing them
with the power to concentrate more and more resources in their own hands.
This phenomenon is not simply a quirk of the sports business; it also is an
outcome of the resurgence of exclusionary capitalism. That said, corporate
welfare is especially pervasive and intense in the sports industry. As expert
Greg LeRoy accurately points out, public subsidization of private stadiums at
the turn of the millennium often covered "most—or *all*—of" development
costs, as opposed to smaller fractions more common in nonstadium deals.
But this distinction is, if anything, a matter of degree. Even if sports leagues
and teams successfully have been siphoning off money from taxpayers, private corporations in other sectors have not been far behind. Consider the
database created by the nonprofit Good Jobs First of more than 370 corporate
subsidy packages of $50 million or more doled out to private firms since the
late 1970s (the database is not exhaustive). The list excludes sports facilities,

yet it contains individual subsidy deals worth up to $8.7 billion, totaling more than $104 billion in corporate welfare (as of January 2017).[58]

The United Center Property-Tax Breaks in Local Context:
Class and Property Taxation in Cook County

The United Center tax breaks also exemplified key local developments in the politics of property taxation in and around Chicago. They were one instance of a larger offensive waged since the 1970s in Cook County by wealthy and well-connected commercial real-estate holders, particularly those in and around the Loop, against a property-tax system that they thought threatened their profit margins in the context of deindustrialization, suburbanization, and federal retrenchment, and that they believed privileged residential home-owners at their expense.

Accelerated deindustrialization after World War II placed officials in inner cities like Chicago in a bind as far as property-tax revenues were concerned. The flight of manufacturing firms to the suburbs, to the Sunbelt, or abroad in search of lower taxes and cheaper labor arrested the growth of urban tax bases. At least as early as 1960, Chicago experienced significant declines in total taxable property values as factories, not to mention the homes of many factory employees, dropped off the tax rolls.[59] Chicago mayor Richard J. Daley and the Cook County Assessor's Office thus faced a difficult situation (Cook County oversaw tax assessment in Chicago and Daley Sr., who simultaneously served as chair of the Cook County Democratic Party, effectively controlled the countywide Democratic machine). They needed some way to compensate for property-tax revenue lost to deindustrialization, but doing so by raising residential property taxes seemed like a dead end, as much of the politicians' appeal to local voters depended on not raising taxes on homeowners.

In fact, much of the Democratic machine's sway with voters rested on an unofficial system of fractional assessment of residential properties—in other words, the valuing of homes at well below market value and, by extension, the suppression of property-tax rates for ordinary homeowners. By the mid-1960s, Richard J. Daley and P. J. Cullerton, the Cook County assessor, had institutionalized this practice of dispensing what sociologist Isaac Martin terms "informal tax privileges" to "keep homeowners in the [Democratic] party fold." Rather than abandon fractional assessment of residential properties, the Daley administration responded to the budgetary strains of deindustrialization with a combination of fiscal restraint, new (nonproperty) taxes, and an increasing dependence on taxation of commercial property such as downtown office space.[60]

At the same time, suburbs in the collar counties surrounding Cook achieved a fiscal balance much more to the liking of commercial landholders. These municipalities used draconian zoning policy, especially strict limits on relatively affordable apartment housing, to limit residential development within their borders to single-family homes occupied exclusively by middle- and upper-class whites. This strategy allowed for the maintenance of relatively low tax rates on homeowners and business largely through the exclusion of low-income residents—a group including disproportionately high numbers of people of color—who local officials feared would increase local fiscal burdens by increasing demand for social welfare services.[61] Outlying suburbs in collar counties like DuPage, Lake, and Will simultaneously engaged in frenzied competition for supplementary commercial and industrial development that would, in theory, depress the property-tax burden shouldered by homeowners even further. What historian Robert Self terms the "savage rivalry" for new investment took the form of a race to the bottom in terms of commercial tax rates, as suburbs in the collar counties attempted to undercut both Chicago and one another in their quest to poach whatever local economic development they could.[62]

By the time Reinsdorf and Wirtz decided to build the United Center in the late 1980s, this tangle of macroeconomic restructuring, local politics, and interurban struggle for investment had yielded a tax structure in which the Cook County border divided two distinct universes (map 6.1). Outside of Cook, municipalities used very low commercial property-tax rates to prove themselves business-friendly. Inside of Cook, Chicago proper and adjacent suburbs struggled to stay afloat amid a hemorrhaging of population and capital (in the case of Chicago) or slower growth (in the case of the Cook suburbs) by taxing commercial property at much higher rates. For example, in 1988, while Chicago and the suburb Burr Ridge (in DuPage County) boasted similar effective property-tax rates on residential property (1.79 percent and 1.71 percent, respectively), the former saddled commercial properties with a rate of 5.21 percent while the latter taxed them at 1.93 percent.

No wonder, then, that the policy analyses produced during the 1980s on behalf of both Cook County's commercial real-estate sector and the Cook County Assessor's Office betrayed profound concern with the rise of the collar counties. A 1983 study written by a tax consultant affiliated with major players in Chicago's commercial real-estate industry noted that "lower effective tax rates" for identical commercial properties in counties like DuPage and Lake

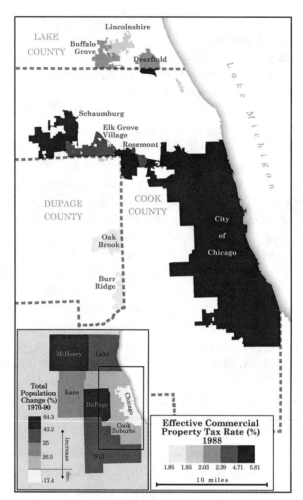

MAP 6.1. Average Effective Commercial Property-Tax Rates in Chicagoland Municipalities for which Data was Available, 1988, and Population Growth in Chicagoland Counties, 1970–1990

Source: Effective tax-rate data from Civic Federation, *Chicagoland—A Fiscal Perspective: 1979–1988* (Chicago: Civic Federation, 1990), 11. Population data for counties from U.S. Census Bureau, "Total Population" tables, 1970, 1980, and 1990. Prepared using *Social Explorer*, accessed January 7, 2015, www .socialexplorer.com/tables/C1990/R10863273. County and place shapefiles obtained from U.S. Census Bureau, *American FactFinder*.

Notes: The Civic Federation defines "effective tax rate" as the ratio of the "actual tax bill of a typical home or business" to the "market value of that property" (see Civic Federation, *Chicagoland—A Fiscal Perspective: 1979–1988*, 11). Several of the mapped municipalities straddle county boundaries and thus did not have uniform property-tax rates. For those for which rate data were not available on both sides of a county border (e.g., Oak Brook), only the portion of the municipality for which data was available is displayed. Some of the municipalities mapped above had ranges of typical tax rates rather than the average. In those cases, I used the midpoint of the range.

threatened growth prospects of Chicago's own real-estate industry. "Concentrations of office space outside Cook County have grown to the point where they now constitute a realistically acceptable alternative to downtown office space for businesses and other activities currently located in downtown Chicago," the study warned. Property-tax disparities were allegedly responsible for the fact that average rental costs for Chicago's downtown office space in 1982 stood at more than $12 per square foot, compared with less than $10 per square foot in suburban Chicagoland.[63]

All this was of particular concern to the commercial real-estate industry in and around the Loop, which witnessed an erosion of its regional dominance by the early 1980s. One industry estimate from that period indicated that in 1965 downtown Chicago housed nearly 98 percent of total metropolitan-area office inventory, but by 1982 the suburban share of that inventory had risen to just below 29 percent. A 1987 study commissioned by the City of Chicago Department of Planning confirmed this trend, noting that the regional market share of commercial office space represented by the inner city "could decline further as more new office centers are built in suburban locations."[64]

The perception, then, among commercial landholders and their tenants in Cook County, and particularly in downtown Chicago, was that the sky was falling. Undoubtedly, they experienced significantly higher property-tax burdens than their peers in the collar counties. Moreover, the ongoing decline in the industrial property-tax base and the ongoing commitment of the Cook County Democratic machine to maintaining low tax rates for homeowners meant a significant shift in relative tax loads from industrial to commercial landholders. Between 1977 and 1983, the percentage of total assessed property value in Cook County represented by commercial real estate jumped from 22 to 26.9 percent, whereas the percentage made up by industrial real estate fell from 18.5 to 16.4 percent. Within city limits, the changes proved even more dramatic, with commercial property moving from 28.8 to 35.9 percent of total assessed value, and industrial property shifting from 17.4 to 12.9 percent.[65] Federal and state policy shifts added to the sense of embattlement in the commercial real-estate industry. State and federal transfers dropped from 34 to 27 percent of total Chicago city revenues between 1982 and 1987 alone. As a result, businesses in the city had reason to worry that local government would try to lean even more heavily on commercial property taxation to pay for the ongoing cost of social welfare programs.[66]

In this context, the United Center property-tax breaks were not simply part of a national shift toward expanded corporate welfare. They were also part of a concerted effort by urban capitalists to realign the risk profile of real-estate investment in central cities like Chicago so that it more closely resembled that of outlying suburbs. Large landholders and trade associations were intent on stopping local policy makers from looking to taxation of commercial property as a way to preserve some semblance of progressive taxation, along with the social services it funded, as the federal government cut corporate taxes and abandoned a system of relatively robust revenue transfers to central cities.[67] In Chicago, this pushback against property taxes was also about the very specific history of property-tax assessment within the city and Cook County more generally. Subsidy deals like the United Center tax breaks were part of a larger rebellion by major commercial real-estate investors in Cook County, and particularly in the Loop, against a system of assessment and taxation that they identified as too progressive in its favoritism toward residential homeowners.[68]

Notably, the class politics of property taxation in and around the Second City after 1970 differed substantially from those in urban California, the region most closely linked in popular historical consciousness to the nationwide property-tax revolt. The anti-property-tax movement in California during the late 1970s was, as Robert Self argues, "one component of a larger attack on [local social-welfare] liberalism"—that is, on a progressive system of state and municipal taxation intended to fund an array of relatively inclusive social and public services—orchestrated largely by affluent homeowners.[69] By contrast, the "revolt" in Illinois was, at least initially, an effort led by social-justice groups and cash-strapped homeowners to preserve and extend a relatively progressive system of taxation in which commercial landholders subsidized ordinary folks' tax privileges. In response, commercial real-estate interests in and around Chicago waged a protracted and multipronged offensive against local property-tax policies throughout the 1980s and 1990s. The United Center property-tax deal was just one piece of this broader campaign to reduce the tax burden shouldered by wealthy commercial landholders in Chicagoland.

The approval by California voters in 1978 of Proposition 13, which restored assessed property values to 1976 levels and capped annual assessment increases at the extremely low rate of 2 percent, was the crowning success of an antitax movement led by relatively wealthy homeowners. These homeowners had grown particularly frustrated in the 1960s and 1970s with "modernization" of property-tax assessment, a process that grew out of a steady stream of public scrutiny of corruption and inconsistency in assessment practices.[70] In response, legislators in California decided to update assessment practices by implementing new qualification requirements for local assessors, mandating more frequent reassessment (to capture inflation), and implementing computerized assessment techniques to foster more objectivity.[71] Modernization in the Golden State ultimately unleashed a massive backlash, as reforms such as computerization meant the end to fractional assessment—the practice was not limited to Cook County—and what Isaac Martin describes as the "social protection from the market" that came with it. The new, less subjective methods resulted in large jumps in assessments across the board, jumps made even worse by steep inflation during the 1970s.[72]

There was far from a consensus among California homeowners about how to respond. Given that residential rates were rising faster than those paid by business, some called for a solution that would shift the property-tax burden to the commercial sector. However, the group that ultimately assumed leadership of California's tax rebels was a mélange of upper-middle-class suburban homeowners and suburban small-business owners who falsely equated high property taxes with the growth in "wasteful state bureaucracy." They set their sights on legislation that would slash property taxes across the board, rather than redistribute the property-tax burden from homeowners to corporations, in the hopes of dismantling urban social-welfare liberalism altogether. As Self explains, these tax rebels settled on "approach[ing] the tax question from the right" instead of "arguing for tax reform as an effort to correct the [increasingly] regressive nature of the state's tax system."[73]

Despite the fact that most major commercial real-estate holders in California opposed the legislation for fear that it would spark a backlash in the form of increased business taxes, Proposition 13 ended up benefiting them the most. According to one estimate, residential homeowners captured approximately 36 percent of property-tax savings resulting from Proposition 13 between 1978 and 1983; the remaining 64 percent accrued to farmers and owners of commercial and industrial properties—in the end, a significant redistribution of wealth to big business.[74]

Popular mobilization around the property tax in Illinois during the 1970s yielded a different outcome. Part of this had to do with a more cautious approach to the modernization of assessment in Illinois. While 1966 legislation passed by the California State Legislature mandated a uniform assessment of all property types—a move that ultimately shifted more of the tax burden onto residential properties—the Illinois General Assembly instituted several property-tax modernization "reforms" in 1969 and 1970 that mostly perpetuated the status quo. These reforms included requirements for more centralization and better training for assessors; however, in what was clearly a deferential nod to Chicago and Cook County, the state also allowed counties of a certain size to continue assessing residential property at lower percentages of full value than commercial and industrial. In addition, Illinois exempted the leadership of the Cook County Assessor's Office from more rigorous qualification requirements, allowing the Democratic machine to maintain its grip over assessment and continue to dole out fractional assessments to homeowners. This meant that through the early 1970s local homeowners, as Isaac Martin puts it, "had comparatively little to complain about." Cook County persisted in its long-running postwar practice of "treat[ing] homes more favorably than businesses."[75]

A different sort of tax rebel emerged from this environment—a variant who viewed property-tax reform as a way to bolster urban social-welfare liberalism rather than undermine it. During the late 1960s and early 1970s, a Chicago-based community organization called the Citizens' Action Program (CAP) pressured legislators to act on behalf of elderly "low- and moderate-income homeowners in the city" who viewed escalating assessments (driven by inflationary pressures) as a "threat to their income security."[76] CAP's grassroots mobilization and exposure of corruption at the Cook County Assessor's Office, namely egregiously low assessments granted to local steel companies, forced state legislators and county officials to act. Between 1970 and 1972, the Illinois General Assembly passed homestead exemption and circuit breaker laws, which decreased and capped, respectively, property-tax payments for low-income, senior citizen homeowners.[77] As the Illinois Economic and Fiscal Commission reported in 1973, lawmakers and activists understood these measures in terms of a progressive vision of social welfare—as "relief to those who most need it, i.e., to those whose incomes are relatively low and whose property taxes are high compared to income."[78]

The Cook County Board, no doubt eager to fend off a broader property-tax revolt and preserve property assessment as a politically valuable patronage mechanism, acted quickly to formalize a system favorable to homeowners. To do so, the board passed an ordinance in 1973 mandating that residential properties be assessed at 22 percent of full market value, apartment buildings at 33 percent, and industrial and commercial properties at 40 percent.[79] By the end of the decade Cook County would reduce the residential percentage to 16 percent but leave rates for other classes unchanged.[80] At the start of the 1980s, local government was going out of its way to privilege ordinary homeowners when it came to property taxes.

This classification system was not new. The Assessor's Office had informally privileged homeowners with preferential rates of assessment for decades. But the formalization of the county classification system sent a louder, clearer message that the local Democratic machine was not about to give up property-tax policy as a means of retaining some vestige of progressive fiscal management.[81] Indeed, the *Tribune* reported that the classification ordinance would "shift more of the property tax burden from [residential] living units to commercial and industrial properties."[82] A 1985 analysis commissioned by then Cook County assessor Thomas Hynes agreed, concluding that the classification system and the array of exemptions instituted over the prior decade had the "net effect" of significantly "shifting" the local property-tax burden from residential to "income producing" (i.e., commercial) properties. The analysis added that by 1980 the total amount of assessed residential property value untaxed as a result of recently implemented, homeowner-friendly exemptions had surpassed $2 billion.[83]

Given the paucity of reliable data on effective tax rates during the 1970s and 1980s, as well as the long history of inconsistent assessment techniques within Cook County (even post-modernization), it is difficult to verify whether the classification ordinance resulted in a further shift of the tax burden to business or simply legalized the status quo of informal homeowner privilege. The Civic Federation, a nonprofit tax watchdog group, consistently argued that "the decision to classify Cook County assessments initially was made so that the commercial/industrial sector would bear a larger share of the tax burden than the residential sector."[84] Sociologist Clarence Lo agrees, pointing out that in contrast to California, tax reform in Illinois achieved a certain measure of "downward distribution." However, a 1986 study completed for the Mayor's Office by a quartet of experts claimed that, according to the city's financial statements, the percentage of the property-tax burden placed on Chicago business remained steady at 64 percent between 1970 and 1984.[85] Whatever the case, the variable classification system meant the persistence of a relatively progressive property-tax system in Cook County. A 1989 report published by the Civic Federation noted that as of 1987 the effective property-tax rate on residential homes in the county stood at 1.5 percent, compared to 5.4 percent for commercial property and 4.8 percent on industrial property.[86] According to separate estimates published by the State of Illinois in 1990, commercial and industrial property accounted for less than a third of total market value of all property in Cook County at the time, yet it generated approximately 59 percent of the county's property-tax revenue.[87]

In the midst of the profit squeeze of the 1970s and growth rates in the 1980s that failed to match the immediate post–World War II boom, the business community in Cook County viewed progressive property taxation as a serious threat. The preface to a 1983 report commissioned by major landholders from downtown Chicago asserted, "A growing imbalance in the allocation of the property tax burden threatens to tip the scales against downtown's buildings and employers so far that they could be seriously damaged unless needed changes are made." The report lambasted the "inequity and destructiveness of the existing system" and suggested that "a greater measure of equity be

restored to the property tax system as it affects downtown Chicago."[88] According to this line of thinking, major commercial landholders were victims
of a property-taxation scheme squarely at odds with national trends toward
business-friendly solutions to slowed growth. Just as the Reagan administration embarked on aggressive cuts to corporate taxes—corporate income
tax as a share of GDP went from 2.4 to 1.5 percent between 1980 and 1984
—commercial real-estate investors in Chicago allegedly found themselves
under a fiscal siege orchestrated by local policy makers.[89]

By the late 1970s influential firms and civic organizations like the Chicago
Central Area Committee were fighting back against the prevailing property-
tax structure. A key component of this pushback consisted of a sleek public
relations and political lobbying campaign underwritten by the commercial
real-estate industry, as well as by banks, law firms, insurance companies,
and advertising firms that leased office space in the Loop. Predictably, the
primary target of this campaign was the classification system. A 1983 policy
study funded by the likes of the Chicago Mercantile Exchange, First National
Bank of Chicago, JMB Realty Corporation (a concern founded by Bulls limited partners Judd Malkin and Robert Judelson), and Prudential Insurance
isolated the Cook County Classification Ordinance of 1974 as a blight on the
commercial real-estate sector. And the Chicago Commercial Club's much-
heralded 1984 report *Jobs for Metropolitan Chicago* proclaimed, "The existing real estate classification system in Cook County is too complex, inhibits
economic growth and is more than a decade old." It went on: "Tax assessment based on the system has an adverse impact on decisions to locate business here."[90]

These reports were only the beginning of a steady stream of data, rhetoric,
and lobbying in support of refashioning the local property-tax system in the
name of more robust profits for businesses in and around the Loop. Subsequent efforts by the likes of the Building Owners and Managers Association
and the Chicago Association of Commerce and Industry (later renamed the
Chicagoland Chamber of Commerce) would strike the same chord.[91] Moreover, the barrage of business-sponsored, anticlassification literature did not
languish in some isolated echo chamber populated only by petulant capitalists; the local press did its part to convince the public of the merit of taxing
those capitalists less. Beginning in 1980, for example, *Crain's Chicago Business*
began running an annual "Property Tax Analyses" feature that aped the business community's complaints about the purported role of property taxes in
driving investment to the suburbs, as well as its arguments in favor of rewriting the classification system.[92]

During the first half of the 1980s the informational and lobbying campaigns started to chip away at the 40 percent assessment rate for business. In 1980 the Cook County Board attempted to placate local business by authorizing steep reductions in assessments for commercial investors building in areas "in need of development." Major developers quickly parlayed the new law into millions in tax savings, despite questions about whether many of the development sites genuinely met the "in need" criteria.[93] By 1984 Cook County had devised at least four such "incentive" programs for commercial and industrial real estate investors, some of which mandated assessment and tax cuts of as much as 60 percent for periods of up to twelve years.[94] The concessions did not stop there. In 1986 Cook County instituted reductions in the assessment level for commercial and industrial property. On the surface, the reductions seemed modest; the assessment rates (i.e., the percentage of "fair market value" used to determine the taxable value of a property) were reduced from 40 percent to 38 percent for commercial property and from 40 percent to 36 percent for industrial property.[95] However, a couple of percentage points could mean hundreds of thousands of dollars in property-tax savings for downtown office towers.

In 2008, more than two decades later and amid ongoing descriptions of classification as an "obstacle to economic growth" by the local real-estate industry, the Cook County Board reduced the statutory assessment levels on commercial and industrial property to 25 percent of market value. While the board simultaneously reduced the official residential assessment level to 10 percent, thus maintaining preferential treatment of homeowners, the gap continued to narrow between statutory assessment rates for commercial and residential. In other words, by 2000, the degree of legal property-tax privilege enjoyed by homeowners was in significant decline.[96]

The *Chicago Tribune*'s Steve Kerch once described the greater corporate pushback against classification as a new "property tax revolt of a quiet kind" in contrast to the "placard-carrying homeowners" of the 1970s.[97] It is only in the context of this "quiet" revolt that the United Center tax deal makes sense. One of the deal's key provisions, reducing the assessment level on the arena from the standard 38 percent to 20 percent, constituted an extension of contemporary business efforts to undermine the classification system's favoritism of regular homeowners and to remove one of the last bulwarks of relatively progressive taxation in Chicago.

This movement placed significant downward pressure on tax rates for commercial real estate. The limited data available on changes in effective tax rates of different classes of property in Chicago city indicate that between the early 1990s and mid-2000s, rates plummeted for commercial and industrial property while holding relatively steady for homeowners (table 6.1). Accord-

TABLE 6.1. Effective Property-Tax Rates, City of Chicago, Tax Years 1987–2012

Tax year	Residential	Commercial	Industrial
1987	1.50	5.40	4.80
1988	1.79	5.21	4.84
1989	1.68	5.81	4.97
1990	1.50	4.53	4.61
1991	1.57	4.38	4.41
1992	1.55	4.31	5.85
No data available 1993–1998			
1999	1.51	4.61	4.34
2000	1.47	3.88	2.91
2001	1.34	3.12	2.95
2002	1.27	3.27	2.05
2003	1.39	3.01	1.76
2004	1.29	2.25	1.90
2005	1.21	2.37	1.84
2006	1.29	1.87	1.24
2007	1.25	2.20	1.49
2008	1.31	2.35	1.61
2009	1.45	2.43	n/a
2010	1.72	4.23	n/a
2011	1.76	3.75	n/a
2012	1.84	4.87	3.23
2013	1.66	3.84	3.62

Source: Civic Federation, Chicagoland—A Fiscal Perspective (Chicago: Civic Federation, 1989–1994),
Municipal Reference Collection, Harold Washington Library Center; Civic Federation, Effective Property
Tax Rates 1999–2008 (2010); Civic Federation, Estimated Effective Property Tax Rates 2000–2009 (2011);
Civic Federation, Estimated Effective Property Tax Rates 2003–2012 (2014); Civic Federation, Estimated
Effective Property Tax Rates 2004–2013 (2015).

Notes: Figures for effective property-tax rates are estimates of the ratio between a typical property's tax bill
and its full market value (i.e., market sale price). For years after 2004, residential rates do not account for
homestead exemptions.

ing to these numbers, by 2006 the commercial rate sat less than .5 percentage points above the residential rate, whereas in the late 1980s the difference
was usually around 3 or 4 points. The trends for commercial and industrial
would reverse after 2006, most likely because the reassessment of properties
lagged behind the fall of property values caused by the 2007 financial crisis
(reassessment by Cook County does not occur every year, which means that
a property's formal assessed value may fail to track sudden declines in market
value). Nevertheless, effective property-tax rates for business remained significantly below levels of the late 1980s.

The war against commercial property taxation waged by the likes of
Reinsdorf and Wirtz had consequences for ordinary Chicagoans that data
on tax rates fail to capture. Nowhere was this more evident than in Chicago

Public Schools (CPS), which, like other districts in Illinois, have remained overly dependent on funding from property taxes. Absent a compensatory rise in residential tax rates in Cook County, the widespread success of the commercial real-estate sector in reducing its property-tax burden has played an important role in what a *Crain's Chicago Business* reporter described in 1998 as the "chronic underfunding" of CPS. By extension, this has contributed to the shuttering of numerous neighborhood schools, educational program cuts, and seemingly constant teacher layoffs in recent decades.[98] It was not just peanut vendors and public-housing residents who found themselves undermined by United Center ownership. In fact, the costs of the arena trickled down in ways that left few Chicagoans untouched.

The United Center, Amusement Taxes, and the Downward Shift of the Tax Burden

In May 1991, Fran Spielman of the *Sun-Times* noted the City Council's decision to exempt 40 percent of the revenue produced by United Center luxury boxes from Chicago's amusement tax, which normally required professional sports facilities and other entertainment venues to transfer 4 percent of ticket sales proceeds to the city. From 2002 to 2007, the only years for which data are available, the breaks in amusement taxes saved Reinsdorf and Wirtz more than $5.2 million (in constant 2016 dollars; see appendix D for calculations).[99] Though small relative to the property-tax abatements, these breaks still resulted in significant long-term savings for the owners. United Center officials insisted that the tax breaks were a prerequisite for private financing of the new arena. "The lenders wouldn't agree to anything less," Reinsdorf's spokesperson Howard Pizer told Spielman right before the City Council approved the amendment.[100] Much like the special assessment formula, the amusement-tax breaks reduced the owners' tax bill and helped them secure cheaper credit.

Situated in the broader history of municipal finance in Chicago, the amusement-tax breaks shielded the team owners from new and higher taxes and fees intended to help the city weather budgetary strain at the end of the twentieth century. The Chicago amusement tax dated to 1947. However, the combination of declines in federal aid to cities, the fall of commercial property-tax rates, and the reticence of local politicians to raise residential property taxes pushed the Mayor's Office and City Council, as well as the Cook County Board, to create new taxes and nontax fees (e.g., permits, fines) and increase existing ones.[101] City parking and cigarette taxes, both instituted in 1972, were two of at least eight taxes and fees created by Chicago over the course of the 1970s. These were followed by a new city sales tax and increased utility taxes in 1982, and the list of taxes—on long-distance phone calls, soft drinks, wine, beer, alcohol, gas, and so on—grew in subsequent years, as did the rates on existing consumption taxes and user fees.[102] Between 1983 and 1992, property-tax levies within the city of Chicago continued to rise, roughly 29 percent when adjusted for inflation, in line with education costs. But over the same period revenues from local nonproperty taxes like sales and excise taxes and user fees went up at a faster rate (33 percent) to help offset the nearly 23 percent fall in receipts from intergovernmental revenue.[103] The flat rates on most of the taxes and fees meant they were regressive, eating up larger shares of earnings for low-income people. That wealthy businessmen like Reinsdorf and Wirtz successfully dodged significant chunks of their statutory liabilities under these levies only exacerbated their regressiveness.[104]

Ordinary Chicagoans, and especially low-income residents, thus found themselves squeezed from both sides by the transformation of local fiscal policy pushed for successfully by urban capitalists. On the one hand, the erosion of commercial property taxes as a central component of the city's fiscal base made it harder to fund basic services like public schools. On the other hand, the new taxes demanded by local officials to sustain what remained of public infrastructure fell disproportionately on the backs of those who could least afford them. This is an important point, as some might identify the maintenance of relatively low residential property taxes as an exception to larger trends of exclusionary capitalism. They were not: maintaining them relied not on redistributing resources from the top down but on preserving a limited amount of privilege for the middle class by further exploiting low-income people.

Reinsdorf and Wirtz were not satisfied with the exemption of 40 percent of skybox revenues. They also lobbied aggressively to block amusement-tax increases by the city and county. Each time the City Council or the County Board considered raising the amusement tax, United Center officials sent irate letters, issued formal complaints at public hearings, made critical statements to the local media, and pressured local officials behind closed doors.[105] The stated rationale for their opposition was simultaneously comical and offensive. In 1996 Andrew Fegelman of the *Tribune* reported that after John Stroger, Cook County Board president, proposed a county-level amusement tax, he "got an angry phone call" from Reinsdorf, who was "upset that Stroger would suggest such a tax when his teams already have been suffering from accusations that their tickets are overpriced." Of course, the tickets were overpriced by most Chicagoans' standards. Reinsdorf opposed the tax because he understood that, given that prices were already as high as local demand would allow, increased amusement taxes would come out of his pockets, not from higher ticket prices. Howard Pizer, correctly assuming that few Chicagoans realized the extent of the tax relief his bosses already enjoyed, added that, as Fegelman put it, "his industry was being asked by government to shoulder too much of a burden."[106]

The history of the amusement-tax breaks confirms that this sort of corporate welfare had as much to do with changes in fiscal policy writ large as with the monopoly powers wielded by pro sports leagues and teams. Investment "incentive" programs that the state debuted during the 1980s and 1990s, such as the Enterprise Zone Program and High Impact Business Program, included exemptions from paying excise and sales taxes. Many major corporations, including Boeing, Sears, and Walmart, availed themselves of the breaks in return for establishing or maintaining a presence in the state. In other words, the amusement-tax breaks granted to the United Center signaled not so much that local policy makers considered themselves hostages of the sports business in particular; rather, they were willing to give arena ownership the same preferential treatment received by the commercial real-estate industry across the board.[107]

*

In June 2013, Reinsdorf told Fran Spielman of the *Sun-Times* that the special property-tax formula "didn't save us millions of dollars. . . . [A]ll we got was predictability and tax certainty. . . . [F]or all I know, we ended up paying more taxes than we would otherwise have paid."[108] This claim, however absurd, nicely encapsulated the new era of stadium financing from which the United Center emerged. As teams like the Bulls touted their "free market" bona fides by pointing to their use of private money to finance new facilities, they engineered complex subsidy deals to ensure that the public bore the bulk of the investment risk. What most distinguished the new generation of stadiums from their predecessors was not the extent of private investment but the extent of private control over expanding stadium-generated revenues. In the end, while Reinsdorf and Wirtz priced out most Chicagoans from the United Center, they demanded that those same Chicagoans subsidize the facility through schemes largely hidden from public view.

As tempting as it is to chalk up this case study and the recent history of stadium finance entirely to monopoly powers specific to the professional sports business, there is more to it. Policy makers' willingness to subsidize Reinsdorf and Wirtz without asking for anything in return increasingly characterized the dealings between the government and capital throughout the economy after the 1970s. More and more, firms from a wide array of sectors flexed their political muscle by way of growing involvement in campaign finance. As a result, they availed themselves of an expanding menu of corporate subsidy programs offered by cities, counties, states, and the federal government, all of which prioritized private profitability over the public good.

In Chicago, the United Center also joined a broad coalition of these firms in fighting back against a local system of property taxation that, in their view, remained stubbornly progressive after the 1970s, particularly in comparison to places like California. Simultaneously, they made every effort to insulate themselves from a growing array of new regressive taxes and fees borne primarily by regular consumers and intended to make up for the gradual reduction of the commercial real-estate sector's property-tax burden. In the end, the Bulls' relationship to the government and fiscal policy represents an acute symptom of systemic problems, not an exception within an otherwise free market.

Conclusion

A few weeks before the Bulls won their fifth NBA title in 1997, traffic cop Stan Mullins voiced what many of his fellow Chicagoans thought about Michael Jordan. "It's amazing how one man could change the face of this city," Mullins stated.[1] He was right. Although the mystique of Jordan never fully eradicated the iconography of Al Capone—today travelers can still purchase Capone-themed shot glasses at Midway Airport or pay $30 to take an "Untouchables tour" of the city—in the eyes of many Chicago was a different place because of His Airness. For Chicagoans, the success of Jordan and the Bulls provided psychological benefits—pride, fun, distraction—that came with living in a championship city and on occasion fostered collective celebration that transformed places like Grant Park into momentary oases of diversity.

Viewed in isolation, these benefits suggest that teams like the Bulls made their respective cities better places to live for everyone. But considered along with the long list of items on the "cost" side of the ledger it is far less clear that, on balance, the team proved a boon to Chicago after Jerry Reinsdorf assumed control of the franchise in 1985. All in the name of increased profits, Bulls ownership made it harder and harder for working- and middle-class fans to attend games, promoted a model of redevelopment on the Near West Side that further marginalized low-income residents, insisted on massive surface parking lots at the United Center that discouraged nearby investment, ruthlessly purged independent peanut and souvenir vendors from around the arena, and refused to pay anything resembling a fair share of taxes in a city already plagued by underfunded schools and social services.

Moreover, the only conceivable economic benefits from the Bulls in this period were marginal at best and had nothing to do with a new arena or any other part of Jerry Reinsdorf's growth strategy. That the team provided a

boost to local tourism was the result of an accident—Michael Jordan's land-
ing in Chicago—unrelated to the construction of the United Center. Boosters were not wrong to characterize the Bulls as exceptional in terms of their
commitment to the community. But what distinguished the team's ownership in this regard was not that they avoided imposing severe socioeconomic
costs on their host city but that they exploited Chicago and Chicagoans a bit
less than was normal for major-league franchises in the New Gilded Age. The
bar, in other words, was incredibly low.

Teams like the Bulls and wealthy urban capitalists like Reinsdorf continue
to inflict on their cities the types of socioeconomic costs discussed in the previous chapters to further enrich themselves. In December 2016, Sarah Lyall
of the *New York Times* reported that the Barclays Center in Brooklyn, home
of the NBA's Nets, was hawking something called the "Brooklyn Sports and
Entertainment Experience." The "experience," which charges fans more than
$6,000 per game for VIP treatment including access to several "not-open-to-
the-public-back areas," exemplifies the ongoing gentrification of sports venues as owners continue to capitalize on staggering levels of income inequality. Other segments of the urban entertainment industry have followed suit.
Movie theaters, for example, increasingly devote seating to IMAX theaters
and costlier "luxury" options like "plush recliners."[2]

Avaricious commercial landholders and their lawmaker allies have continued the assault on independent vendors around stadiums and on city sidewalks more generally. In February 2016, Georgia's Cobb County passed an
ordinance granting MLB's Atlanta Braves the power to prohibit any independent peddling activity around their new stadium.[3] On the other side of the
country, the new millennium ushered in intensified harassment of street vendors by Los Angeles law enforcement— part of the city's ongoing embrace
of "broken windows" policing—despite evidence that the peddlers help the
local economy (on more recent developments in LA, see notes).[4]

The business model of urban capitalists like Reinsdorf, which depends
on reduced taxation and expanded government subsidies for wealthy and
well-connected firms, maintains a firm grip over American cities that shows
few signs of loosening. James Dolan, owner of the New York Knicks and
their home arena, Madison Square Garden, recently fought off an attempt
by reformers to repeal a property-tax break that saves his enterprise around
$50 million annually. And in the 2016 presidential election, nearly 63 million
Americans voted for Donald Trump, a man whose "fortune" derives in large
part from hundreds of millions of dollars in tax breaks on his various real-
estate developments. That much of America respects—some might go so far

as to say "idolizes"—this sort of exploitative accumulation of wealth is cause for great concern. As I was finishing this book, Amazon CEO Jeff Bezos was stoking a national subsidy-bidding war between cities and states bent on securing the privilege of hosting the company's new corporate headquarters. A bill introduced in California's state legislature in October 2017 could result in as much as $1 billion in total tax breaks for Amazon over ten years if it locates the new facility in the Golden State.[5]

If the United States continues down this path, the future will be one of increased insecurity and suffering for most Americans. Economist Thomas Piketty warns that if economic inequality in the United States continues to intensify as it has over the past generation, it could reach world-historic levels by 2030.[6] Even the International Monetary Fund, by no means a bastion of progressive economic thought, asserted in June 2017 that growth in the United States since the financial crisis of 2007–2008 "has been too low and too unequal." The organization went on to note that "in inflation-adjusted terms, more than half of U.S. households [have] a lower income today than they did in 2000," and the United States has "one of the highest" poverty rates among "advanced economies." Chicago persists as a microcosm of these trends, as the current mayor, Rahm Emanuel, clings to what journalist Ben Joravsky aptly describes as an "obsession with downtown development." This was bad news for most Chicagoans but not for Reinsdorf. He officially became a billionaire in 2015.[7]

What is to be done? According to many economists and legal experts, the best tactic for reigning in team owners' ability to exploit host cities is breaking up the major-league cartels into separate, competing leagues by way of more aggressive antitrust enforcement, thereby eliminating teams' exclusive territorial franchises. This proposal, at least in theory, has real merit. Increased competition—that is, more leagues and teams—could help reduce ticket prices through increased supply and arrest the growth of public stadium subsidies by reducing the leverage that any individual franchise has over its host city.[8] With enough public support, along with careful design and implementation, such a reform would likely make a real difference.

Activists have also offered serious, if more radical, solutions, such as public ownership and control of professional sports franchises à la F.C. Barcelona, one of Europe's premier soccer clubs. Barcelona operates as a nonprofit, with a club president elected by "fan members" who each hold very small stakes in the team. According to advocates, this model mitigates problems like extortionate ticket pricing and prioritizes the concerns of ordinary fans over enrichment of owners.[9] Though improbable in the United States because of certain resistance from major-league owners and officials, this scheme deserves serious consideration by those interested in building a serious movement for a less exclusionary professional sports industry.

Initiatives to reign in the power of team owners through local government reform are less fanciful and have even become a reality in some cities. For example, in 2006 voters in Seattle approved an initiative limiting the city's ability to dole out subsidies to professional sports teams and mandating that the city earn a financial return on investing in facilities used by privately owned teams. Such developments are encouraging, but their impact is limited by their modest geographic scope; city ordinances cannot stop counties, states, or nearby suburbs from doling out unconditional subsidies. As the urban historian Colin Gordon rightly argues, organizers will have to replicate such success at regional and national levels to make a serious dent in the ability of urban capitalists to avail themselves of wasteful corporate welfare.[10]

Rather than dismissing any of these approaches, my instinct is to entertain all of them as possible components of a larger effort to create a less exclusionary sports business. All who insist they have a silver bullet should be greeted with skepticism, and those interested in real change would do well to embrace political experimentation. One of the lessons of the recent history of the Bulls is that reform efforts focused exclusively on ending the seemingly special relationship between the government and the sports industry will not be enough. There is no guarantee that simply pushing through a mandate to subject the major leagues to the same degree of antitrust scrutiny and enforcement as other industries will prevent billionaire team owners from continuing to accumulate ever-larger amounts of wealth and power. After all, much of the exclusionary capitalist behavior rampant among teams like the Bulls—namely, the development of parasitic relationships with government and the pricing out of ordinary consumers—pervades the entire economy. With each passing year, industries other than sports that are dominated by predatory monopolies or oligopolies become less and less exceptional. Moreover, putting all of our energy into reforms that only target the legal standing of the major leagues would constitute extremely inefficient politics. Major-league sports remain a tiny slice of the overall American economy, on the order of .001 or .002 percent of U.S. GDP at the end of the twentieth century.[11] By singling out the sports business as the problem, as some orthodox economists do, activists run the risk of directing desperately needed reform efforts away from the rest of the economy, where exclusionary capitalism is also the norm.

With all this in mind, it is important to incorporate attempts to fix the sports industry into broader movements to make our cities (and nation) more inclusive and corporations less powerful: real campaign-finance reform (i.e., publicly funded rather than privately funded campaigns), genuinely progressive taxation, and public spending that prioritizes the economic security of ordinary people. Even without any special focus on the sports business, these types of movements will mitigate many of the exploitative practices of owners like Reinsdorf by redistributing wealth and power downward. A significant downward distribution of wealth, for example, would reduce the incentive to cater to rich consumers. It would also reduce the capacity of urban capitalists to dictate city politics through lobbying and campaign finance.

While it does not offer any easy fixes, the history of the Bulls does suggest important characteristics of a more inclusive pro sports industry: first, more equitable access to games; second, adoption of stadium designs that focus on integrating spectator sport into neighborhoods rather than clearing the way for unobstructed profiteering by team owners; and last, increased democratic control over financing of sports infrastructure.

Under the ownership of Jerry Reinsdorf, the Bulls have provided humanity with a lot of thrills over the past three decades. Any sports fan, and many who are not sports fans, will tell you as much. Fewer know, however, that over the same period the franchise took almost every opportunity to enrich itself at the expense of regular Chicagoans. Reinsdorf decided to do so not to keep a struggling operation afloat but to further pad the bottom line of an already-profitable business. Nonetheless, the mainstream media, and even some academics, heralded the Bulls as a shining example of civic-mindedness within the sports business. This should be of profound concern not just to Chicagoans but to America at large. If the Bulls are the best that the business of professional sport can offer in terms of corporate responsibility, then there is little doubt that the team is part of a fundamentally broken industry and, more broadly, a fundamentally broken economic system. As a society, we are long past due in reshaping this system so that the pleasure sport provides is not contingent on our acceptance of a more unequal society.

Chapter 2 presents a variety of data on the relationship between socioeconomic status and the likelihood of attending live sporting events during the 1990s. This appendix briefly describes the methods behind analyzing some of these data.

In his study on the relationship between social class and sporting event attendance, the sociologist Thomas Wilson applied a statistical technique called multiple classification analysis (also known as factorial analysis of variance, or factorial ANOVA) to data from the 1993 General Social Survey (GSS). Wilson's analysis shows that "those who are richest in cultural capital [measured as education] and those richest in economic capital [measured as income]" are the most likely to attend live sporting events.[1] Wilson employed multiple classification analysis in large part because of the formatting of GSS variables. The survey designers formatted income as an ordinal variable— that is, a variable in which each respondent falls into one of several discrete and ordered ranges like $0–$4,999, $5,000–$9,999, and so on. The variable recording whether a respondent attended a sporting event the previous year has a binary, or dichotomous, format, which allows for only two possible values: 0 when the respondent did not attend, and 1 if the respondent did attend. Factorial ANOVA is well suited for isolating and quantifying relationships between an ordinal variable and a dichotomous variable, hence Wilson's methodological approach.

However, multiple classification analysis cannot produce estimates of the change in the odds of a specific outcome (dependent) variable—in this case, whether someone attended a sporting event—associated with a given change in a predictor (independent) variable (e.g. income).[2] To do so, one would need to convert the predictor variable of interest—for example, income—

into a continuous variable, or a variable that can assume an unlimited number of specific respondent values, like $29,343 and $100,676. I built on Wilson's analysis by performing such a conversion and then using a technique called logistic regression to generate estimates of the quantitative relationship between respondents' odds of having attended a sporting event and a single-unit change in income and education (one dollar and one year, respectively). The logistic regression analysis also generated the predicted probability curves in figures 2.3 and 2.4.[3]

Data and Methods

For the United States, the 1993 GSS was one of three national surveys *not* conducted by private market-research firms that asked respondents about their sport spectatorship habits during the 1990s.[4] The survey employed a nationally representative sample of English-speaking households. The sample excluded populations not living in households (e.g. college dorm residents, military personnel, the homeless, and incarcerated populations). All respondents were at least eighteen years of age.

My analysis consists of five basic logistic regression models with the same dependent variable: whether the respondent attended an amateur or professional sporting event in the year leading up to the survey (1992). The relevant survey question reads:

> Next I'd like to ask about some leisure or recreational activities that people do during their free time. As I read each activity, can you tell me if it is something you have done in the past twelve months? Let's begin with attending an amateur or professional sports event. Did you do that within the past twelve months?[5]

The only restriction on the sample for my models was the exclusion of cases with missing values on the independent, dependent, or cohort variables. For the first model, which uses per capita family income as the sole predictor, 1,464 respondents make up the restricted sample. The second through fifth models, each of which uses years of education as the lone predictor for a different age cohort, relied on samples consisting of 136, 720, 432, and 298 respondents. A previous version of this analysis included only one model containing both family income and education as predictor variables, as well as several other controls.[6] I chose to redo the analysis using these two, simplified models because (1) the lone model suffered from significant multicollinearity as a result of including both income and education as predictors; (2) the simplified models help address the issue of potential interactive effects between

TABLE A.A.1. Descriptive Statistics for General Social Survey Samples

	Mean or percentage	Standard deviation	Minimum	Maximum
Income model (*n* = 1,464)				
Dependent variables				
Individual level				
Attended sporting event in previous year				
Yes	57.42		0	1
No[a]	42.58		0	1
Independent variables				
Household level				
Family income (per capita 1992 dollars)	16,753.86	14,526.84	125.00	103,591.60
Education models				
Dependent variables				
Individual level				
Attended sporting event in previous year by age cohort				
18–24 years old (*n* = 136)				
Yes	69.68		0	1
No[a]	30.32		0	1
25–44 years old (*n* = 720)				
Yes	65.19		0	1
No[a]	34.81		0	1
45–64 years old (*n* = 432)				
Yes	51.19		0	1
No[a]	48.81		0	1
65+ years old (*n* = 298)				
Yes	31.50		0	1
No[a]	68.50		0	1
Independent variables				
Individual level				
Years of education by age cohort				
18–24 years old	12.94	1.87	8	17
25–44 years old	13.80	2.62	5	20
45–64 years old	13.05	3.12	0	20
65+ years old	11.44	3.46	0	20

Source: National Opinion Research Center, *General Social Survey, 1993* (Chicago: University of Chicago, 1993).

Notes: Descriptive statistics for individual-level variables weighted to account for the higher probability of the GSS selecting respondents from smaller households.

[a]Reference category.

family income and household size on the one hand, and between education and age on the other; and (3) my main interest in this case was not isolating specific causal mechanisms so much as describing the order of magnitude of the relationship between different measures of socioeconomic status and sporting event attendance. Table A.A.1 provides descriptive statistics for the independent and dependent variables for all models.

Wilson's analysis does not specify if he used family or respondent income, but I opted for the former in my first model since one would expect that having parents or other immediate family members with higher incomes could affect young-adult or nonworker respondents' ability to attend sporting events. The GSS records income within discrete bands rather than as a continuous variable. Following Michael Hout's work on using GSS income measures, I recoded the bands as a continuous variable using the midpoint of each. I also used an equation offered by Hout to compute a top code based on the frequencies of respondents in the top two income bands (for this data set, $103,591.57).[7] I did not transform the continuous income variable using a natural logarithm, a common practice in econometrics, since its distribution does not display the right skewness typical of most income measures (largely because of the aforementioned top-coding procedure). However, I did divide each respondent's family income (continuous) by the number of people in the respondent's household to generate a new per capita family income variable—the predictor ultimately used in the first regression. Using the per capita variable addresses the fact that large households reliant on a given income are likely to have had less money per person for leisure activities than smaller households with the same income. Therefore, family income per person offers a more precise measurement of an individual respondent's socioeconomic status. The equation for model 1 is as follows:

$$Y_{ij} = \beta_0 + \beta_1 [\text{per capita family income}]_j + \varepsilon_{i,}$$

where Y_{ij} is the binary outcome indicating whether respondent i from household j attended an amateur or professional sporting event, β_0 is the intercept, β_1 is the regression coefficient for the per capita family income variable, and ε_i is the error term. The model is weighted to account for the number of adults in each respondent's household, as the survey design made it less likely that individuals in large households were selected relative to individuals in smaller households.

Respondents' years of education constitutes the predictor of interest for the second through fifth models, each of which restricts the sample to a unique age cohort: 18–24 years old, 25–44 years old, 45–64 years old, or 65 years and older. I disaggregated by age cohort because many younger respondents from more affluent backgrounds had not yet reached the end of their educational histories. As a result, separating by age helps guard against the possibility of a single model confusing young age with low socioeconomic status (i.e. failing to account for the interactive effects of age and education). The equation for models 2–5 is as follows:

$$Y_{ia} = \beta_0 + \beta_1[\text{education}]_i + \varepsilon_i,$$

where Y_{ia} is the binary outcome indicating whether respondent i from age cohort a attended an amateur or professional sporting event, β_0 is the intercept, β_1 is the regression coefficient for the respondent's years of education, and ε_i is the error term. This model is also weighted to account for the number of adults in each respondent's household.

Results

Table A.A.2 lists the results of the logistic regression analyses. In terms of significance and the direction of effects of the independent or predictor variables of interest, the results confirm the conclusions reached by Wilson. In the first model, the exponentiated coefficient for the predictor ($p < 0.001$) indicates that a \$10,000 increase in per capita family income was associated with a 32 percent increase in the odds of attending a sporting event. Figure 2.3 graphs the predicted probabilities of sporting event attendance as a function of per capita family income.

In model 2, the exponentiated coefficients for education are all positive and significant ($p < 0.001$ for all cohorts save 18–24 years old, the coefficient of which is significant at the $p < 0.01$ level). The effect size of education is largest for the youngest cohort: each additional year of education was associated with a 36 percent increase in the odds of attendance. The effect size is smallest for the cohort age 25–44: each additional year of education was associated with a 21 percent increase in the odds of attendance. Figure 2.4 graphs the predicted probabilities of sporting event attendance as a function of years of education for each age cohort.

In interpreting these results, readers should keep in mind that the GSS asked about professional and amateur events. Amateur events are likely to be much cheaper or even free, and thus frequented more by larger families on tighter budgets. This means that had the survey asked only about professional events, the positive associations between socioeconomic status and attendance would have likely been even stronger.

TABLE A.A.2. Logistic Regression of Probability of Having Attended a Sporting Event on Individual- and Household-Level Variables

	β	e^{β}
Income model ($n = 1{,}464$)		
Household level		
Family income (per capita 1992 dollars)	0.000028*** (0.000005)	1.000028
Education models		
Individual level		
Years of education by age cohort		
18–24 years old ($n = 136$)	0.306478** (0.102783)	1.358632
25–44 years old ($n = 720$)	0.190662*** (0.035992)	1.210050
45–64 years old ($n = 432$)	0.215651*** (0.038276)	1.240669
65+ years old ($n = 298$)	0.252504*** (0.048189)	1.287245

Source: National Opinion Research Center, General Social Survey, 1993 (Chicago: University of Chicago, 1993).

Notes: Robust standard errors in parentheses below coefficients. Two things likely explain the relatively large standard error and p-value for the youngest age cohort: 1) the comparatively small sample size; and 2) the fact that there is less variability within the cohort in terms of years of education since it is impossible, for example, for respondents in their late teens to have 20 years of education (the maximum value for the education variable in the survey). Because a discussion of model fit is not particularly relevant to this analysis, I do not report goodness of fit measures (e.g., information criterion).

***$p < 0.001$. **$p < 0.01$.

Appendix B: City of Chicago, Cook County, and Illinois State Campaign Contributions by United Center Ownership and Executives, 1980–2016

The in-text references in chapters 3, 5, and 6 to political campaign contributions by United Center ownership and executives rely on data from microfiche records held by the Illinois State Board of Elections archive in Chicago and online records maintained by the Illinois Sunshine Database. The data are limited to contributions to candidates running for city-level offices in Chicago (e.g., mayor), county-level offices in Cook (e.g., assessor), and state-level offices in Illinois (e.g., attorney general), as these were the levels of government responsible for legislation affecting the profitability of the United Center. In addition to providing tables summarizing these contributions, this appendix addresses two important methodological issues: why the data fail to capture 100 percent of the contributions of interest and how I define the categories of United Center ownership and United Center executives.

Data Issues

Since 2000, the Illinois State Board of Elections has used an electronic filing system, which allows for focused and comprehensive searches of receipts by specific campaign committees and expenditures by specific donors within the state. The Illinois Sunshine Database website offers a user-friendly interface for conducting such searches, and users can be confident that results dealing with years 2000 and later are relatively thorough and accurate (the database also includes manually entered data from 1994 to 1999, but the data are incomplete).[1]

Compiling comprehensive historical data on contributions to political campaigns in Illinois before 2000 presents several methodological challenges. The most significant has to do with the fact that the Illinois State Board of

Elections maintains much of the pre-2000 data, and all pre-1994 data, only in microfiche records organized by individual campaign committees (each candidate and political action committee maintains its own campaign committee, or in some cases multiple campaign committees). The only way to view specific records is to submit requests to view all the microfiche from a specific committee—for example, for everything under the heading "Richard M. Daley Campaign Committee." There are no microfiche records organized by donor. This means that to put together a list of all Illinois campaign contributions from a specific donor pre-2000, researchers have to pull the microfiche for every single campaign committee, then manually comb the microfiche for the donor name. This would require thousands of requests and, as a result, is impossible without a large team of dedicated researchers.

In view of these challenges, I used my preexisting knowledge of the political connections and interests of key figures like Jerry Reinsdorf to conduct a targeted search of specific committee records for evidence of their campaign contribution activity before 2000. For example, given the fact that Reinsdorf and many of his associates had an interest in local property taxation, I requested the microfiche for the committees of all Cook County assessors in office during Reinsdorf's tenure as Bulls chair. The fact that many of these records are handwritten, and often illegible, further complicated the task, as did the tendency of those in charge of reporting for individual committees to *not* alphabetize records according to donor name. These obstacles notwithstanding, after combing through thousands of individual contribution listings in the microfiche, I located ninety-two donations from relevant United Center officials between 1980 and 1999. I went back as far as 1980 to account for the fact that political capital accrues to donors over time, not simply in response to a single contribution.

Fortunately, the Illinois Sunshine Database allows for comprehensive searches of campaign contribution data by donor (the data are incomplete for the period 1994–1999 but complete for 2000 on). This eliminates the need to comb through individual committee records to compile the donation histories of specific contributors. After assembling a list of donors in key ownership and/or executive roles with the United Center, I used the database to identify 964 donations from 1994 to 2016 for inclusion in the final database. Added to the contributions from the microfiche records, this produced a database containing 1,056 total records.

The methodological issues described in this section mean that the estimates of total donations reported in tables below are significant underestimates. They undoubtedly omit significant campaign contribution activity before 2000 that was missed in the research process because I was unable to systematically analyze the records of each and every campaign committee. In other words, all the data and estimates should be viewed as partial, conservative, and suggestive rather than definitive.

Defining United Center "Ownership" and "Executives"

The question of which arena and team officials to include in reports of campaign contributions made with the interests of the United Center in mind is a difficult one. Many people serve, or have served, as high-ranking United Center executives; and many hold, or have held, significant economic stakes in the arena. As of the 2015–2016 season, ownership of the United Center was split between two different teams, the Bulls' board of directors consisted of ten people, and the list of Bulls limited investment partners (exclusive of board members) included seventeen individuals, families, and partnerships. Moreover, membership on the Bulls board of directors has turned over significantly since Reinsdorf took control of the franchise in 1985. Only five of the sixteen board members from the 1985–1986 season remained in 2015–2016.[2] Given these intricacies, a certain amount of subjectivity is inherent in deciding which people and entities to include within the group of campaign donors whose contributions likely placed the United Center in the good graces of city, county, and state policy makers.

I narrowed the list of relevant individual donors to eight people (table A.B.1). The basic criteria for inclusion on the list were (1) a clear financial stake in the economic success of United Center for all or most of Jerry Reinsdorf's tenure as general partner and chairman of the board of the Chicago Bulls limited partnership, and (2) an extensive history of involvement in politics by way of campaign finance. The inclusion of Reinsdorf and William (Bill) Wirtz requires little explanation. As majority owners and chairs of the Bulls and Blackhawks, respectively, they both had large economic stakes in the United Center. Bill Wirtz took over the Blackhawks in 1966, twelve years after his father Arthur purchased the club. Rocky Wirtz, Bill's son, succeeded his father as Blackhawks chair in 2007, and so I included his campaign contributions from 2007 to 2016 in the database.[3]

Robert Judelson and Allan Muchin were also obvious choices, for two reasons. First, in addition to being limited partners (i.e., junior investors) in the Bulls, each has sat continuously on the board of directors since Reinsdorf purchased the team in 1985.[4] Presumably, this has endowed them with long-running public recognition as key Bulls executives—that is, as donors whom politicians recognize as part of Bulls and United Center operations. Second, each has close business ties to Reinsdorf. Judelson has partnered with

TABLE A.B.1. Individual Campaign Contributions by United Center Ownership and Executives, 1980–2016

Individual donor	Position/role	Total contributions
Crown, Steven	Chicago Bulls Board of Directors and representative of family with limited partnership stake in Bulls, 1988–present	$246,000.00
Judelson, Robert	Chicago Bulls Board of Directors and limited partner (Bulls), 1985–present	$171,400.00
Malkin, Judd	Chicago Bulls Board of Directors and limited partner (Bulls), 1988–present	$537,500.00
Muchin, Allan	Chicago Bulls Board of Directors and limited partner (Bulls), 1985–present	$66,745.56
Pizer, Howard	Executive vice president of the Chicago White Sox and United Center	$61,490.00
Reinsdorf, Jerry	Chicago Bulls chairman and Chicago White Sox chairman	$152,897.58
Wirtz, Rocky	Chicago Blackhawks chairman and United Center co-owner, 2007–present	$17,600.00
Wirtz, William	Chicago Blackhawks chairman and United Center co-owner, to 2007; Chicago Stadium owner	$9,300.00
Total		**$1,262,933.14**

Source: Illinois State Board of Elections archives, Chicago; Illinois Sunshine Database, www.illinoissunshine .org/. All raw data and spreadsheets available from author upon request.

Notes: These contributions cover campaigns, successful and unsuccessful, of candidates for city-level offices in Chicago, county-level offices in Cook, and state-level offices in Illinois. Donations to offices that received fewer than $1,000 in total campaign contributions were excluded from the data set. The totals are underestimates since data for years 1980–1999 are incomplete. All totals are the sum of nominal, non-inflation-adjusted values. Judd Malkin's membership on the board may have started pre-1988, but data on board membership in 1986 and 1987 are unavailable.

Reinsdorf on several lucrative real-estate ventures, including Balcor Company and Bojer Financial. Reinsdorf has retained Muchin's law firm, Katten, Muchin, Roseman (formerly Katten, Muchin, Zavis), for a variety of services, including filing appeals to contest the nominal property taxes levied against the United Center.[5]

Judd Malkin's relationship to the Bulls and United Center is only slightly less distinguished than those of Judelson and Muchin. Malkin has served as limited partner and board member since at least 1988. Moreover, he has collaborated extensively with Judelson on real-estate investment, most notably as cofounder of JMB Realty Corporation. More recently, Malkin invested in a joint real-estate concern led by Judelson and Reinsdorf called Michigan Avenue Real Estate Investors. By now he is a mainstay of Bulls leadership, with strong business connections to other key team executives, and he is recognized as such within Chicago.[6] Steven Crown, also a member of the Bulls board since at least 1988, made the list as well. Crown's father, Lester, served on the Bulls board and as a limited partner under Reinsdorf before Steven took over the slot; given the Crown family's consistent involvement in the franchise's decision making and ongoing role as a Bulls limited partner, I included Steven on the list.[7] The list excludes other board members with shorter membership spans and limited partners who are not on the board, as these groups have less of a claim to recognizability and influence than do active Bulls executives. Because the ownership structure of the Blackhawks differs from that of the Bulls—the Blackhawks are a subsidiary of the much larger Wirtz Corporation—I was unable to identify specific investors in the hockey team other than Bill and Rocky Wirtz. Therefore, excepting the Wirtzes, all the franchise investors and board members included in this analysis come from the Bulls side.[8]

Howard Pizer, executive vice president of the United Center, rounds out the list. Although Pizer is not a partner in either of the teams, he has long stood at the forefront of the United Center's political and public relations operations. He began working for Reinsdorf in 1972, and since has regularly served as Reinsdorf's chief lieutenant, fulfilling a variety of roles including negotiator and spokesperson.[9] Within Chicago, he is a well-known representative of Reinsdorf's economic interests, and his campaign contributions should be viewed in that context.

The men listed in table A.B.1 also funneled large sums to political candidates by way of corporate entities under their direct control. These included sports franchises (e.g., Bulls), sports facilities (e.g., United Center), real-estate firms, and liquor distributorships. Political contributions from these entities for the period 1980–2016 are summarized in table A.B.2.

This partial accounting of individual and corporate campaign contributions to candidates for offices within Illinois yields a total dollar value of more than $3 million. Table A.B.3 shows a breakdown of this total by the specific political offices sought by contribution recipients.

TABLE A.B.2. Corporate Campaign Contributions by United Center Ownership and Executives, 1980–2016

Corporate donor	Industry	Bulls/United Center connection	Total contributions
Balcor Company	Real estate	Judelson and Reinsdorf (cofounders)	$23,500.00
Bojer Financial	Real estate	Judelson and Reinsdorf (cofounders)	$2,000.00
CBLS Corp. (Bulls)	Professional sports	Reinsdorf (controlling shareholder)	$219,746.84
Chicago Blackhawks	Professional sports	William/Rocky Wirtz (chairman)	$4,115.00
Chic. Stadium Corp.	Professional sports	William/Rocky Wirtz (owner)	$239,925.00
Chicago White Sox	Professional sports	Reinsdorf (chairman)	$54,863.78
Encounters, Ltd.	Real estate	Judelson and Reinsdorf (cofounders)	$124,600.00
Jerbo Holdings, Inc.	Real estate	Judelson and Reinsdorf (cofounders)	$15,000.00
JMB Realty Corp.	Real estate	Judelson (cofounder) and Malkin (cofounder and executive officer)	$100,000.00
JMR Charities, Inc.	Foundation	Reinsdorf (founder)	$8,048.00
JMR Fund	n/a	Reinsdorf (details unavailable)	$2,500.00
JMR Trust	Real estate	Reinsdorf (founder)	$125,386.48
Judge & Dolph	Liquor distribution	William/Rocky Wirtz (owner)	$250,650.00
Michigan Ave. Real Estate Investors	Real estate	Reinsdorf (founder), Judelson (founder), Malkin (investor)	$7,500.00
United Center Joint Venture	Professional sports	Reinsdorf (co-owner), William/Rocky Wirtz (co-owner)	$61,750.00
Westwood Pointe, Inc.	n/a	Judelson (position unknown), Reinsdorf (president)	$138,200.00
Wirtz Beverage	Liquor distribution	William/Rocky Wirtz (owner)	$245,883.00
Wirtz Corporation	n/a	William/Rocky Wirtz (owner)	$91,057.81
Wirtz Realty Corp.	Real estate	William/Rocky Wirtz (owner)	$51,150.00
Wirtz, Haynie, & Ehrate Realty Corp.	Real estate	Rocky Wirtz (president)	$10,500.00
Total			**$1,776,375.91**

Source: For raw data sources, see Table A.B.1. Information on the specific roles of Bulls and United Center executives in the listed corporations were pieced together from popular press reports, especially Chris Lamberti, "Reinsdorf Made Big Donations to Rauner, Rahm, Other ISFA Influencers," *Baseball Prospectus: South Side,* May 12, 2016, accessed January 28, 2018, southside.locals.baseballprospectus.com/2016/05/12/reinsdorf-made-big-donations-to-rauner-rahm-other-isfa-influencers/, and the search tool at "Corporation/LLC Search," *Office of the Illinois Secretary of State,* accessed June 22, 2017, www.cyberdriveillinois.com/departments/business_services/corp.html.

Notes: Donations listed under "Chicago Bulls/Chicago White Sox" and "Chicago Bulls Professional Sports" were merged into "CBLS Corp." category. Donations listed under "United Center" were merged into "United Center Joint Venture" category. Donations to offices that received fewer than $1,000 in total campaign contributions were excluded from the data set. All totals represent the sum of nominal, non-inflation-adjusted values.

TABLE A.B.3. United Center Ownership and Executives Campaign Contributions by Office, 1980–2016

Electoral office	To Democrats	To Republicans	Total contributions
Chicago City			
City Council	$382,396.76	$1,500.00	$383,896.76
Mayor	$432,400.00	$0.00	$432,400.00
Chicago City Total	**$814,796.76**	**$1,500.00**	**$816,296.76**
Cook County			
Assessor	$110,600.00	$0.00	$110,600.00
Board of Commissioners	$131,574.02	$0.00	$131,574.02
Board of Review	$0.00	$1,000.00	$1,000.00
Circuit Court	$12,647.58	$0.00	$12,647.58
Clerk	$3,250.00	$0.00	$3,250.00
State's Attorney	$57,292.29	$0.00	$57,292.29
Cook County Total	**$315,363.89**	**$1,000.00**	**$316,363.89**
State of Illinois			
Attorney General	$180,108.00	$28,500.00	$208,608.00
Comptroller	$66,250.00	$6,700.00	$72,950.00
Court of Appeals	$3,500.00	$0.00	$3,500.00
Gen. Assembly (House and Senate)	$512,540.00	$398,984.84	$913,524.84
Governor	$289,720.00	$245,645.56	$535,365.56
Lieutenant Governor	$2,500.00	$3,500.00	$6,000.00
Secretary of State	$4,500.00	$4,500.00	$9,000.00
Supreme Court	$76,050.00	$1,000.00	$77,050.00
Treasurer	$10,250.00	$70,400.00	$80,650.00
State of Illinois Total	**$1,145,418.00**	**$759,230.40**	**$1,906,648.40**
Totals (all offices)	**$2,275,578.65**	**$761,730.40**	**$3,039,309.05**

Sources: See Table A.B.1.

Notes: Democratic and Republican categories for "General Assembly," "State of Illinois Total," and "Totals (all offices)" rows do not add up to respective totals because the total column includes donations to third-party candidates. Donations to offices that received fewer than $1,000 in total campaign contributions were excluded from the data set. All totals are the sum of nominal, non-inflation-adjusted values.

Appendix C: United Center Property-Tax Savings

In Cook County, tax liabilities for residential properties depend on four variables. The first is the property's fair market value (FMV), or fair cash value (FCV). Assessors in Cook County employ something called the sales approach to determine the fair market value of homes. This approach uses data on recent sale prices of comparable homes to estimate fair market value.[1] The second variable is the assessment level, or the rate (i.e., percentage of FMV) at which property is assessed. Through tax year 2008, Cook County assessed residential property at 16 percent of FMV, and it has assessed such property at 10 percent of FMV since then.[2] A property's assessed value (AV) is determined by multiplying fair market value by the assessment level. The third variable is the equalization factor (EF), or equalization multiplier. The State of Illinois determines the equalization factor each year to ensure that the assessment level on the total assessed value of properties in all counties equals 33.3 percent (the idea behind the equalization process is to distribute the property-tax burden equally throughout the state). Multiplying the assessed value by the equalization factor yields the equalized assessed value (EAV). The final variable is the actual tax rate. Keep in mind that the Cook County clerk determines the tax rate after taxing bodies like local school districts issue their budget requests, or levies. The clerk's office calculates the tax rate simply by dividing total property-tax levy by total tax base (i.e., total EAV).[3] In the end, the formula for calculating a residential tax bill is as follows:

$$\text{Tax bill}_{residential} = \text{FMV} \times \text{Assessment level} \times \text{EF} \times \text{Tax rate},$$

or, in simplified form:

$$\text{Tax bill}_{residential} = \text{EAV} \times \text{Tax rate}.$$

In Cook County, the formula for determining commercial property-tax obligations differs from the one used for residential properties. Instead of using the sales approach, the assessor employs the income approach. The income approach tries to account for the fact that, unlike residential properties, the value of commercial properties depends in part on their potential to generate future commercial income.[4] To determine fair market value using the income approach, the assessor multiples a commercial property's annual net income (i.e., profits) by a multiplier based on the property's capitalization rate (a measure of rate of return on investment in the property). This multiplier is called the net income multiplier.[5]

Assessment levels for commercial properties also differ from those for residential ones. Through tax year 2008, Cook County assessed commercial properties at 38 percent of fair market value, but that number dropped to 25 percent thereafter. So, the formula for calculating the tax bill for a commercial property is as follows:

$$\text{Tax bill}_{\text{commercial}} = \text{Net income} \times \text{Net income multiplier} \times \text{Assessment level} \times \text{EF} \times \text{Tax rate,}$$

or, in simplified form:

$$\text{Tax bill}_{\text{commercial}} = \text{FMV} \times \text{Assessment level} \times \text{EF} \times \text{Tax rate,}$$

or, further simplified:

$$\text{Tax bill}_{\text{commercial}} = \text{EAV} \times \text{Tax rate.}$$

Legislation passed in 1989 by the Illinois General Assembly mandated that the Cook County assessor value the United Center according to a special formula. This formula included several key provisions that drastically reduced the arena's property-tax bills. First, it fixed the United Center's assessment level at 20 percent, significantly below the 38 percent standard used for commercial properties through tax year 2008 (and below the current rate of 25 percent). The special formula also allowed for the underestimation of the arena's net income, which the assessor used to determine fair market value. It did this by permitting several atypical deductions from the arena's reported net income. These deductions included income taxes, annual replacement and maintenance costs, and mortgage interest. Table A.C.1 shows the degree to which these deductions allowed United Center ownership to claim an adjusted net income that, in certain years, amounted to as little as 3 percent of actual net income.[6]

In addition to the reduced assessment level and net income deductions, the legislation fixed the net income multiplier at 4 (i.e., mandated that the

TABLE A.C.1. Net Income Adjustments for United Center, Fiscal Years
1996–2010

Fiscal year	Actual net income	Adjusted net income	Adjusted/Actual
1996	$19,231,094	$16,133,767	0.84
1997	$21,790,968	$15,066,475	0.69
1998	$20,872,858	$11,438,624	0.55
1999	$29,795,378	$10,483,585	0.35
2000	$31,296,064	$866,078	0.03
2001	$31,564,728	$11,241,461	0.36
2002	$29,583,315	$14,930,172	0.50
2003	$29,003,815	$15,325,901	0.53
2004	$16,153,032	$6,606,170	0.41
2005	$18,117,704	$4,029,693	0.22
2006	$31,233,134	$5,828,709	0.19
2007	$25,943,925	$4,273,254	0.16
2008	$32,446,174	$12,414,808	0.38
2009	$30,443,568	$10,514,329	0.35
2010	$33,335,513	$19,278,344	0.58

Source: Cook County Assessor's Office, Freedom of Information Act Request,
Work Order No. 62939, Transaction No. WCB081711, March 28, 2013.

Notes: All data except "Adjusted/Actual" field transcribed directly from revenue
statements provided to Cook County Assessor by United Center legal counsel.
"Fiscal year" refers to the year during which the net income was generated.
Values not adjusted for inflation.

Assessor's Office multiply net income by 4 to determine fair market value).
The net income multiplier is the inverse of a property's capitalization rate.
The latter is calculated by dividing the net operating income that a property
produces by its market value.[7] In other words:

Capitalization rate = Net operating income / Property value,

and

Net income multiplier = Property value / Net operating income.

By setting the net income multiplier for the arena at 4, the state required
that the Assessor's Office assume 25 percent capitalization for the United Center. We know from income statements that the actual capitalization rate was
significantly lower, ranging from 10 percent to 20 percent between 1999 and
2010. This translated into net income multipliers ranging from 5.0 to 9.7,
well above the value mandated by the state legislation regarding the United
Center. Previous versions of analysis assumed a net income multiplier of 8
for all years based on the investigative reporting of Chuck Neubauer, as I

initially overlooked the fact that I had access to the data necessary to calculate the United Center's capitalization rate and net income multiplier. Using the exact net income multipliers results in a revised tally of property-tax savings for the arena between the lower- and middle-range estimates from my previous work.[8]

The special provisions secured by Reinsdorf and Wirtz yielded a final formula for calculating the arena's tax liabilities that differed considerably from what it would have been under normal procedures for assessing commercial property. In the adjusted formula, the absolute value of net income drops dramatically, and two of the key multipliers—the net income multiplier and the assessment level—also shrink:

Normal tax bill = (Net income × Net income multiplier) × 0.38 × EF × Tax rate,

versus

Adjusted tax bill = (Adjusted net income × 4) × 0.20 × EF × Tax rate.

To reiterate, these formulas reflect property-tax statutes as they existed before 2009, when the assessment level for commercial properties dropped (I adjust for this change in the computations included below).[9]

Applying the formulas outlined here, the total estimated tax bill for 1997–2011 would have totaled approximately $175.5 million (constant 2016 dollars) under normal assessment procedures (table A.C.2).[10] Table A.C.3 shows that the difference between the estimate of what Reinsdorf and Wirtz would have paid normally in the years in question and what they actually paid amounts to more than $147.0 million (constant 2016 dollars).[11] Converted to present value at 1994, the savings totaled $85.9 million (see chapter 6).

TABLE A.C.2. Estimated United Center Tax Liabilities, in Constant 2016 Dollars, under Standard Assessment Procedures, Tax Years 1997–2011

Tax year	Net income	NIM	Fair cash value (Net income × NIM)	Assessed value (FCV × 38 pre-2009, FCV × 25 post-2008)	Equalization factor	Equalized assessed value	Tax rate	Standard tax liability	CPI-U (Chicago MSA)	Standard tax liability (2016 dollars)
1997	$19,231,094.00	6.00	$115,386,564.00	$43,846,894.32	2.15	$94,222,591.20	8.84	$8,332,103.74	161.70	$11,815,510.52
1998	$21,790,968.00	6.00	$130,745,808.00	$49,683,407.04	2.18	$108,304,859.01	8.87	$9,608,807.09	165.00	$13,353,446.57
1999	$20,872,858.00	6.00	$125,237,148.00	$47,590,116.24	2.25	$107,101,556.60	8.54	$9,142,188.87	168.40	$12,448,469.08
2000	$29,795,378.00	5.00	$148,979,361.28	$56,612,157.28	2.22	$125,877,131.72	7.79	$9,803,311.02	173.80	$12,933,940.29
2001	$31,296,064.00	5.30	$165,788,894.64	$62,999,779.96	2.31	$145,516,891.76	7.69	$11,193,159.31	178.30	$14,394,917.65
2002	$31,564,728.00	5.02	$158,519,451.81	$60,237,391.69	2.47	$148,720,096.34	7.28	$10,822,361.41	181.20	$13,695,304.17
2003	$29,583,315.00	5.19	$153,519,734.52	$58,337,499.12	2.46	$143,498,580.33	6.43	$9,231,263.67	184.50	$11,472,884.68
2004	$29,003,815.00	5.46	$158,252,096.16	$60,135,796.54	2.58	$154,891,771.15	6.27	$9,716,360.80	188.60	$11,813,260.68
2005	$16,153,032.00	9.22	$148,937,459.89	$56,596,234.76	2.73	$154,620,913.36	5.98	$9,247,876.83	194.30	$10,913,827.34
2006	$18,117,704.00	9.66	$174,992,956.32	$66,497,323.40	2.71	$180,048,152.84	5.30	$9,546,153.06	198.30	$11,038,587.95
2007	$31,233,134.00	6.71	$209,700,669.04	$79,686,254.23	2.84	$226,619,738.42	4.99	$11,317,389.74	204.82	$12,670,273.62
2008	$25,943,925.00	8.75	$226,911,293.92	$86,226,291.69	2.98	$256,833,632.43	4.82	$12,369,107.74	212.54	$13,344,850.48
2009	$32,446,174.00	7.07	$229,434,038.38	$57,358,509.60	3.37	$193,303,913.19	4.63	$8,944,172.06	210.00	$9,766,501.79
2010	$30,443,568.00	6.60	$200,948,968.93	$50,237,242.23	3.30	$165,782,899.37	4.93	$8,174,754.77	212.87	$8,805,785.77
2011	$33,335,513.00	5.39	$179,577,029.33	$44,894,257.33	2.97	$133,362,880.83	5.05	$6,728,824.15	218.68	$7,055,536.01
Totals										**$175,523,096.60**

Source: Cook County Assessor's Office, Freedom of Information Act Request.

Notes: Inflation adjustments made using the Bureau of Labor Statistics CPI-U for Chicago-Gary-Kenosha area (annual average CPI for 2016 was 229.30).

TABLE A.C.3. Difference between Tax Bills Under Standard Assessment Procedures and Actual Tax Payments for the United Center, in Constant 2016 Dollars, Tax Years 1997–2011

Tax year	Standard tax liability (actual NIMs)	Actual tax payment (per assessor's records)	Standard less Actual	CPI-U (Chicago area)	Standard less Actual (2016 dollars)
1997	$8,332,103.74	$2,382,735.00	$5,949,368.74	161.70	$8,436,624.31
1998	$9,608,807.09	$2,332,645.00	$7,276,162.09	165.00	$10,111,748.60
1999	$9,142,188.87	$1,830,261.00	$7,311,927.87	168.40	$9,956,292.66
2000	$9,803,311.02	$1,452,308.00	$8,351,003.02	173.80	$11,017,846.34
2001	$11,193,159.31	$1,002,830.00	$10,190,329.31	178.30	$13,105,232.15
2002	$10,822,361.41	$1,625,205.00	$9,197,156.41	181.20	$11,638,666.44
2003	$9,231,263.67	$1,737,160.00	$7,494,103.67	184.50	$9,313,891.38
2004	$9,716,360.80	$1,461,588.00	$8,254,772.80	188.60	$10,036,245.57
2005	$9,247,876.83	$1,001,475.00	$8,246,401.83	194.30	$9,731,942.52
2006	$9,546,153.06	$893,788.00	$8,652,365.06	198.30	$10,005,066.13
2007	$11,317,389.74	$1,007,487.00	$10,309,902.74	204.82	$11,542,351.34
2008	$12,369,107.74	$1,013,212.00	$11,355,895.74	212.54	$12,251,710.79
2009	$8,944,172.06	$1,550,108.00	$7,394,064.06	210.00	$8,073,876.42
2010	$8,174,754.77	$1,376,218.00	$6,798,536.77	212.87	$7,323,333.86
2011	$6,728,824.15	$2,498,489.00	$4,230,335.15	218.68	$4,435,735.18
Totals			**$121,012,325.27**		**$146,980,563.69**

Source: Cook County Assessor's Office, Freedom of Information Act Request.

Notes: Inflation adjustments made using the Bureau of Labor Statistics CPI-U for the Chicago-Gary-Kenosha area (annual average CPI for 2016 was 229.30).

Appendix D: United Center Amusement-Tax Savings

Table A.D.1 shows the calculations for determining the savings that accrued to Reinsdorf and Wirtz as a result of the Chicago City Ordinance exempting 40 percent of revenue from luxury suites from the city amusement tax. "Fiscal year" denotes the year in which the taxable revenue was produced. This differs from the label "tax year," which is used to discuss property taxes in appendix C. "Tax year" coincides with the year in which a property assessment was executed, and the assessment is based on income generated by the property in previous years.

TABLE A.D.1. United Center City Amusement Tax Savings in Constant 2016 Dollars, Fiscal Years 2002–2007

Fiscal year	Suite license fees (net)	Amusement-tax rate	Liability absent ordinance (standard)	60% of suite license fees	Actual liability (accounting for ordinance)	Standard less Actual	CPI-U (Chicago MSA)	Standard less Actual (2016 $)
2002	$28,013,933.00	0.07	$1,960,975.31	$16,808,359.80	$1,176,585.19	$784,390.12	181.20	$992,617.13
2003	$28,264,187.00	0.07	$1,978,493.09	$16,958,512.20	$1,187,095.85	$791,397.24	184.50	$983,571.65
2004	$20,654,596.00	0.07	$1,445,821.72	$12,392,757.60	$867,493.03	$578,328.69	188.60	$703,138.52
2005	$17,352,845.00	0.08	$1,388,227.60	$10,411,707.00	$832,936.56	$555,291.04	194.30	$655,323.45
2006	$26,676,637.00	0.08	$2,134,130.96	$16,005,982.20	$1,280,478.58	$853,652.38	198.30	$987,111.44
2007	$24,671,689.00	0.08	$1,973,735.12	$14,803,013.40	$1,184,241.07	$789,494.05	204.82	$883,870.38
Totals								**$5,205,632.57**

Source: Cook County Board of Review, Freedom of Information Act Request no. WCB081711, August 17, 2011; amusement-tax rates collected from press reports.

Notes: Inflation adjustments made using the Bureau of Labor Statistics CPI-U for the Chicago-Gary-Kenosha area (annual average CPI for 2016 was 229.30).

Notes

Introduction

1. Sam Smith, "Bulls Stampede to First Title," *Chicago Tribune*, June 13, 1991, ProQuest.

2. See David Andrews, ed., *Michael Jordan, Inc.: Corporate Sport, Media Culture, and Late Modern America* (Albany, NY: SUNY Press, 2001); Walter LaFeber, *Michael Jordan and the New Global Capitalism*, 2nd ed. (New York: W. W. Norton, 2002).

3. Dennis Coates and Brad Humphreys, "Do Economists Reach a Conclusion on Subsidies for Sports Franchises, Stadiums, and Mega-Events?" *Economic Journal Watch* 5 (2008): 310.

4. Andrew Zimbalist, *May the Best Team Win: Baseball Economics and Public Policy* (Washington, DC: Brookings Institution Press, 2003), 130.

5. Several sociologists and political scientists have gone further than the economics literature in this regard, especially by discussing the implication of recent stadium developments in the displacement of low-income residents by more affluent ones. See Michael Danielson, *Home Team: Professional Sports and the American Metropolis* (Princeton, NJ: Princeton University Press, 1997); Kevin Delaney and Rick Eckstein, *Public Dollars, Private Stadiums: The Battle over Building Sports Stadiums* (New Brunswick, NJ: Rutgers University Press, 2003); Charles Euchner, *Playing the Field: Why Sports Teams Move and Cities Fight to Keep Them* (Baltimore, MD: Johns Hopkins University Press, 1993); Costas Spirou and Larry Bennett, *It's Hardly Sportin': Stadiums, Neighborhoods, and the New Chicago* (DeKalb: Northern Illinois University Press, 2003).

6. Rodney Fort, "Market Power in Pro Sports," in *The Economics of Sports*, ed. William Kern (Kalamazoo, MI: W. E. Upjohn Institute for Employment Research, 2000), 8. See also James Quirk and Rodney Fort, *Hard Ball: The Abuse of Power in Pro Team Sports* (Princeton, NJ: Princeton University Press, 1999); Zimbalist, *May the Best Team Win*.

7. Quirk and Fort, *Hard Ball*, 128.

8. Philip Mattera and Kasia Tarczynska, *Megadeals: The Largest Economic Development Subsidy Packages Ever Awarded by State and Local Governments in the United States* (Washington, DC: Good Jobs First, 2013), 12, accessed January 4, 2017, www.goodjobsfirst.org/sites/default/files/docs/pdf/megadeals_report.pdf.

9. Michael Cieply, "Charging a Premium, at a Cost," *New York Times*, August 1, 2011, ProQuest.

10. Thomas Piketty, *Capital in the Twenty-First Century* (Cambridge, MA: Belknap Press of Harvard University Press, 2014), 291.

11. See, for example, David Harvey, *A Brief History of Neoliberalism* (New York: Oxford University Press, 2005).

12. Jefferson Cowie, *The Great Exception: The New Deal and the Limits of American Politics* (Princeton, NJ: Princeton University Press, 2016), 206, 222.

13. Rodney Fort, "NBA Team Values-Selected," *Rodney's Sports Economics*, accessed February 14, 2016, umich.app.box.com/s/41707f0b2619c0107b8b/1/320023265. Inflation adjustments made using the Bureau of Labor Statistics' Consumer Price Index–Urban (CPI-U) annual averages for the United States, accessed January 23, 2018, www.bls.gov/cpi/tables/historical-cpi-u-201709.pdf.

14. Economic Policy Institute, "Median Household Wealth by Race and Ethnicity, 1983–2010 (2010 Dollars)," *State of Working America*, accessed January 17, 2018, www.stateofworkingamerica.org/chart/swa-wealth-figure-6e-median-household-wealth/.

15. "Chicago Bulls," *Forbes: The Business of Basketball*, accessed August 3, 2017, www.forbes.com/teams/chicago-bulls/.

16. Cowie, *The Great Exception*, 9–17, 224–29.

17. Piketty, *Capital*, 275, 291, 294, 348 (specific values taken from tables S8.2 and S10.1 of the online supplement to Piketty, available at piketty.pse.ens.fr/en/capital21c2); Cowie, *Great Exception*, 115.

18. Saskia Sassen, *Expulsions: Brutality and Complexity in the Global Economy* (Cambridge, MA: Harvard University Press, 2014), 76; Cowie, *Great Exception*, 151, 153–54.

19. Michael Hirsley, "Dick Klein, Bulls' Founder and 1st CEO, Dies at 80," *Chicago Tribune*, October 12, 2000, ProQuest; "Display Ad 41," *Chicago Tribune*, January 29, 1968, ProQuest; Bureau of Labor Statistics, *Area Wage Survey: The Chicago, Illinois, Metropolitan Area, June 1970* (Washington, DC: U.S. Department of Labor, 1970), 42; *The* Chicago Tribune *Book of the Chicago Bulls: A Decade-by-Decade History* (Chicago: Agate Midway, 2016), 8–9. Inflation adjustments made using "Consumer Price Index, All Urban Consumers (CPI-U), Chicago-Gary-Kenosha, Not Seasonally Adjusted," *Bureau of Labor Statistics*, accessed January 16, 2018, data.bls.gov/pdq/SurveyOutputServlet?data_tool=dropmap&series_id=CUURA207SA0,CUUSA207SA0.

20. For an accessible introduction to this history, see Arthur MacEwan and John Miller, *Economic Collapse, Economic Change: Getting to the Roots of the Crisis* (Armonk, NY: M. E. Sharpe, 2011), 33–64.

21. Jefferson Cowie, *Stayin' Alive: The 1970s and the Last Days of the Working Class* (New York: New Press, 2012), 227–36; Piketty, *Capital*, 549.

22. John Bellamy Foster and Robert McChesney, *The Endless Crisis: How Monopoly-Finance Capital Produces Stagnation and Upheaval from the USA to China* (New York: Monthly Review Press, 2012), 67.

23. Piketty, *Capital*, 220, 256, 297–99 (specific values taken from table S8.2 of the online supplement to Piketty available at piketty.pse.ens.fr/en/capital21c2).

24. Piketty, *Capital*, 348 (specific values taken from table S10.1 of the online supplement to Piketty available at piketty.pse.ens.fr/en/capital21c2).

25. John Logan and Harvey Molotch, *Urban Fortunes: The Political Economy of Place*, 2nd ed. (Berkeley: University of California Press, 2007), 2, 20, 99–110; Piketty, *Capital*, 22.

Chapter 1

1. Richard Roeper, "United Crowd Just Happy to Be There," *Chicago Sun-Times*, March 26, 1995, NewsBank; John Husar, "Jordan's Statuesque Presence Draws Thousands to Pregame Pilgrimage," *Chicago Tribune*, May 29, 1997, ProQuest.

2. R. C. Longworth, "A Bull-ish Change: Team Does Bang-Up Job for City's Image," *Chicago Tribune*, June 14, 1997, ProQuest; John Kass, "Michael Jordan Could Become Driving Force on Lakeshore Drive," *Chicago Tribune*, May 4, 1998, ProQuest.

3. On this process, see Costas Spirou and Dennis Judd, *Building the City of Spectacle: Mayor Richard M. Daley and the Remaking of Chicago* (Ithaca, NY: Cornell University Press, 2016), 75–119.

4. Jerry Bonkowski, "Fans Go for Michael-bilia," *USA Today*, May 17, 1996, ProQuest.

5. For a helpful overview of these issues, see Paul Street, *Racial Oppression in the Global Metropolis: A Living Black Chicago History* (Lanham, MD: Rowman & Littlefield, 2007).

6. Street, *Racial Oppression*, 286–91.

7. Barbara Ferman, *Challenging the Growth Machine: Neighborhood Politics in Chicago and Pittsburgh* (Lawrence: University of Kansas, 1996), 95–97, 103–7; Street, *Racial Oppression*, 291–94.

8. Bob Greene, "A Coach, a Team, a Local Anesthetic," *Chicago Tribune*, June 23, 1996, ProQuest.

9. D. Bradford Hunt and John DeVries, *Planning Chicago* (Chicago: American Planning Association, 2013), 24–26, 30, 33–36.

10. Ester Fuchs, *Mayors and Money: Fiscal Policy in New York and Chicago* (Chicago: University of Chicago Press, 1992), 156–65; Kari Lydersen, *Mayor 1%: Rahm Emanuel and the Rise of Chicago's 99%* (Chicago: Haymarket Books, 2013), 40.

11. Street, *Racial Oppression*, 108; Dick Simpson, *Rogues, Rebels, and Rubber Stamps: The Politics of the Chicago City Council 1863 to the Present* (Boulder, CO: Westview, 2001), 153. On the postwar history of public housing in Chicago, see Arnold Hirsch, *Making the Second Ghetto: Race and Housing in Chicago, 1940–1960*, 3rd ed. (Chicago: University of Chicago Press, 1998).

12. Street, *Racial Oppression*, 121, 135.

13. Robert Beauregard, *Voices of Decline: The Postwar Fate of US Cities* (Cambridge, MA: Blackwell, 1993), 164.

14. Arthur M. Louis, "The Worst American City," *Harper's*, January 1975, 71.

15. Fuchs, *Mayors and Money*, 98–99.

16. Anselm Strauss, *Images of the American City* (New York: Free Press, 1961), 33, 50.

17. Simpson, *Rogues, Rebels, and Rubber Stamps*, 111; Marni Pyke, "Suburbs, O'Hare Mark 50-Year Milestone," *Arlington Daily Herald*, April 1, 2013, ProQuest.

18. Commercial Club of Chicago, *Make No Little Plans: Jobs for Metropolitan Chicago* (Chicago, 1984), 19, 27–28, Municipal Reference Collection, Harold Washington Library Center.

19. Ferman, *Challenging the Growth Machine*, 90.

20. Chicago Central Area Committee, *Chicago Central Area Committee News*, Fall 1983, 2–3, Chicago History Museum.

21. Larry Bennett, "Postwar Redevelopment in Chicago: The Declining Politics of Party and the Rise of Neighborhood Politics," in *Unequal Partnerships: The Political Economy of Urban Redevelopment in Postwar America*, ed. Gregory Squires (New Brunswick, NJ: Rutgers University Press, 1991), 170.

22. See Larry Bennett, "Harold Washington and the Black Urban Regime," *Urban Affairs Quarterly* 28, no. 3 (March 1993): 423–40.

23. Rowan Miranda, "Post-Machine Regimes and the Growth of Government: A Fiscal History of the City of Chicago, 1970–1990," *Urban Affairs Quarterly* 28, no. 3 (March 1993): 415–16.

24. Ferman, *Challenging the Growth Machine*, 106; Bennett, "Harold Washington," 432.

25. David Elsner and Bill Barnhart, "Fixing the Gap, Nail by Nail: Business, City Attempt to Revive Once-Strong Tie," *Chicago Tribune*, November 2, 1986, ProQuest; "Up against Downtown? Not Anymore," *Chicago Tribune*, January 25, 1995, ProQuest; Robert Davis, "Daily Life in Chicago Is Far Different from Daley Life of Only a Decade Ago," *Chicago Tribune*, December 7, 1986, ProQuest; John McCarron, "World's Fair Lobby Calling It Quits," *Chicago Tribune*, August, 21, 1987, ProQuest.

26. Joel Rast, *Remaking Chicago: The Political Origins of Urban Industrial Change* (DeKalb, IL: Northern Illinois University Press, 1999), 85.

27. Jason Hackworth, *The Neoliberal City: Governance, Ideology, and Development in American Urbanism* (Ithaca, NY: Cornell University Press, 2007), 21.

28. *Chicago Tribune* quoted in Bennett, "Harold Washington," 424.

29. Chicago Central Area Committee, *1986 Annual Report* (Chicago, 1987), 21, Chicago Central Area Committee Annual Reports, Chicago History Museum.

30. Hunt and DeVries, *Planning Chicago*, 74; Chicago Central Area Committee, Pastora San Juan Cafferty, *The Chicago Project: A Report on Civic Life in Chicago* (Chicago, September 1986), 13, Municipal Reference Collection, Harold Washington Library Center.

31. Manning Marable, *Black Leadership* (New York: Columbia University Press, 1998), 134.

32. Commercial Club of Chicago, *Jobs for Metropolitan Chicago: A Two Year Report* (Chicago, 1987), 13, Municipal Reference Collection, Harold Washington Library Center.

33. Robert Davis, "Mayor's Death Stuns City," *Chicago Tribune*, November 26, 1987, ProQuest.

34. "Chicago Bulls at Milwaukee Bucks Box Score, November 25, 1987," *Basketball-Reference.com*, accessed January 8, 2018, www.basketball-reference.com/boxscores/198711250MIL.html; "Michael Jordan," *Basketball-Reference.com*, accessed January 8, 2018, www.basketball-reference.com/players/j/jordami01.html.

35. Charles Madigan, "Michael: City's Most Valuable Imagemaker," *Chicago Tribune*, June 2, 1991, ProQuest.

36. Larry Bennett, *The Third City: Chicago and American Urbanism* (Chicago: University of Chicago Press, 2012), 95.

37. Bennett, *Third City*, 111; Spirou and Judd, *Building the City of Spectacle*, 120–30.

38. John Hannigan, *Fantasy City: Pleasure and Profit in the Postmodern Metropolis* (New York: Routledge, 1998), 51.

39. As a percentage of gross domestic product, this represented a fall from 3.5 percent to 2.3 percent. White House Office of Management and Budget, *Fiscal Year 2013 Historical Tables* (Washington, DC: U.S. Government Printing Office, 2012), 251, accessed January 20, 2018, www.gpo.gov/fdsys/pkg/BUDGET-2013-TAB/pdf/BUDGET-2013-TAB.pdf.

40. Miriam Greenberg, *Branding New York: How a City in Crisis Was Sold to the World* (New York: Routledge, 2008), 35.

41. Dennis Judd, "Constructing the Tourist Bubble," in *The Tourist City*, ed. Dennis Judd and Susan Fainstein (New Haven, CT: Yale University Press, 1999), 35–36.

42. Costas Spirou, *Urban Tourism and Urban Change: Cities in a Global Economy* (New York: Routledge, 2011), 106.

43. Costas Spirou, "Urban Beautification: The Construction of a New Identity in Chicago," in *The New Chicago: A Social and Cultural Analysis*, ed. John Koval, Larry Bennett, Michael Bennett, Fassil Demissie, Roberta Garner, and Kiljoong Kim (Philadelphia: Temple University Press, 2006), 296–98; John Kass and Thomas Hardy, "Republicans Will Contribute a Fair Portion to the Democrats' Convention," *Chicago Tribune*, July 21, 1994, ProQuest; City of Chicago, Office of Management and Budget, *Program and Budget Summary* (Chicago, 1991–2000), Municipal Reference Collection, Harold Washington Library Center (for exact figures, consult the "Mayor's Office of Special Events" sections); David Mendell, "New Attractions Making Chicago City that Bubbles," *Chicago Tribune*, June 19, 1998, ProQuest; Spirou, *Urban Tourism and Urban Change*, 132–33.

44. Chicago Central Area Committee, *Redraft of Chicago Central Area Plan* (Chicago, 1984), 22–26, Municipal Reference Collection, Harold Washington Library Center; Commercial Club of Chicago, *Make No Little Plans*, 28; Richard Roeper, "A Few Final Thoughts on Bulls and Three Petes," *Chicago Sun-Times*, June 22, 1993, NewsBank.

45. Spirou and Bennett, *It's Hardly Sportin'*, 181.

46. Madigan, "Michael"; Steve Johnson, "Now the Real Fans Can Honor the Bulls," *Chicago Tribune*, June 16, 1992, ProQuest; Richard Roeper, "Brightest Star Gone—Our Skyline Is Dimmer," *Chicago Sun-Times*, October 7, 1993, NewsBank.

47. Longworth, "Bull-ish Change."

48. Irv Kupcinet, "KUP & Company," *Chicago Sun-Times*, December 22, 1991, NewsBank; "Da Skit: What's Da Big Deal?" *Chicago Tribune*, February 17, 1992, ProQuest.

49. Rick Kogan, "Dennis Rodman: A Chicago-Style Hot-Dog," *Chicago Tribune*, October 8, 1995, ProQuest.

50. Count conducted using ProQuest and NewsBank searches. The *Arlington Daily Herald*, *Chicago Defender*, and *Springfield State Journal-Register* all published similar articles as well. Rick Morrissey, "The Joy of Six Awesome Runs Appears to Be on Last Legs," *Chicago Tribune*, June 15, 1998, ProQuest; Richard Roeper, "Jordan Is Not Alone as Young Achiever," *Chicago Sun-Times*, February 19, 1997, NewsBank.

51. Longworth, "Bull-ish Change"; Tom Hundley, "Feeling Constricted by Ties to the Mafia," *Chicago Tribune*, April 19, 2001, ProQuest; Giorgio Viberti, "Rusconi: Jordan, ti ricordi de me?" *La Stampa*, October 15, 1997, LexisNexis; Bill Dedman, "Fans Bid the Bulls Hail (and Farewell?)," *New York Times*, June 17, 1998, ProQuest; *El País*, "Una pacífica división racial," September 3, 2000, LexisNexis.

52. Steven Morris, "Chicago Making Pitch for Global Tourists," *Chicago Tribune*, October 16, 1993, ProQuest; Fran Spielman, "3-Yr. Push Will Tout City's Cultural Offerings," *Chicago Sun-Times*, March 21, 1997, NewsBank; Barbara Sullivan, "$6 Million for Chicago Tourism a New Culture of Cooperation to Market Culture," *Chicago Tribune*, March 21, 1997, ProQuest.

53. Shirley Leung, "Caution to the Wind," *Chicago Tribune*, July 6, 1993, ProQuest; "City's Favorite Landmarks: Anything M.J.," *Arlington Daily Herald*, June 3, 1998, ProQuest; Chicago Office of Tourism, *Passport to Chicago: 1998 Chicago Sightseeing Tours*, pamphlet (Chicago, 1998), Municipal Reference Collection, Harold Washington Library Center; Jennifer Dorsey, "TIA's '98 Pow Wow to Showcase Chicago's Tourist Attraction," *Travel Weekly*, April 7, 1997, accessed January 6, 2018, www.travelweekly.com/Destinations2001-2007/TIA-s-98-Pow-Wow -to-Showcase-Chicago-s-Tourist-Attraction.

54. Richard M. Daley, "Standard of Excellence Will Endure," *Chicago Sun-Times*, April 20, 1998, NewsBank; Chicago Central Area Committee, *Chicago Central Area Plan* (Chicago, 1983), 92, Municipal Reference Collection, Harold Washington Library Center.

55. Longworth, "Bull-ish Change."

56. Mike Wise, "U.S. vs. the World? All-Star Games Should Take a Global Approach," *New York Times*, February 3, 2002, ProQuest; LaFeber, *Michael Jordan and the New Global Capitalism*, 169.

57. See, for example, Spirou and Judd, *Building the City of Spectacle*, 55–65.

58. Author's calculations based on data from U.S. Bureau of Economic Analysis, "Personal Income Summary," *Interactive Data Tables*, table CA1-3, accessed June 27, 2017, www.bea.gov/itable. Inflation adjustments made using the CPI-U annual, national averages.

59. William Testa, "A City Reinvents Itself," in *Global Chicago*, ed. Charles Madigan (Urbana: University of Illinois Press, 2004), 47.

60. Terry Nichols Clark, Richard Lloyd, Kenneth K. Wong, and Pushpam Jain, "Amenities Drive Urban Growth," *Journal of Urban Affairs* 24, no. 5 (Winter 2002): 504; Commercial Club of Chicago, *Make No Little Plans*, 27.

61. World Travel Tourism Council, "Leisure Travel and Tourism Spending," *Economic Data Search Tool*, accessed August 27, 2013, www.wttc.org/wttc/research/economic-data-search-tool/ (link no longer active, but original raw data is available from the author upon request).

62. Hannigan, *Fantasy City*, 107; Susan Fainstein and Robert Stokes, "Spaces of Play: The Impacts of Entertainment Development on New York City," *Economic Development Quarterly* 12, no. 2 (May 1998): 150–51; Mark Rosentraub and Mijin Joo, "Tourism and Economic Development: Which Investments Produce Gains for Regions?" *Tourism Management* 30 (2009): 759–70.

63. Rick Morrissey, "Jordan Had Rare Air for the Dramatic in Chicago," *Chicago Tribune*, January 13, 1999, ProQuest.

64. Steve Rhodes, "Even in Bronze, Jordan Spirit Is a Real Magnet," *Chicago Tribune*, November 7, 1994, ProQuest.

65. Dave Newbart, "Jordan's Now the Big Splash for Tourists," *Chicago Tribune*, November 3, 1997, ProQuest; Philip Franchine, "City Wows Big Shots of Travel Trade," *Chicago Sun-Times*, May 24, 1998, NewsBank.

66. Phil Rosenthal, "Tour Group Has Quite a Yen to See Jordan," *Chicago Sun-Times*, June 6, 1996, NewsBank; Bonkowski, "Fans Go for Michael-bilia."

67. Bob Secter, "Legend Grows around the Globe," *Chicago Tribune*, June 17, 1996, ProQuest; Husar, "Jordan's Statuesque Presence." The popularity of the statue with tourists continued even in the wake of Jordan's departure from Chicago. In 2009, the *Tribune*'s K. C. Johnson reported that, during a single hour of loitering around the statue, he encountered tourists from Miami, New Jersey, San Diego, Spain, Germany, Finland, Italy, and Hong Kong. K. C. Johnson, "The United Center and the Statue Become Ground Zero for a Socioeconomic Renaissance," *Chicago Tribune*, September 10, 2009, ProQuest.

68. The definition of the home market matters. If defined as the central city only, then transfers from suburbs would constitute new economic activity, but if defined as the larger "metro area," they would not. Dennis Coates and Brad Humphreys, "The Stadium Gambit and Local Economic Development," *Regulation* 23, no 2 (2000): 17.

69. Ronald Yates and Nancy Ryan, "Area's Economy Could Take a Hit without Jordan," *Chicago Tribune*, October 7, 1993, ProQuest.

70. Mark Rosentraub, *Major League Losers: The Real Cost of Sports and Who's Paying for It* (New York: Basic Books, 1997), 171.

71. Roger Noll and Andrew Zimbalist, "Economic Impact of Sports Teams and Facilities," in

Sports, Jobs, and Taxes: The Economic Impact of Sports Teams and Stadiums, ed. Roger Noll and Andrew Zimbalist, 55−91 (Washington, DC: Brookings Institution Press, 1997), 73.

72. Some experts have begun to call for the incorporation of team quality into econometric models that analyze the local economic impact of new stadiums and/or franchises. Existing models suggest that, despite little evidence that new stadiums or franchises enhance local growth, a novelty effect may yield positive impacts on growth in a short window right after a stadium or franchise appears. As Geoffrey Propheter explains, if they take novelty effects in these contexts seriously, then it makes sense for economists to "consider [such effects] to not just include when a region acquires a new team but also when an established team experiences gains in quality." Propheter's analysis indicates that the United Center, the new Bulls arena opened in 1994, had a positive, statistically significant impact on the Chicago Metropolitan Statistical Area's (MSA) "share of regional personal income," whereas data that he pooled for a larger sample of NBA arenas suggest that, typically, such arenas do not have such an effect. Propheter postulates that "income transfers from the suburban area around the central city may be responsible" for the exceptional findings related to the United Center. Another possibility, however, is that the dummy variable in Propheter's model indicating when a new arena appeared detected increases in the effects of the global marketing of Jordan and the Bulls in the middle of the 1990s. Geoffrey Propheter, "Are Basketball Arenas Catalysts for Economic Development?" *Journal of Urban Affairs* 34, no. 4 (2012): 451, 457.

73. Craig Depken, II, "The Impact of New Stadiums on Professional Baseball Team Finances," *Public Finance and Management* 6, no. 3 (2006): 445−46, 451, 462−64, 467−68; Zimbalist, *May the Best Team Win*, 132−33.

74. On the geography of gentrification and economic inequality in Chicago during this period, see Nathalie P. Voorhees Center for Neighborhood and Community Improvement, *The Socioeconomic Change of Chicago's Community Areas (1970−2010): Gentrification Index* (Chicago: University of Illinois at Chicago, 2014), accessed January 8, 2018, www.voorheescenter .com/gentrification-index.

75. Alf Siewers, Philip Franchine, and Zay Smith, "Bulls Win It! City Whoops It Up for New NBA Champs!" *Chicago Sun-Times*, June 13, 1991, NewsBank; Sam Smith, "High Five! Bulls Are Champs!" *Chicago Tribune*, June 13, 1991, ProQuest; "What a Week," *Chicago Tribune*, June 16, 1991, ProQuest.

76. Barry Cronin, "Devout Fans Rooting for the Bulls Religiously," *Chicago Sun-Times*, June 2, 1991, NewsBank.

77. American Communities Project, "Racial/Ethnic Composition and Segregation," *Diversity and Disparities*, accessed January 12, 2018, s4.ad.brown.edu/Projects/Diversity/Data/ Download1.htm.

78. Greene, "Coach, a Team, a Local Anesthetic."

79. Siewers, Franchine, and Smith, "Bulls Win It!"; Don Hayner and Angie Chester, "Fans at Rally Show Bulls Their Love Knows No Limit," *Chicago Sun-Times*, June 16, 1991, NewsBank.

80. Bob Secter and James Hill, "1 Down and 2 to Go for the Bulls," *Chicago Tribune*, June 21, 1996, ProQuest; Mary Schmich, "Community Bond Is a Bunch of Bulls," *Chicago Tribune*, June 23, 1993, ProQuest.

81. Paul Street, *Still Separate, Unequal: Race, Place, Policy, and the State of Black Chicago* (Chicago: Urban League, 2005), 146; Street, *Racial Oppression*, 258.

82. According to census figures, the poverty rate fell from 21.6 to 19.6 percent. Author's calculations from John Logan, Zengwang Xu, and Brian Stults, Longitudinal Tract Database, *US*

2010 Project, accessed January 23, 2018, s4.ad.brown.edu/Projects/Diversity/Researcher/LTDB .htm; American Communities Project, "Chicago City: Data for the City Area," *Diversity and Disparities*, accessed January 12, 2018, s4.ad.brown.edu/Projects/Diversity/segregation2010/city .aspx?cityid=1714000.

83. Street, *Racial Oppression*, 197, 200.

84. Strauss, *Images of the American City*, 11.

85. Sam Bass Warner Jr., *Streetcar Suburbs: The Process of Growth in Boston (1870–1900)*, 2nd ed. (Cambridge, MA: Harvard University Press, 1978), x.

86. Cowie, *Stayin' Alive*, 164–65.

87. Michael Rosenfeld, "Celebration, Politics, Selective Looting and Riots: A Micro Level Study of the Bulls Riot of 1992 in Chicago," *Social Problems* 44, no. 4 (November 1997): 488; Raymond Coffey, "Cops' Defense Stars after the Sun Sets," *Chicago Sun-Times*, June 22, 1993, NewsBank.

88. Rosenfeld, "Celebration," 489.

89. Jay Mariotti, "Give the Arrests a Rest and Just Cheer the Bulls," *Chicago Sun-Times*, June 16, 1992, NewsBank; Roeper, "Few Final Thoughts."

90. Jennie Acker, "Koreans Testing Waters in Search of Firmer Ground with Blacks," *Chicago Tribune*, May 26, 1992, ProQuest.

91. Rosenfeld, "Celebration," 491–94.

92. Rosenfeld, "Celebration," 484–85, 493–95. The odds of a "food and liquor" being looted were 132 percent higher than for a "general merchandise and miscellaneous" store (significant at $p < 0.001$).

93. Rosenfeld, "Celebration," 489.

94. Michael Abramowitz, "Bulls NBA Victory Sparks Chicago Riot," *Washington Post*, June 16, 1992, ProQuest.

95. Ironically, the riots probably reduced any positive economic impact that the Bulls brought to the city through negative publicity, damage to public property, and law enforcement and court costs. See Victor Matheson and Robert Baade, "The Paradox of Championships: Be Careful What You Wish For, Sports Fans," Working Paper No. 05-04, College of the Holy Cross, Department of Economics Faculty Research Series (February 2005), accessed January 12, 2018, crossworks.holycross.edu/cgi/viewcontent.cgi?referer=https://scholar.google.com/&httpsredir =1&article=1088&context=econ_working_papers.

96. Nate Silver, "The Most Diverse Cities Are Often the Most Segregated," *FiveThirtyEight*, May 1, 2015, accessed January 26, 2018, fivethirtyeight.com/features/the-most-diverse-cities -are-often-the-most-segregated/; American Communities Project, "Chicago City"; Lauren Nolan, "A Deepening Divide: Income Inequality Grows Spatially in Chicago," *Voorhees Center for Neighborhood & Community Improvement*, March 11, 2015, accessed January 12, 2018, voorheescenter.wordpress.com/2015/03/11/a-deepening-divide-income-inequality-grows -spatially-in-chicago/; Richard Florida, "The High Inequality of U.S. Metro Areas Compared to Countries," *Citylab*, October 9, 2012, accessed January 12, 2018, www.citylab.com/life/2012/ 10/high-inequality-us-metro-areas-compared-countries/3079/; Spirou and Judd, *Building the City of Spectacle*, 157–74.

97. Street, *Racial Oppression*, 289–91; Spirou and Judd, *Building the City of Spectacle*, 13, 64, 119; William Sander and William Testa, "Why Chicago Is Not Detroit," *Federal Reserve Bank of Chicago* (blog), May 2, 2016, accessed January 12, 2018, midwest.chicagofedblogs.org/?p=2557.

98. Chicago Central Area Committee, *1986 Annual Report*, 6, 8; Chicago Central Area Committee, *1987 Annual Report* (Chicago, 1988), 25, Chicago Central Area Committee Annual

Reports, Chicago History Museum; Chicago Central Area Committee, *1988 Annual Report* (Chicago, 1989), 5, Chicago Central Area Committee Annual Reports, Chicago History Museum. The data from the 1988 report uses buildings under construction at the time to project the estimates forward to 1990.

99. Hunt and DeVries, *Planning Chicago*, 74.

100. Spirou and Judd, *Building the City of Spectacle*, 83, 87, 96, 105, 113, 144; Danny Ecker, "Navy Pier Revenue Jumped in 2015," *Crain's Chicago Business*, August 15, 2016, accessed June 7, 2018, www.chicagobusiness.com/article/20160815/NEWS09/160819941/navy-pier-revenue-jumped-in-2015; Judith Grant Long, *Public/Private Partnerships for Major League Sports Facilities* (New York: Routledge, 2013), 21.

101. Merrill Goozner, "Chicago's Bond Rating Upgraded," *Chicago Tribune*, October 3, 1987, ProQuest; Greg Hinz, "Chicago's Bond Rating Suffers Second Downgrade This Week," *Crain's Chicago Business*, August 6, 2010, accessed January 26, 2018, www.chicagobusiness.com/article/20100806/NEWS02/100809908/chicagos-bond-rating-suffers-second-downgrade-this-week; Spirou and Judd, *Building the City of Spectacle*, 174; Jordyn Holman, "Chicago Mayor Pushes Moody's to Rescind City's Junk-Bond Rating," *Bloomberg Markets*, January 11, 2017, accessed January 12, 2018, www.bloomberg.com/news/articles/2017-01-11/chicago-mayor-pushes-moody-s-to-rescind-city-s-junk-bond-rating.

102. Spirou and Judd, *Building the City of Spectacle*, 204, 208.

103. Chicago city consists of approximately eight hundred total census tracts as of this writing. U.S. Census Bureau, American Community Survey 5-Year Estimates (2011–2015), Table S1701: Poverty Status in the Past 12 Months, American FactFinder, accessed June 25, 2017, factfinder.census.gov/faces/nav/jsf/pages/index.xhtml.

104. Jay Mariotti, "It's All Over Now: MJ Walking Away," *Chicago Sun-Times*, January 12, 1999, NewsBank.

105. Chuck Goudie, "With Michael Gone, Capone Sneaks Back In," *Arlington Daily Herald*, June 9, 2000, ProQuest.

106. Kathy Bergen and Robert Channick, "A City in Crisis Seeks Answers," *Chicago Tribune*, February 15, 2013, ProQuest. The increase in Chicago's murder rate outstripped increases in most other U.S. cities. Josh Sanburn and David Johnson, "See Chicago's Deadly Year in 3 Charts," *Time*, January 17, 2017, accessed January 25, 2018, time.com/4635049/chicago-murder-rate-homicides/.

Chapter 2

1. Melissa Isaacson, "'Celebration' Fun for Almost All," *Chicago Tribune*, June 15, 1991, ProQuest; Flynn McRoberts and Elizabeth Chur, "40,000 Bulls Fans Rally in Grant Park to Say: 'We Like Mike and His Friends,'" *Chicago Tribune*, June 17, 1992, ProQuest.

2. George Papajohn and Jodi Wilgoren, "Hundreds of Thousands Reach Out, Touch Bulls," *Chicago Tribune*, June 15, 1991, ProQuest.

3. On the history of Grant Park, see Timothy Gilfoyle, *Millennium Park: Creating a Chicago Landmark* (Chicago: University of Chicago Press, 2006).

4. Richard Rothschild, "They're Gone, but Can't Be Forgotten," *Chicago Tribune*, April 23, 2006, ProQuest; "Bulls Bash to Start at 11 Tomorrow at Grant Park," *Chicago Sun-Times*, June 13, 1991, NewsBank.

5. Rosenfeld, "Celebration," 488; Rob Karwath, "Bulls Bring Out the Champion in Everyone," *Chicago Tribune*, June 16, 1991, ProQuest.

6. Don Hayner and Tom McNamee, "A Bulls Bash," *Chicago Sun-Times*, June 14, 1991, NewsBank; Isaacson, "'Celebration' Fun for Almost All"; Papajohn and Wilgoren, "Hundreds of Thousands Reach Out."

7. For an example of these photos, see Roland Lazenby, *And Now, Your Chicago Bulls! A Thirty-Year Celebration!* (Dallas, TX: Taylor Publishing, 1995), 210.

8. The photo, "Fans Leaving Grant Park after the Bulls Rally Exchange High Fives with People Coming to the Park for the Opening of the Blues Fest," is by Charles Osgood, *Chicago Tribune*, June 16, 1991, sec. 1, 8, Periodicals Reading Room, Harold Washington Library Center.

9. David Karp and William Yoels, "Sport and Urban Life," *Journal of Sport and Social Issues* 14, no. 2 (September 1990): 97.

10. For crowd size estimates for subsequent rallies, see Rosenfeld, "Celebration," 488.

11. "With Citizens United, Now What?" *Chicago Tribune*, November 1, 1997, ProQuest.

12. Isaacson, "'Celebration' Fun for Almost All."

13. Lacy Banks, "Tickets Available, but Buyer Beware," *Chicago Sun-Times*, October 31, 1990, NewsBank. Inflation adjustments made using the CPI-U for Chicago-Gary-Kenosha.

14. Papajohn and Wilgoren, "Hundreds of Thousands Reach Out."

15. Ray Long, "Free-for-All Festivity to Laud Bulls," *Chicago Sun-Times*, June 22, 1993, NewsBank.

16. Jerry Thomas and Paul Salopek, "NBA Champion Chicago Bulls Fan-tastic Day in Grant Park," *Chicago Tribune*, June 19, 1996, ProQuest.

17. Neil Steinberg, "Fan-tastic!—150,000 Cheer Bulls at Lakefront Rally," *Chicago Sun-Times*, June 22, 1993, NewsBank.

18. Isaacson, "'Celebration' Fun for Almost All"; Andrew Gottesman, "Celebration! 150,000 Fans Scream Appreciation of Their 3-Time Champion Bulls Tuesday at Grant Park Rally," *Chicago Tribune*, June 22, 1993, ProQuest; Alex Rodriguez and J. Michael Rodriguez, "'A Wonderful Waltz,'" *Chicago Sun-Times*, June 16, 1998, NewsBank.

19. Leslie Baldacci, "Ups and Downs for Bulls Fans," *Chicago Sun-Times*, June 23, 1996, NewsBank; Rick Telander, "Bulls' Fourth Title Celebration a Timely Affair," *Chicago Sun-Times*, June 19, 1996, NewsBank.

20. "Sound Off Sports Fans!: Bulls' Management Angers Fans," *Chicago Tribune*, November 6, 1973, ProQuest.

21. Don Pierson, "No Shortage of Buyers Yet: Ticket Prices: Outa Sight!" *Chicago Tribune*, March 20, 1977, ProQuest.

22. Neil Milbert, "Cubs, Sox, Bears Tickets Are Endangered Species," *Chicago Tribune*, August 7, 1977, ProQuest.

23. Dave Jones, "Sports Briefing: Bulls Boost Ticket Prices," *Chicago Tribune*, May 7, 1981, ProQuest; "Bulls Raise Ticket Prices," *Chicago Tribune*, June 13, 1985, ProQuest. Jones's article appears, based on comparisons to similar articles published around the same time, to use the label "box seats" as a synonym for courtside seats.

24. Pierson, "Ticket Prices!"

25. Steve Daley, "Reinsdorf Shows He's All Business," *Chicago Tribune*, February 9, 1985, ProQuest. The Bulls franchise is a limited partnership consisting of one general partner (Reinsdorf) with final say over franchise operations, a board of directors (chaired by Reinsdorf), and several limited partners "without any control or say in how the business operates." Melissa Harris and Jared S. Hopkins, "The Chairman and the White Sox," *Chicago Tribune*, July 28, 2013, ProQuest.

26. Bureau of Economic Analysis, "Personal Income Summary." These data are for the Chicago-Joliet-Naperville (IL-IN-WI) metropolitan statistical area, and the years used for comparison are 1985 and 1994. Inflation adjustments made using the CPI-U for Chicago-Gary-Kenosha.

27. Bob Sakamoto, "Upbeat Bulls Go Upscale but Can the Team Move Up in NBA Standings?" *Chicago Tribune*, September 22, 1985, ProQuest.

28. Bob Sakamoto, "Bulls Convert Fast Start Into Ticket Sales," *Chicago Tribune*, November 26, 1986, ProQuest.

29. Lacy Banks, "Hottest Ticket Gets Hotter," *Chicago Sun-Times*, October 30, 1991, NewsBank.

30. "View of Sports," *Chicago Sun-Times*, January 7, 1990, NewsBank.

31. "Union Is Fighting Injustice," *Chicago Sun-Times*, October 26, 1993, NewsBank.

32. John Siegfried and Timothy Peterson, "Who Is Sitting in the Stands? The Income Levels of Sports Fans," in *The Economics of Sports*, ed. William Kern (Kalamazoo, MI: W. E. Upjohn Institute for Employment Research, 2000), 61–63.

33. Thomas Wilson, "The Paradox of Social Class and Sports Involvement," *International Review for the Sociology of Sport* 37, no. 1 (March 2002): 5–16.

34. This is the same as saying that each additional $10,000 in per capita family income increases the odds of having attended a sporting event by a factor of 1.32.

35. Sean Dinces, "The Attrition of the Common Fan: Class, Spectatorship, and Major-League Stadiums in Postwar America," *Social Science History* 40, no. 2 (2016): 344.

36. Lacy Banks, "Suddenly, Bulls Are a Hot Ticket," *Chicago Sun-Times*, February 19, 1988, NewsBank; Merrill Goozner, "Michael Jordan & Co. Fuel Chicago's Bull Market," *Chicago Tribune*, May 1, 1988, ProQuest; Linda Kay, "Odds & INS," *Chicago Tribune*, April 28, 1988, ProQuest; Toni Ginnetti, "Bull Marketers Build for Long-Run Success," *Chicago Sun-Times*, November 1, 1989, NewsBank. The Bulls also cut the number of standing-room-only tickets over the course of the 1990s because of concerns with standing fans obstructing the views of those with seats. Fred Mitchell, "Bulls Stand Up for Seated Fans During Playoffs," *Chicago Tribune*, April 14, 1998, ProQuest.

37. Dinces, "Attrition of the Common Fan," 350, 352.

38. Danielson, *Home Team*, 64–65.

39. Rodney Fort, "NBA Fan Cost Index," *Rodney Fort's Sports Business Data*, data based on estimates from *Team Marketing Report*, accessed August 20, 2013, umich.app.box.com/s/41707f0b2619c0107b8b/1/320022929; Bureau of Economic Analysis, "Personal Income Summary." Inflation adjustments made using the CPI-U for Chicago-Gary-Kenosha.

40. U.S. Bureau of Labor Statistics, "Quintiles of Income before Taxes: Annual Average Expenditures and Characteristics, Consumer Expenditure Survey, 1994," *Consumer Expenditure Survey Expenditure Tables*, 3, accessed January 21, 2018, www.bls.gov/cex/1994/Standard/quintile.pdf.

41. Pamela Scott, Jane Templeman, and Michael Lischer, "Stadiums Designed for the Winning Tradition," *Athletic Business*, September 1988, 82, Amateur Athletic Foundation Library; Andrew Cohen, "Concessions Come of Age," *Athletic Business*, May 1991, 62, Amateur Athletic Foundation Library; Andrew Cohen, "Cashing In on Basketball," *Athletic Business*, July 1994, 26, Amateur Athletic Foundation Library.

42. Ginnetti, "Bull Marketers Build"; Brian Hewitt, "Bulls' Center of Controversy," *Chicago Sun-Times*, March 20, 1994, NewsBank.

43. Hewitt, "Bulls' Center of Controversy."

44. Jeff Borden, "High-Tech Heaven," *Crain's Chicago Business*, November 11, 1996, ProQuest.

45. Melvin Helitzer, *The Dream Job: $port$ Publicity, Promotion and Marketing*, 2nd ed. (Athens, OH: University Sports Press, 1996), 5.

46. Don Pierson, "Dolphin Plan Hits Jackpot," *Chicago Tribune*, April 19, 1987, ProQuest. The Palace also offered three thousand club seats. Bob Ryan and Jackie MacMullan, "Ainge Lost the Touch," *Boston Globe*, June 4, 1988, Factiva; John Helyar, "For Team Owners, More Is Never Enough," *Wall Street Journal*, May 3, 1996, Factiva.

47. Sam Smith, "Bulls Notes," *Chicago Tribune*, December 8, 1988, ProQuest.

48. The twelve arenas "opened" between 1990 and 1996 include new facilities as well as those that underwent major renovation. Data obtained from John Helyar, "Game? What Game? Arenas Emphasize Ambiance and Amenities to Entice Fans," *Wall Street Journal*, March 20, 1991, ProQuest; "Luxury Suite and Club Seating Prices for MLB, NBA, NFL, and NHL," *Team Marketing Report*, March 2000, 5–6, Amateur Athletic Foundation Library; Long, *Public/Private Partnerships*, 22–25.

49. Fran Spielman, "The Puck Stops Here: Bill Wirtz Gives Family New Legacy with Stadium," *Chicago Sun-Times*, August 28, 1994, NewsBank.

50. Anthony Baldo, "Edifice Complex," *Financial World*, November 26, 1991, Factiva.

51. Dennis Zimmerman, "Subsidizing Stadiums: Who Benefits, Who Pays?" in *Sports, Jobs, and Taxes: The Economic Impact of Sports Teams and Stadiums*, ed. Roger Noll and Andrew Zimbalist (Washington, DC: Brookings Institution Press, 1997), 141–42; Robert Baade, "What Explains the Stadium Construction Boom?" *Real Estate Issues* 21, no. 3 (1996): 6; Michael Ozanian, "The $11 Billion Pastime," *Financial World*, May 10, 1994, Factiva.

52. Hewitt, "Bulls' Center of Controversy."

53. Joanne Cleaver, "Hot Boxes," *Crain's Chicago Business*, November 14, 1994, ProQuest.

54. Dennis Conrad and Ray Long, "For Lobbyists, Sports Events Are Just the Ticket to Plead Case to Officials," *Associated Press Newswires*, May 23, 1997, Factiva; Kevin Knapp, "Bagging Grizzlies," *Crain's Chicago Business*, May 1, 2000, ProQuest; Shia Kapos, "Bulls Eye View: United Center Is Playground for City's Power Brokers," *Crain's Chicago Business*, January 9, 2012, ProQuest.

55. Blair Kamin, "Don't Take Me Out to the Mall Game," *Chicago Tribune*, February 5, 1995, ProQuest; Ron Grossman and Flynn McRoberts, "Near West Side Rebounds Like Its Bullish Neighbors," *Chicago Tribune*, June 7, 1998, ProQuest.

56. Hewitt, "Bulls' Center of Controversy."

57. Bob Herguth, "Reinsdorf Talks about His Teams," *Chicago Sun-Times*, May 19, 1996, NewsBank.

58. Frederick H. Low, "Tickets Soar for United Center," *Chicago Sun-Times*, June 29, 1994, NewsBank.

59. John Handley, "Arena Financing No Pie-In-the-Skybox-Deal," *Chicago Tribune*, July 24, 1994, ProQuest.

60. Jeff Borden, "Bulls Play Defense at the Ticket Office," *Crain's Chicago Business*, May 17, 1999, ProQuest.

61. Dinces, "Attrition of the Common Fan," table 5, 356. For NBA arenas alone premium seating went from 5.1 to 19.4 percent of total capacity, and the mean number of nonpremium seats declined by approximately 1,580.

62. Neil deMause, "Angels Exec: We Don't Care about Poor Fans, Because They Don't Buy Enough Hot Dogs," *Field of Schemes* (blog), June 19, 2015, accessed January 17, 2018, www .fieldofschemes.com/2015/06/19/9330/angels-exec-we-dont-care-about-poor-fans-because -they-dont-buy-enough-hot-dogs/; Dan Steinberg and Scott Allen, "Redskins Remove Seats from FedEx Field for Third Time in Five Seasons," *Washington Post*, June 1, 2015, ProQuest.

63. Cornelia Grumman, "Brokers' Prices Are Jumping Higher Than a Certain Bull," *Chicago Tribune*, March 19, 1995, ProQuest; Marla Donato and Michael Martinez, "Demand for No. 45 Sends Sales Skyrocketing," *Chicago Tribune*, March 25, 1995, ProQuest.

64. Michael Gillis, "Bulls Tickets Shoot Up to $9,000 Each," *Chicago Sun-Times*, June 10, 1998, Highbeam Research; Laura Janota, "Caught Up in Ticket Madness? Game 5 Seats Will Cost Bulls Fans a Pretty Penny," *Arlington Daily Herald*, June 12, 1998, ProQuest.

65. U.S. Bureau of Labor Statistics, "Quintiles of Income Before Taxes: Annual Average Expenditures and Characteristics, Consumer Expenditure Survey, 1997," *Consumer Expenditure Survey Expenditure Tables*, accessed January 21, 2018, www.bls.gov/cex/1997/Standard/quintile .pdf.

66. Dan Rozek, "Fans United in Support," *Chicago Sun-Times*, June 9, 1997, NewsBank.

67. Sam Smith, "Bulls Notes," *Chicago Tribune*, December 8, 1988, ProQuest.

68. Bruce Buursma, "A Change in Corporate Playing Field," *Chicago Tribune*, September 16, 1990, ProQuest.

69. Andrew Cohen, "Down in Front," *Athletic Business*, July 1991, 32, Amateur Athletic Foundation Library.

70. Spielman, "Puck Stops Here," *Chicago Sun-Times*, August 28, 1994, NewsBank.

71. Jim Allen, "Reinsdorf: In Long Run, Fans Will Gain From Lockout," *Arlington Daily Herald*, November 11, 1998, ProQuest.

72. On the roots of ballooning TV rights fees, See David Anderson, "The Sports Broadcasting Act: Calling It What It Is—Special Interest Legislation," *Hastings Communication and Entertainment Law Journal* 17 (1995): 945–59.

73. These are nominal values obtained from Rodney Fort, "NBA TV Revenue," *Rodney Fort's Sports Business Data*, updated February 24, 2013, accessed August 20, 2013, umich.app.box .com/s/41707f0b2619c0107b8b/1/320023253.

74. Quirk and Fort, *Hard Ball*, 29–30.

75. Teams rarely, if ever, reveal their internal balance sheets, and the NBA has accused estimates from *Financial World*, and later *Forbes*, of overstating revenues and profits. However, Nate Silver, then of the *New York Times*, reported that leaked financial information from the New Orleans Hornets showed that the estimates "closely match" actual figures. More recent (and better sourced) estimates of team values and revenues by *Bloomberg Business* suggest that, if anything, the data from *Financial World* and *Forbes* underestimate the profits of NBA franchises. Nate Silver, "Calling Foul on N.B.A.'s Claims of Financial Distress," *FiveThirtyEight* (*blog*), July 5, 2011, fivethirtyeight.blogs.nytimes.com/2011/07/05/calling-foul-on-n-b-a-s -claims-of-financial-distress/?_r=0; Wendy Thurm, "Forbes, Bloomberg Battle it Out on MLB Team Valuations," *FanGraphs Baseball* (blog), November 8, 2013, www.fangraphs.com/blogs/ forbes-bloomberg-battle-it-out-on-mlb-team-valuations/.

76. Between the 1989–1990 and 1995–1996 seasons, the average ratio of player costs to total revenue was 34 percent, and it ranged from 26 percent to 43 percent. Rodney Fort, "NBA Income and Expenses," *Rodney Fort's Sports Business Data*, updated March 23, 2013, accessed August 20, 2013, umich.app.box.com/s/41707f0b2619c0107b8b/1/320022939. Inflation adjust-

ments made using CPI-U for the U.S. To put this level of operating margin into perspective, Nike—a very profitable company—currently posts operating margins in the low-to-mid teens. "NKE Company Financials," *Nasdaq*, accessed January 17, 2018, www.nasdaq.com/symbol/nke/financials?query=ratios. Operating margin indicates the percentage of each dollar a company earns that is left over after operating costs are deducted, and thus how well a firm controls costs. When comparing firms, operating income is a better metric than net income because the former deals with revenue before taxes and debt service. Because debt service and tax liabilities can vary widely from firm to firm depending on the year in question, comparing net income (or profit margins based on net income) may not be useful in gauging relative profitability. Aaron Brenner, "Financial Analysis for Union Researchers," presentation given at the Strategic Corporate Research Summer School, Summer 2013, Cornell University, Ithaca, New York.

77. Fort, "NBA Income and Expenses."

78. Quirk and Fort, *Hard Ball*, 89. On the relationship between salaries and ticket prices, also see James Quirk and Rodney Fort, *Pay Dirt: The Business of Professional Team Sports* (Princeton, NJ: Princeton University Press, 1992), 219–23; Zenon Zygmont, "Why Professional Athletes Make So Much Money," in *Sport and Public Policy*, ed. Charles Santo and Gerard Mildner (Champaign, IL: Human Kinetics, 2010), 33–46.

79. Paul D. Staudohar, "Labor Relations in Basketball: The Lockout of 1998–99," *Monthly Labor Review* (April 1999): 4–5, 8; Conrad, *The Business of Sports*, 138.

80. "Chicago Bulls Franchise Index," *Basketballreference.com*, n.d., accessed August 20, 2013, www.basketball-reference.com/teams/CHI/.

81. David Sharos, "Stadium Seats with High Hopes for the Fall Season," *Chicago Tribune*, August 23, 1999, ProQuest.

82. During these three years, the Bulls' average ticket price ranked sixth, eighth, and twelfth most expensive out of twenty-nine teams. Rodney Fort, "NBA Ticket Prices," *Rodney Fort's Sports Business Data*, based on data from *Team Marketing Report*, February 27, 2013, accessed August 20, 2013, umich.app.box.com/s/41707f0b2619c0107b8b/1/320023271.

83. Econometric research confirms that changes in NBA payrolls from season to season have no statistically significant impact on ticket prices. See Patrick Rishe and Michael Mondello, "Ticket Price Determination in Professional Sports: An Empirical Analysis of the NBA, NFL, NHL, and Major League Baseball," *Sport Marketing Quarterly* 13, no. 2 (2004): 104–12, Amateur Athletic Foundation Library.

84. Quirk and Fort, *Hard Ball*, 89.

85. "Word from the Field," *Team Marketing Report*, August 1996, 8, Amateur Athletic Foundation Library; Rodney Fort, "NBA Attendance," *Rodney Fort's Sports Business Data*, updated May 24, 2013, accessed August 20, 2013, umich.app.box.com/s/41707f0b2619c0107b8b/1/320022885.

86. Quirk and Fort, *Hard Ball*, 92.

87. Lawrence Mishel, Josh Bivens, Elise Gould, and Heidi Shierholz, *The State of Working America*, 12th ed. (Ithaca, NY: Cornell University Press, 2012), 174–75; Saskia Sassen, "A Global City," in *Global Chicago*, ed. Charles Madigan (Urbana: University of Illinois Press, 2004), 21, 23.

88. Household income data include government transfers like Social Security. Family income and household income are not identical measures; average measures of the latter tend to skew lower because they include households made up of unrelated individuals like young, single roommates. In this paragraph, the two labels refer to distinct data and measurements. Mishel et al., *State of Working America*, 54–56, 173–74.

89. Juliet Schor, *The Overworked American: The Unexpected Decline of Leisure* (New York: Basic Books, 1992), 28–38.

90. Mishel et al., *State of Working America*, 56.

91. Robert Frank, *Luxury Fever: Why Money Fails to Satisfy in an Era of Excess* (New York: Free Press, 1999), 19–27.

92. Baade, "What Explains the Stadium Construction Boom," 8.

93. Cohen, "Cashing In," 26; Russell Granik, "NBA Overcomes Financial Woes, Meets Drug Problem, TV Contracts, Expansion Head On," *Sportsbil* (January 1990), n.p., Amateur Athletic Foundation Library.

94. Helitzer, *The Dream Job*, 32–34.

95. Bill Gloede and C. L. Smith Muniz, "NBA Goes Global," *Sports Inc.: The Sports Business Weekly*, November 16, 1987, 29, Amateur Athletic Foundation Library; Merrill Goozner, "Michael Jordan & Co. Fuel Chicago's Bull Market," *Chicago Tribune*, May 1, 1988, ProQuest; "NBA Finals TV Ratings, 1974–2008," *TV by the Numbers*, May 22, 2009, accessed August 20, 2013, tvbythenumbers.zap2it.com/2009/05/22/nba-finals-tv-ratings-1974–2008/19324/.

96. "Will 'Super Bowl' TV Viewership Set Another Record?" *TV by the Numbers*, January 28, 2011, accessed January 17, 2018, tvbythenumbers.zap2it.com/2011/01/28/will-super-bowl-tv-viewership-set-another-record-poll-ratings-history/80597/.

97. "Renting Your Facility Can Maximize Space Use and Generate Revenues," *Athletic Business*, August 1984, 86, Amateur Athletic Foundation Library.

98. Carla Nielsen, "Bull Market in Show-Biz," *Chicago Sun-Times*, October 31, 1990, NewsBank; "Chicago Bulls Make Moves to Get Personal with Season Ticket Buyers," *Team Marketing Report*, November 1992, 2, Amateur Athletic Foundation Library; Matthew J. Robinson, interview with Steve Schanwald, executive vice president of business operations, Chicago Bulls, *Sport Marketing Quarterly* 15, no. 1 (2006): 5, Amateur Athletic Foundation Library; Mark Mandernach, "A Bull Marketer," *Chicago Tribune*, April 14, 1996, ProQuest.

99. Steve Schanwald, "Beyond Michael: The Bulls Use Today's Marketing Strategies to Generate Long-Term Interest in Team," *Team Marketing Report*, November 1991, 8, Amateur Athletic Foundation Library.

100. Ray Sons, "New Stadium, Old Memories," *Chicago Sun-Times*, May 14, 1991, NewsBank; Hewitt, "Bulls' Center of Controversy"; Rick Reilly, "Last Call?" *Sports Illustrated: Vault*, May 11, 1998, accessed January 8, 2018, www.si.com/vault/1998/05/11/242928/last-call-the-greatest-sports-dynasty-of-the-90s-may-or-may-not-be-about-to-hang-it-up-but-behind-the-scenes-the-chicago-bulls-season-has-certainly-felt-like-a-farewell-tour.

101. Philip Franchine, "1.7 Million Dial, but Few Ring Up 6,000 Bulls Tickets," *Chicago Sun-Times*, June 4, 1991, NewsBank.

102. Michael Hirsley, "Yes, Even the Lordly Bulls Must Do a Little Marketing," *Chicago Tribune*, May 9, 1997, ProQuest; Christopher Condon, "The Red Sox Nurture a 'Sellout' Streak," *Bloomberg Businessweek*, July 29, 2010, accessed January 17, 2018, www.bloomberg.com/news/articles/2010–07–29/the-red-sox-nurture-a-sellout-streak.

103. Neil deMause, "Maple Leaf Ticket Prices Aren't Part of a Grand Conspiracy, Except for the Usual Ones," *Field of Schemes* (blog), March 15, 2017, accessed January 20, 2017, www.fieldofschemes.com/2017/03/15/12219/maple-leafs-ticket-prices-arent-part-of-a-grand-conspiracy-except-for-the-usual-ones/. Economists who have studied the subject offer some qualifications of this view, arguing, for example, that the availability of local television broadcasts of sports games can reduce the impact of local monopoly power on ticket prices. They

also note that teams may not set ticket prices in strict accordance with their monopoly position, because they might believe that it is more profitable to get fans in the door with slightly cheaper tickets, then saddle them with high-priced concessions (i.e., to implement monopoly pricing in the market for concessions rather than for tickets). See Dennis Coates and Brad Humphreys, "Ticket Prices, Concessions and Attendance at Professional Sporting Events," *International Journal of Sport Finance* 2 (2007): 161–70.

104. Derek Thomson, "How Did Broadway Tickets Get So Expensive? Blame the 1%," *Atlantic*, June 11, 2012, accessed January 17, 2018, www.theatlantic.com/business/archive/2012/06/how-did-broadway-tickets-get-so-expensive-blame-the-1/258346/.

105. See, for example, Quirk and Fort, *Hard Ball*, 8.

106. Mike Davis, *City of Quartz: Excavating the Future in Los Angeles* (New York: Verso, 2006), 223, 231. On increased prices at Broadway plays, see Thompson, "How Did Broadway Tickets Get So Expensive?" On increased prices at concerts, see Alan Krueger, "Land of Hope and Dreams: Rock and Roll, Economics, and Rebuilding the Middle Class," Remarks of the Chairman of the President's Council of Economic Advisers, Cleveland, OH, June 12, 2013, accessed January 17, 2018, obamawhitehouse.archives.gov/blog/2013/06/12/rock-and-roll-economics-and-rebuilding-middle-class. On increased prices at museums, see Mostafa Heddaya, "The Price of Admission: The New Whitney and Museum Tickets in New York," *BlouinArtInfo International*, May 11, 2015, accessed January 17, 2018, www.blouinartinfo.com/news/story/1152388/the-price-of-admission-the-new-whitney-and-museum-tickets-in.

107. Jim Kirk, "A Franchise on the Rise but Reinsdorf Insists Estimates Way Off," *Chicago Tribune*, June 23, 1997, ProQuest.

108. Barry Cronin, "Devout Fans Rooting for the Bulls Religiously," *Chicago Sun-Times*, June 2, 1991, NewsBank. As Andrew Zimbalist notes, even television access to major-league sports has become increasingly gentrified in recent decades, with a higher and higher proportion of games migrating from major networks to cable channels. Zimbalist, *May the Best Team Win*, 147.

109. "President Obama Talks Basketball with Marv Albert," May 25, 2010, accessed August 20, 2013, www.youtube.com/watch?v=bnLEd7b6uqk. Coincidentally, Obama attributes high prices to high player salaries.

Chapter 3

1. Tom Fitzpatrick, "Sox Out to Cash In," *Chicago Sun-Times*, July 9, 1986, NewsBank.

2. Fran Spielman, "New Home Delay for Families Routed by Sox," *Chicago Sun-Times*, October 6, 1989, NewsBank; Ben Joravsky, "The Stadium Game: Who Loses If the White Sox Win?" *Chicago Reader*, April 21, 1988, accessed January 8, 2018, www.chicagoreader.com/chicago/the-stadium-game-who-loses-if-the-white-sox-win/Content?oid=872098.

3. Earnest Gates quoted in Luke Cyphers, "Room with a View," *New York Daily News*, August 23, 1998, LexisNexis.

4. Robert Mier, "A Stadium Deal That Won't Leave Residents in the Cold," *Crain's Chicago Business*, July 8, 1991, LexisNexis.

5. Spirou and Bennett, *It's Hardly Sportin'*, 156–64.

6. The City of Chicago uses community-area boundaries for data collection purposes. Sociologists mapped the original seventy-five community areas—there now are seventy-seven—in the 1920s. Bennett, *Third City*, 26–30.

7. Transcript of Public Hearing in the Matter of the Chicago Bears Stadium, February 6,

1988, Malcolm X Community College, box 17, folder 7, 74–75, Robert Mier Papers, Chicago History Museum.

8. See Chicago Department of Planning, "Analysis of Potential Sites for Domed Sports Stadium: Report to the Mayor's Advisory Committee on a New Sports Stadium," October 1985, box 21, folder 7, Robert Mier Papers, Chicago History Museum; hand-written notes by Robert Mier, box 21, folder 7, Robert Mier Papers, Chicago History Museum.

9. This figure refers to the northwestern quarter (tracts 2804–2816). Statistic generated using "Create a Report" function and 1980 census data at *Social Explorer*, accessed January 23, 2018, www.socialexplorer.com /a9676d974c /explore.

10. Alex Kotlowitz, *There Are No Children Here: The Story of Two Boys Growing Up in the Other America* (New York: Anchor Books, 1991), 12.

11. Ed Shurna, interview by author, August 15, 2011, transcript available from author upon request.

12. Fran Spielman, "City Accused of Stadium Land Grab," *Chicago Sun-Times*, October 1, 1987, NewsBank.

13. Spirou and Bennett, *It's Hardly Sportin'*, 151.

14. Earnest Gates, interview by author, August 10, 2011, transcript available from author by request.

15. Stephen Steinhoff, *Making the Link: Directing Economic Benefits of the Proposed West Side Stadium to Local Neighborhood Development*, Nathalie P. Voorhees Center for Neighborhood and Community Improvement (Chicago, IL: University of Illinois at Chicago, 1988), cover sheet (n.p.), 21–23, Municipal Reference Collection, Harold Washington Library Center.

16. Transcript of Public Hearing in the Matter of the Chicago Bears Stadium, Malcolm X Community College, 40.

17. Interfaith Organizing Project, *The Better Alternative: Near West Side Neighborhood Revitalizing Plan* (Chicago, June 1987), secs. II and IV.A.3, Municipal Reference Collection, Harold Washington Library Center; Fran Spielman, "Bears Stadium Foes to Lobby in Springfield," *Chicago Sun-Times*, June 25, 1987, NewsBank.

18. Interfaith Organizing Project, *The Better Alternative*, secs. III, IV.A.1, and VI.

19. *Living in Greater Chicago: The Buyers and Renters Guide! 1994 Edition* (Deerfield, IL: GAMS Publishing, 1994), 73, Bound Periodicals, Harold Washington Library Center.

20. For early indications of the move of historic preservationists into Tri-Taylor, see Celeste Buck, "Bringing Buildings Back to Life," *Chicago Sun-Times*, June 6, 1986, NewsBank; Celeste Buck, "Chicago Area Rehab Lives Despite Cut in Tax Credit," *Chicago Sun-Times*, November 14, 1986, NewsBank; Maureen Hart, "History Walks with Neighborhood Tours," *Chicago Tribune*, May 10, 1987, ProQuest.

21. Spirou and Bennett, *It's Hardly Sportin'*, 148–49; William Purdy Jr. (Bears Counsel) to Thomas Tully (Wirtz Counsel), May 12, 1988, box 17, folder 9, Robert Mier Papers, Chicago History Museum; Thomas Tully to William Purdy, Jr., May 19, 1988, box 17, folder 9, Robert Mier Papers, Chicago History Museum; Ed Shurna, interview by author. The fact that during the final months of 1988 city officials devoted most of their energy to mediating the conflict between the Bears and Wirtz, rather than the conflict between the Bears and the IOP, corroborates Shurna's account. See correspondence between city officials and legal counsel for Wirtz and the Bears, box 18, folder 3, Robert Mier Papers, Chicago History Museum.

22. Ray Sons, "Stadium Feud," *Chicago Sun-Times*, July 24, 1988, NewsBank; Fran Spielman, "New Arena Set-Wirtz-Secret Talk with Gov Reported," *Chicago Sun-Times*, October 7, 1988, NewsBank.

23. Ed Shurna, interview by author; Interfaith Organizing Project, *The New "West Side Story": The Story of the Interfaith Organizing Project* (Chicago, 1992), 31, Associated Mennonite Biblical Seminary Library; Fran Spielman, "Ministers Hit Wirtz Stadium Plan," *Chicago Sun-Times*, May 9, 1989, NewsBank.

24. Spielman, "Ministers Hit Wirtz Stadium Plan"; John McCarron, "Daley Blows a Whistle on Plans by Hawks, Bulls for New Arena," *Chicago Tribune*, May 23, 1989, ProQuest; Charles Wheeler III and Mark Brown, "Senate Backs a New Bulls-Hawks Stadium," *Chicago Sun-Times*, June 23, 1989, NewsBank; Gates, interview by author; Shurna, interview by author.

25. This is the sum of the nominal contribution amounts. Schedule A Forms for Richard M. Daley Campaign Committee, Illinois State Board of Elections microfiche archives, Chicago. Because of the complexity of citing individual contributions, I indicate only the campaign committee in the footnotes. Individual donation records are available from the author upon request.

26. Ben Joravsky, "Reinsdorf's Secret Weapon," *Chicago Reader*, September 19, 1996, accessed January 17, 2018, www.chicagoreader.com/chicago/reinsdorfs-secret-weapon/Content?oid=891597; Shurna, interview by author.

27. Shurna, interview by author.

28. Gates, interview by author.

29. Aggregate statistic for tracts 2804–2816. Statistic generated using "Create a Report" function and 1990 census data at *Social Explorer*, accessed January 23, 2018, www.socialexplorer.com/a9676d974c/explore.

30. White House Office of Management and Budget, "Summary Comparison of Total Outlays for Grants to State and Local Governments: 1940–2016," *Historical Tables*, Fiscal Year 2012, table 12.1, accessed January 23, 2018, www.whitehouse.gov/omb/budget/Historicals.

31. Shurna quoted in M. W. Newman and Lillian Williams, "People Power: Chicago's Real Clout," *Chicago Sun-Times*, April 8, 1990, NewsBank; Shurna, interview by author; Interfaith Organizing Project, *New "West Side Story,"* 31; Joravsky, "Reinsdorf's Secret Weapon."

32. Interfaith Organizing Project, *New "West Side Story,"* 3, 32–34; Mary Schmich, "Land War Turns to Mutual Respect," *Chicago Tribune*, June 24, 1992, ProQuest; Patrick Reardon, "Stadium Agreement Has Winning Look," *Chicago Tribune*, May 10 1991, ProQuest.

33. Maudlyne Ihejirika, "New Stadium a Moving Event," *Chicago Sun-Times*, March 29, 1992, NewsBank.

34. Reardon, "Stadium Agreement Has Winning Look."

35. Interfaith Organizing Project, *New "West Side Story,"* 3, 26.

36. See Interfaith Organizing Project, *Better Alternative.*

37. Alexander von Hoffman, *House by House, Block by Block: The Rebirth of America's Urban Neighborhoods* (New York: Oxford University Press, 2003), 113, 144; Rod McCullom, "Playing Ball: West-Siders and Stadium Developers Make Up a New Set of Rules," *Chicago Reader*, April 9, 1992, accessed January 21, 2018, www.chicagoreader.com/chicago/playing-ball-west-siders-and-stadium-developers-make-up-a-new-set-of-rules/Content?oid=879483.

38. Logan and Molotch, *Urban Fortunes*, 39.

39. Terry Wilson, "W. Side Plan Draws Discontent," *Chicago Tribune*, April 22, 1987, Pro Quest.

40. William Wallace, *The Better Alternative (Target Area I): An Update* (Chicago, December 1991), prepared for the Interfaith Organizing Project, n.p. (26th page, beginning count with "Preface"), Municipal Reference Collection, Harold Washington Library Center.

41. Ihejirika, "New Stadium a Moving Event"; Maudlyne Ihejirika, "Residents Win Fair Deal the Hard Way," *Chicago Sun-Times*, March 29, 1992, NewsBank.

42. Grant Pick, "The Importance of Being Earnest," *Crain's Chicago Business*, April 4, 1994, ProQuest.

43. Gates quoted in Joravsky, "Reinsdorf's Secret Weapon."

44. Spirou and Bennett, *It's Hardly Sportin'*, 162.

45. John Handley, "In Play: West Side Story Getting Positive Rewrite with Help of New Stadium," *Chicago Tribune*, July 24, 1994, ProQuest.

46. "Editorial Background: The United Center's Impact on its Community," supplement to official United Center news release, February 1, 1995, 1, 5, Municipal Reference Collection, Harold Washington Library Center; Janita Poe, "It's a 'United' Effort," *Chicago Tribune*, February 27, 1995, ProQuest.

47. Patricia Wright, Thomas Chefalo, and John Cabral, *A Report on the City of Chicago Strategic Neighborhood Action Program* (Chicago: Center for Urban Economic Development, University of Illinois at Chicago, March 1994), 18, Municipal Reference Collection, Harold Washington Library Center; Handley, "In Play"; Cheryl Ririe-Kurz, "West Side Story," *Chicago Sun-Times*, August 6, 1995, NewsBank; Ellen Rooney Martin, "Bouncing Back: Businesses and Developers Bring a Gritty Community Back to Life," *Chicago Tribune*, August 24, 1996, ProQuest.

48. Gates, interview by author; Shurna, interview by author; Spirou and Bennett, *It's Hardly Sportin'*, 161–62.

49. Burney Simpson, "City Plots New West Side Story," *Chicago Reporter*, 25, no. 8 (December 1996): 8, bound periodicals, Cudahy Library, Loyola University, Chicago.

50. Gates, interview by author.

51. Lee Bey and William Smith, "Near West Side Is Reborn—Multimillion-Dollar Projects Spark Development Boom," *Chicago Sun-Times*, April 11, 1996, NewsBank; Brenda Warner Rotzoll, "Residents Near United Center Grapple with Cost of Housing," *Chicago Sun-Times*, January 6, 1997, NewsBank; "Residential Sales Transactions," *Chicago Tribune*, January 27, 2008, ProQuest.

52. *Living in Greater Chicago: The Buyer's and Renter's Guide! 1996 Edition* (Chicago: GAMS Publishing, 1996), R-11, R-15, Bound Periodicals, Harold Washington Library Center; Harry Golden Jr. and Fran Spielman, "2 Final W. Side Site Plans Picked for Bears Stadium," *Chicago Sun-Times*, January 22, 1988, NewsBank.

53. Janita Poe, "Jordan Center Not Slam Dunk for All," *Chicago Tribune*, April 27, 1997, ProQuest; Interfaith Organizing Project, *Better Alternative*, sec. III. See Rachel Weber, "Extracting Value from the City: Neoliberalism and Urban Redevelopment," *Spaces of Neoliberalism*, ed. Neil Brenner and Nik Theodore (Malden, MA: Blackwell, 2002), 172–93.

54. Reverend George Daniels quoted in Spirou and Bennett, *It's Hardly Sportin'*, 162.

55. Devereux Bowly Jr., *The Poorhouse: Subsidized Housing in Chicago, 1895–1976* (Carbondale: Southern Illinois University Press, 1978), 112–13; Janet Smith, "Public Housing Transformation: Evolving National Policy," in *Where Are Poor People to Live?*, ed. Larry Bennett, Janet Smith, and Patricia Wright (Armonk, NY: M. E. Sharpe, 2006), 19–25; Bill Wilen, "The Horner Model: Successfully Redeveloping Public Housing," *Northwestern Journal of Law and Social Policy* 1, no. 1 (Summer 2006): 65.

56. Court records quoted in Wilen, "The Horner Model," 68. See *Horner Mother's Guild v. Chicago Housing Authority*, No. 91 C 3316, 1991 U.S. Dist. LEXIS 16632 (N. Dist. Ill., East. Div., Nov. 12, 1991). Vacancy data from Chicago Housing Authority, "HQS Inspection Report: December, 1991," Public Housing Management Assessment Program (PHMAP) Certification

(Chicago, March 2, 1992), Chicago Housing Authority Development Records, 1948–1992, box 3, Chicago History Museum.

57. Wilen, "The Horner Model," 68; Memorandum from Kristin R. Anderson, CHA Office of External Affairs, to Robert Whitfield, CHA Chief Operating Officer, March 2, 1992, 6, Public Housing Management Assessment Program: Appeal of Management Assessment Rating, May 11, 1992, Chicago Housing Authority Development Records, 1948–1992, box 3, Chicago History Museum.

58. D. Bradford Hunt, *Blueprint for Disaster: The Unraveling of Chicago Public Housing* (Chicago: University of Chicago Press, 2009), 6.

59. Smith, "Public Housing Transformation," 24.

60. See Hirsch, *Making the Second Ghetto*.

61. Hunt, *Blueprint for Disaster*, 185; Susan Popkin, Victoria Gwiasda, Lynn Olson, Dennis Rosenbaum, and Larry Buron, *The Hidden War: Crime and the Tragedy of Public Housing in Chicago* (New Brunswick, NJ: Rutgers University Press, 2000), 2.

62. Bowly, *Poorhouse*, 182.

63. Smith, "Public Housing Transformation," 30–31; Chicago Housing Authority, "CHA Is Suspending Registrations for the Section 8 Rent Subsidy Program on May 31, 1985," CHA News (press release), May 30, 1985, Chicago Housing Authority Development Records, 1948–1992, box 19, folder 4, Chicago History Museum.

64. Perkins and Will, *Chicago Sports Center: A Concept Plan for Near Westside Revitalization and a New Bears Football Stadium* (Chicago, April 1987), Special Collections, Harold Washington Library Center.

65. Transcript of Public Hearing in the Matter of the Chicago Bears Stadium, Malcolm X Community College, 80; Patrick Reardon, "Stadium Could Fill Urban Void," *Chicago Tribune*, April 14, 1987, ProQuest; David Ibata, "$20 Million Plan a First Step in Revitalizing the West Side," *Chicago Tribune*, June 3, 1985, ProQuest.

66. Interfaith Organizing Project, *Better Alternative*, "Executive Summary"; Transcript of Public Hearing in the Matter of the Chicago Bears Stadium, Malcolm X Community College, 40.

67. According to court documents, between November 1981 and July 1991, the vacancy rate at Horner ballooned from 2.3 to 49.3 percent—by far, the highest vacancy rate of any CHA high-rise development with more than 1,000 units. *Horner Mothers Guild v. Chicago Housing Authority*, No. 91 C 3316, 1993 U.S. Dist. LEXIS 7432 (N. Dist. Ill., East. Div., May 26, 1993), 5. The 1991 vacancy rate figures offered in the court documents vary slightly—by less than 1 percentage point—with those cited above from original CHA publications.

68. *Horner Mothers Guild v. Chicago Housing Authority*, No. 91 C 3316, 1991 U.S. Dist. LEXIS 16632 (N. Dist. Ill., East. Div., Nov. 12, 1991), 1; *Horner Mothers Guild*, 1993 U.S. Dist. LEXIS 7432, 5; Wilen, "The Horner Model," 69. On the legal history of the de facto demolition concept, see Catherine Fennell, *Last Project Standing: Civics and Sympathy in Post-Welfare Chicago* (Minneapolis: University of Minnesota Press, 2015), 83–99.

69. Jonah Newman, "Dismantling the Towers," *Chicago Reporter*, March 13, 2015, accessed January 22, 2018, chicagoreporter.com/dismantling-the-towers/.

70. During these years much evidence emerged in support of the plaintiffs' accusations. After the tenants filed the suit in 1991, inspectors from Chicago's Department of Buildings recorded a total of 570 "dangerous and hazardous" code violations at Horner. Despite Horner residents' exposure to some of the worst physical deterioration and highest vacancy rates among CHA projects, CHA officials had consistently overlooked the development when distributing

federal money for rehabilitation during the late 1980s and early 1990s. *Horner Mother's Guild*, 1993 U.S. Dist. LEXIS 7432, 8.

71. Fran Spielman, "Fingers Pointed over Demolition Plan," *Chicago Sun-Times*, July 29, 1994, NewsBank.

72. Thomas Gradel and Dick Simpson, *Corrupt Illinois: Patronage, Cronyism, and Criminality* (Urbana: University of Illinois Press, 2015), 144.

73. Dorothy Collin and Mike Conklin, "Bidders Starting to Pipe Up for Stadium's Organ," *Chicago Tribune*, May 18, 1994, ProQuest; Spielman, "Fingers Pointed."

74. Stacy Springfield, "Horner Annex Reborn," *Our Voices* (blog), June 15, 1997, accessed January 22, 2018, wethepeoplemedia.org/uncategorized/horner-annex-reborn/; Maudlyne Ihejirika and Gilbert Jimenez, "CHA Wants to Raze Annex—Residents in Stadium Shadow Face Move," *Chicago Sun-Times*, August 4, 1994, NewsBank; Flynn McRoberts, "CHA Wants to Demolish Three Horner Buildings Near New Stadium," *Chicago Tribune*, August 4, 1994, ProQuest.

75. Maudlyne Ihejirika, "Arena Neighbors Wonder Why CHA Plays Hardball," *Chicago Sun-Times*, August 8, 1994, NewsBank; Maudlyne Ihejirika, "Horner Annex Residents, CHA OK Relocation," *Chicago Sun-Times*, August 10, 1994, NewsBank. Thom Finerty, who attended meetings about the redevelopment of Horner in his capacity as a CHA official during the early 1990s, confirms that Pizer pressed the CHA to have the annex demolished. Thom Finerty, interviews by author, August 24, 2011 and December 21, 2011, transcripts available upon request from author. The interviews with Finerty and William Wilen (see below) were conducted simultaneously because of scheduling constraints.

76. Chinta Strausberg, "Hendon Wants Bulls Boycott," *Chicago Defender*, November 2, 1995, 1, 10, Periodicals Microform Reading Room, Harold Washington Library Center; Mark Weinberg, *Career Misconduct: The Story of Bill Wirtz's Greed, Corruption, and the Betrayal of Blackhawks' Fans* (Chicago: Blueline Publishing, 2001), 38–44.

77. Micah Maidenberg, "Reinsdorf-Founded Firm Plans West Loop Apartments," *Crain's Chicago Business*, August 22, 2012, accessed January 22, 2018, www.chicagobusiness.com/realestate/20120822/CRED03/120829935/reinsdorf-founded-firm-plans-west-loop-apartments; Micah Maidenberg, "Reinsdorf-Backed Developer Plans 61 More Apartments on West Side," *Crain's Chicago Business*, April 4, 2013, accessed January 22, 2018, www.chicagobusiness.com/realestate/20130404/CRED03/130409890/reinsdorf-backed-developer-plans-61-more-apartments-on-west-side; "Warren Ashland Place," *West Loop Luxury Apartments*, accessed June 25, 2016, westloopluxuryapartments.com/properties/warren-ashland-place/?utm_source=michavegroup.com&utm_medium=referral&utm_campaign=michavegroup.

78. Euchner, *Playing the Field*, 135, 156–58.

79. Ihejirika and Jimenez, "CHA Wants to Raze Annex."

80. Lane quoted in Maudlyne Ihejirika, "Horner Annex Residents Face 2-Year Housing Wait," *Chicago Sun-Times*, August 11, 1994, NewsBank.

81. McRoberts, "CHA Wants to Demolish"; Ihejirika, "Arena Neighbors Wonder"; Maudlyne Ihejirika, "Horner Resident Fights for Home," *Chicago Sun-Times*, August 14, 1994, NewsBank.

82. Flynn McRoberts, "HUD Blocks a Move to Demolish CHA Homes Near Stadium," *Chicago Tribune*, September 10, 1994, ProQuest.

83. Zagel approved the consent decree in April 1995 and approved an amended version in September of the same year. Wilen, "The Horner Model," 69–70.

84. Hunt and DeVries, *Planning Chicago*, 155. The initial decree called for the rehabilitation

of some of the high-rises. On why this changed, see Wilen, "The Horner Model," 69–71; William Wilen, "Horner Residents Negotiate Housing Redevelopment Plans," *Illinois Welfare News*, December 2001, 3–4, 10.

85. Yan Zhang and Gretchen Weismann, "Public Housing's Cinderella: Policy Dynamics of HOPE VI in the Mid-1990s," in *Where Are Poor People to Live? Transforming Public Housing Communities* (Armonk, NY: M. E. Sharpe, 2006), 44–45; Susan Popkin, Bruce Katz, Mary Cunningham, Karen Brown, Jeremy Gustafson, and Margery Turner, *A Decade of HOPE VI: Research Findings and Policy Changes* (Washington, DC: Urban Institute, 2004), 17, accessed December 20, 2016, www.urban.org/sites/default/files/alfresco/publication-pdfs/411002-A-Decade -of-HOPE-VI.PDF; U.S. General Accounting Office, *HOPE VI Leveraging Has Increased, but HUD Has Not Met Annual Reporting Requirement*, Report to the Chairman, Subcommittee on Housing and Transportation, Committee on Banking, Housing, and Urban Affairs, U.S. Senate, GAO-03-91, December 2002, accessed January 23, 2018, www.gao.gov/assets/240/236352.html.

86. Janet Smith, "Mixed-Income Communities: Designing Out Poverty or Pushing Out the Poor?" in *Where Are Poor People to Live?*, ed. Larry Bennett, Janet Smith, and Patricia Wright (Armonk, NY: M. E. Sharpe, 2006), 260–65.

87. Smith, "Public Housing Transformation," 35–36.

88. On these policy shifts, see the selections in Adolph Reed Jr., ed., *Without Justice for All: The New Liberalism and Our Retreat from Racial Equality* (Boulder, CO: Westview, 1999).

89. Kathe Newman and Philip Ashton, "Neoliberal Urban Policy and New Paths of Neighborhood Change in the American Inner City," *Environment and Planning A* 36 (2004): 1151–72.

90. Congress permanently repealed the law in 1998. Wilen, "Horner Residents Negotiate Housing Redevelopment Plans," 3.

91. William Wilen, interviews by author, August 24, 2011 and December 21, 2011, transcripts available form author upon request. William Wilen and Rajesh Nayak, "Relocated Public Housing Residents Have Little Hope of Returning: Work Requirements for Mixed-Income Public Housing Developments," in *Where Are Poor People to Live?*, ed. Larry Bennett, Janet Smith, and Patricia Wright (Armonk, NY: M. E. Sharpe, 2006), 221, 227; Mark Joseph, "Creating Mixed-Income Developments in Chicago: Developer and Service Provider Perspectives," *Housing Policy Debate* 20, no. 1 (January 2010): 102.

92. Maudlyne Ihejirika, "Near West Side Group Honored," *Chicago-Sun Times*, June 13, 1997, NewsBank; Byron P. White, "Housing Plan May Go Westward," *Chicago Tribune*, April 16, 1996, ProQuest; Finerty, interviews by author.

93. Finerty, interviews by author.

94. Maudlyne Ihejirika, "Crusade by Horner Moms Pays Off," *Chicago Sun-Times*, August 4, 1995, NewsBank.

95. Of the new units, 200 sat on the site of demolished Horner high-rises, 261 were "scattered site" units dispersed throughout the immediate neighborhood, and 90 were rehabilitated Horner Annex units; 233 of the new units went to public housing residents from outside the area. These figures do not include additional, publicly subsidized housing units reserved for relatively higher-income families (those earning "between 50 and 80 percent of area median income") built as part of phase 1 to simultaneously satisfy a separate consent decree dating back to the 1970s (this decree originated from the *Gautreaux et al. v Chicago Housing Authority* case). Wilen, "Horner Model," 68–71; Wilen, "Horner Residents Negotiate Housing Redevelopment Plans," 3.

96. Preston Smith II, *Racial Democracy and the Black Metropolis: Housing Policy in Postwar Chicago* (Minneapolis: University of Minnesota Press, 2012), xvi.

97. Janita Poe, "A Meeting of Motives," *Chicago Tribune*, August 9, 1996, ProQuest.

98. Don Adams, "Replacement Housing or Replacing People," *Our Voices*, June 15, 1997, accessed January 23, 2018, wethepeoplemedia.org/uncategorized/replacement-housing-or -replacing-people/.

99. Leon Pitt, "Reinsdorf Offers Aid in CHA Dispute," *Chicago Sun-Times*, June 12, 1997, NewsBank; Ihejirika, "Near West Side Group Honored."

100. Springfield, "Horner Annex Reborn."

101. Flynn McRoberts, "Judge Won't Join Battle over Tenants for Horner," *Chicago Tribune*, June 18, 1997, ProQuest.

102. Springfield, "Horner Annex Reborn."

103. Don Adams, "Working to Improve Horner Homes," letter to the editor, *Chicago Tribune*, October 11, 1999, ProQuest.

104. Gates, interview by author; Wilen, interviews by author; Frederick Lowe, "Keeping the Faith: Saint Malachy's Never Gave Up on the West Side," *Chicago Reader*, May 11, 2000, accessed September 15, 2013, www.chicagoreader.com/chicago/keeping-the-faith/Content?oid=902248; Shurna, interview by author. For a superb analysis of intraracial class politics in the postwar United States more broadly, see Adolph Reed Jr., *Stirrings in the Jug: Black Politics in the Post-Segregation Era* (Minneapolis: University of Minnesota Press, 1999).

105. Fennell, *Last Project Standing*, 8, 181, 186–93; Wilen, interviews by author; "Near West Side Home Visitors Program: Staff Directory," *LISC Chicago New Communities Program*, n.d., accessed January 23, 2018, www.newcommunities.org/cmadocs/hvpstaff.pdf.

106. Melita Marie Garza, "Old Problems Plague New Low-Rises," *Chicago Tribune*, September 20, 1999, ProQuest; Celeste Garrett, "Changes to Public Housing Spur State Street Revival," *Chicago Tribune*, July 30, 2003, ProQuest.

107. Smith, *Racial Democracy*, xviii.

108. Philip Klinker, "Bill Clinton and the Politics of the New Liberalism," in *Without Justice for All: The New Liberalism and Our Retreat from Racial Equality*, ed. Adolph Reed Jr. (Boulder, CO: Westview, 1999), 12.

109. Bill Clinton, "Our American Community," speech to the Democratic Leadership Council, New Orleans, May 2, 1992, in *Preface to the Presidency: Selected Speeches of Bill Clinton, 1974–1992*, ed. Stephen A. Smith (Fayetteville: University of Arkansas Press, 1996), 148.

110. Gates, interview by author; Dawn Turner Trice, "Leader Stayed Loyal to West Side," *Chicago Tribune*, September 6, 2010, ProQuest.

111. Fennell, *Last Project Standing*, 174–75, 181.

112. Near West Side Community Development Corporation and Local Initiatives Support Corporation, *More Than Bricks and Mortar: A Quality of Life Plan for West Haven* (Chicago, 2002), 13, accessed January 24, 2018, www.newcommunities.org/cmadocs/WestHaven -QofLplan2002.pdf.

113. Hunt and DeVries, *Planning Chicago*, 156–57, 160–65; Larry Bennett, Nancy Hudspeth, and Patricia Wright, "A Critical Analysis of the ABLA Redevelopment Plan," in *Where Are Poor People to Live?*, ed. Larry Bennett, Janet Smith, and Patricia Wright (Armonk, NY: M. E. Sharpe, 2006), 199.

114. Hunt and DeVries, *Planning Chicago*, 162–65.

115. "Telling Our Story," *Chicago Video Project*, 2009, accessed January 20, 2017, chicagovideo .com/videos/; Bennett, Hudspeth, and Wright, "Critical Analysis," 205.

116. Wilen, "Horner Model," 80.

117. Newman, "Dismantling the Towers"; Bennett, Hudspeth, and Wright, "Critical Analysis," 203–4.

118. See "Telling Our Story," *Chicago Video Project*; Wilen, "Horner Model."

119. Chicago Housing Authority, "Authorization to Enter into a Predevelopment Loan Agreement with BMH-I, LLC," February 12, 2014, accessed January 25, 2014, www.thecha.org/assets/1/20/4-Horner_Superblock171.pdf.

120. Chicago Housing Authority, "Authorization to Enter"; Jonah Newman, e-mail message to author, May 19, 2015; Fennell, *Last Project Standing*, 245–46.

121. Newman, "Dismantling the Towers."

122. Transcript of the Public Hearing in the Matter of the Chicago Bears Stadium, City of Chicago Department of Human Services, Kedzie Avenue Branch, February 6, 1988, box 17, folder 7, 4–10, Robert Mier Papers, Chicago History Museum.

123. Logan and Molotch, *Urban Fortunes*, 145.

Chapter 4

1. John Byrne, "For Daley, Goodbyes Begin," *Chicago Tribune*, April 8, 2011, ProQuest.

2. Elizabeth Brackett, "Community Redevelopment Reforms Spark Funding Concerns," *PBS Online NewsHour* (April 7, 2005), television transcript, accessed May 13, 2013, www.pbs.org/newshour/bb/economy/jan-june05/housing_4–7.html (link no longer active, but PDF copy available from author upon request).

3. Near West Side Community Development Corporate and Local Initiatives Support Corporation, *West Haven: Rising Like the Phoenix, LISC Chicago's New Communities Program* (October 2007), 4, accessed May 13, 2013, www.newcommunities.org/cmadocs/WHaven_NCP_Plan_07.pdf. For the purposes of this chapter, "West Haven" refers to the neighborhood surrounding the United Center—not just the redeveloped Horner site that goes by the same name.

4. Spirou and Bennett, *It's Hardly Sportin'*, 175.

5. Patrick Reardon, "Stadium Could Fill Urban Void," *Chicago Tribune*, April 14, 1987, ProQuest.

6. Stephen Steinhoff, *A New Sports Stadium: Can It Bring Economic Benefits to Residents of the Near West Side?*, Technical Report No. 4-87 (Chicago: Nathalie P. Voorhees Center for Neighborhood and Community Improvement, University of Illinois at Chicago, 1988), 16, Municipal Reference Collection, Harold Washington Library Center.

7. Daley quoted in Patrick Reardon, "Stadium Agreement Has a Winning Look," *Chicago Tribune*, May 10, 1991, ProQuest.

8. Matt Smith quoted in Lee Bey and William Smith, "Near West Side Is Reborn," *Chicago Sun-Times*, April 11, 1996, NewsBank; Greg Longhini quoted in John Handley, "United Front," *Chicago Tribune*, June 30, 1996, ProQuest.

9. Cyphers, "Room with a View."

10. "United Center's Helping Hand," *Chicago Sun-Times*, February 5, 1995, NewsBank.

11. Burney Simpson, "City Plots New West Side Story," 1, 6–10; Ron Grossman and Flynn McRoberts, "Near West Side Rebounds Like Its Bullish Neighbors," *Chicago Tribune*, June 7, 1998, ProQuest.

12. *Chicago 96*, promotional magazine for Chicago's campaign to host the 1996 Democratic National Convention (Chicago: Committee for '96, 1994), 3, Municipal Reference Collection, Harold Washington Library Center.

13. Scott Fornek, "Near West Side," *Chicago Sun-Times*, December 30, 1996, NewsBank; Grossman and McRoberts, "Near West Side Rebounds."

14. Local Initiatives Support Corporation MetroEdge, *Westhaven Market Study* (November 5, 2007), 17, accessed January 24, 2018, www.newcommunities.org/cmadocs/Westhaven _MetroEdge_FINAL.pdf; Local Initiatives Support Corporation MetroEdge, *West Haven Information Profile* (Chicago: Near West Chamber of Commerce, May 2010), accessed May 13, 2013, www.lisc-chicago.org/uploads/lisc-chicago/documents/westhaven-metroedge.pdf, 17. The income statistic refers to the area bounded by Kinzie Street to the north, the Eisenhower Expressway to the south, Rockwell Street to the west, and Ashland Avenue to the east.

15. Near West Side Community Development Corporation and Local Initiatives Support Coalition, *More Than Bricks and Mortar*, 17; Handley, "In Play."

16. Near West Side Community Development Corporation and Local Initiatives Support Coalition, *More Than Bricks and Mortar*, 2.

17. Grossman and McRoberts, "Near West Side Rebounds."

18. Near West Side Community Development Corporation and Local Initiatives Support Coalition, *More Than Bricks and Mortar*, 1, 13.

19. Hoffman, *House by House*, 137, 144, 158.

20. Rosalind Rossi and Jon Schmid, "Chicago Schools Add More Latinos, Asians," *Chicago Sun-Times*, January 4, 1998, NewsBank.

21. Evan Osnos, "West Town's Revival Not Without a Price," *Chicago Tribune*, July 12, 1996, ProQuest.

22. Geographic Information Systems (GIS) software makes this possible by linking data from the U.S. Census to digital boundary files at multiple scales (e.g., census block, census tract, city). For historians of neighborhoods, using GIS can be tricky, because census tract boundaries shifted repeatedly during the twentieth century. If a historian defines a "neighborhood" as a set of tracts as drawn in one census year, it becomes difficult to gauge accurately change over time within that original neighborhood if the tract boundaries shrank or expanded in subsequent decades. To visualize why this could pose a problem, imagine that two of the edge tracts in a "neighborhood" expand to include additional area from one census to another. The net population of the tracts in the first census was 1,500, and the net population of the tracts in the subsequent census was 2,000. We have no way of knowing whether the population gain represents longtime residents from the new areas incorporated into the expanded tracts or an influx of new residents into the area covered by the old tract boundaries. To address this, sociologists John Logan, Zengwang Xu, and Brian Stults developed a "longitudinal tract database" that standardizes census tract boundaries and data across years from 1970 to 2010. See John Logan, Zengwang Xu, and Brian Stults, "Interpolating US Decennial Census Tract Data from as Early as 1970 to 2010: A Longitudinal Tract Database," *Professional Geographer* 66, no. 3 (2014): 412–20.

23. "West Haven" refers to the area bounded by Kinzie Street to the North, the Eisenhower Expressway to the South, Rockwell Street to the West, and Ashland Avenue to the East. This is the official boundary delineated by the Near West Side Community Development Corporation. See "Community Directory," *Near West Side Community Development Corporation*, accessed May 13, 2013, www.nearwestsidecdc.org/directory/index.html (link no longer active but digital copy available from author upon request); Near West Side Community Development Corporation, "Our Story," accessed October 21, 2017, nearwestsidecdc .org/our-story/; Local Initiatives Support Corporation, *West Haven Information Profile*, 6. An earlier NWSCDC planning document (from 2002) excluded the strip between Western Avenue

and the western border of the Near West Side community area from its technical definition of the neighborhood—that is, it defined West Haven as having the same exact geography as the "Better Alternative Area," with Western as the westernmost border (instead of Rockwell). However, I used the broader boundary for three reasons: First, even though the earlier document technically excluded the aforementioned strip from the official West Haven boundary, it included the strip along with notes on prospective development there in its neighborhood map, and there were no other areas outside the delineated border included in the map. Second, local press reports indicate that residents from the strip and local community organizers active there talked as if the area belonged to the neighborhood surrounding the United Center. Third, the existence of railroad tracks and fencing on the western edge of the strip created barriers between the strip and neighborhoods to the east. See Near West Side Community Development Corporation and Local Initiatives Support Corporation, *West Haven: Rising Like the Phoenix,* "Contents" page; Grant Pick, "Turf War," *Chicago Reader,* July 9, 1998, accessed January 22, 2018, www.chicagoreader.com/chicago/turf-war/Content?oid=896776; Michael Abramowitz and David Aldridge, "On Chicago's Near West Side, Poverty Surrounds the Bulls," *Washington Post,* June 9, 1992, ProQuest.

24. Geographers Elvin Wyly and Daniel Hammel reported in 1998 that, "on the west side, gentrification extends outward from downtown along two corridors: one toward a large medical complex just west of Ashland Avenue and another toward the new United Center." Elvin Wyly and Daniel Hammel, "Modeling the Context and Contingency of Gentrification," *Journal of Urban Affairs* 20, no. 3 (October 1998): 308.

25. Nathalie P. Voorhees Center for Neighborhood and Community Improvement, *The Socioeconomic Change of Chicago's Community Areas,* 14.

26. See map 3.5 for the geography of Tri-Taylor. As of 1990, the total population of these two pockets was 817 persons, 209 of which were black (based on the raw data used to construct map 1.1). Because the demographic analysis in this chapter focuses primarily on change in black population—in particular, black population decline—throughout West Haven, the relatively miniscule number of African Americans in these pockets cannot exert a significant impact.

27. Author calculations based on data in Chicago Metropolitan Agency for Planning (CMAP), *Land Use Inventory, 1990* (Chicago: Chicago Metropolitan Agency for Planning, 2001), accessed May 17, 2013, www.cmap.illinois.gov/land-use-inventory.

28. Author calculations based on data in CMAP, *Land Use Inventory, 1990.*

29. Sean Dinces, "Bulls Markets: Power, Place, and Professional Sport in Late Twentieth-Century Chicago" (PhD diss., Brown University, 2014), 241–52.

30. Wyly and Hammel, "Modeling the Context and Contingency of Gentrification," 315–16.

31. Pick, "The Importance of Being Earnest"; Fennell, *Last Project Standing,* 138.

32. Sean Zielenbach, "Understanding Community Change: A Look at Low-Income Chicago Neighborhoods in the 1990s," *Neighborhood Change in Urban America,* no. 4 (February 2005): 1, accessed January 13, 2012, www.urban.org/sites/default/files/publication/51516/311151 -understanding-community-change.pdf.

33. Chicago Housing Authority, *Statistical Profile: 1991 to 1992* (Chicago, n.d.), 5, Municipal Reference Collection, Harold Washington Library Center; Bowly, *Poorhouse,* 119–21; Fennell, *Last Project Standing,* 42. Although Rockwell sat just outside the western edge of the original "Better Alternative Area," it makes sense to consider it part of West Haven because the NWSCDC incorporated it into its official area of operations after breaking with the IOP. Moreover, given that rail lines to the west formed a barrier between the housing project and East Garfield Park, Rockwell melded more seamlessly into the neighborhood around the United

Center. Near West Side Community Development Corporation, "Community Directory." For other evidence that Gates and the NWSCDC considered Rockwell as part of the neighborhood, see Pick, "Turf War"; Near West Side Community Development Corporation and Local Initiatives Support Corporation, *More Than Bricks and Mortar.*

34. The larger loss indicated by the CHA numbers likely has to do either with the influx of new residents into non-CHA residential structures in the tract during the 1990s or with challenges associated with establishing a complete census count in very low-income areas.

35. This coincided with a decline in units designated for public housing residents from 1,136 to 71. Micah Maidenberg, "The Rockwell Review," *Chicago Journal,* April 29, 2009, accessed May 13, 2013, www.chicagojournal.com/News/In-The-Paper/04–29–2009/The_Rockwell_review.

36. Casey Sanchez, "Just Moving On: After Years of Waiting and Struggling to Meet New Requirements, Thousands of CHA Residents May Not Return to New Mixed-Income Housing," *Chicago Reporter* 35, no. 3 (May/June 2006): 22–27, bound periodicals, Cudahy Library, Loyola University, Chicago.

37. Patricia Wright, "Community Resistance to CHA Transformation: The History, Evolution, Struggles, and Accomplishments of the Coalition to Protect Public Housing," in *Where Are Poor People to Live? Transforming Public Housing Communities,* ed. Larry Bennett, Janet Smith, and Patricia Wright (Armonk, NY: M. E. Sharpe, 2006), 126.

38. Hackworth, *Neoliberal City,* 59. See Sanchez, "Just Moving On."

39. Near West Side Community Development Corporation and Local Initiatives Support Corporation, *More Than Bricks and Mortar,* 13; Vernon Ford, *A Draft Commentary on the Proposed Westside Stadium Site and Issues Faced by Local Community Residents, City Administration, the Private Development Sector and the Black Middle Class* (report submitted by mail to Robert Mier, June 4, 1987), box 17, folder 5, 1, Robert Mier Papers, Chicago History Museum.

40. Wilen, "The Horner Model," 71–72.

41. Local Initiatives Support Corporation MetroEdge, *Westhaven Market Study,* 26; Gates, interview by author.

42. Susan Popkin, Mary K. Cunningham, and Martha Burt, "Public Housing Transformation and the 'Hard to House,'" *Housing Policy Debate* 16, no. 1 (2005): 1; Chicago Housing Authority, *The Plan for Transformation: An Update on Relocation* (Chicago, April 2011), 23, accessed January 24, 2018, www.thecha.org/assets/1/22/4_14_11_Report_FINAL_appendices_(1).pdf.

43. Todd Sink and Brian Ceh, "Relocation of Urban Poor in Chicago: HOPE VI Policy Outcomes," *Geoforum* 42, no. 1 (2011): 71, 81.

44. Susan Popkin, *The HOPE VI Program—What about the Residents?* (Washington, DC: Urban Institute, 2002), 4, accessed January 24, 2018, webarchive.urban.org/UploadedPDF/310593_HopeVI.pdf.

45. Newman and Ashton, "Neoliberal Urban Policy and New Paths of Neighborhood Change," 1154–55; Elvin Wyly, Thomas Cooke, Daniel Hammel, Steven Holloway, and Margaret Hudson, "Low- to Moderate-Income Lending in Context: Progress Report on the Neighborhood Impacts of Homeownership Policy," *Housing Policy Debate* 12, no. 1 (2001): 87–92.

46. Wyly et al., "Low- to Moderate-Income Lending in Context," 88.

47. Local Initiatives Support Corporation MetroEdge, *Westhaven Market Study,* 12.

48. Don Terry, "Democrats Bring a Fleeting Sense of Peace to a Neighborhood," *New York Times,* August 30, 1996, ProQuest; Grossman and McRoberts, "Near West Side Rebounds."

49. Bennett, Hudspeth, and Wright, "A Critical Analysis," 201; Near West Side Community Development Corporation and Local Initiatives Support Corporation, *West Haven: Rising Like the Phoenix,* 16.

50. Bill Rumbler, "City Values Climb across the Board," *Chicago Sun-Times*, June 23, 1996, NewsBank; Martin, "Bouncing Back."

51. Sean Zielenbach, *The Art of Revitalization: Improving Conditions in Distressed Inner-City Neighborhoods* (New York: Garland, 2000), 113–14.

52. Kirsten Miller, "Olympic Opportunity? Real Estate Interests Assess Washington Park," *Chicago Sun-Times*, January 5, 2007, NewsBank; Mark Boyer, "Urban Planning Folly: The United Center and the Near West Side," *Curbed Chicago*, May 9, 2011, accessed May 17, 2013, chicago.curbed.com/archives/2011/05/09/urban-planning-folly-the-united-center-and-the -near-west-side.php.

53. M. W. Newman, "West Side Story: Bears and Blight," *Chicago Sun-Times*, April 19, 1987, NewsBank.

54. Danuzio Lima and Stephen Steinhoff, *Community Resources Book*, Technical Report No. 1-87, prepared for the Interfaith Organizing Project (Chicago: Nathalie P. Voorhees Center for Neighborhood and Community Improvement, University of Illinois at Chicago, August 1987), 76, Municipal Reference Collection, Harold Washington Library Center.

55. Steinhoff, *New Sports Stadium*, 18.

56. Greg Longhini and Pat Dowell-Cerasoli, internal memo to Robert Giloth and David Mosena, Chicago Department of Planning, May 28, 1987, box 17, folder 4, 1, Robert Mier Papers, Chicago History Museum.

57. David Ibata, "Westgate Mill: New Life for Old Neighborhood," *Chicago Tribune*, June 9, 1985, ProQuest; Patrick Barry, "Ring around the Loop," *Chicago Magazine*, April 1986, 140, 158, Bound Periodicals, Harold Washington Library Center; Newman, "West Side Story"; Patrick Reardon, "Stadium Could Fill Urban Void," *Chicago Tribune*, April 14, 1987, ProQuest.

58. Don DeBat and Gary Meyers, "Near West Side Property Values Get High Grades," *Chicago Sun-Times*, June 22, 1990, NewsBank; Newman, "West Side Story."

59. Kotlowitz, *There Are No Children Here*, 158.

60. Annie Kostiner, interview by author, August 25, 2011, transcript available upon request; Lewis Kostiner, interview by author, August 25, 2011, transcript available upon request. Because of scheduling constraints, I conducted the interviews with Annie and Lewis simultaneously.

61. William Mullen, "West Side Story from Skid Row's Ashes," *Chicago Tribune*, February 16, 1986, ProQuest.

62. City of Chicago Department of Planning and Development, *Chicago Neighborhood Development: New Construction 1987–1990* (Chicago, February 1992), 231–41, Municipal Reference Collection, Harold Washington Library Center.

63. Fran Spielman, "Stadium 'Only Chance' for Area," *Chicago Sun-Times*, April 17, 1987, NewsBank.

64. Martin, "Bouncing Back"; Jane Adler, "Biz Inches West toward United Center," *Crain's Chicago Business*, May 5, 1997, ProQuest; Local Initiatives Support Corporation MetroEdge, *Westhaven Market Study*, 3.

65. Spirou and Bennett, *It's Hardly Sportin'*, 160.

66. Dean Baker, *Plunder and Blunder: The Rise and Fall of the Bubble Economy* (Sausalito, CA: Polipoint, 2009), 36–37. Median income gains were driven primarily by rises in productivity, not redistribution. See Brookings Institution Center on Urban and Metropolitan Policy, *Chicago in Focus: A Profile from Census 2000* (Washington, DC: Brookings Institution, 2003), 57, accessed January 22, 2018, www.brookings.edu/wp-content/uploads/2016/07/chicago2.pdf.

67. Annie Kostiner, interview by author; Lewis Kostiner, interview by author.

68. Spirou and Bennett, *It's Hardly Sportin'*, 157, 168.

69. Greg Hinz, "Owners Say United Center Is Worth $2 Billion a Year to Local Economy," *Crain's Chicago Business*, July 23, 2015, accessed January 22, 2018, www.chicagobusiness.com / article / 20150723 / BLOGS02 / 150729890 / owners-say-united-center-is-worth-2-billion-a-year -to-local-economy.

70. Delaney and Eckstein, *Public Dollars, Private Stadiums*, 115; Quirk and Fort, *Hard Ball*, 156.

71. Long, *Public/Private Partnerships*, 38.

72. Blair Kamin, "The Big Fix," *Chicago Tribune*, August 4, 1996, ProQuest.

73. David Roeder and Fran Spielman, "Madison St. in Play," *Chicago Sun-Times*, September 19, 2006, NewsBank.

74. Adler, "Biz Inches West."

75. Gates, interview by author.

76. Kelly Virella, "Black and White, Seeing Red All Over: Major Retailer's Search for Green Kicks Up Racial Tension in Chicago's Gentrifying Areas," *Chicago Reporter* 38, no 5 (September– October 2009): 11, bound periodicals, Cudahy Library, Loyola University, Chicago.

77. Bennett, Hudspeth, and Wright, "Critical Analysis," 204.

78. Charles Leroux and Ron Grossman, "West Side Stories," *Chicago Tribune*, August 26, 1996, ProQuest; Eran Ben-Joseph, *Rethinking a Lot: The Design and Culture of Parking* (Boston: MIT Press, 2012), 120; Gates, interview by author.

79. CMAP, *Land Use Inventory, 2001*; Gates, interview by author.

80. Robert Baade, Mimi Nikolova, and Victor Matheson, "A Tale of Two Stadiums: Comparing the Economic Impact of Chicago's Wrigley Field and U.S. Cellular Field," College of the Holy Cross, Economics Department Working Paper No. 6-08 (August 2006), accessed January 20, 2018, crossworks.holycross.edu /cgi /viewcontent.cgi?article=1069&context=econ_working _papers.

81. Jon Hilkevitch, "Work Grinds on at Loyola Stop: When Will It End?" *Chicago Tribune*, November 19, 2012, ProQuest; A. J. LaTrace, "Sweet Vintage Map Shows Chicago Rapid Transit Lines in 1946," *Curbed Chicago*, June 4, 2014, accessed January 20, 2018, chicago.curbed.com / 2014/6/4/10091558/vintage-map-shows-chicago-rapid-transit-lines-from-1946.

82. City of Chicago, Regional Transportation Authority, Metropolitan Planning Council, and HNTB, *Final Recommendations Report* (Chicago: Reconnecting Neighborhoods, December 2008), W-2, accessed May 17, 2013, reconnectingneighborhoods.org/resources/pdfs/ WestExConReport_May6_2008.pdf (link no longer active, but digital copy available from author upon request). In early 2017, the city finally announced plans to build a new Green Line stop at Damen Avenue. Greg Hinz, "CTA to Open New El Stop by United Center," *Crain's Chicago Business*, February 9, 2017, accessed January 22, 2018, www.chicagobusiness.com /article/ 20170209/BLOGS02/170209841/cta-to-open-new-el-stop-by-united-center.

83. "Option 7: Bulls & Kids," *Chicago Tribune*, May 7, 2008, ProQuest.

84. Boyer, "Urban Planning Folly."

85. Interfaith Organizing Project, *Better Alternative*, sec. V.B.

86. City of Chicago, Regional Transportation Authority, Metropolitan Planning Council, and HNTB, *Existing Conditions Report: Near West Study Area* (Chicago: Reconnecting Neighborhoods, February 2008), 5, 9, 11, 13, 15, accessed May 17, 2013, reconnectingneighborhoods .org/resources/pdfs/ WestExConReport_May6_2008.pdf (link no longer active but digital copy available from author upon request).

87. Euchner, *Playing the Field*, 64, 29.

88. City of Chicago, Regional Transportation Authority, Metropolitan Planning Council, and HNTB, *Final Recommendations Report*, W-6.

89. Damien Cox, "Build Arena with Character and They Will Come," *Toronto Star*, November 16, 1996, LexisNexis.

90. John Siegfried and Andrew Zimbalist, "The Economics of Sports Facilities and Their Communities," *Journal of Economic Perspectives* 14, no. 3 (Summer 2000): 103, 109.

91. Cook County Board of Review, Freedom of Information Act Request No. WCB081711, submitted August 17, 2011, fulfilled September 23, 2011.

92. Zimbalist, *May the Best Team Win*, 127–28.

93. Celeste Garrett, "Singing the DNC Blues," *Chicago Sun-Times*, September 11, 1996, NewsBank.

94. Interfaith Organizing Project, *Better Alternative*, sec. 2.

95. Interfaith Organizing Project, *Better Alternative*, sec. 2.

96. Bennett, *Third City*, 149.

Chapter 5

1. Jeff Borden, "High-Tech Heaven: United Ctr.'s Gee-Whiz Gizmos," *Crain's Chicago Business*, November 11, 1996, LexisNexis.

2. Barbara Sullivan, "Wirtz Scion Takes Aim at Big Goal," *Chicago Tribune*, May 20, 1996, ProQuest.

3. City of Chicago, *Journal of the Proceedings of the City Council of the City of Chicago, Illinois* (October 2, 1995), 8258–59, Municipal Reference Collection, Harold Washington Library Center.

4. Quirk and Fort, *Hard Ball*, 118; Long, *Public/Private Partnerships*, 43–45. For a historical overview of baseball's antitrust exemption, see Zimbalist, *May the Best Team Win*, 15–33. MLB is one of a handful of industries with an official exemption from certain types of antitrust enforcement. Louis Jacobson, "Liberal Group Says Health Insurance, Baseball Are Only Industries Exempt from Antitrust Laws," *Politifact*, October 13, 2009, accessed January 22, 2018, www.politifact.com/truth-o-meter/statements/2009/oct/13/americans-united-change/liberal-group-says-health-care-baseball-are-only-i/.

5. Quirk and Fort, *Hard Ball*, 134; Long, *Public/Private Partnerships*, 43–44; Gregg Easterbrook, "How Taxpayers Keep the NFL Rich," *Atlantic*, December 8, 2015, accessed January 22, 2018, www.theatlantic.com/entertainment/archive/2015/12/how-taxpayers-keep-the-nfl-rich/418971/. For brief overviews of antitrust law and professional sports, see Gary Roberts, "Professional Sports and the Antitrust Laws," in *The Business of Professional Sports*, ed. Paul Staudohar and James Mangan (Urbana: University of Illinois Press, 1991), 135–41; Fort, "Market Power in Pro Sports."

6. "The Surrender of America's Liberals," *Bill Moyers & Company*, transcript of interview of Adolph Reed Jr. by Bill Moyers, February 25, 2014, accessed January 22, 2018, billmoyers.com/segment/the-surrender-of-americas-liberals/.

7. Charlie Beyer, interview by author, September 2, 2011, transcript available from author upon request.

8. Ben Joravsky, "Warts and All," *Chicago Reader*, October 11, 2007, accessed January 22, 2018, www.chicagoreader.com/chicago/warts-and-all/Content?oid=926119; Beyer, interview;

Ben Joravsky, "Working for Peanuts," *Chicago Reader*, October 12, 1995, accessed January 22, 2018, www.chicagoreader.com /chicago/working-for-peanuts/Content?oid=888718. The figure of "48 Black vendors who sell outside of the United Center" comes from Weinberg, quoted in Chinta Strausberg, "Beavers Tangles with Peanut Vendors," *Chicago Defender*, September 28, 1995, 5, Periodicals Microform Reading Room, Harold Washington Library Center.

9. Roger G. Noll and Andrew Zimbalist, "'Build the Stadium—Create the Jobs,'" in *Sports, Jobs, and Taxes: The Economic Impact of Sports Teams and Stadiums*, ed. Roger G. Noll and Andrew Zimbalist (Washington, DC: Brookings Institution Press, 1997), 8.

10. Tom Barnes, "Stadium Vendors Report Brisk Business: Ordinance Restricting Novelty Sellers Outside Boosts Union Sales Inside," *Pittsburgh Post-Gazette*, December 21, 1995, Lexis-Nexis Academic; "Fenway Squeeze Play," *Boston Globe*, December 18, 1998, HighBeam; Kevin Simpson, "Game-Day Vendors Singing Blake Street Blues," *Denver Post*, April 9, 1996, ProQuest.

11. Ray Hanania, "Ald. Hansen Tells Wrigley Peddlers to Take a Hike," *Chicago Sun-Times*, September 14, 1989, NewsBank; Fran Spielman, "Wrigley Area Vendors Lose—Council Bars 44th Ward Street Peddlers," *Chicago Sun-Times*, June 8, 1990, NewsBank; Municipal Code of Chicago, Chapter 4-244-130, accessed January 23, 2018, www.amlegal.com /codes/client/chicago _il/.

12. Robert Davis, "Council Might Throw Street Vendors a Curve," *Chicago Tribune*, March 4, 1993, ProQuest; Municipal Code of Chicago, Chapter 4-244-145, accessed January 23, 2018, www.amlegal.com /codes/client/chicago_il/.

13. Beyer, interview by author.

14. Robert Davis, "World Cup Spurs Peddler-Ban Vote," *Chicago Tribune*, April 12, 1994, ProQuest; Municipal Code of Chicago, Chapter 4-244-140, accessed January 23, 2018, www .amlegal.com /codes/client/chicago_il/.

15. Mark Weinberg, interview by author, August 7, 2011, transcript available from author upon request.

16. Beyer, interview by author.

17. *Elliott v. United Center*, No. 95 C 5440, 1996 U.S. Dist. LEXIS 1177 (N. Dist. Ill., East. Div., Feb. 2, 1996), 2.

18. Joravsky, "Working for Peanuts."

19. Weinberg, interview by author.

20. Jerry Reinsdorf, Oral History Interview, June 25, 2007, Chicago History Museum.

21. Weinberg, *Career Misconduct*, 125.

22. Weinberg, interview by author. See Reinsdorf, Oral History Interview, Chicago History Museum.

23. "Peanut Vendors Sue United Center," *Chicago Tribune*, September 23, 1995, ProQuest; *Elliott*, 1996 U.S. Dist. LEXIS 1177, 5; See Appeal No. 96-3002, entire case file, filed November 4, 1996, Records of the U.S. Circuit Court of Appeals Cases, Northern District of Illinois, Eastern Division, National Archives Record Center, Chicago.

24. Quoted definitions are taken from the introduction of *Elliott*, 1996 U.S. Dist. LEXIS 1177, 10.

25. Ellis W. Hawley, *The New Deal and the Problem of Monopoly: A Study in Economic Ambivalence* (Princeton, NJ: Princeton University Press, 1966), 6.

26. *Fishman v. Estate of Wirtz*, Nos. 85-1453 and 85-1545, 1986 U.S. App. LEXIS 34177 (7th Cir., Nov. 21, 1986), 3.

27. See *Elliott*, 1996 U.S. Dist. LEXIS 1177; *Fishman v. Wirtz*, Nos. 74 C 2814 and 78 C 3621,

1981 U.S. Dist. LEXIS 9998 (N. Dist. Ill., East. Div., Oct. 28, 1981); *Fishman v. Estate of Wirtz,* 1986 7th Cir. LEXIS 34177; Weinberg, *Career Misconduct,* 20 – 23.

28. *Elliott,* 1996 U.S. Dist. LEXIS 1177, 8.

29. *Elliott v. United Center,* No. 96-3002, 1997 U.S. App. LEXIS 27221 (7th Cir., Oct. 3, 1997), 4.

30. *Elliott,* 1996 U.S. Dist. LEXIS 1177, 10. Because Pallmeyer heard the case as a magistrate judge, another U.S. district court judge had to uphold her opinion before the case could make its way to a circuit court of appeals. District court judge James Holderman did so in July 1996 (magistrate rulings serve as a sort of initial screening in the district court system). See *Elliott v. United Center,* No. 95 C 5440, 1996 U.S. Dist. LEXIS 9846 (N. Dist. Ill., East. Div., July 12, 1996).

31. *Elliott,* 1996 U.S. Dist. LEXIS 1177, 8.

32. *Elliott,* 1996 U.S. Dist. LEXIS 1177, 7.

33. *Elliott,* 1997 U.S. App. LEXIS 27221, 3.

34. *Elliott,* 1997 U.S. App. LEXIS 27221, 3.

35. Weinberg, *Career Misconduct,* 44 – 45.

36. Alan Brinkley, *The End of Reform: New Deal Liberalism in Recession and War* (New York: Vintage, 1995), 113; Rudolph Peritz, *Competition Policy: History, Rhetoric, Law,* rev. ed. (New York: Oxford University Press, 2000), 12; Robert Reich, *Saving Capitalism: For the Many, Not the Few* (New York: Vintage, 2015), 46 – 47.

37. Andrew Wender Cohen, *The Racketeer's Progress: Chicago and the Struggle for the Modern American Economy, 1900 – 1940* (New York: Cambridge University Press, 2004), 164, 171, 192, 235, 244.

38. Brinkley, *End of Reform,* 5; Peritz, *Competition Policy,* 58; Edward Herman, "A Brief History of Mergers and Antitrust Policy," in *Real World Micro,* 18th ed., ed. Smriti Rao, Bryan Snyder, and Chris Sturr (Boston: Economic Affairs Bureau, 2009), 140; Reich, *Saving Capitalism,* 46 – 47.

39. Cohen, *Racketeer's Progress,* 265 – 67; Hawley, *The New Deal,* 452; Cowie, *The Great Exception,* 104 – 5, 118.

40. Brinkley, *End of Reform,* 106 – 36; Peritz, *Competition Policy,* 112 – 13.

41. Brinkley, *End of Reform,* 118, 267 – 68.

42. Herman, "A Brief History," 140 – 41.

43. Peritz, *Competition Policy,* 202 – 5.

44. John Bellamy Foster, Robert McChesney, and R. Jamil Jonna, "Monopoly and Competition in Twenty-First Century Capitalism," *Monthly Review* 62, no. 11 (April 2011): 30; William Kovacic, "The Antitrust Paradox Revisited: Robert Bork and the Transformation of Modern Antitrust Policy," *Wayne Law Review* 36 (1990): 1413 – 71.

45. Foster, McChesney, and Jonna, "Monopoly and Competition," 30.

46. Milton Friedman, *Capitalism and Freedom* (Chicago: University of Chicago Press, 1962), 119. For the purposes of this chapter, "Chicago School" refers specifically to the cadre of legal theorists led by jurists like Bork and Posner. While the political motivations of these theorists overlapped a great deal with those of the Chicago School of economics that rose to prominence during the same period and is most closely associated with Friedman, there were some notable theoretical divides between the two groups. For more on this, see Foster, McChesney, and Jonna, "Monopoly and Competition."

47. Joseph Persky, "Lange and Von Mises, Large-Scale Enterprises, and the Economic Case for Socialism," *Journal of Economic Perspectives* 5, no. 4 (Fall 1991): 231; James Livingston, *Against Thrift: Why Consumer Culture Is Good for the Economy, the Environment, and Your Soul* (New York: Basic Books, 2011), 20 – 21.

48. Herman, "A Brief History," 141.

49. *Elliott*, 1996 U.S. Dist. LEXIS 1177, 11.

50. *Elliott*, 1996 U.S. Dist. LEXIS 1177, 12.

51. "Supreme Court Justice Oliver Wendell Holmes, Jr., Explains Why Baseball Is Not Subject to Antitrust Laws, 1922," in *Major Problems in American Sports History*, ed. Steven Riess (Stamford, CT: Cengage, 2015), 215–16; Quirk and Fort, *Hard Ball*, esp. chapters 6–8; Zimbalist, *May the Best Team Win*, 15–33.

52. Zimbalist, *May the Best Team Win*, 28–30, 145; Quirk and Fort, *Hard Ball*, 134; Long, *Public/Private Partnerships*, 43–44.

53. Reich, *Saving Capitalism*, 29–47. The scope of this campaign's success is evident in the fact that President Bill Clinton appointed Diane Wood to the bench of the Seventh Circuit Court in 1995, and two years later he appointed Rebecca Pallmeyer to work alongside Wood (recall that Pallmeyer initially heard the vendor case as a magistrate judge). By the 1990s, even Democrats like Clinton were happy to stack the courts with apologists for the predatory ranks of big business. Sheryl Gay Stolberg, "Judicial Bouts Reveal Power of Persuasion," *New York Times*, April 21, 2010, ProQuest; "Senate Confirms 3 Judgeships, U.S. Attorney," *Chicago Tribune*, October 22, 1998, ProQuest.

54. Quirk and Fort, *Hard Ball*, 8, 177–78, 182.

55. Foster and McChesney, *Endless Crisis*, 71; Quirk and Fort, *Hard Ball*, 24.

56. See *Elliott v. United Center*, No. 97-1188, U.S. Sup. LEXIS 1866 (March 23, 1998).

57. City of Chicago, *Journal of the Proceedings of the City Council of the City of Chicago, Illinois* (August 2, 1995), 6135–36, Municipal Reference Collection, Harold Washington Library Center; Joseph Kirby, "Street Vendors Dealt Blow at United Center," *Chicago Tribune*, September 28, 1995, ProQuest.

58. City of Chicago, *Journal of the Proceedings of the City Council* (October 2, 1995), 8258–59; Kirby, "Street Vendors Dealt Blow."

59. John Carpenter and Charles Nicodemus, "How City Hall Banned Vendors Near Arenas," *Chicago Sun-Times*, January 11, 1998, NewsBank; Walter Burnett Jr., interview by author, August 29, 2011, transcript available from author upon request; Strausberg, "Hendon Wants Bulls Boycott"; Weinberg, *Career Misconduct*, 38–44.

60. Schedule A Forms for Friends of Walter Burnett Jr., Illinois State Board of Elections microfiche archives, Chicago. On the definition of "United Center ownership," see appendix B. Campaign contributions directly from corporations were legal in Illinois. Simpson, *Rogues, Rebels, and Rubber Stamps*, 281.

61. Dan Clawson, Alan Neustadtl, and Mark Weller, *Dollars and Votes: How Business Campaign Contributions Subvert Democracy* (Philadelphia: Temple University Press, 1998), 19.

62. This is the sum of nominal donation values based on author's calculations using data from Schedule A Forms for Friends of Walter Burnett Jr., Illinois State Board of Elections microfiche archives, Chicago; "Illinois Sunshine: Search," *Illinois Campaign for Political Reform*, accessed January 14, 2016, illinoissunshine.org/search/. (Searchable committees "controlled" by Burnett include Friends of Walter Burnett Jr. and 27th Ward Regular Democratic Organization.)

63. Simpson, *Rogues, Rebels, and Rubber Stamps*, 254.

64. Schedule A Forms for Patrick M. Huels Campaign Fund, Illinois State Board of Elections microfiche archives, Chicago.

65. Carpenter and Nicodemus, "How City Hall Banned Vendors."

66. Schedule A Forms for Patrick M. Huels Campaign Fund.

67. City of Chicago, *Journal of the Proceedings of the City Council* (October 2, 1995), 8258–

59; Gary Washburn and Andrew Martin, "Huels Feels the Heat, Resigns as Alderman," *Chicago Tribune*, October 22, 1997, ProQuest.

68. Carpenter and Nicodemus, "How City Hall Banned Vendors"; Fran Spielman and Pablo Martinez Monsivais, "Loopholes Undermine New Ethics Ordinance," *Chicago Sun-Times*, October 19, 1997, NewsBank; Simpson, *Rogues, Rebels, and Rubber Stamps*, 275.

69. Simpson, *Rogues, Rebels, and Rubber Stamps*, 107–58, 247–48; Lydersen, *Mayor 1%*, 40.

70. Simpson, *Rogues, Rebels, and Rubber Stamps*, 140, 195–96, 222–24, 247; Gradel and Simpson, *Corrupt Illinois*, 76–77.

71. Simpson, *Rogues, Rebels, and Rubber Stamps*, 247–49, 251, 270, 281, 287.

72. Simpson, *Rogues, Rebels, and Rubber Stamps*, 248–49, 269–70, 272.

73. "Illinois Sunshine Search," *Illinois Campaign for Political Reform*, accessed January 14, 2016.

74. For sources, see appendix B.

75. "Alderman Edward M. Burke," *City of Chicago*, accessed July 13, 2017, www.cityofchicago .org/city/en/about/wards/14/alderman_burke_sbiography.html. For source information on contributions, see appendix B.

76. "Don't Push the Street Vendors Out," *Chicago Tribune*, September 30, 1995, ProQuest.

77. David Harvey, *The Enigma of Capital and the Crises of Capitalism* (New York: Oxford University Press, 2010), 10; Johnna Montgomerie and Karel Williams, "Financialised Capitalism: After the Crisis and beyond Neoliberalism," *Competition and Change* 13, no. 2 (June 2009): 101; Fran Spielman, "Bulls Give Students a $3.5 Million Boost," *Chicago Sun-Times*, November 11, 1998, NewsBank; Municipal Code of Chicago, Chapter 4-244-147, accessed January 23, 2018, www.amlegal.com/codes/client/chicago_il/.

78. Reich, *Saving Capitalism*, 179–80.

79. Based on author's calculations using ArcGIS software.

80. Davis, "Daily Life in Chicago."

81. Fran Spielman, "Daley Backs Plan to Pull Permits on Newsstands," *Chicago Sun-Times*, January 29, 1992, NewsBank; Robert Davis, "City Decides to Get Serious About Enforcing Newsstand Ordinance," *Chicago Tribune*, May 15, 1992, ProQuest.

82. The author obtained a consolidated list of this legislation, based on the Chicago Municipal Code, from the City of Chicago Office of the City Clerk, Freedom of Information Act Request, submitted November 13, 2014, fulfilled November 19, 2014. The Chicago City Council has passed at least eleven additional antipeddling ordinances or amendments since Daley left office in 2011.

83. Ryan Thomas Devlin, "'An Area That Governs Itself': Informality, Uncertainty and the Management of Street Vending in New York City," *Planning Theory* 10, no. 1 (2011): 59; Mitchell Duneier, *Sidewalk* (New York: Farrar Straus & Giroux), 235, 237–38.

84. Duneier, *Sidewalk*, 235, 237–38, 248, 252, 317; Devlin, "'Area That Governs Itself'," 59.

85. Duneier, *Sidewalk*, 125–26, 158, 259.

86. Duneier, *Sidewalk*, 158–59, 286–89, 312. George Kelling and James Wilson, "Broken Windows: The Police and Neighborhood Safety," *Atlantic*, March 1982, accessed January 10, 2018, www.theatlantic.com/magazine/archive/1982/03/broken-windows/304465/.

87. Duneier, *Sidewalk*, 43.

88. Beyer, interview by author.

89. Yvonne Yen Liu, Patrick Burns, and Daniel Fleming, *Sidewalk Stimulus: Economic and Geographic Impact of Los Angeles Street Vendors* (Los Angeles: Economic Roundtable, 2015), 5,

accessed January 22, 2018, economicrt.org/publication/sidewalk-stimulus/. Also see Alfonso Morales, Steven Balkin, and Joseph Persky, "The Value of Benefits of a Public Street Market: The Case of Maxwell Street," *Economic Development Quarterly* 9, no. 4 (November 1995): 304–20.

90. Zimbalist, *May the Best Team Win*, 127–28.

91. Duneier, *Sidewalk*, 255–56.

92. "Baseball Candor via Air Vent," *Sports Illustrated*, September 22, 1958, accessed January 8, 2018, www.si.com/vault/1958/09/22/568820/baseball-candor-via-air-vent.

93. Euchner, *Playing the Field*, 11.

94. Reinsdorf, Oral History Interview, Chicago History Museum. Emphasis added.

95. Vernon Ford, *A Draft Commentary*, 30, 36.

96. Rachel Weber, interview with WBEZ Chicago, May 9, 2011, accessed January 22, 2018, www.wbez.org/shows/eight-fortyeight/examining-how-the-united-center-has-impacted-chicagos-near-west-side/1bcb28b4-893c-4682-86e6-a480e2c825c6.

97. Beyer, interview by author.

98. See Kevin Kruse, "The Politics of Race and Public Space: Desegregation, Privatization, and the Tax Revolt in Atlanta," *Journal of Urban History* 31, no. 5 (July 2005): 610–33.

99. Thomas Frank, "Chicago Is the Future," *Harper's*, December 2013, 9. The process of "transposing" privatization back onto the central city also had earlier precedents. As Benjamin Lisle documents in his history of the development of Busch Memorial Stadium in St. Louis, by the 1960s some central-city growth coalitions were already pursuing this strategy. However, at the time, such developments remained relatively exceptional. See Benjamin Lisle, *Modern Coliseum: Stadiums and American Culture* (Philadelphia: University of Pennsylvania Press, 2017), 193–228.

100. *Weinberg v. City of Chicago*, No. 02-1372, 2002 U.S. App. LEXIS 23878 (7th Cir., Nov. 20, 2002).

101. "Invoking Terrorism Threat Bad Way to Win Argument," *Pantagraph* (Bloomington, IL), September 19, 2003, ProQuest.

102. James K. Galbraith, *The Predator State: How Conservatives Abandoned the Free Market and Why Liberals Should Too* (New York: Free Press, 2009), 132.

Chapter 6

1. Quotation taken from Handley, "In Play."

2. Long, *Public/Private Partnerships*, 35, 88.

3. Harvey, *A Brief History*, 164–65.

4. Handley, "In Play."

5. "Editorial: A Tale of Two Deals—One Touchdown, One Fumble," *Crain's Chicago Business*, May 26, 1997, ProQuest.

6. Quirk and Fort, *Hard Ball*, 150–51; Raymond Keating, "It's Time to Get Government Out of the Sports Business," *USA Today Magazine*, March 1, 2000, Factiva. Some sources put the amount of public funding for infrastructure closer to $30 million. See Robert Baade and Allen Sanderson, "Bearing Down in Chicago: Location, Location, Location," in *Sports, Jobs and Taxes*, ed. Roger Noll and Andrew Zimbalist (Washington, DC: Brookings Institution Press, 1997), 327.

7. Ben Joravsky, "Welcome to U.S. Cellular Field, Home of the Sweetheart Deal," *Chicago Reader*, April 23, 2013, accessed January 10, 2018, www.chicagoreader.com/chicago/taxpayers-subsidize-white-sox-park/Content?oid=9371315.

8. Bondholders accept lower interest rates on tax-exempt bonds because they do not pay taxes on earned interest. Local governments reduce debt service by locking in these lower interest rates, and the federal government subsidizes the arrangement by way of forgone tax revenues. On the Tax Reform Act and stadium finance, see Neil deMause and Joanna Cagan, *Field of Schemes: How the Great Stadium Swindle Turns Public Money Into Private Profit* (Lincoln: University of Nebraska Press, 2008), 50–52.

9. Long, *Public/Private Partnerships*, 18–19, 33–34; Sean Dinces, "Nothing but Net Profit: Property Taxes, Public Dollars, and Corporate Philanthropy at Chicago's United Center," *Radical History Review* no. 125 (October 2016): 16–17.

10. Long, *Public/Private Partnerships*, xiii, 4–7, 35–37.

11. Long, *Public/Private Partnerships*, 24.

12. Figures for the cost of the infrastructural development vary by source. Charles Wheeler III and Mark Brown, "Senate Backs a New Bulls-Hawks Stadium," *Chicago Sun-Times*, June 23, 1989, NewsBank; Charles Wheeler III, "Stadium Plan up to Governor," *Chicago Sun-Times*, July 1, 1989, NewsBank; Lynn Sweet, "Daley Wary of Bears South Loop Stadium," *Chicago Sun-Times*, July 27, 1989, NewsBank; Keating, "It's Time to Get Government Out"; Baade and Sanderson, "Bearing Down in Chicago," 327.

13. State of Illinois, 86th General Assembly, House of Representatives, transcription of debate on Amendment 1 to House Bill 2321, June 30, 1989, Illinois State Archives, Springfield.

14. Chuck Neubauer, "Stadium Snares Huge Tax Breaks under State Law," *Chicago Sun-Times*, April 16, 1995, NewsBank.

15. State of Illinois, 86th General Assembly, House of Representatives, transcription of debate on Amendment 1 to House Bill 2321; Cook County Assessor's Office, Freedom of Information Act Request, Order No. 62939, Transaction No. 62013, March 28, 2013 (fulfilled in person).

16. Cook County Assessor's Office, Freedom of Information Act Request, Order No. 62939.

17. League of Women Voters of Chicago, *A Guide through Chicago's Tax Maze* (Chicago: September 1987), 7, Municipal Reference Collection, Harold Washington Library Center. See table 6.1 for commercial tax rate data. To compute the property-tax rate, I divided the estimated standard tax liabilities listed in table A.C.2 (third column from the left) by the value of the United Center. To adjust the value of the United Center for each year post-1994, I followed Long's methodology by inflating the original building cost using the Turner building cost index and subtracting accumulated straight-line depreciation. Long, *Public/Private Partnerships*, 75; "Turner Building Cost Index," *Data 360*, accessed July 17, 2017, www.data360.org/dsg.aspx?Data_Set_Group_Id=850; "Cost Index," *Turner Construction*, accessed July 17, 2017, www.turnerconstruction.com/cost-index. Baseline building costs figure taken from Judith Grant Long, "Public Funding for Major League Sports Facilities (3): National Basketball Association," Edward J. Bloustein School of Planning and Public Policy Working Paper, 76, accessed July 17, 2017, web.archive.org/web/20061012080835/http://policy.rutgers.edu:80/faculty/long/DataSeriesNBA2of3.pdf.

18. Kurt Badenhausen, "Full List: The World's 50 Most Valuable Sports Teams 2017," *Forbes*, July 12, 2017, accessed January 22, 2018, www.forbes.com/sites/kurtbadenhausen/2017/07/12/full-list-the-worlds-50-most-valuable-sports-teams-2017/#19fde11f4a05; Rodney Fort, "NBA Team Values-Selected," *Rodney's Sports Economics*, accessed July 17, 2017, umich.app.box.com/s/41707f0b2619c0107b8b/1/320023265. Reported team values are nominal.

19. Neil deMause, "Will Marlins Park Cost Taxpayers 'Billions,' or Mere Hundreds of Millions?" *Field of Schemes* (blog), January 25, 2013, accessed January 22, 2018, www.fieldofschemes

.com/2013/01/25/4433/will-marlins-park-cost-taxpayers-billions-or-mere-hundreds-of
-millions/. For a helpful overview of present value, see "Time Value of Money: Six Functions
of a Dollar," *California State Board of Equalization*, accessed January 22, 2018, www.boe.ca.gov/
info/tvm/index.html.

20. Long, *Public/Private Partnerships*, 24, 144; Baade and Sanderson, "Bearing Down in Chi-
cago," 327. The formula for computing the present value of cash flows is $PV_1 = \sum_{j=1}^{k} \frac{F_j}{(1+i)^{j-1}}$,
where PV_1 is the net present value of a series of flows at period 1, F is the nominal cash
flow at period j, k is the final period, and i is the nominal discount rate. For more, see Anthony E.
Boardman and David H. Greenberg, "Discounting and the Social Discount Rate," in *Handbook
of Public Finance*, ed. Fred Thompson and Mark T. Green (New York: Marcel Decker, 1998),
269–318. I use the 1994 annual interest rate on a twenty-year Treasury bill (7.5 percent) as the
discount rate. Data on annual Treasury bill rates obtained from U.S. Federal Reserve, "Selected
Interest Rates (daily): H.15," accessed July 27, 2015, www.federalreserve.gov/releases/h15/data
.htm. I estimate tax savings in years for which I do not have data on actual payments by using a
linear trend line through the 1997–2011 data to extrapolate into past and future years (I exclude
2005 and 2006 when computing the trend line because payments in those years skewed low as a
result of the reduction in United Center net income caused by the 2004–2005 NHL lockout). I
also divide the extrapolated value for 1994 by four to reflect the fact that the arena operated for
only a quarter of that year.

21. Author's calculations using individual present value computations for investments after
1994 (applying the same annual interest rate cited in previous note) and individual future value
computations for investments before 1994 (applying the annual twenty-year Treasury rate for
1993, as rates for 1991–1992 are not available). I did not perform a detailed present value comparison of the sum of the amounts in table 4.2 with the total value of property-tax abatements
because it is unclear whether several of the major items in table 4.2 met both of the following
criteria: created benefits for people other than United Center ownership and would not have
occurred in the absence of the United Center. For example, the publicly funded infrastructural
upgrades around the United Center authorized in 1989 were, in all likelihood, limited primarily
to projects that increased the arena's operational efficiency (e.g., road upgrades enhancing accessibility to parking lots). Regarding the public investment brought by the Democratic National
Convention, the evidence presented in chapters 1 and 4 suggests that a considerable portion may
have eventually happened even if the city did not host the event (especially in neighborhoods in
and around the Loop). Nevertheless, even if the present values of the figures in table 4.2 (minus
the stadium-specific infrastructure investment) were summed with those in table 4.1, the total
would remain considerably below the sum of property tax savings.

22. Long, *Public/Private Partnerships*, 11–13, 80, 88–91, 114. Accounting for such hidden
costs, Long pegs the actual public share of United Center financing at 41 percent. This is likely
a considerable underestimate since she did not have access to data on the various tax breaks
enjoyed by the owners.

23. Neubauer, "Stadium Snares Huge Tax Breaks."

24. Across all leagues the average real, absolute public contributions to new stadiums went
from $216 million for those opened in the first half of the 1990s to $334 million for those opened
in the second half of the 2000s. Long, *Public/Private Partnerships*, 35, 88–96; Delaney and Eckstein, *Public Dollars, Private Stadiums*, 24; Quirk and Fort, *Hard Ball*, 144.

25. A statement of compliance from the city was required since the legislation indicated that
the city might be called upon to use eminent domain to secure land for the new arena. *Journal of*

the Proceedings of the City Council of the City of Chicago, May 22, 1991, 185, Municipal Reference Collection, Harold Washington Library Center.

26. Long, *Public/Private Partnerships*, 153. On the recent outcry in Chicago over the opacity, corruption, and inequity of the local property tax system, see a recent *Tribune* series of investigative reports at "The Tax Divide," *Chicago Tribune*, accessed January 25, 2018, www .chicagotribune.com/news/watchdog/taxdivide/.

27. Fort, "Market Power in Pro Sports," 8.

28. For informative treatments of this issue, see deMause and Cagan, *Field of Schemes*; Euchner, *Playing the Field*; Quirk and Fort, *Hard Ball*.

29. Reinsdorf quoted in Euchner, *Playing the Field*, 134.

30. Long, *Public/Private Partnerships*, 88–96.

31. Long, *Public/Private Partnerships*, 5–6.

32. On the definition and history of "business climate" rhetoric, see Greg LeRoy, *The Great American Jobs Scam: Corporate Tax Dodging and the Myth of Job Creation* (San Francisco: Berrett-Koehler Publishers, 2005), 68–91.

33. On the organizational and institutional histories of the right-wing resurgence, see Kim Phillips-Fein, *Invisible Hands: The Making of the Conservative Movement from the New Deal to Reagan* (New York: Norton, 2009); Nancy MacLean, *Democracy in Chains: The Deep History of the Radical Right's Stealth Plan for America* (New York: Viking, 2017). On the rise of supply-side economics and conservative tax policy, see Bruce Bartlett, *The New American Economy: The Failure of Reaganomics and a New Way Forward* (New York: Palgrave Macmillan, 2009).

34. Piketty, *Capital*, 499 (specific values taken from table S14.1 of the online supplement to Piketty available at piketty.pse.ens.fr/en/capital21c2).

35. Bartlett, *New American Economy*, 120–21, 141, 155–57; Kapo Yuen, "Determining the Severity of Macroeconomic Stress Scenarios," *Governors of the Federal Reserve System*, June 24, 2015, accessed January 21, 2018, www.federalreserve.gov/bankinforeg/determining-the-severity -of-macroeconomic-stress-scenarios.htm; Douglas Holtz-Eakin, "Analyzing the Economic and Budgetary Effects of a 10 Percent Cut in Income Tax Rates," Economic and Budget Issue Brief, *Congressional Budget Office*, December 1, 2005, accessed January 21, 2018, www.cbo.gov/sites/ default/files/109th-congress-2005-2006/reports/12-01-10percenttaxcut.pdf; Thomas Hungerford, "Taxes and the Economy: An Economic Analysis of the Top Tax Rates since 1945," *Congressional Research Service*, September 14, 2012, accessed January 21, 2018, www.dpcc.senate.gov/ files/documents/CRSTaxesandtheEconomy%20Top%20Rates.pdf.

36. LeRoy, *Great American Jobs Scam*, 1–2, 71–73; "Industrial Revenue Bonds," *Good Jobs First*, accessed August 3, 2015, www.goodjobsfirst.org/accountable-development/industrial -revenue-bonds; Kenneth Thomas, *Competing for Capital: Europe and North America in a Global Era* (Washington, DC: Georgetown University Press, 2000), 150–61; Timothy Bartik, *A New Panel Database on Business Incentives for Economic Development Offered by State and Local Governments in the United States* (Kalamazoo, MI: W. E. Upjohn Institute for Employment Research, February 2017), 65–78, accessed January 28, 2018, research.upjohn.org/cgi/viewcontent .cgi?article=1228&context=reports.

37. LeRoy, *Great American Jobs Scam*, 79–84; Harvey, *A Brief History*, 47.

38. William Domhoff, *Who Rules America? Power, Politics, and Social Change*, 5th ed. (New York: McGraw-Hill, 2006), 147–48.

39. "PAC Count: 1977 to Present," *Federal Election Commission*, accessed January 8, 2018, classic.fec.gov/press/paccnt_grph.html; "PAC Activity Increases in 1995–96 Election Cycle," Federal Election Commission press release, April 22, 1997, accessed January 10, 2018, www.fec

.gov/updates/pac-activity-increases-in-1995-96-election-cycle-2/. Numbers not adjusted for inflation.

40. Martin Gilens and Benjamin Page, "Testing Theories of American Politics: Elites, Interest Groups, and Average Citizens," *Perspectives on Politics* 12, no. 3 (September 2014): 575.

41. Piketty, *Capital*, 335.

42. Jay Fitzgerald an Kevin McDermott, "Big Bucks, Political Power Playing the Contribution Game," in *Illinois for Sale: Do Campaign Contributions Buy Influence?*, ed. Dana Heupel (Springfield: University of Illinois at Springfield Press, 1997), 121; "Illinois Enacts Sweeping Campaign Finance Reform," *National Conference on State Legislatures*, accessed January 23, 2017, www.ncsl.org/research/elections-and-campaigns/illinois-enacts-campaign-contribution-limits.aspx.

43. Dana Heupel, "The Story behind the Story: An Introduction," in *Illinois for Sale: Do Campaign Contributions Buy Influence?*, ed. Dana Heupel (Springfield: University of Illinois at Springfield Press, 1997), 2.

44. Schedule A Forms for Friends of Michael Madigan, Illinois State Board of Elections microfiche archives, Chicago; "Illinois Sunshine: Search," *Illinois Campaign for Political Reform*, accessed January 14, 2016, www.illinoissunshine.org/search/.

45. Litsey quoted in Fitzgerald and McDermott, "Big Bucks," 122.

46. State of Illinois, 86th General Assembly, House of Representatives, transcription of debate on Amendment 1 to House Bill 2321.

47. Schedule A Forms for Citizens for Jim Thompson, Illinois State Board of Elections microfiche archives, Chicago; "Illinois Sunshine: Search," *Illinois Campaign for Political Reform*, accessed January 14, 2016, www.illinoissunshine.org/search/.

48. Schedule A Forms for Citizens for Thomas C. Hynes, Illinois State Board of Elections microfiche archives, Chicago; Schedule A Forms for Citizens for James M. Houlihan, Illinois State Board of Elections microfiche archives, Chicago; "Illinois Sunshine: Search," *Illinois Campaign for Political Reform*, accessed January 14, 2016, www.illinoissunshine.org/search/.

49. Bernard Schoenburg, "Double-Donation Game Common among State Contractors: Contributors Give to Both Major Parties," in *Illinois for Sale: Do Campaign Contributions Buy Influence?*, ed. Dana Heupel (Springfield: University of Illinois at Springfield Press, 1997), 72–80.

50. Clawson, Neustadtl, and Weller, *Dollars and Votes*, 154–57.

51. Christi Parsons, "Internet Stalkers Can Go to Prison: Cyberstalking Law Gives Up to 3 Years for the 1st Offense," *Chicago Tribune*, August 2, 2001, ProQuest.

52. On the origins of TIF in Illinois, see Civic Federation, *Chicagoland—A Fiscal Perspective: 1977–1986* (Chicago: Civic Federation, 1988), 23–26, Municipal Reference Collection, Harold Washington Library Center. On state enterprise zones, see Jeff McCourt and Greg LeRoy, *A Better Deal for Illinois: Improving Economic Development Policy* (Washington, DC: Good Jobs First, January 2003), 1, accessed January 23, 2018, www.goodjobsfirst.org/sites/default/files/docs/pdf/il.pdf; John Gorman, "Illinois Gears Up to Land GM's Saturn Project," *Chicago Tribune*, January 24, 1985, ProQuest. On the High Impact Business Program, see "Informational Bulletin FY86–50," *Illinois Department of Revenue*, April 1986, accessed January 23, 2018, www.revenue.state.il.us/publications/bulletins/1986/FY86–50.PDF; McCourt and LeRoy, *A Better Deal for Illinois*, 1; Bill Barnhart and Sally Saville Hodge, "Inside Business: Some Development Bills Escaped Hostage Taking," *Chicago Tribune*, July 8, 1985, ProQuest; Harlan Draeger, "3,000 New Jobs—Motorola to Build Libertyville Plant," *Chicago Sun-Times*, November 4, 1989, NewsBank. On the BDPIP, see "Illinois Compiled Statutes: Finance (30 ILCS 750/) Build Illinois Act," *Illinois General Assembly*, accessed July 19, 2017, www.ilga.gov/legislation/ilcs/ilcs4.asp?DocName

=003007500HArt%2E+8&ActID=567&ChapterID=7&SeqStart=1800000&SeqEnd=3100000; "Public Act to Bill Conversion Table," *Illinois General Assembly*, accessed July 19, 2017, www .ilga.gov/reports/static/PA88.pdf; Pat Clawson, "Development Pact with 3COM OKd," *Chicago Tribune*, October 15, 1997, ProQuest. On EDGE, see Merrill Goozner, "Governments Rethink Corporate Tax Breaks," *Chicago Tribune*, March 14, 2000, ProQuest.

53. Nancy Ryan, "City, State Tax Breaks Keep Nabisco," *Chicago Tribune*, December 15, 1993, ProQuest; Greg Trotter, "Laid Off Oreo Bakery Workers Question Mondelez CEO on Job Cuts," *Chicago Tribune*, May 19, 2016, accessed January 25, 2018, www.chicagotribune.com/business/ ct-oreo-workers-question-ceo-0519-biz-20160518-story.html; Fran Spielman, "Ford to Build S. Side Facility," *Chicago Sun-Times*, September 7, 2000, NewsBank; Good Jobs First, "Summary of State and Local Awards: Illinois," *Subsidy Tracker*, accessed October 6, 2017, subsidytracker .goodjobsfirst.org/prog.php?statesum=IL.

54. Philip Mattera, Kasia Tarczynska, and Greg LeRoy, *Tax Breaks and Inequality: Enriching Billionaires and Low-Road Employers in the Name of Economic Development* (Washington, DC: Good Jobs First, 2014), 6, accessed January 24, 2018, www.goodjobsfirst.org/sites/default/files/ docs/pdf/taxbreaksandinequality.pdf; "Beginners Guide," *Good Jobs First*, accessed December 12, 2015, www.goodjobsfirst.org/accountable-development/beginners-guide; John Chase and Danny Ecker, "Pier Pressure: How City Power Players Diverted $55 Million in Blight-Fighting TIF Cash to Navy Pier," July 21, 2017, accessed January 23, 2018, www.chicagobusiness.com/ article/20170721/ISSUE01/170729970/how-chicago-power-players-diverted-tif-funds-to-navy -pier. For a state-by-state breakdown of the conditions attached to property-tax abatements, see Daphne Kenyon, Adam Langley, and Bethany Paquin, *Rethinking Property Tax Incentives for Business* (Cambridge, MA: Lincoln Land Institute, 2012), 66–71.

55. City of Chicago Department of Planning and Development, Freedom of Information Act Request, submitted November 30, 2015, fulfilled December 3, 2015.

56. Gilfoyle, *Millennium Park*, 157; TIF is the one type of property tax incentive about which evidence "is more mixed," though the implementation of TIF programs varies widely across states. Kenyon, Langley, and Paquin, *Rethinking Property Tax Incentives*, 30–44; LeRoy, *Great American Jobs Scam*, 57–64.

57. Greg LeRoy, *No More Candy Store: States and Cities Making Job Subsidies Accountable* (Washington, DC: Good Jobs First, 1997), 17; LeRoy, *Great American Jobs Scam*, 168, 176–78.

58. LeRoy, *Great American Jobs Scam*, 158; Philip Mattera and Kasia Tarczynska, "Mega- deals," *Good Jobs First*, accessed January 18, 2017, www.goodjobsfirst.org/megadeals. The data- base reports all subsidies in nominal dollars. The literature on the proliferation of corporate- friendly tax policy and the expansion of corporate welfare in recent decades—a literature largely ignored by sports economists—is expansive. See, for example, Dean Baker, *The Conser- vative Nanny State: How the Wealthy Use the Government to Stay Rich and Get Richer* (Washing- ton, DC: Center for Economic and Policy Research, 2006); Galbraith, *Predator State*; David Cay Johnston, *Free Lunch: How the Wealthiest Americans Enrich Themselves at Government Expense (and Stick You With the Bill)* (New York: Portfolio, 2007); David Cay Johnston, *Perfectly Legal: The Covert Campaign to Rig Our Tax System to Benefit the Super Rich—and Cheat Everybody Else* (New York: Portfolio, 2003); Thomas, *Competing for Capital*; Kenneth Thomas, *Investment Incentives and the Global Competition for Capital* (New York: Palgrave Macmillan, 2011).

59. Fuchs, *Mayors and Money*, 164–65. For exemplary historical treatments of property taxes in locales other than Chicago, see Robert Self, *American Babylon: Race and the Struggle for Postwar Oakland* (Princeton, NJ: Princeton University Press, 2003); Colin Gordon, *Mapping*

Decline: St. Louis and the Fate of the American City (Philadelphia: University of Pennsylvania Press, 2008).

60. Isaac Martin, *The Permanent Tax Revolt: How the Property Tax Transformed American Politics* (Stanford, CA: Stanford University Press, 2008), 7, 57, 63; Fuchs, *Mayors and Money,* 173.

61. See Gordon, *Mapping Decline,* 112–52.

62. Self, *American Babylon,* 131, 319; Illinois Economic and Fiscal Commission, *Property Tax in Illinois: Selected Problems and Proposals* (Springfield, IL, May 1973), 18–19, Municipal Reference Collection, Harold Washington Library Center.

63. Shlaes & Co., *Real Property Appraisal in Downtown Chicago: Current Problems and Suggested Solutions* (Chicago: December 1983), iv, 14, Chicago History Museum. The report does not disaggregate rental costs in Cook County suburbs from collar-county suburbs. Also see Donald Haider and Thomas Jacobs, *Cook County, Illinois Analysis of Property Classification for Tax Assessment Purposes* (Chicago: Office of the Assessor of County of Cook, Illinois, October 1985), 77–95, Municipal Reference Collection, Harold Washington Library Center.

64. Shlaes & Co., *Real Property Appraisal,* 1, 13, addendum C (table C-1) (this study defines "downtown" or "central business district" as the "area between the Chicago River and Lake Michigan, extending from Congress Parkway to Oak Street"); Shlaes & Co., *Office and Residential Space Demand Potential in the Chicago Central Area,* Working Paper No. 3 in Chicago Zoning Bonus Study (Chicago: City of Chicago Department of Planning, 1987), 9, Municipal Reference Collection, Harold Washington Library Center.

65. Haider and Jacobs, *Cook County,* 43, 45. Whether this fiscal landscape posed an existential threat to Chicago's commercial real-estate industry is open to debate. Growth in new office-space construction in the Loop slowed dramatically at the end of the 1970s, but this probably owed less to property taxes than to a market correction in response to a massive boom in downtown construction during the early 1970s and the lagged effects of a national recession in the middle of the decade. See Shlaes & Co., *Office and Residential Space Demand,* esp. 2–8. Moreover, by the start of the 1980s the contraction had reversed as a result of robust growth in downtown service and financial-sector employment, as well as the entrance en masse of "pension funds, tax shelter syndicators and foreign investors" into downtown real estate markets. See Shlaes & Co., *Real Property Appraisal,* iv-v.

66. Civic Federation, *Chicagoland—A Fiscal Perspective: 1978–1987* (Chicago: Civic Federation, 1989), 18, Municipal Reference Collection, Harold Washington Library Center.

67. Gordon, *Mapping Decline,* 54–55.

68. As Robert Self notes, homeowners in urban America "were an occupationally varied lot" who "were diverse in class background and place of origin." The list of beneficiaries of the relatively low residential tax rates institutionalized in Cook County during the 1950s and 1960s through fractional assessment included not just the elderly homeowner struggling to hold on to a two-bedroom home on Chicago's South Side. It also included, for example, the relatively affluent family living in a luxurious residence in suburban Evanston. Despite this heterogeneity, it seems reasonable to generalize Cook County commercial landholders' assault against the property-tax privileges of residential landholders as a class conflict between urban capitalists and working- and middle-class homeowners (although, as I argue later, low-income residents, rather than ordinary homeowners, suffered most from this conflict). Consider that in 1970 the average housing-unit value for owner-occupied units in Cook County stood at less than $28,000 (the median was undoubtedly lower). Holding such modest assets, though not insignificant, clearly distinguished most homeowners from major commercial real-estate investors like Reinsdorf

and Wirtz. Self, *American Babylon*, 98; "Average Value of Owner-Occupied Housing Unit, Census 1970, Cook County, IL," *Social Explorer*, accessed January 21, 2018, www.socialexplorer.com/.

69. Self, *American Babylon*, 317.

70. California Tax Data, "What Is Proposition 13?" *California Property Tax Information*, accessed September 12, 2015, www.californiataxdata.com/pdf/Prop13.pdf; Clarence Lo, *Small Property versus Big Government: Social Origins of the Property Tax Revolt* (Berkeley: University of California Press, 1990), 154–58.

71. Martin, *Permanent Tax Revolt*, 12, 44–46; Lo, *Small Property*, 13.

72. Martin, *Permanent Tax Revolt*, 12, 51, 56–57, 65–66; Self, *American Babylon*, 293; Illinois Economic and Fiscal Commission, *Report to the Illinois General Assembly on Property Tax* (Springfield, IL, April 9, 1990), 11, Municipal Reference Collection, Harold Washington Library Center.

73. Self, *American Babylon*, 317–20.

74. Lo, *Small Property*, 20–21; Self, *American Babylon*, 325.

75. Dean Tipps, "California's Great Property Tax Revolt: The Origins and Impact of Proposition 13," in *State and Local Tax Revolt: New Directions for the 80's*, ed. Dean Tipps and Lee Webb (Washington, DC: Conference on Alternative State and Local Policies, 1980), 68; Martin, *Permanent Tax Revolt*, 57, 62–67.

76. Martin, *Permanent Tax Revolt*, 65.

77. Martin, *Permanent Tax Revolt*, 63–64, 112; Clarence Lo, *Small Property*, 18; "Home Owners, 65 and Older, Get Tax Break," *Chicago Tribune*, January 5, 1970, ProQuest; Thomas Buck, "Homestead Tax Relief Forms Going into Mail," *Chicago Tribune*, May 23, 1972, ProQuest. For a helpful summary of this legislation, see John McCarron, "Property Taxes: Reach for a Pain Reliever," *Chicago Tribune*, May 10, 2010, ProQuest; Illinois Economic and Fiscal Commission, *Report to the Illinois General Assembly on Property Tax* (Springfield, IL, December 1997), 5, Municipal Reference Collection, Harold Washington Library Center.

78. Illinois Economic and Fiscal Commission, *Property Tax in Illinois*, 74.

79. "County Board Alters Tax Assessing System," *Chicago Tribune*, December 18, 1973, ProQuest.

80. State of Illinois Economic and Fiscal Commission, *Report to the Illinois General Assembly on Property Tax* (Springfield, IL, April 9, 1990), 142; Jack Mabley, "Those Equalizers Tax Payer's Brain," *Chicago Tribune*, June 19, 1978, ProQuest; William Juneau, "Tax Break a Headache for County," *Chicago Tribune*, June 26, 1980, ProQuest. Despite the previous push for "modernization," assessors working for the county quickly routinized an unofficial practice of valuing residential properties at closer to 10 percent of market value. According to at least one local expert, they also informally valued many commercial properties well below 40 percent, although it is unclear if this undervaluation proved as systematic as it did in the case of residential properties. Either way, the larger point holds that the classification system further entrenched relative favoritism for homeowners. See Laura Janota and Lorilyn Rackl, "Tax Changes Could Weigh on Homeowners," *Arlington Daily Herald*, December 18, 1998, ProQuest; Cass Cliatt and Shruti Date, "Why Homeowners Might Be Losers in Property Tax Fight," *Arlington Daily Herald*, October 1, 2001, ProQuest; Ashley Wiehle, "Cook Assessment Plan Goes to Senate," *Chicago Tribune*, April 10, 2008, ProQuest; Don Haider, "Why You Might Sit Down for This Bill," *Chicago Tribune*, April 29, 2010, ProQuest.

81. The Illinois State Constitution of 1970 explicitly allowed Cook County to classify different types of property for assessment purposes. According to the local press, between 1970 and

1973, Cook County had informally assessed residential properties at slightly more than 22 percent and commercial ones at slightly less than 40 percent. Civic Federation, *The Cook County Property Assessment Process: A Primer on Assessment, Classification, Equalization and Property Tax Exemptions* (Chicago, April 5, 2010), 10–11, accessed July 10, 2013, www.civicfed.org/sites/default/files/100405_CookCountyAssessmentPrimer.pdf; Thomas Buck, "Succeeds Tully: Swain New Assessor Deputy," *Chicago Tribune*, May 19, 1973, ProQuest; Stanley Ziemba, "New Property-Tax Categories Used," *Chicago Tribune*, November 15, 1973, ProQuest. It is unclear from the local reporting exactly how much the new formal rates differed from the informal ones, because it does not specify whether the change was in "percentage" or "percentage points." See "Tax Plan Would Ease Homeowner's Bill," *Chicago Tribune*, June 30, 1973, ProQuest. The Cook County classification ordinance was part of a broader collection of "reforms" instituted by the county in 1973, including the adoption of more standardized training and qualification requirements, as well as computerized assessment. These reforms placed enough upward pressure on property tax bills to mobilize a new set of more middle-class (and more antistate) tax rebels in Illinois during the second half of the 1970s. While they secured the extension of some of the state legislation protecting senior citizens from rampant tax increases to the population at large—Illinois passed a general homestead exemption in 1978—they failed to push through the sort of measures achieved by their counterparts in California. Property classification in Cook County, which dampened the severity of property-tax increases for residential homeowners across the board, likely played an important role in this story. Illinois Economic and Fiscal Commission, *Property Tax in Illinois*, 25; Robert Kuttner, *Revolt of the Haves: Tax Rebellions and Hard Times* (New York: Simon & Schuster, 1980), 300–301; Douglas Whitley, "Is Proposition 13 for Illinois?" *Illinois Parks and Recreation* 25 (May–June 1979), accessed January 22, 2018, www.lib.niu.edu/1979/ip790508.html.

82. "Tax Plan Would Ease Homeowner's Bill," *Chicago Tribune*; Gary Washburn, "Tax Structure Threatens City's Future: Experts," *Chicago Tribune*, July 22, 1973, ProQuest.

83. Haider and Jacobs, *Cook County*, 46.

84. Civic Federation, *Chicagoland—A Fiscal Perspective: 1976–1985* (Chicago: Civic Federation, 1987), 12, Municipal Reference Collection, Harold Washington Library Center; Civic Federation, *Chicagoland—A Fiscal Perspective: 1980–1989* (Chicago: Civic Federation, 1991), 12, Municipal Reference Collection, Harold Washington Library Center.

85. Lo, *Small Property*, 18, 20–21, 30–31; Terry Nichols Clark, Karen Lee Curtis, Katie Cox, and Susan Herhold, *Business and Taxes in Chicago: A Report to the City of Chicago*, April 15, 1986, 40, Municipal Reference Collection, Harold Washington Library Center.

86. Steve Kerch, "Its Appeal Is Growing," *Chicago Tribune*, November 25, 1990, ProQuest.

87. State of Illinois Economic and Fiscal Commission, *Report to the Illinois General Assembly on Property Tax* (Springfield, IL, April 9, 1990), 147. These statistics likely overstate the relative tax burden of commercial and industrial property in Cook County at the time. The same report explains that local assessors regularly underestimated the fair market value of commercial properties (94–95). This is discussed in more detail in "Cook County Tax Squeeze," *Chicago Tribune*, November 10, 1985, ProQuest; Tim Novak and Mark Skertic, "Are Your Property Taxes Making You Say, 'Ouch'?" *Chicago Sun-Times*, July 5, 2002, NewsBank; and Mark Brown, "County Property Taxes Just Don't Add Up," *Chicago Sun-Times*, July 10, 2002, NewsBank.

88. Shlaes & Co., *Real Property Appraisal in Downtown Chicago*, i, 56.

89. Dean Baker, *The United States Since 1980* (New York: Cambridge University Press, 2007), 67.

90. David Ibata, "Downtown Office Boom Takes Timeout," *Chicago Tribune*, January 18,

1988, ProQuest; Shlaes & Co., *Real Property Appraisal*, iii, x; Commercial Club of Chicago, *Make No Little Plans*, 26.

91. Howard Builta, "Real Estate Tax," *Chicago Tribune*, March 30, 1988, ProQuest. On the Association of Commerce and Industry, see Haider and Jacobs, *Cook County*, 88–89.

92. The *Crain's* series is discussed in Haider and Jacobs, *Cook County*, 89. As an example, they cite, "Good Tax News Doesn't Hide Cook County's Flaws," *Crain's Chicago Business*, August 13, 1985, 52.

93. The ordinance allowed for a drop in the assessment level from 40 percent to 16 percent for the first thirteen years. "A Tax-Incentive Rulebook," *Chicago Tribune*, September 5, 1981, ProQuest. On specific examples of developers taking advantage of the ordinance, see John McCarron and Stanley Ziemba, "Developers Win 1st Tax Reduction," *Chicago Tribune*, October 15, 1983, ProQuest; Stanley Ziemba, "West Side Center for Northern," *Chicago Tribune*, July 13, 1988, ProQuest.

94. For a detailed list of these incentives, see Haider and Jacobs, *Cook County*, 90–91.

95. Larry Cose, "Businesses Get Assessment Cut," *Chicago Sun-Times*, May 20, 1986, NewsBank.

96. Allison Kaplan, "Forum Prevails as Cook Prepares to Simplify Tax Bill," *Arlington Daily Herald*, February 20, 1999, ProQuest; Haider, "Why You Might Sit Down." Again, it is difficult to know to what degree this change shifted the tax burden back to homeowners, as local assessors had continued to informally undervalue residential and commercial property on an inconsistent basis. The consensus among the local press was that the shift would be significant. See also Janota and Rackl, "Tax Changes Could Weigh on Homeowners"; Cliatt and Date, "Why Homeowners Might Be Losers"; Greg Hinz, "Biz Tax Load Gets Lighter," *Crain's Chicago Business*, August 16, 2006, ProQuest; Haider, "Why You Might Sit Down."

97. Kerch, "It's Appeal Is Growing."

98. Kevin Knapp, "Selling School Spirit," *Crain's Chicago Business*, June 27, 1998, ProQuest. In CPS, property taxes alone account for almost 40 percent of total funding. Chicago Public Schools, *Understanding the Chicago Public Schools Budget: A Citizen's Guide*, 4, accessed September 15, 2015, www.cps.edu/SiteCollectionDocuments/CitizensGuide.pdf. On the overreliance of Illinois districts on property taxes, see Matthew Gardner, Robert Lynch, Richard Sims, Ben Schweigert, and Amy Meek, *Balancing Act: Tax Reform Options in Illinois* (Washington, DC: Institute of Taxation and Economic Policy 2002), accessed January 24, 2018, itep.org/wp-content/uploads/ilfinal.pdf; Illinois State Board of Education, *Fact Sheet: Illinois Ranks Last in State Contribution to P-12 Funding* (Springfield, IL, February 2013), accessed January 24, 2018, http://206.166.105.35/budget/FY14/fact-sheet4-efab.pdf.

99. Fran Spielman, "$160 Million Plan for a New Stadium," *Chicago Sun-Times*, May 9, 1991, NewsBank; Cook County Board of Review, Freedom of Information Act Request No. WCB081711. The savings figure would have been considerably higher had the NHL not suffered a work stoppage during 2004 and 2005.

100. Fran Spielman, "Aldermen Join Stadium Push," *Chicago Sun-Times*, May 21, 1991, NewsBank.

101. Gary Washburn, "Chicago to Take Lesser Cut So It Won't Lose Big Shows," *Chicago Tribune*, March 10, 1999, ProQuest; "Budget Uses Levies for Leverage," *Chicago Tribune*, November 20, 1983, ProQuest.

102. League of Women Voters of Chicago, *A Guide through Chicago's Tax Maze* (Chicago: September 1987), 26; League of Women Voters of Chicago, *A Guide through Chicago's Tax Maze*

(Chicago: September 1997), 28, Municipal Reference Collection, Harold Washington Library Center; Nichols Clark, Lee Curtis, Fox, and Herhold, *Business and Taxes in Chicago*, 39; Civic Federation, *Chicagoland—A Fiscal Perspective: 1978–1987*, 17; Nancy Ryan and John Kass, "Daley Budget Plan OK'd," *Chicago Tribune*, November 16, 1995, ProQuest; Mark Brown, "County Board OKs $43 Million Hike in '97 Budget," *Chicago Sun-Times*, November 23, 1996, News-Bank; Jim Allen, "With No New Taxes in Store, Daley Unveils New Budget," *Arlington Daily Herald*, October 9, 1997, ProQuest; Fran Spielman, "Budget Woes," *Chicago Sun-Times*, October 6, 2004, NewsBank; Fran Spielman, "Daley Planning More Taxes, Fees," *Chicago Sun-Times*, September 17, 2005, NewsBank.

103. These levies include all taxing bodies, including parks, schools, community colleges, and so on. Civic Federation, *Chicagoland—A Fiscal Perspective, 1983–1992* (Chicago: Civic Federation, September 1994), 25–27, 72, 78, accessed January 8, 2018, www.civicfed.org/civic-federation/publications/chicagoland-fiscal-perspective-1983-1992.

104. By the end of the century, Illinois depended far more than most states on "extremely regressive" taxes. Gardner et al., *Balancing Act*, 2–3, 49.

105. Fran Spielman, "Pro Sports Execs Balk at 'Fun Tax' Hike," *Chicago Sun-Times*, December 4, 1992, NewsBank; John Kass, "Aldermen Become Fans," *Chicago Tribune*, December 4, 1992, ProQuest; "Daley Asks Fun-Seekers to Help City Pay Bills," *Chicago Sun-Times*, October 11, 1994, NewsBank.

106. Andrew Fegelman, "Some Not Amused by County Tax," *Chicago Tribune*, November 16, 1996, ProQuest.

107. McCourt and LeRoy, *A Better Deal for Illinois*, 1; Good Jobs First, "Summary of State and Local Awards: Illinois," *Subsidy Tracker*, accessed August 24, 2017, subsidytracker.goodjobsfirst.org/prog.php?statesum=IL; Fran Spielman, "Daley Backs Off on Tax-Theater, Sports Pressure Works," *Chicago Sun-Times*, October 23, 1994, NewsBank; Robert Davis, "City Passes Tax Hike That Spreads Pain," *Chicago Tribune*, November 11, 1994, ProQuest.

108. Fran Spielman, "Bulls, Rahm Break Ground on New $25 Million Practice Facility on United Center Parking Lot," *Chicago Sun-Times*, June 10, 2013, NewsBank.

Conclusion

1. John Husar, "Jordan's Statuesque Presence Draws Thousands to Pregame Pilgrimage," *Chicago Tribune*, May 29, 1997, ProQuest.

2. Sarah Lyall, "Chauffeur, Shootaround and Boneless Chicken Wings: Living Large with the Nets," *New York Times*, December 14, 2016, ProQuest; Brent Lang, "Movie Ticket Prices Hit Record High with Popularity of 3D Titles, Rise of Luxury Seating," *Variety*, July 22, 2015, accessed January 17, 2018, variety.com/2015/film/news/movie-ticket-prices-record-high-2015-summer-blockbusters-1201545600/.

3. Neil deMause, "Cobb County Lets Braves Ban Vendors around New Stadium, Doesn't Cite 'Safety' This Time," *Field of Schemes* (blog), July 11, 2016, accessed January 17, 2018, www.fieldofschemes.com/2016/07/11/11347/cobb-county-lets-braves-ban-vendors-around-new-stadium-doesnt-cite-safety-this-time/.

4. Liu, Burns, and Fleming, *Sidewalk Stimulus*, 17. In an interesting twist to this story, the LA City Council decriminalized street vending in early 2017 amid fears that ongoing criminalization would make undocumented vendors easy marks for immigration enforcement officials under the Trump administration. Hailey Branson-Potts, "Council Passes Vending Law," *Los Angeles Times*, February 16, 2017, ProQuest.

5. Nathaniel Vinton, "Tax Exemption Saves Madison Square Garden Chairman Dolan $48.5 Million for 2016 Fiscal Year," *New York Daily News*, April 6, 2016, accessed January 17, 2018, www.nydailynews.com/sports/basketball/knicks/tax-exemption-saves-msg-chairman-dolan-48–5m-fiscal-yr-article-1.2589753; "Presidential Election Results: Donald J. Trump Wins," *New York Times*, January 4, 2017, accessed January 21, 2018, www.nytimes.com/elections/results/president; Charles Bagli, "Trump Built his Empire as King of the Tax Break," *New York Times*, September 18, 2016, ProQuest; Leanna Garfield, "Amazon Just Revealed the Top Cities for HQ2—Here Are the Ones Throwing Hundreds of Millions to Land It," *Business Insider*, January 18, 2018, accessed January 21, 2018, www.businessinsider.com/amazon-hq2-cities-developers-economic-tax-incentives-2017–10/#memphis-tennessee-60-million-1.

6. Piketty, *Capital*, 264.

7. "2017 Article IV Consultation with the United States of America—Concluding Statement of the IMF Mission," *International Monetary Fund*, June 27, 2017, accessed January 21, 2018, www.imf.org/en/News/Articles/2017/06/27/ms062717–2017-article-iv-consultation-with-the-united-states-of-america; Ben Joravsky, "Rahm's Obsession with Downtown Development Isn't Really about Fostering Neighborhood Growth," *Chicago Reader*, June 14, 2017, accessed January 21, 2018, www.chicagoreader.com/chicago/mayor-rahm-emanuel-neighborhood-opportunity-fund-downtown-development/Content?oid=27060797; Chris Smith, "Surging NBA Team Values Create Two New Billionaires," *Forbes*, January 22, 2015, accessed January 21, 2018, www.forbes.com/sites/chrissmith/2015/01/22/surging-nba-team-values-create-two-new-billionaires/#79a38063498c.

8. Stephen Ross and Stefan Szymanski, *Fans of the World Unite! A (Capitalist) Manifesto for Sports Consumers* (Stanford, CA: Stanford Economics and Finance, 2008), 153–61, 207. Ross and Szymanski look beyond this solution by proposing a "promotion and relegation" system like the one employed in European professional soccer, which would sustain more teams per city. The setup would be akin to allowing minor league teams to move into the "majors" on the basis of good performance, and vice versa. Given the painstaking detail of their proposal and the lengthy summary required to do it justice, I have omitted a discussion of the plan.

9. Bruce Schoenfeld, "F.C. Barcelona: By the Fans, for the Fans," *Sports Business Journal*, May 29, 2000, accessed January 21, 2018, www.sportsbusinessdaily.com/Journal/Issues/2000/05/20000529/No-Topic-Name/FC-Barcelona-By-The-Fans-For-The-Fans.aspx; David Conn, "Barcelona's Model of Integrity Shows Right Is Might," *The Guardian*, May 16, 2006, accessed January 21, 2018, www.theguardian.com/football/2006/may/17/championsleague.europeanfootball.

10. Angela Galloway, "Initiative 91: Seattle Rejects Sports Subsidies," *Seattle Post-Intelligencer*, November 7, 2006, accessed January 21, 2018, www.seattlepi.com/news/article/Initiative-91-Seattle-rejects-sports-subsidies-1219229.php; Gordon, *Mapping Decline*, 227.

11. Foster and McChesney, *Endless Crisis*, 67–72; Roger Noll, "Economic Perspectives on the Athlete's Body," *Stanford Humanities Review* 6, no. 2 (1998), accessed January 21, 2018, web.stanford.edu/group/SHR/6-2/html/noll.html.

Appendix A

1. Thomas Wilson, "The Paradox of Social Class and Sports Involvement," *International Review for the Sociology of Sport* 37, no. 1 (March 2002): 5.

2. For more on multiple classification analysis, see Melissa Hardia and Chardie Baird, "Mul-

tiple Classification Analysis (MCA)," in *The Sage Encyclopedia of Social Science Research Methods*, ed. Michael Lewis-Beck, Alan Bryman, and Tim Futing Liao (Thousand Oaks, CA: Sage, 2004), 685–86.

3. In statistical analysis, odds and probability are distinct but related measures. The odds of an event happening are computed by dividing the probability by the difference between one and the probability.

4. The Bureau of Labor Statistic's Consumer Expenditure Survey and the National Endowment for the Humanities' Survey of Public Participation in the Arts are the other two.

5. "GSS Frequently Asked Questions," *GSS Data Explorer*, accessed December 24, 2016, https://gssdataexplorer.norc.org/pages/show?page=gss%2Ffaq; National Opinion Research Center, *Ballot A Questionnaire, 1993 General Social Survey* (Chicago: University of Chicago, 1993), 59.

6. Dinces, "Bulls Markets," 423.

7. Michael Hout, "Getting the Most out of the GSS Income Measures," *GSS Methodological Report 101* (July 2004). In the 1993 GSS, the highest category is "$75,000 and above," and the open-ended nature of this category precludes easy determination of the midpoint. Hout offers two approaches to determining this midpoint, or "top code." The first involves arbitrarily setting the top code at some fixed amount above $75,000. The second involves the formula alluded to in the text, or equation 2 in the aforementioned paper by Hout. However, the formula for equation 2 is printed incorrectly in the original publication; the entire equation must be divided by 2 to yield the correct results.

Appendix B

1. "About," *Illinois Sunshine Database*, accessed June 16, 2017, www.illinoissunshine.org/about/.

2. *2015–16 Media Guide: Celebrating the 50th Season of Chicago Bulls Basketball* (Chicago: Chicago Bulls, 2015), 7, accessed June 13, 2017, i.cdn.turner.com/drp/nba/bulls/sites/default/files/bulls_mg_1516.pdf; *Chicago Bulls Official Media Guide and Yearbook 1985–1986* (Maywood, IL: Saltzman Printers, n.d.), 4, author's personal copy.

3. Trevor Jensen and Neil Milbert, "Bill Wirtz: 1929–2007," *Chicago Tribune*, September 27, 2007, ProQuest.

4. *2015–16 Media Guide*, 7; *Chicago Bulls Official Media Guide*, 4.

5. On the business partnerships between Judelson and Reinsdorf, see Charles Storch, "In Business, Reinsdorf Earns More than Praise," *Chicago Tribune*, October 10, 1993, ProQuest. On Muchin's legal work on behalf of United Center ownership, see Dinces, "Bulls Markets," 393–94.

6. "Real Estate Management and Development Company Overview of JMB Realty Corporation," *Bloomberg*, accessed June 15, 2017, www.bloomberg.com/research/stocks/private/snapshot.asp?privcapId=916311; Andrew Schroedter and Eddie Baeb, "Balcor Band Reunites," *Crain's Chicago Business*, August 22, 2009, accessed January 23, 2012, www.chicagobusiness.com/article/20090822/ISSUE01/100032306/balcor-band-reunites.

7. I use the phrase "at least" because I do not have access to reliable data on the makeup of the board for the 1986–1987 and 1987–1988 seasons. Among the team media guides that I have reviewed, Steven Crown's name appears first in *Chicago Bulls 1988/89 Yearbook*, Chicago History Museum. The 1985–1986 guide lists his father, Lester, as a board member. *Chicago Bulls Official Media Guide*, 4.

8. "Company Overview of Wirtz Corporation," *Bloomberg*, accessed January 26, 2018, www .bloomberg.com/research/stocks/private/snapshot.asp?privcapid=939641.

9. Joravsky, "Reinsdorf's Secret Weapon."

Appendix C

1. Illinois Department of Revenue, *The Illinois Property Tax System: A General Guide to the Local Property Tax Cycle*, 10–11, accessed July 10, 2010, tax.illinois.gov/publications/localgovernment/ptax1004.pdf.

2. Civic Federation, *The Cook County Property Assessment Process*, 12.

3. The Cook County clerk calculates the tax rate applied to assessed values for a given tax year—and the Clerk's Office send bills and accepts payments—during the following year. For example, the Clerk's Office would mail property-tax bills based on 2017 tax-year assessments in 2018. See Cook County Clerk's Office, "Clerk Orr Releases 2012 Tax Rates," press release, accessed January 24, 2018, www.cookcountyclerk.com/sites/default/files/pdfs/2012%20Tax %20Rate%20Report.pdf.

4. Illinois Department of Revenue, *The Illinois Property Tax System*, 10–11.

5. Dennis Carr, Jeff Lawson, and J. Carl Schultz, *Mastering Real Estate Appraisal* (Chicago: Dearborn Financial Publishing, 2003), 344. There are additional time lags involved in the commercial property tax cycle. The net income figures on which commercial property assessments are based come from the preceding fiscal year. In other words, commercial assessments for tax year 2012 are based on income data from fiscal year 2011. This means that actual billing and payment executed during 2013 is based on net income data from at least two years prior ("at least" because not all properties are reassessed every year; in fact, in Cook County most properties are reassessed once every three years). See Illinois Department of Revenue, *Illinois Property Tax System*.

6. Amendment 1 to House Bill 2321, June 30, 1989, Illinois State Archives, Springfield, Illinois. Although the language is ambiguous, the amendment suggests that, unlike typical properties in Cook (which are reassessed every three years), the United Center receives a yearly reassessment. This is corroborated by the documents containing United Center income data from the Cook County Assessor's Office. Cook County Assessor's Office, Freedom of Information Act Request, Order No. 62939.

7. On the relationship between net income and capitalization rate, see Carr, Lawson, and Schultz, *Mastering Real Estate Appraisal*, 344.

8. Cook County Assessor's Office, Freedom of Information Act Request, Work Order No. 62939; Neubauer, "Stadium Snares Huge Tax Breaks"; Dinces, "Nothing but Net Profit," 18–19; Sean Dinces and Carol Caref, *Nothing but Net Profits: Jerry Reinsdorf, Property Tax Relief, and Corporate School Reform on Chicago's Near West Side* (Chicago: Chicago Teachers Union, 2013), 13–17, accessed January 22, 2018, www.ctunet.com/quest-center/research/position-papers/text/NothingButNetReportFull.pdf.

9. Civic Federation, *The Cook County Property Assessment Process*, 12.

10. For tables A.C.2 and A.C.3 I match CPI index year to the tax year. Because billing and payment are technically executed in the year following the tax year, there is an argument for adjusting for inflation by using the CPI index for year X + 1 when adjusting data from tax year X. However, for the sake of simplicity I match CPI year X with tax year X.

11. It is also worth noting that, according to their own internal documentation, Reinsdorf

and Wirtz appear to have violated the law in tax year 2006. To smooth the passage of the 1989 legislation, the two owners agreed to pay a minimum of $1 million in annual property taxes, even when the adjusted net income dropped below the threshold needed to produce a $1 million tax bill. In 2006, they paid only $900,000, but there is no record of any repercussions. Illinois 86th General Assembly, Amendment 1 to House Bill 2321, June 30, 1989, Illinois State Archives, Springfield.

Index

Page numbers followed by "f" indicate figures and tables.